THE GREEN STUDIES READER

The Green Studies Reader is a fantastically comprehensive selection of critical texts which address the connection between ecology, culture and literature. It offers a complete guide to the growing area of 'ecocriticism' and a wealth of material on green issues from the romantic period to the present.

The most important aspects of this field are covered in depth:

- Romantic ecology and its legacy
- The earth, memory and the critique of modernity
- Nature/culture/gender
- Ecocritical principles
- Environmental literary history
- The nature of the text

Appearing in this collection are extracts from today's leading ecocritics and figures from the past who pioneered a green approach to literature and culture. As a whole the reader encourages a reassessment of the development of criticism and offers a radical prospect for its future.

The book includes extracts from: William Wordsworth, Henry David Thoreau, John Ruskin, William Morris, Virginia Woolf, D. H. Lawrence, Theodor Adorno, Martin Heidegger, Raymond Williams, Theodore Roszak, Claude Lévi-Strauss, Jean-François Lyotard, Jonathan Bate, Kate Soper, Gary Snyder, Terry Gifford, Louise Westling, Richard Kerridge and Jhan Hochman.

Laurence Coupe is Senior Lecturer in English at Manchester Metropolitan University, where he teaches a course in ecological literary theory. He is the author of the 'Ecocriticism' and 'Myth' sections of the *Annotated Bibliography for English Studies*, the editor of *Green Letters*, and the author of *Myth* (Routledge, 1997).

The
GREEN STUDIES
READER

From Romanticism to Ecocriticism

Edited by

Laurence Coupe

With a foreword by

JONATHAN BATE

London and New York

First published 2000
by Routledge
11 New Fetter Lane, London EC4P 4EE

Simultaneously published in the USA and Canada
by Routledge
29 West 35th Street, New York, NY 10001

Routledge is an imprint of the Taylor & Francis Group

© 2000 Laurence Coupe

Typeset in Garamond and Univers by Florence Production Ltd,
Stoodleigh, Devon
Printed and bound in Great Britain by
TJ International Ltd, Padstow, Cornwall

British Library Cataloguing in Publication Data
A catalogue record for this book is available from the British Library

Library of Congress Cataloging in Publication Data
The green studies reader : from Romanticism to ecocriticism /
[edited by] Laurence Coupe.
p.   cm.
Includes bibliographical references (p.) and index.
1. English literature – 19th century – History and criticism.
2. Nature in literature.   3. English literature – 20th century –
History and criticism.   4. American literature – History and
criticism.   5. Environmental protection in literature.
6. Romanticism – Great Britain.   7. Ecology in literature.
I. Coupe, Laurence, 1950–
PR468.N3 G74 2000
820.9′36–dc21   00–028064

ISBN 0–415–20407–0 (pbk)
ISBN 0-415-20406-2 (hbk)

In memory of John Danby

Contents

CONTENTS

SECTION TWO   GREEN THEORY

Part III   Nature/Culture/Gender

Part IV Ecocritical Principles

CONTENTS

SECTION THREE   GREEN READING

Contents

Preface

This reader joins a distinguished list of academic anthologies published by Routledge. At first glance, it might seem to offer a contrast to the *Cultural Studies Reader*, since its recurrent focus is on the theme of nature. However, as I hope will soon become clear, it is the very boundary between 'culture' and 'nature' that the contents of the present reader elucidate. Again, it might seem to be radically distinct from the *Post-Colonial Studies Reader*, since it does not seem designed to promote awareness of particular historical and political issues. However, a good deal of the material gathered here addresses the connection between the domination, pollution and threatened destruction of the planet and the oppression of human beings. Meanwhile, we may point to the exploitation of the developing world and we may remind ourselves of the oppressive dualism by which both 'nature' and 'native' are subordinated.

So *The Green Studies Reader* is designed to complement the previous readers. Moreover, like them, it is intended to be a pioneering publication. The fact that literary and cultural studies departments in United Kingdom universities have begun only recently to introduce courses in 'ecocriticism' means that the subject is in need of clarification and organisation. I was tempted to say 'definition', but that would be fatal. This is a wide-ranging and open-ended anthology because green connections really do stop nowhere, and what is required is a good selection of material that might form the basis of further definition, controversy and revaluation.

The structure of the reader is loosely chronological in that the first section covers the romantic and modern ages, while the second and third cover the contemporary, which for me is the distinctively 'ecocritical age'. However, as one impulse behind the volume is to repudiate linear, progressive thinking, the chronology is not meant to indicate that certain preoccupations of earlier ecological theorists have now been 'dealt with' or superseded. Rather, it is hoped that the contributions of Wordsworth and Ruskin, for example, will seem more relevant than ever by setting them in the context of today's ecocritics.

The stylistic conventions applied here are easily explained. The material having come from both Britain and the United States, I have not imposed standardised spelling, except where failing to alter a word would look like a typing error to a British reader (for example, 'practicing'). This editorial control does not extend to the way information is presented by authors in their own footnotes; though, in order to prevent the reader becoming clogged by extraneous material, I have taken the liberty of removing all 'matters arising' or authorial speculations from them. Again, where lists of works cited have been given, these have been standardised. As is customary in readers, I have enjoyed the editor's privilege of retitling extracts in order to indicate their relevance to the part in which they are included; and where appropriate, I have introduced my own subheadings [in square brackets].

I cannot emphasise enough the provisional and exploratory aspect of this anthology. If readers regret the exclusion of material they regard as important, or if they fail at first to see the significance of particular extracts, I ask that they consider the material gathered here as intended to stimulate debate about the 'nature' of criticism and to give green studies some much-needed bearings. It is hoped that the volume will be consulted by anyone engaged in literary and cultural criticism, regardless of whether they are specialising in green studies. If it is used as a set text on an ecocritical course, the division of the volume into three sections of two parts each is intended to facilitate course organisation; but of course tutors and students will select the material that seems most appropriate in the context of their other work.

Acknowledgements

Anyone working in the field of green studies owes a debt to Jonathan Bate, but I am especially grateful to him for the personal interest he has taken in this reader from the days when it was only a proposal. Another longstanding supporter to whom I am grateful is Dominic Head, whose advice has always been worth taking. I am also indebted to Richard Kerridge and Greg Garrard for effectively launching the British branch of the Association for the Study of Literature and Environment (ASLE) with their 'Culture and Environmentalism' conference at Bath, and for enabling me to make many contacts useful to this project. One of these was Terry Gifford, who has been a great help and example to me.

Green studies in the United Kingdom would not have been possible without the inspiration of the original ASLE, launched in the United States. I am especially grateful to two members of that organisation. First, there is Cheryll Glotfelty, who effectively founded it: she has been a supportive and cooperative correspondent. Second, there is Scott Slovic, editor of *ISLE* (*Interdisciplinary Studies in Literature and Environment*): I cannot thank him enough for the time and trouble he has taken to enable me to include important articles from that journal, and for his general encouragement.

I am indebted to my wife, Margaret, for her advice, patience and good will. Also, I would like to acknowledge invaluable help from my friend and neighbour Simon Butler, who was always available when my word-processing went awry, and from Ian Reed of Manchester Metropolitan University, who gave detailed technical guidance. Special thanks must go to Talia Rodgers at Routledge, who had the vision to see the necessity for a green reader when literary and cultural studies still seemed predominantly grey. Nor should I overlook Rosie Waters, also at Routledge, who has been an extremely helpful adviser.

I gratefully acknowledge permission to reprint extracts from the following books, given by the publishers and, where living, the authors and/or translators. Theodor W. Adorno, *Aesthetic Theory* (ed. G. Adorno and R. Tiedman; trans. R. Hullot-Kentor), London and Mineapolis, MN: Athlone Press/University of Minnesota Press, 1997, pp. 61–2, 65–6, 73–4. English translation copyright 1997 by the Regents of the University of Minnesota. Original, German-language edition copyright 1970 by Suhrkamp Verlag. Theodor W. Adorno and

Max Horkheimer, *Dialectic of Enlightenment* (trans. J. Cumming), London: Verso, 1972, pp. 8–9, 32–4, 57. Jonathan Bate, *Romantic Ecology: Wordsworth and the Environmental Tradition*, London and New York: Routledge, 1991, pp. 1–4, 17–22, 56. Lawrence Buell, *The Environmental Imagination: Thoreau, Nature Writing, and the Formation of American Culture*, Cambridge, MA: Harvard University Press, 1995, pp. 84–8, 98–9, 285–9. Verena Andermatt Conley, *Ecopolitics: The Environment in Post-Structuralist Thought*, London and New York: Routledge, 1997, pp. 123–9, 139–40. Patrick Curry, *Defending Middle-Earth: Tolkien, Myth and Modernity*, Edinburgh: Floris Books, 1997, pp. 69–77. John F. Danby, *Shakespeare's Doctrine of Nature: A Study of 'King Lear'*, London: Faber & Faber, 1975, pp. 44–6, 52–3, 125–6, 131–2, 138. John F. Danby, *The Simple Wordsworth: Studies in the Poems 1797–1807*, London: Routledge & Kegan Paul, 1960, pp. 6–7, 10–11, 12–14, 97–8, 99–100, 122–3, 125–7. John Elder, *Imagining the Earth: Poetry and the Vision of Nature*, Urbana and Chicago, IL: University of Illinois Press, 1985, pp. 26–34. Terry Gifford, *Pastoral*, London and New York: Routledge, 1999, pp. 86–7, 134–5, 169–71. Cheryll Glotfelty, 'Flooding the Boundaries of Form: Terry Tempest Williams' Ecofeminist *Unnatural History*', in Stephen Tchudi (ed.) *Change in the American West: Exploring the Human Dimension*, Reno, NV: University of Nevada Press, 1996, pp. 158–67. (Special permission granted by the editors of *Halcyon*, in which this material first appeared.) Donna J. Haraway, *Primate Visions: Gender, Race, and Nature in the World of Modern Science*, New York and London: Routledge, 1989, pp. 10–13. Robert Pogue Harrison, *Forests: The Shadow of Civilization*, Chicago and London: University of Chicago Press, 1992, pp. 100–5, 148–52. Martin Heidegger, '. . . Poetically Man Dwells . . . ', in *Poetry, Language, Thought* (trans. A. Hofstadter), New York: Harper & Row, 1971, pp. 213–22, 227–9. William Howarth, 'Some Principles of Ecocriticism', in C. Glotfelty and H. Fromm (eds) *The Ecocriticism Reader: Landmarks in Literary Ecology*, Athens, GA and London: University of Georgia Press, 1996, pp. 69, 76–82. (Permission rests with author.) Richard Kerridge, 'Ecological Hardy', in Karla Armbruster and Kathleen Wallace (eds) *Beyond Nature Writing*, Charlottesville, VA: University of Virginia Press, 2000 (in press). D. H. Lawrence, 'Pan in America', in *Phoenix: The Posthumous Papers of D. H. Lawrence* (ed. E. D. McDonald), London: William Heinemann, 1936, pp. 22–4, 31. (Permission also given by Laurence Pollinger Ltd and the Estate of Frieda Lawrence Ravagali.) F. R. Leavis and Denys Thompson, *Culture and Environment: The Training of Critical Awareness*, London: Chatto & Windus, 1964, pp. 91–7. (Permission rests with Random House and with the Leavis Literary Estate.) Claude Lévi-Strauss, 'Structuralism and Ecology', in *The View from Afar* (trans. J. Neugroschel and P. Hoss), Oxford and New York: Blackwell/Basic Books, 1985, pp. 113–15, 118–20. (English translation copyright *c.* 1985 by Basic Books, Inc. Reprinted by Permission of Basic Books, a member of Perseus Books, L.L.C.) Jean-François Lyotard, 'Oikos', in *Political Writings* (trans. B. Readings and K. P. Geiman), London: UCL Press, 1993, pp. 101–2, 103–4, 104–7. (Permission also rests with Diane Elam.) Leo Marx,

ACKNOWLEDGEMENTS

The Machine in the Garden: Technology and the Pastoral Ideal in America, London and New York: Oxford University Press, 1964, pp. 11–12, 13–14, 24–32. Patrick D. Murphy, *Literature, Nature, and Other: Ecofeminist Critiques*, Albany, NY: State University of New York Press, 1995, pp. 3–5, 11–12, 17. (The chapter concerned originally appeared as 'Prolegomenon for an Ecofeminist Dialogue', in Dale M. Bauer and Susan J. McKinistry (eds) *Feminism, Bakhtin, and the Dialogic Voice*, Albany, NY: State University of New York Press, 1992.) Theodore Roszak, *Where the Wasteland Ends: Politics and Transcendence in Post-Industrial Society*, New York: Doubleday, 1972, pp. 313–18, 462–5. (Permission rests entirely with author.) Gary Snyder, 'Language Goes Two Ways', in *A Place in Space: Ethics, Aesthetics, and Watersheds*, Washington, DC: Counterpoint, 1995, pp. 173–82. Kate Soper, *What is Nature? Culture, Politics and the Non-Human*, Oxford and Cambridge, MA: Blackwell, 1995, pp. 98–107, 149–52, 155–7. Raymond Williams, *The Country and the City*, London: Hogarth Press, 1985. (Permission rests with Random House and the Raymond Williams Estate.) Virginia Woolf, 'Dorothy Wordsworth', in *The Common Reader: Second Series* (ed. A. McNeillie), London: Hogarth Press, 1986. (Permission also rests with the Estate of Virginia Woolf, represented by the Society of Authors.)

I gratefully acknowledge permission to reprint extracts from the following articles, given either by the journal editors or the authors, or by both. Karla Armbruster, 'Blurring Boundaries in Ursula Le Guin's "Buffalo Gals, Won't You Come Out Tonight?": A Poststructuralist Approach to Ecofeminist Criticism', *ISLE*, 3(1), 1996, pp. 18–19, 29–46. Jonathan Bate, 'Living with the Weather', *Studies in Romanticism*, 35(3), 1996, pp. 434–5, 439–47. (Special permission given by the Trustees of Boston University.) Kenneth Burke, 'Why Satire – with a Plan for Writing One', *Michigan Quarterly Review*, 13(4), 1974, pp. 307–24, 329–30. Carol H. Cantrell, 'The Locus of Compassibility: Virginia Woolf, Modernism, and Place', *ISLE*, 5(2), 1998, pp. 26–8, 32–9. Greg Garrard, 'Radical Pastoral?', *Studies in Romanticism*, 35(3), 1996, pp. 451–4, 462–5. (Special permission given by the Trustees of Boston University.) Terry Gifford, 'The Social Construction of Nature', *ISLE*, 3(2), 1996, pp. 29–34. Dominic Head, 'Problems in Ecocriticism and the Novel', *Key Words*, 1, 1998, pp. 60–1, 64–71. Jhan Hochman, '*The Silence of the Lambs*: A Quiet Bestiary', *ISLE*, 1(2), 1993, pp. 75–9. Jhan Hochman, 'Green Cultural Studies: An Introductory Critique of an Emerging Discipline', *Mosaic*, 30(1), 1997, pp. 81–2, 88–94. (*Mosaic* is a journal for the interdisciplinary study of literature.) Richard Kerridge, 'Ecothrillers: Environmentalism in Popular Culture', *English Review*, 8(3), 1998, pp. 32–5. Richard Kerridge, 'BSE Stories', *Key Words: A Journal of Cultural Materialism*, 2, 1999, pp. 111–21. Betty and Theodore Roszak, 'Deep Form in Art and Nature', *Resurgence*, 176 (May–June), 1996, pp. 20–3. (Permission rests solely with authors. Address of journal: Ford House, Hartland, Bideford, Devon EX39 6EE, UK.) Scott Slovic, 'Ecocriticism: Containing Multitudes, Practising Doctrine', *ASLE News*, 11(1), 1999, pp. 4–5. Louise H. Westling, 'Thoreau's Ambivalence Towards Mother Nature', *ISLE*, 1(1), 1993, pp. 145–50.

ACKNOWLEDGEMENTS

Every effort has been made to obtain permission to reprint all the extracts included. If any copyright holder has been inadvertently omitted, please apply in writing to the publisher.

Foreword

The starting point of Laurence Coupe's admirable *Green Studies Reader* is the Romantic critique of the Enlightenment's aspiration to master the natural world and set all things to work for the benefit of human commerce. Romanticism and its afterlife – with its search for a symbiosis between mind and nature, the human and the non-human – offers a challenge within the realms of both political and scientific ecology.

Part two turns to the critique of modernity. The Great War's destruction of individual spirits, established social orders and vast tracts of land led to a profound sense of alienation. It was in this context that D. H. Lawrence looked back to the energies of myth and F. R. Leavis to the imagined 'organic communities' of the past. But, as Coupe's selections powerfully show, the mid-twentieth-century critique of modernity by means of the memory – or the imagination – of a more unified relationship with the earth was by no means a solely English phenomenon: Heidegger and Adorno in Germany and later, in subtly different ways, Kenneth Burke and Leo Marx in America, worked in the same broad territory.

The relationship between nature and culture is the key intellectual problem of the twenty-first century. A clear and critical thinking of the problem will be crucial to humankind's future in the age of biotechnology. Part three of this book reveals how figures from very different disciplines offer fresh insights in this area: philosophers, poets, anthropologists, postmodern theorists.

Part four introduces some of the principles of a more specifically literary 'ecocriticism'. These are then taking up in parts five and six, where a rich variety of close readings reveal the range of texts and cultural formations which may be illuminated anew by being considered from a 'green' perspective.

The Green Studies Reader should take its place as a central text in any course on the relationship between literature and questions of ecology and environment. The editor has done a superb job in terms of both extracts chosen and organisational principles. For the first time, it is possible to see both the continuity and the variety of the traditions in which 'green thinking' has emerged within literary culture.

The theoretical, historical and practical exemplars collected in this book will stimulate new generations of students into new and vital reanimations and rethinkings of their literary inheritance.

Professor Jonathan Bate
Author of *The Song of the Earth*

General Introduction

An early follower of the Zen school of Buddhism reflected on his under-standing of nature as follows:

> Before I had studied Zen for thirty years, I saw mountains as moun-tains, and waters as waters. When I arrived at a more intimate know-ledge, I came to the point where I saw that mountains are not mountains, and waters are not waters. But now that I have got its very substance I am at rest. For it's just that I see mountains once again as mountains, and waters once again as waters.[1]

At first Ching-yuan had naively taken nature for granted. Later it occurred to him that in effect nature existed inside his mind, in that it found its shape and significance only as he made sense of it. But now he understands that it is equally mistaken to take nature for granted and to try and subsume it within his own mental operations. The point is to learn from nature, to enter into its spirit, and to stop trying to impose upon it the arbitrary constraints which result from our belief in our own importance. This wisdom may remind us of William Wordsworth's invitation to 'Come forth into the light of things', made in his poem 'The Tables Turned'. Far from assuming that whatever lies outside human consciousness is chaos, to which that consciousness gives order, he implies that human beings discover meaning – are illuminated – when they suspend the 'meddling intellect' which 'misshapes the beauteous forms of things' and attune themselves with a larger enlightenment, which includes mountains and waters as well as minds. As John G. Rudy explains:

> To encounter 'the light of things' themselves, one must shed the notion of light as emerging from a separate source. Indeed, one must relinquish the idea of separateness itself. To come into the light of things, one must become the things themselves, must see through things as things.[2]

Beyond duality, beyond the opposition of mind and matter, subject and object, thinker and thing, there is the possibility to 'realise' nature. Rudy

1

suggests that the word 'realise' may be read simultaneously as 'actualise' and 'understand': our ability to perceive things means that they 'realise' (actualise) themselves in us, and this in turn is the only way we can 'realise' (understand) the fact that those things are realising themselves in us.[3] But of course, though nature needs human minds to achieve 'self-realisation', and though at that moment all notions of separation appear redundant, the process implies that something is already there, asking to be actualised or understood.

Since the mid-1970s, much critical theory seems to have been dedicated to repudiating any such 'realisation'. In various schools – formalist, psychoanalytic, new historicist, deconstructionist, even Marxist – the common assumption has been that what we call 'nature' exists primarily as a term within a cultural discourse, apart from which it has no being or meaning. That is to say, it is a sign within a signifying system, and the question of reference must always be placed in emphatic parentheses. To declare that there is 'no such thing as nature' has become almost obligatory within literary and cultural studies. The great fear has been to be discovered committing what might be called 'the referential fallacy'. On the one hand, the scepticism of theory has proved salutary: too often previous critics assumed that their preferred works of literature told the 'truth' about the world. On the other hand, it has encouraged a heavy-handed culturalism, whereby suspicion of 'truth' has entailed the denial of non-textual existence. It is a mistake easily made, perhaps, once one has recognised the crucial role language plays in human sense-making. But it should still be pointed out that, in failing to move beyond the linguistic turn, theory has been stuck at Ching-yuan's second stage of enlightenment. In seeking to avoid naïvety, it has committed what might be called 'the semiotic fallacy'.[4] In other words, it has assumed that because mountains and waters are human at the point of delivery, they exist only as signified within human culture. Thus they have no intrinsic merit, no value and no rights. One function of green studies must be to resist this disastrous error: it belongs, whatever the claims of the theorist to reject the legacy of western 'Man', to 'the arrogance of humanism'.[5] As Bill McKibben puts it in his lament over the subordination of the non-human world by the human: 'Nature's independence *is* its meaning; without it there is nothing but us.'[6]

However, it is not being suggested here that we should counter this arrogance simply by insisting that, for example, Wordsworth's 'I wandered lonely as a cloud' is simply 'about' daffodils after all. Just as it is necessary to query critics' claims for 'truth' on behalf of texts, so we must avoid reducing complex linguistic performance to the level of merely pointing at things. However, it is perhaps a sign of the times, in these times of the sign, that it has become necessary to remind ourselves that, whatever else Wordsworth's poem is concerned with (the creativity of perception, the uses of memory, the restorative power of imagination), it makes no sense unless we concede the existence of a certain kind of flower. For, if we emphasise signification

2

to the exclusion of reference, we may be as guilty of treating the non-human environment with the same contempt as are those destructive forces which we might wish to condemn.

If that seems an exaggerated claim, consider the consequences of suppressing the referent. Suppose one is reading John Clare's 'bird' poems: 'The Sky Lark', 'The Yellowhammer's Nest', 'Hedge Sparrow', and so on. Or suppose one is listening to Ralph Vaughan Williams's orchestral work, *The Lark Ascending*. The semiotic fallacy declares the existence of the creature evoked to be incidental; these words, these sounds, have nothing finally to do with actual, existing birds. That being the case, there is no reason to be disturbed when one subsequently reads the following statistics: in Britain, between 1972 and 1999 the population of skylarks fell by 60 per cent, the population of yellowhammers also fell by 60 per cent, and the population of tree sparrows fell by 87 per cent. But is it so naïve to ask whether Clare's poetry and Vaughan Williams's music will have the same significance when the cereal monoculture of intensive agriculture (aided by inappropriate housing developments) have finally destroyed all the habitats of these creatures, and there is nowhere for them to live? Does the devastation of bird populations not matter because they are, after all, only referents? If critical theory answers in the negative, then it surely colludes with 'agribusiness' and its remorseless suppression of biodiversity.

So green studies does not challenge the notion that human beings make sense of the world through language, but rather the self-serving inference that nature is nothing more than a linguistic construct. Kate Soper, who is well represented in this reader, makes the point dramatically: 'In short, it is not language which has a hole in its ozone layer; and the real thing continues to be polluted and degraded even as we refine our deconstructive insights at the level of the signifier.'[7] More modestly, we may say that green studies negotiates what 'the real thing' might involve. It is no easy task. For, as Raymond Williams famously observed: 'Nature is perhaps the most complex word in the language.'[8] It might be no exaggeration to say that green studies as a discipline hinges on the recognition of the complexity of that word and of our relation to whatever it denotes. Here it is worth bearing in mind Jhan Hochman's differentiation between 'Nature' and 'nature'. While the former is a rhetorically useful principle, it has often been associated with 'the highly suspect realms of the otherworldly or transcendental'. The latter is to be preferred in that it is more 'worldly': it denotes no more – but certainly no less – than the collective name for 'individual plants, nonhuman animals, and elements'. However, such careful differentiation should not become a rigid distinction: 'For example, how classify apparently sensible, universal, N/natural patterns? Is number nature or Nature? Are life and death nature or Nature?' Moreover, the main aim should be kept in mind: to differentiate between 'nature' and 'culture', so that 'culture does not easily confuse itself with nature or Nature, or claim to know nature as a rationale for replacing [it] with itself and its constructions.'[9] Let me illustrate Hochman's twofold differentiation by pointing out that, while it is necessary to see the medieval 'chain of being' as an idealist construction of Nature which served the interests of feudalism, it does not follow that nature has no existence apart from culture: indeed, such a conclusion has been used to sanction, for example, large-scale deforestation in the short-term interests of the 'fast food' culture of corporate capitalism.

It should be clear from this last observation that, if we may be said to entering 'the ecocritical age', we must understood that epithet in its fullest sense. While I prefer the more inclusive term, 'green studies', the more specific term, 'ecocriticism', has the advantage of reminding us to register the 'critical' quality of these times. For we are not only concerned with the status of the referent and the need to do it justice, in the sense of taking it seriously as something more than linguistic; we are also concerned with the larger question of justice, of the rights of our fellow-creatures, of forests and rivers, and ultimately of the biosphere itself. That is to say, green studies is much more than a revival of mimesis: it is a new kind of pragmatics. While carefully addressing the 'nature' of criticism, in the sense of examining how 'nature' is referred to by critics, it seeks to go further: to use nature as a 'critical' concept. It does this in two related senses. First, in invoking nature, it challenges the logic of industrialism, which assumes that nothing matters beyond technological progress. Thus, it offers a radical alternative to both 'right' and 'left' political positions, both of which assume that the means of production must always be developed, no matter what the cost.[10] Second, in insisting that the non-human world matters, it challenges the complacent culturalism which renders other species, as well as flora and fauna, subordinate to the human capacity for signification. Thus, it queries the validity of treating nature as something which is 'produced' by language.[11] Denying both assumptions, industrialism and culturalism, it sees planetary life as being in a 'critical' condition; and it is to this sense of 'crisis' that it offers a response. If green studies does not have an effect on this way of thinking, does not change behaviour, does not encourage resistance to planetary pollution and degradation, it cannot be called fully 'ecocritical'.

Thus, the appeal to ecology is ultimately a matter of ethics. As Aldo Leopold long ago reminded us: 'All ethics so far evolved rest upon a single premise: that the individual is a member of a community of interdependent parts. . . . The land ethic simply enlarges the boundaries of the community to include soils, waters, plants, and animals, or collectively: the land.' Green studies may not want always to invoke a 'land ethic', but it will usually concur with Leopold's conclusion: '[A] thing is right when it tends to preserve the integrity, stability and beauty of the biotic community. It is wrong when it tends to do otherwise.'[12] For the point is not just to speak *about* nature but also to speak *for* nature. Green studies makes no sense unless its formulation of theory contributes to the struggle to preserve the 'biotic community'. Lawrence Buell succinctly defines ecocriticism as follows: 'study of the relation between literature and environment conducted in a spirit of commitment to environmental praxis.'[13] More broadly, and in the light of Hochman's differentiation, green studies debates 'Nature' in order to defend nature.

The focus of any praxis is on the future; with green studies what is at stake is the future of the planet itself. In that sense, it is the most radical of critical activities. Class, race and gender are important dimensions of both literary and cultural studies; but the survival of the biosphere must surely rank as even more important, since without it there are no issues worth addressing. Paul Virilio might be accused of hyperbole when he declares that the ecological battle is 'the only one worth fighting',[14] but one sees what he means. With no planet, there is no future, and so no other battles to be fought. This fact seemed suddenly to dawn on the world's media in late November and early December 1999, when the World Trade Organisation staged a 'ministerial meeting' in Seattle. The aim was to affirm the principle of globalisation by way of 'free trade'; but about 50,000 citizens from all walks of life and all parts of the world protested so effectively for four days that at one point the convention was nearly cancelled. The protests were the biggest witnessed in the United States since the Vietnam War, and the theme that united the demonstrators was the need to protect the earth. Globalisation was denounced as not only 'market liberalisation', that is, the lowering of trade barriers in the interests of the rich and at the expense of the poor, but also the overriding of local laws and customs which favoured the rights of ecosystems. Vandana Shiva, director of the Research Foundation for Science and Ecology, New Delhi, reflected soon after on the significance of the event:

> The WTO has earned itself names such as World Tyranny Organisation because it enforces anti-people, anti-nature decisions to enable corporations to steal the world's harvests through secretive, undemocratic structures and processes. It institutionalises forced trade, not free trade. . . . The rules set by the secretive WTO violate principles of human rights and ecological survival. They violate rules of justice and sustainability. They are rules of warfare against the people and the planet. Changing these rules is the most important struggle of our times. It is a matter of survival.[15]

The demonstrators knew that it is impossible to separate defence of people from defence of the planet, human rights from ecological survival, justice from sustainability. Suddenly a struggle that had seemed eccentric was recognised as central, as fundamental, as crucial.

Interestingly, the methods used by the majority of demonstrators were those of civil disobedience (notably passive resistance), first proclaimed by Henry David Thoreau in the middle of the nineteenth century. It is no coincidence that Thoreau is included in this volume, as a pioneer of ecocriticism. Thus, the word 'radical' reminds us that green studies is also about getting back, with an appropriate pun, to the 'grassroots' of culture. It remembers both the nature from which culture emerged and, within culture, the past efforts of those who in their time tried to speak for the earth. That is why over a third of the contents collected here predates our own 'ecocritical age'. Far from considering early reflections on the name and nature of 'nature' to be merely a naïve and vague prefiguration of ecocriticism proper, this reader is designed to encourage speculation about where and when, in the context of the humanities, green studies effectively began. Obviously, English ecocritics are correct to see their discipline as being officially launched by Jonathan Bate's *Romantic Ecology* (1991); and they are correct to give due recognition to the pioneering work of Raymond Williams in *The Country and the City* (1973). But would either work have made sense without John Ruskin's *Modern Painters* Volume III (1856), or Wordsworth's 'Preface' to *Lyrical Ballads* (2nd edn, 1800)? I am aware that for many non-green theorists, there is no fate worse than being accused of being 'out of date'. But green studies reminds us that place matters as much as time, geography as much as history, being as much as becoming, permanence as much as change. In so doing, it unsettles the linear assumption made by so many contemporary theorists, for whom Hades' instruction to Orpheus, on no account to look back, is universally sound advice.

Indeed, it is with the contemporary 'green turn' that we see how vital is the continuity between the language and symbolism of poets such as Wordsworth and contemporary environmentalism. The interest, then, is in deciding how far the spirit of romanticism needs restating in order to give it newly ecological significance, how far the original meaning still stands as a challenge to our times. Sometimes we may have the feeling that we are only just catching up with Wordsworth; sometimes we will be consciously enlisting him for the campaign through appropriate citation and quotation. Moreover, if the tension between original meaning and subsequent significance is at stake, we need not confine ourselves to romanticism, but may find that Shakespeare, say, will offer visions of nature that are as relevant as they are remote, while modernist writers suddenly turn out to be engaged in a radical mimesis where once they were taken to be preoccupied with the primacy of the signifier.

A similar dialectic may apply to the critical canon. Green studies being concerned with permanence as much as with change, it allows us to reflect upon the literary or cultural text in the context of the slow evolution of the biosphere. Thus, it would be absurd were it to applaud novelty for its own sake in the field of theory, given that it is that very way of thinking which threatens us with catastrophe. Thus, one important purpose of this volume is to recover from obscurity literary critics whose substantial contribution to our understanding of nature has been overshadowed by academic fashions: John Middleton Murry, Kenneth Burke and John Danby, for example. Again, it is hoped that thinkers whose reputations are secure will nevertheless take on ecocritical significance: Martin Heidegger, F. R. Leavis, Theodor Adorno and Max Horkheimer, for example. Not that this effort of recuperation on behalf of past writers should be taken to denote a hostility to postmodernism:

it is precisely because green studies addresses the consequences of the technological project of modernity, with its accompanying intellectual arrogance, that it finds hope in postmodernism's provisionality and pluralism, given ecology's emphasis on the creativity of organic life and on the need for biodiversity. At the same time, it is committed to resisting the global theme park which we call 'postmodernity', and so must be especially careful to distinguish this condition from that complex body of ideas, potentially more favourable to ecology than to consumerist capitalism, which we call 'postmodernism'. Of course, we should bear in mind Charlene Spretnak's distinction between 'deconstructive postmodernism', which fosters 'a nihilistic disintegration of all values' and 'ecological or reconstructive postmodernism', which seeks opportunities for creativity and growth. The one merely plays amidst the ruins of modernity; the other works to open up possibilities for both people and planet.[16] Unfortunately, it is the former version that is widely known, thanks to a fashionable taste for the cynical complicity of such thinkers as Jean Baudrillard, who dismisses complaints about the pollution and despoilation of the planet as irrelevant in a world of 'simulation'. Hence we need to remind ourselves that the theoretical tradition should be kept as healthy as possible, that present fashions are to be judged in perspectives long and deep, lest we surrender to an impoverished view of what constitutes nature and so of what constitutes culture.

Thus, the concern of green studies is with the living connection between past and future. This reader is intended to answer the present need, which is to ensure both dimensions are comprehended, in the interests of those 'mountains and waters' which we now know to exist. Moreover, since our responsibilities towards the biotic community to which they belong are not vague options but are urgent obligations, it is hoped that this volume will be used to ensure that planetary life at long last takes its rightful place at the centre of that discipline which we might still call, though with appropriate hesitation, the humanities.

NOTES

1   Quoted by Alan Watts in *The Way of Zen*, London: Arkana, 1990, p. 146.
2   John G. Rudy, *Wordsworth and the Zen Mind: The Poetry of Self-Emptying*, Albany, NY: State University of New York Press, 1996, p. 109.
3   Ibid.
4   A comparable principle is Paul Ricoeur's 'ideology of the absolute text', which he sees as resulting from concentration on semiotics at the expense of semantics. See his 'What is a Text?', in *A Ricoeur Reader: Reflection and Imagination* (ed. Mario J. Valdes), New York and London: Harvester Wheatsheaf, 1991, p. 47.
5   See David Ehrenfeld, *The Arrogance of Humanism*, New York: Oxford University Press, 1978.
6   Bill McKibben, *The End of Nature*, Harmondsworth: Penguin, 1990, p. 54.
7   Kate Soper, *What is Nature?*, Oxford: Blackwell, 1995, p. 151.

8 Raymond Williams, *Keywords: A Vocabulary of Culture and Society*, London: Fontana, 1983 (revised edn), p. 219.

9 Jhan Hochman, *Green Cultural Studies: Nature in Film, Novel, and Theory*, Moscow, ID: University of Idaho Press, 1998, pp. 2–3.

10 See Andrew Dobson, *Green Political Thought*, London and New York: Routledge, 1995 (2nd edn).

11 This is an issue which is debated by contributors to Part III, but which is also raised throughout the volume. The term 'culturalism' is usually used positively, but I am here casting doubt upon it, without advocating a simplistic 'naturalism'.

12 Aldo Leopold, *A Sand County Almanac*, Oxford: Oxford University Press, 1949, pp. 204, 224–5.

13 Lawrence Buell, *The Environmental Imagination: Thoreau, Nature Writing, and the Formation of American Culture*, Cambridge, MA: Harvard University Press, p. 430.

14 Quoted by Verena Andermatt Conley in *Ecopolitics: The Environment in Poststructuralist Thought*, London and New York: Routledge, 1997, p. 80.

15 Vandana Shiva, 'This round to the citizens', *Society*, supplement to the *Guardian*, 8 December 1999, pp. 4–5.

16 Charlene Spretnak, *States of Grace: The Recovery of Meaning in a Postmodern Age*, San Francisco: HarperCollins, 1991, pp. 12–22.

SECTION ONE

Green Tradition

PART I

*Romantic Ecology
and its Legacy*

Introduction

It was Jonathan Bate who popularised the phrase 'romantic ecology', in his book of that title published in the early 1990s (see Chapter 30 for extract). There he applied it to Wordsworth in particular, but more generally to an 'environmental tradition' running from him that included John Ruskin, William Morris and Edward Thomas. The debate since then has been how 'green' romanticism was generally, apart from Wordsworth. Here I have included some important figures, from the end of the eighteenth to the end of the nineteenth centuries, who deepen and extend our understanding of 'romantic ecology'. Following them we have important critical voices of the twentieth century who predate ecocriticism but who show a preoccupation with what the final contributor calls the 'green language' of romanticism.

William Blake has not usually been thought of as an environmentally minded poet. Indeed, it has been customary to categorise him as a 'gnostic' visionary who treated the natural or 'vegetative' world with contempt. But we must bear in mind that it was the dead universe of Newton's physics that he was rejecting; what he believed in, by contrast, was nature as a mode of revelation. William Wordsworth also had a religious respect for nature, but in his 1800 'Preface' to *Lyrical Ballads* we see how subtle is his understanding of the relation between human 'pleasure', poetic 'purpose' and the 'primary laws' sustaining both human and non-human nature. Nor is that essay merely descriptive: his astute remarks on the 'savage torpor' which results when human beings dissociate themselves from those 'laws' remind us that he was engaged in an ecological campaign. Coleridge was an ally here, even if his laudable attempt to formulate a theory of the imagination that would accommodate both the human mind and the natural world remained subservient to his metaphysical systematising. This tendency was influential on North American 'Transcendentalism', which flourished in the early to mid-nineteenth century: when Ralph Waldo Emerson wrote on nature he was concerned chiefly with the potential of a transcendent self to commune with a transcendent divinity lying beyond natural phenomena. Emerson is not represented here, but we need to know of him in order to appreciate the more Wordsworthian emphasis of his protégé Henry David Thoreau. In the extract offered here Thoreau reflects on the need for external and internal 'wildness' so that culture might not lose touch with nature, and so that literature should remain vital.

Meanwhile, back in England, John Ruskin, another admirer of Wordsworth, had been attempting to improve upon early romantic concepts of the relationship between art and the environment. The third volume of his ambitious *Modern Painters* (1856) is remarkable for its contradictions and even its confusions, but there is a persuasive logic running through the two extracts provide here: the first insists on the need to subordinate the self to the representation of nature; the second proclaims that a regard for nature is a guarantee of an ethical sense which is inextricably bound up with religious principles. If we recall the three stages of apprehending 'mountains and waters' comprehended by Zen, as discussed in the General Introduction, we might roughly equate Ruskin's 'pathetic fallacy' with Ching-yuan's second stage, a disregard for nature's autonomy, and his 'moral of landscape' with Ching-yuan's third stage, a humble openness to nature's revelation. For Ruskin, this last was undoubtedly the complement of Christian faith, but his disciple William Morris was more ambivalent: on the one hand, as an admirer of Karl Marx as well as of Ruskin, he looked forward to a future in which human life would flourish without religion, which was the expression of class-based society; on the other hand he was himself a great decorator and restorer of churches. The important point is that he shared Ruskin's concern for an 'organic' way of living and he agreed that industrial capitalism was a denial of that fundamental human need. With Morris, the legacy of romantic ecology fuses with that of socialist ecology.

The green aspect of romanticism did not become a central object of study until Bate's book, mentioned above. However, earlier critics had already shown an interest in what the romantics had demonstrated about the interaction of human and non-human nature. The modernist writer Virginia Woolf was an admirer of not only William Wordsworth but also his sister Dorothy: indeed, as early as the 1920s she was suggesting what is now widely accepted in feminist scholarship, that the *Grasmere Journals* is as important a founding text of romanticism as is anything written by her brother, particularly in its imaginative response to natural scenes and the minute particulars of landscape. Indeed, the very style of her essay on Dorothy Wordsworth, written at the end of the 1920s, is indebted to romanticism: critical appreciation of the text and imaginative empathy with its author, her companions and her environment coalesce. Similarly, John Middleton Murry, a contemporary of Woolf and a friend of another novelist, D. H. Lawrence, not only admired the romantics but also saw himself as reviving romanticism: Murry felt that the classicism of writers such as T. S. Eliot was arresting the development of English literature, and that the only way forward was to resume and extend the tradition of Wordsworth. In the material reproduced here we see him making a pioneering case for 'the peasant poet' John Clare as equal to, and in some respects superior to, Wordsworth in his expression of affection for his environment. But then, Murry's literary responses were themselves always intense: indeed, later in his life he was inspired by his reading of the romantics to commit himself to pacifism and to make various attempts at establishing a rural commune.

Bold as Woolf's and Murry's insights were, academic literary criticism also was to make its audacious claims on behalf of the romantics. In 1960 John F. Danby wrote a pioneering study called *The Simple Wordsworth*. Here we see him attempt to parallel the relationship between mind and natural object, as articulated by Wordsworth, and the relationship between the constituents of a chemical reaction. This demonstration reminds us that romanticism should never be severed from its historical context – in this case, the growth of scientific knowledge effected by Wordsworth's friend Humphrey Davy, by which the poet was fascinated. Thus, we should not see romanticism simply as a retreat from the world: rather, it was a new way of comprehending the world. However, another academic critic, Raymond Williams, argued convincingly in his influential *The Country and the City* (1973) that if we trace 'the green language' through Wordsworth and Clare, we witness a crisis of sensibility by which nature becomes idealised in the face of its threatened destruction. Working under the influence of Marx, Williams might have been expected to expose remorselessly the romantic 'ideology': actually, we are more aware of his sympathy for the poets concerned as here we see him trace sensitively the 'structure of feeling' (the emergent pattern of general experience) they and many of their contemporaries shared. There is a case to be made for *The Country and the City* as the most important work to have anticipated British ecocriticism. Certainly Bate's *Romantic Ecology*, while it rejects the Marxist emphasis, benefits from its opening up of the question of a native green tradition.

1

Nature as Imagination

WILLIAM BLAKE*

I FEEL THAT a Man may be happy in This World. And I know that This World Is a World of Imagination & Vision. I see Everything I paint In This World, but Every body does not see alike. To the Eyes of a Miser a Guinea is far more beautiful than the Sun, & a bag worn with the use of Money has more beautiful proportions than a Vine filled with Grapes. The tree which moves some to tears of joy is in the Eyes of others only a Green thing which stands in the way. Some see Nature all Ridicule & Deformity, & by these I shall not regulate my proportions; & some scarce see Nature at all. But to the Eyes of the Man of Imagination, Nature is Imagination itself. As a man is, so he sees. As the Eye is formed, such are its Powers. You certainly Mistake, when you say that the Visions of Fancy are not to be found in This World. To Me This World is all One continued Vision of Fancy or Imagination, & I feel Flatter'd when I am told so. What is it sets Homer, Virgil & Milton in so high a rank of Art? Why is the Bible more Entertaining & Instructive than any other book? Is it not because they are addressed to the Imagination, which is Spiritual Sensation, & but mediately to the Understanding or Reason? Such is True Painting, and such was alone valued by the Greeks & the best modern Artists.

*From Blake's letter to the Revd Dr Trusler (23 August 1799), in *Complete Writings* (ed. Geoffrey Keynes), London: Oxford University Press, 1925.

2

Primary Laws

WILLIAM WORDSWORTH*

[PURPOSE]

THE PRINCIPAL OBJECT then which I proposed to myself in these Poems was to make the incidents of common life interesting by tracing in them, truly though not ostentatiously, the primary laws of our nature: chiefly as far as regards the manner in which we associate ideas in a state of excitement. Low and rustic life was generally chosen because in that situation the essential passions of the heart find a better soil in which they can attain their maturity, are less under restraint, and speak a plainer and more emphatic language; because in that situation our elementary feelings exist in a state of greater simplicity and consequently may be more accurately contemplated and more forcibly communicated; because the manners of rural life germinate from those elementary feelings; and from the necessary character of rural occupations are more easily comprehended; and are more durable; and lastly, because in that situation the passions of men are incorporated with the beautiful and permanent forms of nature. The language too of these men is adopted (purified indeed from what appear to be its real defects, from all lasting and rational causes of dislike or disgust) because such men hourly communicate with the best objects from which the best part of language is originally derived; and because, from their rank in society and the sameness and narrow circle of their intercourse, being less under the action of social vanity they convey their feelings and notions in simple and unelaborated expressions. Accordingly such a language arising out of repeated experience and regular feelings is a more permanent and a far more philosophical language than that which is frequently substituted for it by Poets, who think that they are conferring honour upon themselves and their art in proportion as they separate themselves from the sympathies of men, and indulge in arbitrary and capricious habits of expression in order to furnish food for fickle taste and fickle appetites of their own creation.

I cannot be insensible of the present outcry against the triviality and meanness both of thought and language, which some of my contemporaries have occasionally

*From 'Preface' to *Lyrical Ballads* (2nd edn, 1800), in *Poetical Works of William Wordsworth* (ed. Ernest de Selincourt), London: Oxford University Press, 1936.

introduced into their metrical compositions; and I acknowledge that this defect, where it exists, is more dishonorable to the Writer's own character than false refinement or arbitrary innovation, though I should contend at the same time that it is far less pernicious in the sum of its consequences. From such verses the Poems in these volumes will be found distinguished at least by one mark of difference, that each of them has a worthy *purpose*. Not that I mean to say, that I always began to write with a distinct purpose formally conceived; but I believe that my habits of meditation have so formed my feelings, as that my descriptions of such objects as strongly excite those feelings, will be found to carry along with them a *purpose*. If in this opinion I am mistaken I can have little right to the name of a Poet. For all good poetry is the spontaneous overflow of powerful feelings; but though this be true, Poems to which any value can be attached, were never produced on any variety of subjects but by a man who being possessed of more than usual organic sensibility had also thought long and deeply. For our continued influxes of feeling are modified and directed by our thoughts, which are indeed the representatives of all our past feelings; and as by contemplating the relation of these general representatives to each other, we discover what is really important to men, so by the repetition and continuance of this act feelings connected with important subjects will be nourished, till at length, if we be originally possessed of much organic sensibility, such habits of mind will be produced that by obeying blindly and mechanically the impulses of those habits we shall describe objects and utter sentiments of such a nature and in such connection with each other, that the understanding of the being to whom we address ourselves, if he be in a healthful state of association, must necessarily be in some degree enlightened, his taste exalted, and his affections ameliorated. . . .

I will not suffer a sense of false modesty to prevent me from asserting, that I point my Reader's attention to this mark of distinction far less for the sake of these particular Poems than from the general importance of the subject. The subject is indeed important! For the human mind is capable of excitement without the application of gross and violent stimulants; and he must have a very faint perception of its beauty and dignity who does not know this, and who does not further know that one being is elevated above another in proportion as he possesses this capability. It has therefore appeared to me that to endeavour to produce or enlarge this capability is one of the best services in which, at any period, a Writer can be engaged; but this service, excellent at all times, is especially so at the present day. For a multitude of causes unknown to former times are now acting with a combined force to blunt the discriminating powers of the mind, and unfitting it for all voluntary exertion to reduce it to a state of almost savage torpor. The most effective of these causes are the great national events which are daily taking place, and the increasing accumulation of men in cities, where the uniformity of their occupations produces a craving for extraordinary incident which the rapid communication of intelligence hourly gratifies. To this tendency of life and manners the literature and theatrical exhibitions of the country have conformed themselves. The invaluable works of our elder writers, I had almost said the works of Shakespeare and Milton, are driven into neglect by frantic novels, sickly and stupid German

Tragedies, and deluges of idle and extravagant stories in verse. When I think upon this degrading thirst after outrageous stimulation I am almost ashamed to have spoken of the feeble effort with which I have endeavoured to counteract it; and reflecting upon the magnitude of the general evil, I should be oppressed with no dishonorable melancholy, had I not a deep impression of certain inherent and indestructible qualities of the human mind, and likewise of certain powers in the great and permanent objects that act upon it which are equally inherent and indestructible; and did I not further add to this impression a belief that the time is approaching when the evil will be systematically opposed by men of greater powers and with far more distinguished success. . . .

[PLEASURE]

. . . Aristotle, I have been told, hath said, that Poetry is the most philosophic of all writing: it is so: its object is truth, not individual and local, but general, and operative; not standing upon external testimony, but carried alive into the heart by passion; truth which is its own testimony, which gives strength and divinity to the tribunal to which it appeals, and receives them from the same tribunal. Poetry is the image of man and nature. The obstacles which stand in the way of the fidelity of the Biographer and Historian, and of their consequent utility, are incalculably greater than those which are to be encountered by the Poet who has an adequate notion of the dignity of his art. The Poet writes under one restriction only, namely, that of the necessity of giving immediate pleasure to a human Being possessed of that information which may be expected from him, not as a lawyer, a physician, a mariner, an astronomer or a natural philosopher, but as a Man. Except this one restriction, there is no object standing between the Poet and the image of things; between this, and the Biographer and Historian there are a thousand.

Nor let this necessity of producing immediate pleasure be considered as a degradation of the Poet's art. It is far otherwise. It is an acknowledgement of the beauty of the universe, an acknowledgement the more sincere, because it is not formal, but indirect; it is a task light and easy to him who looks at the world in the spirit of love: further, it is a homage paid to the native and naked dignity of man, to the grand elementary principle of pleasure, by which he knows, and feels, and lives, and moves. We have no sympathy but what is propagated by pleasure: I would not be misunderstood; but wherever we sympathize with pain it will be found that the sympathy is produced and carried on by subtle combinations with pleasure. We have no knowledge, that is, no general principles drawn from the contemplation of particular facts, but what has been built up by pleasure, and exists in us by pleasure alone. The Man of Science, the Chemist and Mathematician, whatever difficulties and disgusts they may have had to struggle with, know and feel this. However painful may be the objects with which the Anatomist's knowledge is connected, he feels that his knowledge is pleasure; and where he has no pleasure he has no knowledge. What then does the Poet? He considers man and the objects that surround him as acting and re-acting upon each other, so as to produce an infinite complexity of pain and pleasure; he considers man in his own nature and in his ordinary life as contemplating this with a certain quantity of immediate knowledge, with certain convictions, intuitions, and deductions which by habit become of the nature of intuitions; he considers him as looking upon this complex scene of ideas and sensations, and finding everywhere objects that immediately excite in him sympathies which, from the necessities of his nature, are accompanied by an overbalance of enjoyment.

To this knowledge which all men carry about with them, and to these sympathies in which without any other discipline than that of our daily life we are fitted to take delight, the Poet principally directs his attention. He considers man and nature as essentially adapted to each other, and the mind of man as naturally the mirror of the fairest and most interesting qualities of nature.

3

The Dialectic of Mind and Nature

Samuel Taylor Coleridge*

[THE SUBJECTIVE & OBJECTIVE]

NOW THE SUM of all that is merely OBJECTIVE, we will henceforth call NATURE, confining the term to its passive and material sense, as comprising all the *phaenomena* by which its existence is made known to us. On the other hand the sum of all that is SUBJECTIVE, we may comprehend in the name of the SELF OR INTELLIGENCE. Both conceptions are in necessary antithesis. Intelligence is conceived of as exclusively representative, nature as exclusively represented; the one as conscious, the other as without consciousness. Now in all acts of positive knowledge there is required a reciprocal concurrence of both, namely of the conscious being, and of that which is in itself unconscious. Our problem is to explain this concurrence, its possibility and its necessity.

During the act of knowledge itself, the objective and subjective are so instantly united, that we cannot determine to which of the two the priority belongs. There is here no first, and no second; both are coinstantaneous and one. While I am attempting to explain this intimate coalition, I must suppose it dissolved. I must necessarily set out from the one, to which therefore I give hypothetical antecedence, in order to arrive at the other. But as there are but two factors or elements in the problem, subject and object, and as it is left indeterminate from which of them I should commence, there are two cases equally possible.

1. EITHER THE OBJECTIVE IS TAKEN AS THE FIRST, AND THEN WE HAVE TO ACCOUNT FOR THE SUPERVENTION OF THE SUBJECTIVE, WHICH COALESCES WITH IT. . . .
2. OR THE SUBJECTIVE IS TAKEN AS THE FIRST, AND THE PROBLEM THEN IS, HOW THERE SUPERVENES TO IT A COINCIDENT OBJECTIVE. . . .

*From *Biographia Literaria* (1817) (ed. J. Shawcross), Oxford: Oxford University Press, 1907.

21

Now the apparent contradiction, that the former position, namely, the existence of things without us, which from its nature cannot be immediately certain, should be received as blindly and as independently of all grounds as the existence of our own being, the Transcendental philosopher can solve only by the supposition, that the former is unconsciously involved in the latter; that it is not only coherent but identical, and one and the same thing with our own immediate self consciousness. To demonstrate this identity is the office and object of his philosophy. . . .

[IMAGINATION]

The Imagination then I consider either as primary, or secondary. The primary Imagination I hold to be the living power and prime agent of all human perception, and as a repetition in the finite mind of the eternal act of creation in the infinite I AM. The secondary Imagination I consider as an echo of the former, coexisting with the conscious will, yet still as identical with the primary in the *kind* of its agency, and differing only in *degree*, and in the *mode* of its operation. It dissolves, diffuses, dissipates, in order to recreate: or where this process is rendered impossible, yet at all events it struggles to idealize and to unify. It is essentially *vital*, even as all objects (*as* objects) are essentially fixed and dead.

FANCY, on the contrary, has no other counters to play with, but fixities and definites. The fancy is indeed no other than a mode of memory, emancipated from the order of time and space; while it is blended with, and modified by that empirical phenomenon of the will, which we express by the word *choice*. But equally with the ordinary memory of the Fancy must receive all its materials ready made from the law of association. . . .

. . . The poet, described in ideal perfection, brings the whole soul of man into activity, with the subordination of its faculties to each other, according to their relative worth and dignity. He diffuses a tone and spirit of unity that blends and (as it were) fuses, each into each, by that synthetic and magical power to which we have exclusively appropriated the name of imagination. This power, first put in action by the will and understanding, and retained under their irremissive, though gentle and unnoticed controul . . . reveals itself in the balance or reconciliation of opposite or discordant qualities: of sameness, with difference; of the general, with the particular; the idea, with the image; the individual, with the representative; the sense of novelty and freshness, with old and familiar objects; a more than usual state of emotion, with more than usual order; judgement ever awake and steady self-possession, with enthusiasm and feeling profound or vehement; and while it blends and harmonizes the natural with the artificial, still subordinates art to nature; the manner to the matter; and our admiration of the poet to our sympathy with the poetry.

4

Writing the Wilderness

HENRY DAVID THOREAU*

THE WEST OF which I speak is but another name for the Wild; and what I have
been preparing to say is, that in Wildness is the preservation of the World. . . .

In literature it is only the wild that attracts us. Dullness is but another name
for tameness. It is the uncivilized free and wild thinking in Hamlet and the Iliad,
in all the scriptures and mythologies, not learned in the schools, that delights
us. As the wild duck is more swift and beautiful than the tame, so is the wild –
the mallard – thought, which 'mid falling dews wings its way above the fens.
A truly good book is something as natural, and as unexpectedly and unaccount-
ably fair and perfect, as a wild-flower discovered on the prairies of the West or in
the jungles of the East. Genius is a light which makes the darkness visible, like the
lightning's flash, which perchance shatters the temple of knowledge itself – and not
a taper lighted at the hearthstone of the race, which pales before the light of
common day.

English literature, from the days of the minstrels to the Lake Poets – Chaucer
and Spenser and Milton, and even Shakespeare, included – breathes no quite fresh
and, in this sense, wild strain. It is an essentially tame and civilized literature,
reflecting Greece and Rome. Her wilderness is a greenwood, her wild man a Robin
Hood. There is plenty of genial love of Nature, but not so much of Nature herself.
Her chronicles inform us when her wild animals, but not when the wild man in
her, became extinct.

The science of Humboldt is one thing, poetry is another thing. The poet
today, notwithstanding all the discoveries of science, and the accumulated learning
of mankind, enjoys no advantage over Homer.

Where is the literature which gives expression to Nature? He would be a poet
who could impress the winds and streams into his service, to speak for him; who
nailed words to their primitive senses, as farmers drive down stakes in the spring,
which the frost has heaved; who derived his words as often as he used them –
transplanted them to his page with earth adhering to their roots; whose words were

*From 'Walking' (1862), in *Essays and Other Writings* (ed. Will H. Dircks), London: Walter
Scott Ltd, 1895.

23

so true and fresh and natural that they would appear to expand like the buds at the approach of spring, though they lay half smothered between two musty leaves in a library – aye, to bloom and bear fruit there, after their kind, annually, for the faithful reader, in sympathy with surrounding Nature.

I do not know of any poetry to quote which adequately expresses this yearning for the Wild. Approached from this side, the best poetry is tame. I do not know where to find in any literature, ancient or modern, any account which contents me of that Nature with which even I am acquainted. You will perceive that I demand something which no Augustan nor Elizabethan age, which no *culture*, in short, can give. Mythology comes nearer to it than anything. How much more fertile a Nature, at least, has Grecian mythology its root in than English literature! Mythology is the crop which the Old World bore before its soil was exhausted, before the fancy and imagination were affected with blight; and which it still bears, wherever its pristine vigor is unabated. All other literatures endure only as the elms which overshadow our houses; but this is like the great dragon-tree of the Western Isles, as old as mankind, and, whether that does or not, will endure as long; for the decay of other literatures makes the soil in which it thrives.

The West is preparing to add its fables to those of the East. The valleys of the Ganges, the Nile, and the Rhine having yielded their crop, it remains to be seen what the valleys of the Amazon, the Plate, the Orinoco, the St. Lawrence, and the Mississippi will produce. Perchance, when, in the course of ages, American liberty has become a fiction of the past – as it is to some extent a fiction of the present – the poets of the world will be inspired by American mythology.

The wildest dreams of wild men, even, are not the less true, though they may not recommend themselves to the sense which is most common among Englishmen and Americans today. It is not every truth that recommends itself to the common sense. Nature has a place for the wild clematis as well as for the cabbage. Some expressions of truth are reminiscent, others merely *sensible*, as the phrase is, others prophetic. Some forms of disease, even, may prophesy forms of health. The geologist has discovered that the figures of serpents, griffins, flying dragons, and other fanciful embellishments of heraldry, have their prototypes in the forms of fossil species which were extinct before man was created, and hence, 'indicate a faint and shadowy knowledge of a previous state of organic existence'. The Hindus dreamed that the earth rested on an elephant, and the elephant on a tortoise, and the tortoise on a serpent; and though it may be an unimportant coincidence, it will not be out of place here to state, that a fossil tortoise has lately been discovered in Asia large enough to support an elephant. I confess that I am partial to these wild fancies, which transcend the order of time and development. They are the sublimest recreation of the intellect. The partridge loves peas, but not those that go with her into the pot.

In short, all good things are wild and free. There is something in a strain of music, whether produced by an instrument or by the human voice – take the sound of a bugle in a summer night, for instance – which by its wildness, to speak without satire, reminds me of the cries emitted by wild beasts in their native forests. It is so much of their wildness as I can understand. Give me for my friends and neighbors wild men, not tame ones. The wildness of the savage is but a faint symbol of the awful ferity with which good men and lovers meet. . . .

There are other letters for the child to learn than those which Cadmus invented. The Spaniards have a good term to express this wild and dusky knowledge, *Gramatica parda*, tawny grammar.

5

Landscape, Mimesis and Morality

JOHN RUSKIN*

THE PATHETIC FALLACY

NOW, THEREFORE, PUTTING these tiresome and absurd words quite out of our way, we may go on at our ease to examine the point in question, – namely, the difference between the ordinary, proper, and true appearances of things to us; and the extraordinary, or false appearances, when we are under the influence of emotion, or contemplative fancy; false appearances, I say, as being entirely un-connected with any real power or character in the object, and only imputed to it by us. For instance –

> The spendthrift crocus, bursting through the mould
> Naked and shivering, with his cup of gold.
>
> (O. W. Holmes, Astraea)

This is very beautiful, and yet very untrue. The crocus is not a spendthrift, but a hardy plant; its yellow is not gold, but saffron. How is it that we enjoy so much the having it put into our heads that it is anything else than a plain crocus?

It is an important question. For, throughout our past reasonings about art, we have always found that nothing could be good or useful, or ultimately plea-surable, which was untrue. But here is something pleasurable in written poetry which is nevertheless *un*true. And what is more, if we think over our favourite poetry, we shall find it full of this kind of fallacy, and that we like it all the more for being so.

It will appear also, on consideration of the matter, that this fallacy is of two principal kinds. Either, as in this case of the crocus, it is the fallacy of wilful fancy, which involves no real expectation that it will be believed; or else it is a fallacy caused by an excited state of the feelings, making us, for the time, more or less irrational. Of the cheating of the fancy we shall have to speak presently; but, in

*From *Modern Painters*, Volume III, Chapters 12–13 and Chapter 17 (1856), London: J. M. Dent, 1906.

this chapter, I want to examine the nature of the other error, that which the mind admits when affected strongly by emotion. Thus, for instance, in *Alton Locke*,

> They rowed her in across the rolling foam –
> The cruel, crawling foam.

The foam is not cruel, neither does it crawl. The state of mind which attributes to it these characters of a living creature is one in which the reason is unhinged by grief. All violent feelings have the same effect. They produce in us a falseness in all our impressions of external things, which I would generally characterize as the 'pathetic fallacy'.

Now we are in the habit of considering this fallacy as eminently a character of poetical description, and the temper of mind in which we allow it, as one eminently poetical, because passionate. But I believe, if we look well into the matter, that we shall find the greatest poets do not often admit this kind of falseness, – that it is only the second order of poets who much delight in it.[1]

Thus, when Dante describes the spirits falling from the bank of Acheron 'as dead leaves flutter from a bough' (*Inferno*, III, 112), he gives the most perfect image possible of their utter lightness, feebleness, passiveness, and scattering agony of despair, without, however, for an instant losing his own clear perception that *these* are souls, and *those* are leaves; he makes no confusion of one with the other. But when Coleridge speaks of

> The one red leaf, the last of its clan,
> That dances as often as dance it can
>
> (*Christabel*, Pt I)

he has a morbid, that is to say, a so far false, idea about the leaf; he fancies a life in it, and will, which there are not; confuses its powerlessness with choice, its fading death with merriment, and the wind that shakes it with music. Here, however, there is some beauty, even in the morbid passage; but take an instance in Homer and Pope. Without the knowledge of Ulysses, Elpenor, his youngest follower, has fallen from an upper chamber in the Circean palace, and has been left dead, unmissed by his leader or companions, in the haste of their departure. They cross the sea to the Cimmerian land; and Ulysses summons the shades from Tartarus. The first which appears is that of the lost Elpenor. Ulysses, amazed, and in exactly the spirit of bitter and terrified lightness which is seen in Hamlet ['Well said, old mole! can'st work in the ground so fast?' (I, V)], addresses the spirit with the simple, startled words:

> Elpenor? How camest thou under the shadowy darkness?
> Hast thou come faster on foot than I in my black ship?
>
> (*Odyssey*, XII, 56)

Which Pope renders thus:

> O, say, what angry power Elpenor led
> To glide in shades, and wander with the dead?
> How could thy soul, by realms and seas disjoined,
> Outfly the nimble sail, and leave the lagging wind?

I sincerely hope the reader finds no pleasure here, either in the nimbleness of the sail, or the laziness of the wind! And yet how is it that these conceits are so painful now, when they have been pleasant to us in the other instances?

For a very simple reason. They are not a *pathetic* fallacy at all, for they are put into the mouth of the wrong passion – a passion which never could possibly have spoken them – agonized curiosity. Ulysses wants to know the facts of the matter; and the very last thing his mind could do at the moment would be to pause, or suggest in anywise what was *not* a fact. The delay in the first three lines, and conceit in the last, jar upon us instantly like the most frightful discord in music. No poet of true imaginative power could possibly have written the passage.

Therefore we see that the spirit of truth must guide us in some sort, even in our enjoyment of fallacy. Coleridge's fallacy has no discord in it, but Pope's has set our teeth on edge. . . .

I believe these instances are enough to illustrate the main point I insist upon respecting the pathetic fallacy, – that so far as it *is* a fallacy, it is always the sign of a morbid state of mind, and comparatively of a weak one. Even in the most inspired prophet it is a sign of the incapacity of his human sight or thought to bear what has been revealed to it. In ordinary poetry, if it is found in the thoughts of the poet himself, it is at once a sign of his belonging to the inferior school; if in the thoughts of the characters imagined by him, it is right or wrong according to the genuineness of the emotion from which it springs; always, however, implying necessarily *some* degree of weakness in the character. . . .

My reason for asking the reader to give so much of his time to the examination of the pathetic fallacy was, that, whether in literature or in art, he will find it eminently characteristic of the modern mind; and in the landscape, whether of literature or art, he will also find the modern painter endeavouring to express something which he, as a living creature, imagines in the lifeless object, while the classical and mediaeval painters were content with expressing the unimaginary and actual qualities of the object itself. It will be observed that, according to the principle state long ago, I use the words painter and poet quite indifferently, including in our inquiry the landscape of literature, as well as that of painting; and this the more because the spirit of classical landscape has hardly been expressed in any other way than by words.

Taking, therefore, this wide field, it is surely a very notable circumstance, to begin with, that this pathetic fallacy is eminently characteristic of modern painting. For instance, Keats, describing a wave breaking out at sea, says of it:

Down whose green back the short-lived foam, all hoar,
Bursts gradual, with a wayward indolence.

(Endymion, II, 350)

That is quite perfect, as an example of the modern manner. The idea of the peculiar action with which foam rolls down a long, large wave could not have been given by any other words so well as by this 'wayward indolence'. But Homer would never have written, never thought of, such words. He could not by any possibility have lost sight of the great fact that the wave, from the beginning to the end of it, do what it might, was still nothing else than salt water; and that salt water could not be either wayward or indolent. He will call the waves 'over-roofed', 'full-charged', 'monstrous', 'compact-black', 'dark-clear', 'violet-coloured', 'wine-coloured', and so on. But every one of these epithets is descriptive of pure physical nature. 'Over-roofed' is the term he invariably uses of anything – rock, house, or wave – that nods over at the brow; the other terms need no explanation; they are as accurate and intense in truth as words can be, but they never show the slightest feeling of anything animated in the ocean. Black or clear, monstrous or violet-coloured, cold salt water it is always, and nothing but that.

Well, but the modern writer, by his admission of the tinge of fallacy, has given an idea of something in the action of the wave which Homer could not, and surely, therefore, has made a step in advance? Also there appears to be a degree of sympathy and feeling in the one writer, which there is not in the other; and as it has been received for a first principle that writers are great in proportion to the intensity of their feelings, and Homer seems to have no feelings about the sea but that it is black and deep, surely in this respect also the modern writer is the greater?'

Stay a moment. Homer had some feeling about the sea; a faith in the animation of it much stronger that Keats's. But all this sense of something living in it, he separates in his mind into a great abstract image of a Sea Power. He never says the waves rage, or the waves are idle. But he says there is somewhat in, and greater than, the waves, which rages, and is idle, and that he calls a god.

THE MORAL OF LANDSCAPE

... [Though] the absence of the love of nature is not an assured condemnation, its presence is an invariable sign of goodness of heart and justness of moral perception, though by no means of moral practice; that in proportion to the degree in which it is felt, will probably be the degree in which all nobleness and beauty of character will also be felt; that when it is originally absent from any mind, that mind is in many other respects hard, worldly, and degraded; that where, having been originally present, it is repressed by art or education, that repression appears to have been detrimental to the person suffering it; ... and that wherever the feeling exists, it acts for good on the character to which it belongs, though, as it may often belong to characters weak in other respects, it may carelessly be mistaken for a source of evil in them.

29

. . . [As,] by the accident of education, the love of nature has been, among us, associated with wilfulness, so, by the accident of time, it has been associated with faithlessness. I traced, above, the peculiar mode in which this faithlessness was indicated; but I never intended to imply, therefore, that it was an invariable concomitant of the love. [For we must not] forget there was once a time when 'the Lord answered Job out of the whirlwind' (Job xxxviii.1). And if we now take final and full view of the matter, we shall find that the love of nature, wherever it has existed, has been a faithful and sacred element of human feeling; that is to say, supposing all circumstances otherwise the same with respect to two individuals, the one who loves nature most will be always found to have more faith in God than the other. It is intensely difficult, owing to the confusion and counter influences which always mingle in the data of the problem, to make this abstraction fairly; but so far as we can do it, so far, I boldly assert, the result is constantly the same: the nature-worship will be found to bring with it such a sense of the presence and power of a Great Spirit as no mere reasoning can either induce or controvert; and where that nature-worship is innocently pursued, – i.e. with due respect to other claims on time, feeling, and exertion, and associated with the higher principles of religion, – it becomes the channel of certain sacred truths, which by no other means can be conveyed. . . .

The great mechanical impulses of the age, of which most of us are so proud, are a mere passing fever, half-speculative, half-childish. People will discover at last that royal roads to anything can no more be laid in iron than they can in dust; that there are, in fact, no royal roads to anywhere worth going to; that if there were, it would that instant cease to be worth going to, – I mean, so far as the things to be obtained are in any way estimable in terms of price. For there are two classes of precious things in the world: those that God gives us for nothing – sun, air, and life (both mortal life and immortal); and the secondarily precious things which He gives us for a price: these secondarily precious things, worldly wine and milk, can only be bought for definite money; they never can be cheapened. No cheating nor bargaining will ever get a single thing out of nature's 'establishment' at half-price. Do we want to be strong? – we must work. To be hungry? – we must starve. To be happy? – we must be kind. To be wise? – we must look and think. No changing of place at a hundred miles an hour, nor making of stuffs a thousand yards a minute, will make us one whit stronger, happier, or wiser. There was always more in the world than men could see, walked they ever so slowly; they will see it no better for going fast. And they will at last, and soon too, find out that their grand inventions for conquering (as they think) space and time, do, in reality, conquer nothing; for space and time are, in their own essence, unconquerable, and besides did not want any sort of conquering; they wanted using. A fool always wants to shorten space and time: a wise man wants to lengthen both. A fool wants to kill space and kill time: a wise man, first to gain them, then to animate them. Your railroad, when you come to understand it, is only a device for making the world smaller: and as for being able to talk from place to place, that is, indeed, well and convenient; but suppose you have, originally, nothing to say. We shall be obliged at last to confess, what we should long ago have known, that the really precious things are thought and sight, not pace. It does a bullet no good to go fast; and a man, if he be truly a man, no harm to go slow; for his glory is not at all in going, but in being.

'Well; but railroads and telegraphs are so useful for communicating knowledge to savage nations.' Yes, if you have any to give them. If you know nothing but railroads, and can communicate nothing but aqueous vapour and gunpowder, – what then? But if you have any other thing than those to give, then the railroad is of use only because it communicates that other thing; and the question is – what that other thing may be. Is it religion? I believe if we had really wanted to communicate that, we could have done it in less than 1800 years, without steam. Most of the good religious communication that I remember, has been done on foot; and it cannot be easily done faster than at foot pace. Is it science? But what science – of motion, meat, and medicine? . . . Gradually, thinking on from point to point, we shall come to perceive that all true happiness and nobleness are near us, and yet neglected by us; and that till we have learned how to be happy and noble we have not much to tell, even to Red Indians. The delights of horse-racing and hunting, of assemblies in the night instead of the day, of costly and wearisome music, of costly and burdensome dress, of chagrined contention for place or power, or wealth, or the eyes of the multitude; and all the endless occupation without purpose, and idleness without rest, of our vulgar world, are not, it seems to me, enjoyments we need be ambitious to communicate. And all real and wholesome enjoyments possible to man have been just as possible to him, since first he was made of the earth, as they are now; and they are possible to him chiefly in peace. To watch the corn grow, and the blossoms set; to draw hard breath over ploughshare or spade; to read, to think, to love, to hope, to pray, – these are the things that make men happy; they have always had the power of doing these, they never will have power to do more. The world's prosperity or adversity depends upon our knowing and teaching these few things: but upon iron, or glass, or electricity, or steam, in no wise. . . .

NOTE

1   I admit two orders of poets, but no third; and by these two orders I mean the Creative (Shakespeare, Homer, Dante), and the Reflective or Perceptive (Wordsworth, Keats, Tennyson).

6

Art, Socialism and Environment

WILLIAM MORRIS*

NOW ONCE MORE I will say that we well-to-do people, those of us who love Art, not as a toy, but as a thing necessary to the life of man, as a token of his freedom and happiness, have for our best work the raising of the standard of life among the people; or in other words establishing the claim I made for Labour – which I will now put in a different form, that we may try to see what chiefly hinders us from making that claim good and what are the enemies to be attacked. Thus I put the claim again:

> *Nothing should be made by man's labour which is not worth making; or which must be made by labour degrading to the makers.*

Simple as that proposition is, and obviously right as I am sure it must seem to you, you will find, when you come to consider the matter, that it is a direct challenge to the death to the present system of labour in civilized countries. That system, which I have called competitive Commerce, is distinctly a system of war; that is of waste and destruction: or you may call it gambling if you will, the point of it being that under it whatever a man gains he gains at the expense of some other man's loss. Such a system does not and cannot heed whether the matters it makes are worth making; it does not and cannot heed whether those who make them are degraded by their work: it heeds one thing and only one, namely, what it calls making a profit; which word has got to be used so conventionally that I must explain to you what it really means, to wit the plunder of the weak by the strong! Now I say of this system, that it is of its very nature destructive of Art, that is to say of the happiness of life. Whatever consideration is shown for the life of the people in these days, whatever is done which is worth doing, is done in spite of the system and in the teeth of its maxims; and most true it is that we do, all of us, tacitly at least, admit that it is opposed to all the highest aspirations of mankind.

*From 'Art and Socialism', in *Selected Writings* (ed. G. D. H. Cole), London: Nonesuch Press, 1934.

Do we not know, for instance, how those men of genius work who are the salt of the earth, without whom the corruption of society would long ago have become unendurable? The poet, the artist, the man of science, is it not true that in their fresh and glorious days, when they are in the heyday of their faith and enthusiasm, they are thwarted at every turn by Commercial war, with its sneering question 'Will it pay?' Is it not true that when they begin to win worldly success, when they become comparatively rich, in spite of ourselves they seem to us tainted by the contact with the commercial world?

Need I speak of great schemes that hang about neglected; of things most necessary to be done, and so confessed by all men, that no one can seriously set a hand to because of the lack of money; while if it be a question of creating or stimulating some foolish whim in the public mind, the satisfaction of which will breed a profit, the money will come in by the ton. Nay you know what an old story it is of the wars bred by Commerce in search of new markets, which not even the most peaceable of statesmen can resist; an old story and still it seems for ever new, and now become a kind of grim joke, at which I would rather not laugh if I could help it, but am even forced to laugh from a soul laden with anger.

And all that mastery over the powers of nature which the last hundred years or less has given us: what has it done for us under this system? In the opinion of John Stuart Mill, it was doubtful if all the mechanical inventions of modern times have done anything to lighten the toil of labour: to be sure there is no doubt, that they were not made for that end, but to 'make a profit'. Those almost miraculous machines, which if orderly forethought had dealt with them might even now be speedily extinguishing all irksome and unintelligent labour, leaving us free to raise the standard of skill of hand and energy of mind in our workmen, and to produce afresh that loveliness and order which only the hand of man guided by his soul can produce – what have they done for us now? Those machines of which the civilized world is so proud, has it any right to be proud of the *use* they have been put to by Commercial war and waste?

I do not think exultation can have a place here: Commercial war has made a profit of these wonders; that is to say it has by their means bred for itself millions of unhappy workers, unintelligent machines as far as their daily work goes, in order to get cheap labour, to keep up its exciting but deadly game for ever. Indeed that labour would have been cheap enough – cheap to the Commercial war generals, and deadly dear to the rest of us – but for the seeds of freedom which valiant men of old have sowed amongst us to spring up in our own day into Chartism and Trades Unionism and socialism, for the defence of order and a decent life. Terrible would have been our slavery, and not of the working classes alone, but for these germs of the change which must be.

Even as it is, by the reckless aggregation of machine-workers and their adjoints in the great cities and the manufacturing districts, it has kept down life amongst us, and keeps it down to a miserably low standard; so low that any standpoint for improvement is hard to think of even. By the means of speedy communication which it has created, and which should have raised the standard of life by spreading intelligence from town to country, and widely creating modest centres of freedom of thought and habits of culture – by the means of the railways and the like it has gathered to itself fresh recruits for the reserve army of competing lack-alls on which its gambling gains so much depend, stripping the country-side of its population, and extinguishing all reasonable hope and life in the lesser towns.

Nor can I, an artist, think last or least of the outward effects which betoken this rule of the wretched anarchy of Commercial war. Think of the spreading sore of London swallowing up with its loathsomeness field and wood and heath without mercy and without hope, mocking our feeble efforts to deal even with its minor evils of smoke-laden sky and befouled river: the black horror and reckless squalor of our manufacturing districts, so dreadful to the senses which are unused to them that it is ominous for the future of the race that any man can live among it in tolerable cheerfulness: nay in the open country itself the thrusting aside by miser-able jerry-built brick and slate of the solid grey dwellings that are still scattered about, fit emblems in their cheery but beautiful simplicity of the yeomen of the English field, whose destruction at the hands of yet young Commercial war was lamented so touchingly by the high-minded More and the valiant Latimer. Everywhere in short the change from old to new involving one certainty, whatever else may be doubtful, a worsening of the aspect of the country.

This is the condition of England: of England the country of order, peace and stability, the land of common sense and practicality; the country to which all eyes are turned of those whose hope is for the continuance and perfection of modern progress. There are countries in Europe whose aspect is not so ruined outwardly, though they may have less prosperity, less wide-spread middle-class wealth to balance the squalor and disgrace I have mentioned: but if they are members of the great Commercial whole, through the same mill they have got to go, unless some-thing should happen to turn aside the triumphant march of War Commercial before it reaches the end.

That is what three centuries of Commerce have brought that hope to which sprung up when feudalism began to fall to pieces. What can give us the day-spring of a new hope? What, save general revolt against the tyranny of Commercial war? The palliatives over which many worthy people are busying themselves now are useless: because they are but unorganized partial revolts against a vast wide-spreading grasping organization which will, with the unconscious instinct of a plant, meet every attempt at bettering the condition of the people with an attack on a fresh side; new machines, new markets, wholesale emigration, the revival of grovelling superstitions, preachments of thrift to lack-alls, of temperance to the wretched; such things as these will baffle at every turn all partial revolts against the monster we of the middle classes have created for our own undoing.

I will speak quite plainly on this matter, though I must say an ugly word in the end if I am to say what I think. The one thing to be done is to set people far and wide to think it possible to raise the standard of life. If you think of it, you will see clearly that this means stirring up *general discontent*.

And now to illustrate that I turn back to my blended claim for Art and Labour, that I may deal with the third clause in it: here is the claim again:

It is right and necessary that all men should have work to do –
First – *Work worth doing;*
Second – *Work of itself pleasant to do;*
Third – *Work done under such conditions as would make it neither over-*
wearisome nor over-anxious.

With the first and second clauses, which are very nearly related to each other, I
have tried to deal already. They are as it were the soul of the claim for proper
labour; the third clause is the body without which that soul cannot exist. I will
extend it in this way, which will indeed partly carry us over ground already covered:

No one who is willing to work should ever fear want of such employment as
would earn for him all due necessaries of mind and body.

All due necessaries – what are the due necessaries for a good citizen?

First, *honourable and fitting work*: which would involve giving him a chance
of gaining capacity for his work by due education; also, as the work must be worth
doing and pleasant to do, it will be found necessary to this end that his position
be so assured to him that he cannot be compelled to do useless work, or work in
which he cannot take pleasure.

The second necessity is *decency of surroundings*: including (*a*) good lodging;
(*b*) ample space; (*c*) general order and beauty. That is (*a*) our houses must be well
built, clean and healthy; (*b*) there must be abundant garden space in our towns,
and our towns must not eat up the fields and natural features of the country; nay
I demand even that there be left waste places and wilds in it, or romance and
poetry – that is Art – will die out amongst us. (*c*) Order and beauty means, that
not only our houses must be stoutly and properly built, but also that they be orna-
mented duly: that the fields be not left only for cultivation, but also that they be
not spoilt by it any more than a garden is spoilt: no one for instance to be allowed
to cut down, for mere profit, trees whose loss would spoil a landscape: neither on
any pretext should people be allowed to darken the daylight with smoke, to befoul
rivers, or to degrade any spot of earth with squalid litter and brutal wasteful disorder.

The third necessity is *leisure*. You will understand that in using that word I
imply first that all men must work for some portion of the day, and secondly that
they have a positive right to claim a respite from that work: the leisure they have
a right to claim, must be ample enough to allow them full rest of mind and body:
a man must have time for serious individual thought, for imagination – for
dreaming even – or the race of men will inevitably worsen. Even of the honourable
and fitting work of which I have been speaking, which is a whole heaven asunder
from the forced work of the Capitalist system, a man must not be asked to give
more than his fair share; or men will become unequally developed, and there will
still be a rotten place in Society.

Here then I have given you the conditions under which work worth doing,
and undegrading to do, can be done: under no other conditions can it be done:

if the general work of the world is not worth doing and undegrading to do it is a mockery to talk of civilization.

Well then can these conditions be obtained under the present gospel of Capital, which has for its motto 'The devil take the hindmost'?

Let us look at our claim again in other words:

In a properly ordered state of Society every man willing to work should be ensured –
First – *Honourable and fitting work*;
Second – *A healthy and beautiful house*;
Third – *Full leisure for rest of mind and body.*

Now I don't suppose that anybody here will deny that it would be desirable that this claim should be satisfied: but what I want you all to think is that it is *necessary* that it be satisfied; that unless we try our utmost to satisfy it, we are but part and parcel of a society founded on robbery and injustice, condemned by the laws of the universe to destroy itself by its own efforts to exist for ever. Furthermore, I want you to think that as on the one hand it is possible to satisfy this claim, so on the other hand it is impossible to satisfy it under the present plutocratic system, which will forbid us even any serious attempt to satisfy it: the beginnings of Social Revolution must be the foundations of the re-building of the Art of the People, that is to say of the Pleasure of Life.

7

Dorothy Wordsworth: The Spirit of Appearances

VIRGINIA WOOLF*

SPRING PASSED; SUMMER came; summer turned to autumn; it was winter, and then again the sloes were in blossom and hawthorns green and spring had come. But it was spring in the North now, and Dorothy was living alone with her brother in a small cottage at Grasmere in the midst of the hills. Now after the hardships and separations of youth they were together under their own roof; now they could address themselves undisturbed to the absorbing occupation of living in the heart of Nature and trying, day by day, to read her meaning. . . .

It is strange how vividly all this is brought before us, considering that the diary is made up of brief notes such as any quiet woman might make of her garden's changes and her brother's moods and the progress of the seasons. It was warm and mild, she notes, after a day of rain. She met a cow in a field. 'The cow looked at me, and I looked at the cow, and whenever I stirred the cow gave over eating.' She met an old man who walked with two sticks – for days on end she met nothing more out of the way than a cow eating and an old man walking. And her motives for writing are common enough – 'because I will not quarrel with myself, and because I shall give William pleasure by it when he comes home again'. It is only gradually that the difference between this rough notebook and others discloses itself; only by degrees that the brief notes unfurl in the mind and open a whole landscape before us, that the plain statement proves to be aimed so directly at the object that if we look exactly along the line that it points we shall see precisely what she saw. 'The moonlight lay upon the hills like snow.' 'The air was become still, the lake of a bright slate colour, the hills darkening. The bays shot into the low fading shores. Sheep resting. All things quiet.' 'There was no one waterfall above another – it was the sound of waters in the air – the voice of the air.' Even in such brief notes one feels the suggestive power which is the gift of the poet rather than of the naturalist, the power which, taking only the simplest facts, so orders them that the whole scene comes before us, heightened and composed, the lake in its quiet, the hills in their splendour. Yet she was no descriptive writer in the usual sense.

*From 'Dorothy Wordsworth' (1929), in *The Common Reader: Second Series* (ed. Andrew McNeillie), London: Hogarth Press, 1986.

Her first concern was to be truthful – grace and symmetry must be made subordinate to truth. But then truth is sought because to falsify the look of the stir of the breeze on the lake is to tamper with the spirit which inspires appearances. It is that spirit which goads her and urges her and keeps her faculties for ever on the stretch. A sight or a sound would not let her be till she had traced her perception along its course and fixed it in words, though they might be bald, or in an image, though it might be angular. Nature was a stern taskmistress. The exact prosaic detail must be rendered as well as the vast and visionary outline. Even when the distant hills trembled before her in the glory of a dream she must note with literal accuracy 'the glittering silver line on the ridge of the backs of the sheep', or remark how 'the crows at a little distance from us became white as silver as they flew in the sunshine, and when they went still further, they looked like shapes of water passing over the green fields'. . . .

Always trained and in use, her powers of observation became in time so expert and so acute that a day's walk stored her mind's eye with a vast assembly of curious objects to be sorted at leisure. How strange the sheep looked mixed with the soldiers at Dumbarton Castle! For some reason the sheep looked their real size, but the soldiers looked like puppets. And then the movements of the sheep were so natural and fearless, and the motion of the dwarf soldiers was so restless and apparently without meaning. It was extremely queer. Or lying in bed she would look up at the ceiling and think how the varnished beams were 'as glossy as black rocks on a sunny day cased in ice'. Yes, they

> crossed each other in almost as intricate and fantastic a manner as I have seen the underboughs of a large beech-tree withered by the depth of the shade above. . . . It was like what I should suppose an underground cave or temple to be, with a dripping or moist roof, and the moonlight entering in upon it by some means or other, and yet the colours were more like melted gems. I lay looking up till the light of the fire faded away. . . . I did not sleep much.

Indeed, she scarcely seemed to shut her eyes. They looked and they looked, urged on not only by an indefatigable curiosity but also by reverence, as if some secret of the utmost importance lay hidden beneath the surface. Her pen sometimes stammers with the intensity of the emotion that she controlled, as De Quincey said that her tongue stammered with the conflict between her ardour and her shyness when she spoke. But controlled she was. Emotional and impulsive by nature, her eyes 'wild and starting', tormented by feelings which almost mastered her, still she must control, still she must repress, or she would fail in her task – she would cease to see. But if one subdued oneself, and resigned one's private agitations, then, as if in reward, Nature would bestow an exquisite satisfaction. 'Rydale was very beautiful, with spear-shaped streaks of polished steel. . . . It calls home the heart to quietness. I had been very melancholy', she wrote. For did not Coleridge come walking over the hills and tap at the cottage door late at night – did she not carry a letter from Coleridge hidden safe in her bosom?

Thus giving to Nature, thus receiving from Nature, it seemed, as the arduous and ascetic days went by, that Nature and Dorothy had grown together in perfect sympathy – a sympathy not cold or vegetable or inhuman because at the core of it burnt that other love for 'my beloved', her brother, who was indeed its heart and inspiration. William and Nature and Dorothy herself, were they not one being? Did they not compose a trinity, self-contained and self-sufficient and independent whether indoors or out? . . .

. . . It was a strange love, profound, almost dumb, as if brother and sister had grown together and shared not the speech but the mood, so that they hardly knew which felt, which spoke, which saw the daffodils or the sleeping city; only Dorothy stored the mood in prose, and later William came and bathed in it and made it into poetry. But one could not act without the other. They must feel, they must think, they must be together. So now, when they had lain out on the hillside they would rise and go home and make tea, and Dorothy would write to Coleridge, and they would sow the scarlet beans together, and William would work at his 'Leech Gatherer', and Dorothy would copy the lines for him. Rapt but controlled, free yet strictly ordered, the homely narrative moves naturally from ecstasy on the hills to baking bread and ironing linen and fetching William his supper in the cottage.

The cottage, though its garden ran up into the fells, was on the highroad. Through her parlour window Dorothy looked out and saw whoever might be passing – a tall beggar woman perhaps with her baby on her back; an old soldier; a coroneted landau with touring ladies peering inquisitively inside. The rich and the great she would let pass – they interested her no more than cathedrals or picture galleries or great cities; but she could never see a beggar at the door without asking him in and questioning him closely. Where had he been? What had he seen? How many children had he? She searched into the lives of the poor as if they held in them the same secret as the hills. A tramp eating cold bacon over the kitchen fire might have been a starry night, so closely she watched him; so clearly she noted how his old coat was patched 'with three bell-shaped patches of darker blue behind, where the buttons had been', how his beard of a fortnight's growth was like 'grey *plush*'. And then as they rambled on with their tales of seafaring and the pressgang and the Marquis of Granby, she never failed to capture the one phrase that sounds on in the mind after the story is forgotten: 'What, you are stepping westward?' 'To be sure there is great promise for virgins in Heaven.' 'She could trip lightly by the graves of those who died when they were young.' The poor had their poetry as the hills had theirs. But it was out of doors, on the road or on the moor, not in the cottage parlour, that her imagination had freest play. Her happiest moments were passed tramping beside a jibbing horse on a wet Scottish road with certainty of bed or supper. All she knew was that there was some sight ahead, some grove of trees to be noted, some waterfall to be inquired into. . . .

. . . At last they reached the waterfall. And then all Dorothy's powers fell upon it. She searched out its character, she noted its resemblances, she defined its differences, with all the ardour of a discoverer, with all the exactness of a naturalist, with all the rapture of a lover. She possessed it at last – she had laid it up in her mind for ever. It had become one of those 'inner visions' which she could call to mind at any time in their distinctness and in their particularity. It would come back to her long years afterwards when she was old and her mind had failed her; it would come back stilled and heightened and mixed with all the happiest memories of her past – with the thought of Racedown and Alfoxden and Coleridge reading 'Christabel', and her beloved, her brother William. It would bring with it what no human being could give, what no human relation could offer – consolation and quiet. If, then, the passionate cry of Mary Wollstonecraft had reached her ears – 'Surely something resides in this heart that is not perishable – and life is more than a dream' – she would have had no doubt whatever as to her answer. She would have said quite simply, 'We looked about us, and we felt that we were happy'.

8

John Clare,
Love Poet of Nature

JOHN MIDDLETON MURRY*

. . . [THE] EAGERNESS WITH which we welcome this collection of Clare's poetry [*Poems,* selected and edited by Edmund Blunden and Alan Porter, 1921] is likely to be so genuine and so justified as to disturb our sense of proportion. Into a generation of poets who flirt with nature suddenly descends a true-nature poet, one whose intimate and self-forgetful knowledge of the ways of birds and beasts and flowers rises like the scent of open fields from every page. Surely the only danger is that the enthusiasm of our recognition may be excessive; the relief overpowering with which we greet a poet who not only professes, but proves by the very words of his profession, that his dream of delight is

> To note on hedgerow baulks, in moisture sprent
>   The jetty snail creep from the mossy thorn,
> With earnest heed and tremulous intent,
>   Frail brother of the morn,
> That from the tiny bents and misted leaves
>   Withdraws his timid horn,
>   And fearful vision weaves.

We have indeed almost to be on our guard against the sweet, cool shock of such a verse; the emotional quality is so assured and individual, the language so simple and inevitable, the posture of mind so unassuming and winning, that one is tempted for a moment to believe that while Wordsworth was engaged in putting the poetry of nature wrong by linking it to a doubtful metaphysic, John Clare was engaged in putting it right.

And so in a sense it was. As a poet of nature Clare was truer, more thoroughly subdued to that in which he worked than Wordsworth. Wordsworth called upon the poet to keep his eye upon the object; but his eye was hardly so penetrating and keen as Clare's. Yet Wordsworth was a great poet, and Keats, with whom Clare's kinship was really closer, was a great poet, and Clare was not; and it is important

*From 'The Poetry of John Clare', *Countries of the Mind*, London: Hudson, 1922.

41

in the case of a poet whose gifts and qualities are so enchanting as Clare's are to bear in mind from the outset the vital difference between them. Wordsworth belongs to another sphere than Clare in virtue of the range of his imaginative apprehension: Keats in virtue not only of his imagination, but also of his art. In one respect Clare was a finer artist than Wordsworth, he had a truer ear and a more exquisite instinct for words; but he had nothing of the principle of inward growth which gives to Wordsworth's most careless work a place within the unity of a great scheme. Wordsworth's incessant effort to comprehend experience would itself have been incomprehensible to Clare; Keat's consuming passion to make his poetry adequate not merely in content but also in the very mechanism of expression to an emotional experience more overwhelming even than Wordsworth's would have been like a problem of metaphysics to a ploughboy.

Clare was indeed a singer born. His nature was strangely simple, and his capacity for intense emotion appears at first sight to have been almost completely restricted to a reaction to nature. The intensity with which he adored the country which he knew is without a parallel in English literature; of him it seems hardly a metaphor to say he was an actual part of his countryside. Away from it he pined; he became queer and irresponsible. With his plants and birds and bees and fields he was among his own people. The spiked thistle, the firetail, the hare, the white-nosed and the grandfather bee were his friends. Yet he hardly humanised them; he seems rather to have lived on the same level of existence as they, and to have known them as they know each other. We feel that it is only by an effort that he manages to make himself conscious of his emotion towards them or of his own motive in singing of it. In those rare moments he conceives of the voice of Nature as something eternal, outlasting all generations of men, whispering to them to sing also. Thus, while he sits under the huge old elm which is the shepherd's tree, listening to 'the laugh of summer leaves above',

> The wind of that eternal ditty sings,
> Humming of future things that burn the mind
> To leave some fragment of itself behind.

That is the most imaginative statement Clare ever made of his own poetic purpose. He, the poet, is one more of Nature's voices. . . .

When we have touched the unique emotional core which persists throughout the work of a true poet, we have come perhaps as near as we can to his secret. We stand as it were at the very source of his creation. In the great poetic artist we may follow out the intricacies and ramifications of the intellectual structure by which he makes the expression of his central emotion complete, and the emotion itself permanent. In Clare the work is unnecessary. The emotion is hardly mediated at all. The poetic creation is instinctive and impulsive; the love is poured out, and the bird, the beast, the flower is made glorious. It is the very process which Stendhal described, with fitting brilliancy, as *la cristallisation de l'amour*.

We may therefore most truly describe Clare as the love poet of nature; and we need not pause to explore the causes why nature and not a human being was turned to crystal by the magical process of his love. Those who care to know may find the story woven in among the narrative of Mr. Blunden's sympathetic introduction; they can discover for themselves the reason why Clare appears in the world of grown men and women as a stranger and a changeling; why the woman of his dreams is disembodied; why, when he calls to her in his *Invitation to Eternity,* the present is 'marred with reason' –

> The land of shadows wilt thou trace
> Nor look nor know each other's face;
> The present marred with reason gone
> And past and present both as one?
> Say, maiden, can thy life be led
> To join the living and the dead?
> Then trace thy footsteps on with me:
> We are wed to one eternity.

In eternity perhaps a woman, but in the actual Nature was Clare's mistress; her he served and cherished with a tenderness and faithful knowledge unique in the poetry of nature. Like a true lover he stammered in long speeches, but he spoke to her the divinest and most intimate things. Assuredly his lines were cast so that he had no need of woman even in eternity, and perhaps the truest words he ever wrote of himself are those of the poem by which he is most generally known:

> I long for scenes where man has never trod;
>   A place where woman never smiled nor wept;
> There to abide with my creator, God,
>   And sleep as I in childhood sweetly slept:
> Untroubling and untroubled where I lie;
>   The grass below – above the vaulted sky.

9

William Wordsworth: Poetry, Chemistry, Nature

JOHN F. DANBY*

[AFTER NEWTON]

THE NEWTONIAN UNIVERSE is familiar to us now (and we might still be inclined to summarize it so) in terms of its limitations. It opened out awesomely into Pascal's two infinities, it then proceeded to measure and domesticate these by the newly invented calculus. Everything in this universe was explicable except existence itself. Voltaire, therefore, was serious when he joked that if God did not exist he would have to be invented. Again, the God needed to maintain the cosmic clock need only be a clockmaker, and an absentee. Regarded in its total perfection the universe bore witness to a Supreme Architect, and He could be deduced from and then identified with the marvellous whole. All the same, as Auden has pointed out, God could not enter into His creation in any of its parts. Incarnation was inconceivable. Literally, as Blake perceived, Voltaire's God was Nobody's Daddy. And along with incarnation, the possibility of those instants of revelation and participation which Wordsworth experienced was also excluded:

> There is a field, of many, one,
> A single tree that I have looked upon.

– Wordsworth's tree, for the eighteenth century, would be as unthinkable as the burning bush. Change, growth, emergence of the unique – all were reduced to aggregation, rearrangement, alteration of position. Space and time in this universe were *continua* of basically uniform points: though Blake would assert there was one moment of each day Satan-Newton could not catch, and that that moment opened into Eternity. . . .

. . . It has been only too easy to turn away from Wordsworth's poems to his 'theories', his 'philosophy'. To illustrate at the same time his revolutionary position

*From *The Simple Wordsworth: Studies in the Poems 1797–1807*, London: Routledge & Kegan Paul, 1960.

in literature and philosophy, let us compare Wordsworth's 'A Rainbow' with some lines written on the rainbow in 1727.

In that year Sir Isaac Newton died and James Thomson wrote at length in blank verse to honour the occasion:

> . . . Even Light itself, which everything displays,
> Shone undiscover'd till his brighter mind
> Untwisted all the shining robe of day;
> And, from the whitening undistinguish'd blaze,
> Collecting every ray into his kind,
> To the charm'd eye educ'd the gorgeous train
> Of Parent-colours. . . .

Thomson wrote in the golden age of the Newtonian assurance: in the age of Physics. Wordsworth writes, if we might indulge the fancy, in the age of Chemistry. The difference between the two sciences in Wordsworth's time was exciting, more apparent then than later in the nineteenth century. In physics one worked with mathematics and measurement. Chemists, of course, in the long run, were to do so too. But in the late eighteenth century the chemist is someone capable of being portrayed, as Dalton was, kneeling beside a bog collecting marsh gas, helped by a small boy and his tiddlers'-jar. In chemistry two different things are brought together, a sudden interaction takes place, and instead of the two things there is a third completely different from either. The universe of Newton was a complete, settled thing. Man's relation to it was either that of spectator or of fixed part in a stable whole. The universe of chemistry is a universe of action and re-action, of formation and transformation. Man in this universe is not a spectator. He is an identity both acting and re-acting, formed and formative.

It may be fanciful to describe Wordsworth's as the poetry of chemistry, romantically understood. He did himself, however, use the language of action and reaction to define the experience put into his poetry. And the chemical analogy is useful to suggest the difference between Thomson's world and his, between the lines 'To the Memory of Sir Isaac Newton' and 'A Rainbow':

> My heart leaps up when I behold
>   A rainbow in the sky:
> So was it when my life began;
>   So is it now I am a man;
> So be it when I shall grow old,
>   Or let me die!
> The Child is father of the Man,
>   And I would wish my days to be
> Bound each to each by natural piety.

In Wordsworth's poem there is the rainbow and the man and the re-action that takes place when the two come together. Wordsworth is not arranging products

45

that have been passed on to him from some other centre of truth-making for tastefully decorative treatment. The emphasis is on action between, on what it would be maybe fashionable to call 'dialogue'. Things can and do happen in the universe. The universe involves process, formation, and transformation. Because of this Wordsworth starts with the 'now' of particular experience. Then, since persons are themselves growing things involved in the process of a unified life, he recalls his first childhood's reaction and immediately after looks forward to old age. Then, he hopes, the capacity to respond, or at least to remember, will still be with him. Or else let him die: for will he not be already dead? – We hardly ever read the poem with full understanding because of its overquoted and over-misunderstood lines:

> The Child is father of the Man:
>   And I would wish my days to be
> Bound each to each by natural piety.

'Natural piety' has nothing to do with 'nature' in the hikers' sense. And the piety is not church-bound. Wordsworth is thinking, as the psychiatrists do, of how one lived experience interacts with all the others, and how the unified and harmonious mind is ideally one in which youth, maturity, and age continue to reflect and regenerate each other. The child *is* father of the Man. The parent principle of continuing growth *is* the power of fresh response. On this man depends still for all those moments of renewable experience he is capable of. While this remains with him his days can be bound each to each, in that relation of mutual trust and respect which constitutes 'pietas'.

WORDSWORTH AND 'NATURE'

. . . To see Wordsworth as a 'nature-poet' properly in his place we might consider the modes of 'nature-writing' already practised, the types of writing Wordsworth was transcending.

A rough scale of 'nature-poetry' can be constructed. The first level is that of 'nature-notes', the counting of the streaks of the tulip, observations like 'black as the ash-buds in the front of March' or like 'willows *whiten*, aspens quiver'. Tennyson is a notorious repository of such detachable and detailed accuracies, Wordsworth – surprisingly – less so. His characteristic poetry is not predominantly visual. . . . Few Wordsworth passages are comparable with the following from Coleridge's 'This Lime-Tree Bower My Prison' (of June 1797):

> The roaring dell, o'erwooded, narrow, deep,
> And only speckled by the mid-day sun;
> Where its slim trunk the ash from rock to rock
> Flings arching like a bridge; – that branchless ash,
> Unsunn'd and damp, whose few poor yellow leaves
> Ne'er tremble in the gale, yet tremble still

Fann'd by the water-fall! And there my friends
Behold the dark green file of long dank weeds,
That all at once (a most fantastic sight!)
Still not and drip beneath the dripping edge
Of the blue lay-stone.

This is the kind of attention to detail that Dorothy had and Wordsworth can be imagined as relying on her to supply. Wordsworth was not pre-eminently a note-taker in front of objects. If he ever had been his mature habit was to suppress or ignore the visual. He deplores the time when he was in that state

In which the eye was master of the heart
(Prelude, Bk XI, ll. 105–20)

The eye as such is

in every stage of life
The most despotic of our senses.
(Prelude, Bk XI, ll. 171–4)

The second level is that at which the observer sees not only single details but is interested in drawing the whole scene. The words *draw* and *scene* are significant here. 'Scenery' was invented for the theatre before it was discovered in the world at large. 'Draw' indicates the nearness of the poet to the painter in the art of composition. The eighteenth century abounds in nature-poetry of this sort. It is, among other things, the century of the picturesque. Poets painted their scenes as painters composed their pictures. Even the standard browns and varnished yellows overflow from the easel on to the page of print: in Akenside, for example:

. . . Autumnal spoils
Luxuriant, spreading to the rays of morn,
Blushed o'er the cliffs whose half-encircling mound,
As in a sylvan theatre, enclosed
That flowery level. On the river's brink
I spied a fair pavilion, which diffused
Its floating umbrage 'mid the silver shade
Of osiers. Now the western sun revealed,
Between two parting cliffs, his golden orb,
And poured across the shadow of the hills,
On rocks and floods, a yellow stream of light
That cheered the solemn scene.
(The Pleasures of the Imagination, 1744, Bk II, ll. 288–98)

This is the interest in 'scenery' of the old-fashioned Camera Club – an interest Wordsworth practically never gives way to in his poetry, or not for long.

At a third level we have to do with Ruskin's 'pathetic fallacy'. Now there is the whole scene, maybe closely observed, presented with due regard to composition, but in addition made the vehicle for feelings originating in the beholder. The result, vulgarly, is 'atmosphere'. Dickens is an obvious master of this manner (the second chapter of *Bleak House*), and so of course are Virginia Woolf and D. H. Lawrence; in poetry, among the romantics, Keats and Shelley, among the Victorians Tennyson especially. The opening of 'The Lotos Eaters' is a good instance of what was to become almost a model for 'poetic' description in the nineteenth century. There is nothing comparable with 'The Lotos Eaters' in Wordsworth. In the Tennyson passage the variations of pictorial image only emphasize the sameness and averageness of the supporting mood. Tennyson requires us to surrender to the hypnotic melancholy. Wordsworth insists on the opposite: that we should become awake and aware adjusting our selves to things, not things to us.

This brings us to the fourth level of interest in 'nature'. The three so far indicted are possible in anyone of average capacities. The threshold between the third and the fourth levels, however, seems to be more than usually steep. And it is over this threshold that the peculiarly Wordsworthian is found. The difference is not so much between two different kinds of writing as between two radically different mental attitudes, or kinds of mind. The attitude beyond the threshold Wordsworth himself described as 'wise passiveness'. . . .

Wordsworth's central achievement is a curious composedness *in himself*. He was a man, Coleridge said (making a theological joke) for whom it was good that he should be alone. 'The Solitary Reaper' is one of Wordsworth's largest and most complex statements concerning the alone-ness in which he found his balance. . . .

The largeness and complexity of the poem consist in the kind of solitariness Wordsworth is relating himself to, and the relation he enjoys with it. . . . [This relates to] the recognition of . . . permanence and inescapability: the recognition, too, that the girl's situation is not singular to her, but is Wordsworth's and everybody's:

> Whate'er the theme, the Maiden sang
> As if her song could have no ending;
> I saw her singing at her work
> And o'er her sickle bending.

Wordsworth avoids all the commonplace sentimentalities the situation of the poem might lend itself to. He neither compassionates, nor envies, nor condescends, nor idealizes. He is not the town-dweller finding simple happiness in the countryside. He is not the literary man with a nostalgia for the 'rootedness' of workers in the fields. (The girl is singularly not 'rooted', not 'a part of', or 'at one with', or 'at home in' Nature.) Neither is he at all inclined to rush to relieve the girl's loneliness or the hardness of her lot. Wordsworth is not concerned to alter in any way the situation he contemplates. His toughness as well as his tenderness are equivalent to those he responds to in the girl. Nor is he stoically impassive; and complacent indifference to the girl's situation is the last thing that could be alleged. Neither comfort nor discomfort are adequate to define the complexity of what we are left with at the end. Nor is solitude the right word for what Wordsworth sees as the pathos of the Solitary Reaper: for the solitude, to repeat, is not a singular thing. Something metaphysical rather than psychological seems required to do the perceptions justice. Adapting a sentence of Coleridge's we might say that the medium whereby spirits communicate is the solitude and freedom they have in common, and that this is what Wordsworth's poem is defining.

Wordsworth, at the end, turns his back on the girl. I think his revision of the final verse was a mistake. We need the deep sense of satisfaction that the song has brought with it – the sense of repletion which sets Wordsworth free to turn away, on his own axis, and continue in his own vast orbit:

> I listened till I had my fill,
> And, as I mounted up the hill,
> The music in my heart I bore
> Long after it was heard no more.

'I have learned', Wordsworth wrote in 1798,

> To look on nature, not as in the hour
> Of thoughtless youth; but hearing oftentimes
> The still sad music of humanity.

What this last line means can only be understood in terms of such poems as 'The Solitary Reaper'. Neither man nor nature are opposed. Nor are they one. Both are related to a fuller context that includes them, the expression of which is the song the girl sang. Wordsworth's symbol for the containing situation is commonly not a scene but a monolithic figure in an empty landscape. And that figure (either Michael, or the Leech-Gatherer, or the Highland girl) is the metaphysical 'I' – the 'I' which insulates us and yet is the very means whereby we have communion with things and with other I's.

'The Solitary Reaper' indicates the kind of link there is between such poems as 'The Reverie of Poor Susan' and 'Tintern Abbey'. These last are complementary. They emanate from the Wordsworthian centre in which both 'nature' and 'humanity' are thought of as one.

10

The Green Language

RAYMOND WILLIAMS*

[WORDSWORTH]

THERE IS THE separation of possession: the control of a land and its prospects. But there is also a separation of spirit: a recognition of forces of which we are part but which we may always forget, and which we must learn from, not seek to control. In these two kinds of separation the idea of Nature was held and transformed.

> 'Why', asked Addison, 'may not a whole Estate be thrown into a kind of garden by frequent Plantations. A man might make a pretty Landskip of his own Possessions.'

Wordsworth, almost a century later, took as the centre of his world not a possessive man but a wondering child:

> Frail creature as he is, helpless as frail,
> An inmate of this active universe:
> For feeling has to him imparted power
> That through the growing faculties of sense
> Doth like an agent of the one great Mind
> Create, creator and receiver both,
> Working but in alliance with the works
> Which it beholds.

Two principles of Nature can then be seen simultaneously. There is nature as a principle of order, of which the ordering mind is part, and which human activity, by regulating principles, may then rearrange and control. But there is also nature as a principle of creation, of which the creative mind is part, and from which we may learn the truths of our own sympathetic nature.

*From *The Country and the City* (1973), London: Hogarth Press, 1985.

This active sympathy is the real change of mind, the new consciousness if only in a minority, in the very period in which the willed transformation of nature, not only of land and water but of its raw materials and its essential elements, was to enter a new phase, in the processes we now call industrial. The agrarian confidence of the eighteenth century had been counterpointed, throughout, by feelings of loss and melancholy and regret: from the ambivalence of Thomson to the despair of Goldsmith. Now, with Wordsworth, an alternative principle was to be powerfully asserted: a confidence in nature, in its own workings, which at least at the beginning was also a broader, a more humane confidence in men.

This movement is not, at first sight, very easy to distinguish from what, in the second half of the eighteenth century, is an evident alteration of taste. It is significant and understandable that in the course of a century of reclamation, drainage and clearing there should have developed, as a by-product, a feeling for unaltered nature, for wild land: the feeling that was known at the time as 'picturesque'. It is well known how dramatically the view of the Alps altered, from Evelyn's 'strange, horrid and fearful crags and tracts', in the mid-1640s, or Dennis's 'Ruins upon ruins, in monstrous Heaps, and Heaven and Earth confounded' in 1688, to the characteristic awed praise of mid and later eighteenth-century and nineteenth- and twentieth-century travellers:

Not a precipice, not a torrent, not a cliff but is pregnant with religion and poetry.

(Gray, 1739)

Motionless torrents! silent cataracts!
Who made you glorious as the Gates of Heaven
Beneath the keen full moon?

(Coleridge, 1802)

In the course of the change, comparable districts in Britain – the Lake District, from the 1760s under the influence of Dalton and Brown; the Wye Valley and South Wales, the Scottish Highlands, North Wales, the New Forest, from the 1780s, under the direct influence of William Gilpin – became places of fashionable visiting and even of pilgrimage. Johnson's attitude to the Highlands –

the appearance is that of matter, incapable of form or usefulness, dismissed by nature from her care and left in its original elemental state

– seemed left far behind. That Nature was an improver; the new Nature is an original. But we are bound to remember that most, though not all, of these tours to wild places were undertaken by people who were able to travel because 'nature' had not left their own lands in an 'original elemental state'. The picturesque journeys – and the topographical poems, journals, paintings and engravings which promoted and commemorated them – came from the profits of an improving agriculture and from trade. It is not, at this level, an alteration of sensibility; it is strictly an addition of taste. Like the landscaped parks, where every device was employed to produce a natural effect, the wild regions of mountain and forest were for the most part objects of conspicuous aesthetic consumption: to have been to the named places, to exchange and compare the travelling and gazing experiences, was a form of fashionable society. That in the course of the journeys some other experiences came we know well enough from Wordsworth and others; but it is Wordsworth who makes what for him is the vital distinction:

> even in pleasure pleased
> Unworthily, disliking here, and there
> Liking, by rules of mimic art transferred
> To things above all art; but more – for this,
> Although a strong infection of the age,
> Was never much my habit – giving way
> To a comparison of scene with scene,
> Bent overmuch on superficial things,
> Pampering myself with meagre novelties
> Of colour and proportion: to the moods
> Of time or season, to the moral power,
> The affections and the spirit of the place
> Insensible.

The conventional 'awe' of wild places, that Johnson in the Highlands had described as

> terror without danger . . . one of the sports of fancy, a voluntary agita-
> tion of the mind, that is permitted no longer than it pleases

is something that Wordsworth had known, when he

> sought *that* beauty, which, as Milton sings,
> Hath terror in it.

But he had learned a more general perception:

> When every day brought with it some new sense
> Of exquisite regard for common things.
> And all the earth was budding with these gifts
> Of more refined humanity . . .
> . . . a spirit, there for me enshrined
> To penetrate the lofty and the low.

It is a complicated movement, including many feelings which were already familiar, but now united, even forced, into a principle of human respect and human community.

It is right to stress some continuity from Thomson and the eighteenth-century tradition. There is the use of the country, of 'nature', as a retreat and solace from human society and ordinary human consciousness:

> I well remember that those very plumes,
> Those weeds, and the high spear-grass on that well,
> By mist and silent rain-drops silvered o'er,
> As once I passed, into my heart conveyed
> So still an image of tranquillity,
> So calm and still, and looked so beautiful
> Amid the uneasy thoughts which filled by mind,
> That what we feel of sorrow and despair
> From ruin and from change, and all the grief
> That passing shows of Being leave behind,
> appeared an idle dream.

Characteristically, in this, it is the lonely observer who 'passes', and what he sees is a 'still life': an image against stress and change.

There is also continuity in a different dimension: the recognition, even the idealisation, of 'humble' characters, in sympathy, in charity and in community. *Michael* is subtitled 'a pastoral poem', and it is so in the developed sense of the description of a rural independence – the shepherd and his family who are

> as a proverb in the vale
> For endless industry

– and its dissolution by misfortune, lack of capital, and final sale:

> The Cottage which was nam'd the Evening Star
> Is gone, the ploughshare has been though the ground
> On which it stood; final changes have been wrought
> In all the neighbourhood. . . .

It is significant that Wordsworth links the 'gentle agency' of Nature with the fellow-feeling which binds him to such men as Michael: the link we observed in Thomson. Wordsworth often came closer to the actual men, but he saw them also as receding, moving away into a past which only a few surviving signs, and the spirit of poetry, could recall. In this sense the melancholy of loss and dissolution, which had been so marked in late eighteenth-century country writing, is continued in familiar terms.

But there is also an important development in Wordsworth: a new emphasis, corresponding to just this view of history, on the dispossessed, the lonely wanderer, the vagrant. It is here that the social observation is linked to the perceptions of the lonely observer, who is also the poet. The old Cumberland beggar, in the poem of that title, is a later version of the old man whom Crabbe had observed, but the change of viewpoint is remarkable. He is not now evidence of the lack of community – of the village as a life of pain. On the contrary, more truly separated from its life in any direct way, he concentrates in himself, in his actual vagrancy, the community and charity which are the promptings of nature. It is in giving to him that fellow-feeling is kept alive. It is 'Nature's law' that none should exist divorced from:

> a spirit and pulse of good,
> A life and soul to every mode of being
> Inseparably link'd.

The beggar is the agent of this underlying, almost lost community:

> And while, in that vast solitude to which
> The tide of things has led him, he appears
> To breathe and live but for himself alone,
> Unblam'd, uninjur'd', let him bear about
> The good which the benignant law of heaven
> Has hung around him, and, while life is his,
> Still let him prompt the unletter'd Villagers
> To tender offices and pensive thoughts.

The spirit of community, that is to say, has been dispossessed and isolated to a wandering, challenging if passive, embodiment in the beggar. It is no longer from the practice of community, or from the spirit of protest at its inadequacy, but from

> this solitary being,
> This helpless wanderer

that the instinct of fellow-feeling is derived. Thus an essential isolation and silence and loneliness have become the only carriers of nature and community against the rigours, the cold abstinence, the selfish ease of ordinary society. . . .

[CLARE]

> Accursed Wealth! o'er-bounding human laws,
> Of every evil thou remains't the cause:
> Victims of want, those wretches such as me,
> Too truly lay their wretchedness to thee:
> Thou are the bar that keeps from being fed,
> And thine our loss of labour and of bread.

As a way of seeing the dispossession of labour by capital, this is exact. But it is set in a structure of feeling in which what wealth is most visibly destroying is 'Nature':

that complex of the land as it was, in the past and in childhood, which both ageing and alteration destroy. There are the scenes of what is really an older agriculture –

> Thou far fled pasture, long evanish'd scene!
> Where nature's freedom spread the flow'ry green . . .
> . . . Where lowing oxen roam'd to feed at large,
> And bleeting there the Shepherd's woolly charge . . .

– alongside the more primitive land which is being directly altered: the brooks diverted, the willows felled, in drainage and clearance.

Over a century and a half I can recognise what Clare is describing: particular trees, and a particular brook, by which I played as a child, have gone in just this way, in the last few years, in an improved use of marginal land. And then what one has to consider is the extension of this observation – one kind of loss against one kind of gain – into a loss of 'Nature'. It is not only the loss of what can be called – sometimes justly, sometimes affectedly – a piece of 'unspoiled' country. It is also, for any particular man, the loss of a specifically human and historical landscape, in which the source of feeling is not really that it is 'natural' but that it is 'native':

> Dear native spot! Which length of time endears . . .
> Nay e'en a post, old standard, or a stone
> Moss'd o'er by age, and branded as her own
> Would in my mind a strong attachment gain,
> A fond desire that they might there remain;
> And all old favourites, fond taste approves,
> Griev'd me at heart to witness their removes.

And then what is most urgently being mourned – the 'old favourites' approved by 'fond taste' – is a loss of childhood through a loss of its immediate landscape:

> But now, alas! Those scenes exist no more;
> The pride of life with thee, like mine, is o'er.

It is wholly understandable that this was written at the age of sixteen. A way of seeing has been connected with a lost phase of living, and the association of happiness with childhood has been developed into a whole convention, in which not only innocence and security but peace and plenty have been imprinted, indelibly, first on a particular landscape, and then, in a powerful extension, on a particular period of the rural past, which is now connected with a lost identity, lost relations and lost certainties, in the memory of what is called, against a present consciousness, Nature. The first feeling is so urgent that it inevitably connects widely with other experience:

> His native scenes! O sweet endearing sound!
> Sure never beats a heart, howe'er forlorn,

But the warm'd breast has soft emotions found
To cherish the dear spot where he was born:
E'en the poor hedger, in the early morn
Chopping the pattering bushes hung with dew,
Scarce lays his mitten on a branching thorn,
But painful memory's banish'd thoughts in view
Remind him, when 'twas young, what happy days he knew.

And the transition is then almost unnoticed, as in *Joys of Childhood*:

Dull is that memory, vacant is that mind,
Where no sweet vision of the past appears.

Living in this connecting feeling, Clare recognised, even while he created, the conversion of particular memories into the generalising 'sweet vision of the past'. His most crucial recognition, relating quite centrally to the tradition we have been examining, comes in another verse of the same poem:

Fancy spreads Edens wheresoe'er they be;
The world breaks on them like an opening flower,
Green joys and cloudless skies are all they see;
The hour of childhood is a rose's hour . . .

The natural images of this Eden of childhood seem to compel a particular connection, at the very moment of their widest generality. Nature, the past and childhood are temporarily but powerfully fused:

In nature's quiet sleep as on a mother's breast.

The plough that disturbs this nature connects with the hardest emotions of maturity: dispossession, the ache of labour, the coldness of the available world: a complex of feeling and imagery in the experience of this man and of everyone; of each personal generation and of this generation in history. But what is then achieved, against this experience of pain, is a way of feeling which is also a way of writing:

A language that is ever green

— the language of what Clare now recreates as 'pastoral poesy', in the title of the poem from which the line comes. This is a radical development of language and of the idea of literature; its strength in its connecting feelings of human warmth and community, in a time of real dispossession, eviction and social division; its paradoxical weakness in the making of this connection through withdrawal into 'nature', into the 'Eden' of the heart, and into a lonely, resigned and contemplative love of men:

Unruffled quietness hath made
A peace in every place,
And woods are resting in their shade
Of social loneliness.

It is wholly understandable, this development of responses to a disturbing history and an altering landscape: the real scenes of both at once dissolved and recreated in images which carry the meanings and yet compose a way of seeing that suppresses them. As so often in romantic poetry, it is the survival of human feeling in a factual dispossession:

While threshing in the dusty barn
Or squashing in the ditch to earn
A pittance that would scarce allow
One joy to smooth my sweating brow
Where drop by drop would chase and fall
Thy presence triumphed over all.

The presence is poetry, speaking to and for the humanity of the hedger, the thresher, the man actually altering the landscape in the service and for the gain of others; but distorted by its very loneliness into an opposition to that noise of the world, the noise of actual exploitation and, ironically, of direct response to it:

Bred in a village full of strife and noise,
Old senseless gossips, and blackguarding boys,
Ploughmen and threshers, whose discourses led
To nothing more than labour's rude employs,
'Bout work being slack, and rise and fall of bread
And who were like to die, and who were like to wed.

It is from this actual village, where a community lives under pressure, that the poet withdraws to the quiet of nature, where he can speak for his own and others' humanity, through remembered ballads and contemplated scenes; a speaking silence from which he is torn, bitterly and desperately, to put what he has written back into the noise of the market: profit, malice, envy; a fashionable contempt for his simplicity; and then again, but now virtually breaking the mind, into the speaking silence of the neglected poet, the man alone with nature and with poverty, recreating world in his green language:

I am, but what I am
Who cares or knows?

It was as far as the mind could go, within that structure. Any new direction required an alteration of structure and of essential convention. Clare marks the end of pastoral poetry, in the very shock of its collision with actual country experience.

He could not accept Lamb's characteristic advice, which had tamed so many: 'transplant Arcadia to Helpstone. The true rustic style, the Arcadian English, I think is to be found in Shenstone.' He is, rather, the culmination, in broken genius, of the movement which we can trace from a century before him: the separation of Nature from the facts of the labour that is creating it, and then the breaking of Nature, in altered and now intolerable relations between men. What we find in Clare is not [Ben] Jonson's idealisation of a landscape yielding of itself, nor Thomson's idealisation of a productive order that is scattering and guarding plenty. There was a conscious reaction to this, in Goldsmith, in Langhorne, and in Crabbe. But there was also an unconscious reaction, to a country from which any acceptable social order had been decisively removed. Clare goes beyond the external observation of the poems of protest and of melancholy retrospect. What happens in him is that the loss is internal. It is to survive at all, as a thinking and feeling man, that he needs the green language of the new Nature.

WORDSWORTH: WORKS CITED

Page
50 *Prelude,* Bk II (1850)
51 *Correspondence of Thomas Gray* (ed. Paget Toynbee and L. Whibble), Oxford, 1935, rev. edn 1971, Vol. I, 128.
51 *Hymn before Sunrise, in the Vale of Chamouni* (1802), in Coleridge, *Select Poetry and Prose* (ed. S. Potter), London, 1950.
51 Johnson, cit. C. Hussey, *The Picturesque*, London, 1927, 112.
52 *Prelude*, Bk XII (1850).
52 Johnson, cit. Hussey, *op. cit.*, 113.
52 *Prelude*, Bk XIV (1850).
53 Ibid.
53 *Michael*, in Wordsworth, *Poetical Works* (ed. E. Selincourt and H. Darbishire), Oxford, 1949, Vol. II.
53 Ibid.
54 *The Old Cumberland Beggar, op. cit.*, Vol. IV.

CLARE: WORKS CITED

54 *Helpstone*, in *Poems of John Clare* (ed. J. W. Tibble), 2 vols, London, 1935, Vol. II.
55 *The Village Minstrel,* CVI, *op. cit.*
56 *Joys of Childhood, op. cit.*
56 *Pastoral Poesy, op. cit.*
57 *The Progress of Rhyme, op. cit.*
57 *I am, op. cit.*

PART II

*The Earth, Memory and
the Critique of Modernity*

Introduction

In 1943 the Cambridge academic E. M. W. Tillyard produced a short book summarising briefly the view of the cosmos which would have been inherited from feudalism and still widely accepted in Shakespeare's time. Written in the middle of the Second World War, when the modern faith in democracy and technological progress had been thrown into doubt by the rise of totalitarianism and global warfare, *The Elizabethan World Picture* was no neutral work of scholarship. Having explained the 'chain of being', with its allocation of each creature, plant and mineral to a divinely ordained 'order', Tillyard concluded by suggesting that even in mid-twentieth-century England there was a need to maintain the memory of that picture, for 'the ignoring of [it] by our scientifically minded intellectuals has helped not a little to bring the world into its present conflicts and distresses.'[1] Those working within the field of green studies today will wish to point out that Tillyard was really talking about Nature rather than nature: in the face of the 'present conflicts and distresses', a traditional cultural construction was being commended as the proper way of understanding humanity's place in the universe. However, they might hesitate to dismiss such speculation as 'reactionary': rather, they will see it in the context of that widespread, and hugely important, critique of modernity which in many ways anticipated our 'ecocritical age'. In the selection of material that follows, we find that that critique really does have something to say about nature, whatever else it may be saying about Nature.

Our selection begins quietly enough with the early-twentieth-century poet Edward Thomas's advice on 'nature study' in schools. However, this ostensibly modest request turns out to be a rather more ambitious project: Thomas is insisting on the need to remember what nature has meant in order that modern human beings are not uprooted imaginatively as well as physically. His case for giving children an understanding and appreciation of nature is made in the context of past literature (romanticism), the present crisis (the growth of urbanisation) and future hopes (an increase in understanding of the environment comparable to the growth of scientific knowledge). Thomas is usually called 'modern' but not 'modernist', on the grounds of the modesty of his formal experimentation as a poet; but there is no doubt that he is responding critically to 'modernity', or the modern condition.

61

However, we usually think of the modernists as the writers who actively challenged modernity in the early twentieth century. In doing so they demonstrated their continuity with late romantics such as Ruskin and Morris. That may sound paradoxical, but we must remind ourselves that modernity, which stemmed from the eighteenth-century 'Enlightenment', with its faith in intellectual and in material progress, had already been resisted by a 'counter-Enlightenment' which usually went under the name of romanticism. Modernism was in many respects a complex, self-conscious kind of post-romanticism. If it has been associated with formal experimentation and the autonomy of the aesthetic object, that in itself reminds us that one of its chief impulses was the repudiation of the vulgarity of modernity. But beyond that, we should also note its developing concern for the environment. For example, in 1919 T. S. Eliot had repudiated Wordsworth's definition of poetry as 'emotion recollected in tranquillity' by insisting that the task of the 'individual talent' was 'conformity' to 'tradition', conceived as an 'impersonal' pattern of 'monuments', an 'ideal order' which was not to be understood referentially.[2] Twenty years later, as an orthodox Christian, he was still using the same term, 'conformity', but now to repudiate rather than defend formalism. He declared without reservation that religion 'implies a life in conformity with nature'. As with Tillyard, he meant Nature; but he did also offer a trenchant critique of industrial capitalism's abuse of nature. He condemned 'the exploitation of the earth ... for commercial profit: immediate benefits leading to dearth and desert.'[3]

But not all modernists took their time coming round to an ecological vision. Our second extract comes from an essay by D. H. Lawrence, who was way ahead of Eliot as a green writer. The differences between the two – the one orthodox and neo-classical, the other heretical and neo-romantic, the one a devout servant of God, the other a prophet of a new religion of 'Life' – indicate how complex a phenonemon was modernism. In the essay included here, in stark contrast to Eliot's measured tones, Lawrence offers a vividly unconventional celebration of nature as a repressed force, a forgotten deity. Ultimately, this counts as Nature rather than nature, perhaps; but as always with Lawrence the immediate impression is that of a strong feel for the earth and its non-human inhabitants. His impact on the academy may be indicated by the work of F. R. Leavis, who was eventually to write two books celebrating his genius, having become increasingly disillusioned with Eliot's arid 'impersonality'. But even early on, in the book Leavis co-wrote with his friend Denys Thompson in 1933, we find Lawrence invoked in an attack on the modern urban trend towards 'standardisation', 'levelling down' and 'substitute living'. A founding text of the discipline we now call cultural studies, *Culture and Environment* also merits attention within green studies, given its provocative contrast between a traditional, rural 'organic community', in touch with the natural 'environment', and a modern, urban mechanical 'civilization'. Though Leavis emphasises at the end of this extract that there can be 'no mere turning back', his attempt to keep the memory of the 'organic community' alive was from the start criticised by Marxists, including finally his own student Raymond Williams, on the grounds that he was idealising the past and ignoring the history of rural exploitation. However, one should bear in mind that nostalgia is not the same thing as sentimentality: indeed, until the twentieth century it still carried its etymological force of 'homesickness' – the pain (Greek, *algos*) arising from the need for a 'return home' (*nostos*), the earth being our home or 'household' (Greek, *oikos*). Moreover, early English Marxism was itself informed by powerful memories of pre-industrial society, as with William Morris's attempt to revive medieval craftsmanship and its respect for natural materials.

As for Marx himself: his early writings, partly indebted to romanticism, were dedicated to 'the realized naturalism of man and the realized humanism of nature'; but the later, 'scientific' Marx referred disparagingly to nature as a mere 'tool house' or 'larder' which capitalism was justified in exploiting, given its necessary role in expanding the means of production.[4] Such pronouncements led two leading twentieth-century Marxists, Theodor Adorno and Max Horkheimer, who now appear as indispensable figures in the tradition of socialist ecology, to repudiate the facile progressivism of Marx. For them he was, in so far as he advocated technological advance by appeal to the needs of history, representative of the negative Enlightenment legacy. In their corrective to the Enlightenment project itself, reprinted here, they insist that culture grows from nature, and they appeal to the idea of a repressed memory of nature in order to criticise modernity, characterised as it is by estrangement from both humanity's natural impulses and from natural scenes and seasons. It is true that, under the influence of Freud, they emphasise the former; but they differ from him in their affirmation of external nature as a source of meaning. In the material from his later work reprinted here, Adorno specifically criticises the exclusion of natural beauty from modern aesthetics, based as it is on the celebration of that which is 'man-made' and so 'radically opposed to nature'. For him, nature is both a repressed memory and a radical promise, both the 'no longer' of capitalist technological society and the 'not yet', both paradise lost and paradise regained. This idea was in a sense anticipated by John F. Danby in his study of *King Lear*, written shortly after the end of the Second World War. Radically historicising 'Nature', Danby, in the extract given here, argues that, though Lear's feudal Nature is overtaken by Edmund's capitalist Nature, Cordelia offers an alternative vision of a utopian, socialist Nature which redeems the first from those very errors and injustices which allowed the second to flourish. Nor can any of the three be considered apart from the actual treatment of nature, of the earth itself, that they imply: hence Danby's reference to the wanton mining and aggressive colonisation carried out by 'new men' like Edmund, and the irreverence for the earth that they displayed.

The critique of modernity, then, has often been informed by the memory of a nature which has been lost, polluted, neglected or denied. It will be noticed that both the critique and the memory cut across conventional ideological divisions. Adorno is associated with Marxism, Danby with Christian socialism, Leavis with agnostic liberalism, Eliot with Christian conservatism, and Lawrence with neo-pagan authoritarianism. Green studies must acknowledge the fact that the rejection of modern industrialism has been known to go hand in hand with left, centrist and right-wing politics, but will not be deterred by such labels. It has a good test-case in Martin Heidegger, who was actually a member of the Nazi party in his early career, but who went on to write thoughtful essays about the relation between literature, language and nature – one of which is represented here. Interestingly, in reading Heidegger's ecological reflections, one is struck by the extent to which they complement those of Leavis and Adorno, even though the former showed little interest in him and the latter wrote a book criticising him. His essay's key term is 'dwelling', which denotes the essential feature of human existence as far as he is concerned: learning to find a place on the earth which does not dominate, manipulate, pollute or destroy it. Only poetry can ensure this, for poetry ('making') is the ground of any 'building' we undertake. If this is not immediately reminiscent of Leavis and Adorno, note that he goes on to argue that poetry can rescue us from the dead language of modernity, and restore us to the richness of our etymological origins. Through keeping memory alive, we 'dwell on the earth' in full awareness of its past meaning and present significance. Though Heidegger's own language is painstakingly circumspect as is fitting for someone who radically associates etymology with ecology, we cannot afford to ignore the power of his special kind of 'thinking', substantiating as it does the insights of other writers included in this section.

Indeed, when we turn to Kenneth Burke, perhaps the finest liberal intelligence of the United States in the twentieth century, we find parallels with Heidegger that permit us to see the latter's fascist beginnings as an error that might possibly be redeemed. For Burke, who has been the subject of a scholarly comparison with Heidegger,[5] demonstrates that it is possible to refuse the logic of 'hyper-technologism' without subscribing to a reactionary politics. If anything, we know Burke as the critic who taught us how to forgive ourselves and others for our dangerous 'perfectionism', while at the same time becoming sufficiently self-critical to prevent the danger being realised in either totalitarian politics or totalising technology – each of them a likely means to ecological catastrophe. For Burke, the human being is not only the 'symbol-using animal' but also the 'symbol-misusing animal': for, 'separated from his natural condition by instruments of his own making' (above all, words), he is 'goaded by the spirit of hierarchy' and is never content to leave well enough alone. In short, he is, in Burke's memorable phrase, 'rotten with perfection'.[6] In his article, 'Why Satire', most of which is reprinted here (Chapter 18), he may lament the capacity of humankind to create a 'perfect' realm of 'counter-nature', a 'Helhaven', but puts his faith in its other capacity, to speak out for nature. Here he shows how the creative use of language, evident even (or especially) in the form of satire, can serve to counter the destructive use of language, evident in the form of the pseudo-rhetoric of industrialism. His bold rewriting of the Bible and of Dante's *Divine Comedy*, as well as his drawing on the reserves of the satirical tradition, remind us that the critique of modernity is impossible without memory.

However, the history charted by the academic critic Leo Marx in *The Machine in the Garden* is a reminder how vigilant that memory must be. His book is a study of the development of the pastoral genre in North America after the intrusion of technology into the paradisal landscape initially found by the European settlers. Marx's point is that the sentimental, popular 'pastoral ideal' always has to look back to an idyllic past, to Arcadia or Eden, in order to have a framework within which to condemn the present; but 'pastoral design' of sophisticated literary writing includes a strong sense of reality, whereby the necessity of returning from the idyllic retreat suggests a critique of escapism as much as of the world escaped from. In this respect, we might see Burke's 'Helhaven' project as a special kind of 'design': a critique of the evasion by the rich of the havoc they wreak on the environment of the poor; their 'lunar bubble' would be the 'ideal' in its extreme, unthinking form, to which Burke's satire is the necessary riposte. This, of course, only enforces the idea that the writer who challenges modernity needs memory, informed by culture and responsible to nature. This certainly seems to be the conviction of another North American writer, Thedore Roszak, who was a leading spokesperson of the counter-culture in the 1960s and early 1970s and who is now a leading ecocritic. In the extract included here from his early work *Where the Wasteland Ends*, Roszak invokes a radical romantic tradition which both looks back to the 'old gnosis', the forgotten wisdom of the ancients, and looks forward to green anarchism. He offers a useful ending to this first section in that he takes us back to the idea it began with, namely, the living legacy of romantic ecology.

NOTES

1   E. M. W. Tillyard, *The Elizabethan World Picture* (1943), Harmondsworth: Penguin, 1975, p. 117.

2   T. S. Eliot, 'Tradition and the Individual Talent', in *Selected Essays*, London: Faber & Faber, 1932, pp. 13–22.

3   T. S. Eliot, *The Idea of a Christian Society*, London: Faber & Faber, 1939, p. 18.

4   Karl Marx, *Economic and Philosophical Manuscripts* (trans. T. B. Bottomore), quoted in M. H. Abrams, *Natural Supernaturalism: Tradition and Revolution in Romantic Literature*, New York and London: W. W. Norton, 1971, p. 315; Karl Marx, *Capital*, Vol. I (trans. Ben Fowkes), New York: Vintage, 1977, p. 285.

5   See Samuel B. Southwell, *Kenneth Burke and Martin Heidegger*, Gainesville, FL: University of Florida Press, 1987.

6   Kenneth Burke, 'Definition of Man', in *Language as Symbolic Action*, Berkeley, CA: University of California Press, 1966, p. 16.

11

Studying Nature

EDWARD THOMAS*

WHAT IS TO come of our Nature-teaching in schools? What does it aim at? Whence does it arise? In part, no doubt, it is due to our desire to implant information. It is all very well for the poet to laugh 'When Science has discovered something more / We shall be happier than we were before'; but that is the road we are on at a high rate of speed. If we are fortunate we shall complete our inventory of the contents of heaven and earth by the time when the last man or woman wearing the last pair of spectacles has decided that, after all, it is a very good world and one which it is quite possible to live in. That, however, is an end which would not in itself be a sufficient inducement to push on towards it; still less can such a vision have set us upon the road.

Three things, perhaps, have more particularly persuaded us to pay our fare and mount for somewhere – three things which are really not to be sharply distinguished, though it is convenient to consider them separately. First, the literary and philosophical movement imperfectly described as the romantic revival and return to Nature of the eighteenth and nineteenth centuries. Poets and philosophers need private incomes, State porridge and what not, but literature and philosophy is a force, and for a century it has followed a course which was entered in the period of the French Revolution. This literature shows man in something like his true position in an infinite universe, and shows him particularly in his physical environment of sea, sky, mountain, rivers, woods, and other animals. Second, the enormous, astonishing, perhaps excessive, growth of towns, from which the only immediate relief is the pure air and sun of the country, a relief which is sought by the urban multitudes in large but insufficient numbers and for too short a time. Third, the triumph of science, of systematized observation. Helped, no doubt, by the force of industrialism – to which it gave help in return – science has had a great triumph. At one time it was supposed to have fatally undermined poetry, romance, religion, because it had confused the minds of some poets and critics. These three things considered, Nature-study is inevitable. Literature sends us to Nature principally for joy, joy of the senses, of the whole frame, of the

*From *The South Country*, London: Dent, 1909.

contemplative mind, and of the soul, joy which if it is found complete in these several ways might be called religious. Science sends us to Nature for knowledge. Industrialism and the great town sends us to Nature for health, that we may go on manufacturing efficiently, or, if we think right and have the power, that we may escape from it. But it would be absurd to separate joy, knowledge and health, except as we separate for convenience those things which have sent us out to seek for them; and Nature-teaching, if it is good, will never overlook one of these three. Joy, through knowledge, on a foundation of health, is what we appear to seek.

There is no longer any need to hesitate in speaking of joy in connection with schools, yet might we not still complain, as Thomas Traherne did two hundred and fifty years ago:

> There was never a tutor that did professly teach Felicity, though that be the mistress of all other sciences. Nor did any of us study these things but as aliena, which we ought to have studied as our enjoyments. We studied to inform our Knowledge, but knew not for what end we so studied. And for lack of aiming at a certain end we erred in the manner.

If we cannot somehow have a professor of Felicity we are undone. Perhaps Nature herself will aid. Her presence will certainly make for felicity by enlarging her pupil for a time from the cloistered life which modern towns and their infinite conveniences and servitudes encourage. Tolstoy has said that in the open air 'new relations are formed between pupil and teacher: freer, simpler and more trustful'; and certainly his walk on a winter night with his pupils, chatting and telling tales (see *The School at Yasnaya Polyana,* by Leo Tolstoy), leaves an impression of electrical activity and felicity in the young and old minds of that party which is hardly to be surpassed. And how more than by Nature's noble and uncontaminated forms can a sense of beauty be nourished? Then, too, the reading of great poetry might well be associated with the study of Nature, since there is no great poetry which can be dissevered from Nature, while modern poets have all dipped their pens in the sunlight and wind and great waters, and appeal most to those who most resemble them in their loves. The great religious books, handed down to us by people who lived in closer intercourse with Nature than many of us, cannot be understood by indoor children and adults. Whether connected with this or that form of religion or not, whether taken as 'intimations of immortality' or not, the most profound and longest remembered feelings are often those derived from the contact of Nature with the child's mind.

Of health, though there are exactly as many physicians as patients, it is unnecessary to say anything, except that one of the pieces of knowledge – I do not speak of information – which science has left to us is that movement and the working of the brain in pure air and sunlight is good for body and soul, especially if joy is aiding.

Knowledge aids joy by discipline, by increasing the sphere of enjoyment, by showing us in animals, in plants, for example, what life is, how our own is related to theirs, showing us, in fact, our position, responsibilities and debts among the other inhabitants of the earth. Pursued out of doors where those creatures, moving and still, have their life and their beauty, knowledge is real. The senses are invited there to the subtlest and most delightful training, and have before them an immeasurable fresh field, not a field like that of books, full of old opinions, but one with which every eye and brain can have new vital intercourse. It is open to all to make discoveries as to the forms and habits of things, and care should be taken to preserve the child from the most verbose part of modern literature, that which repeats in multiplied ill-chosen words stale descriptions of birds and flowers, etc., coupled with trivial fancies and insincere inventions. Let us not take the study, the lamp and the ink out of doors, as we used to take wild life – having killed it and placed it in spirits of wine – indoors. Let us also be careful to have knowledge as well as enthusiasm in our masters. Enthusiasm alone is not enthusiasm. There must, at some stage, be some anatomy, classification, pure brain-work; the teacher must be the equal in training of the mathematician, and he must be alive, which I never heard was a necessity for mathematicians. But not anatomy for all, perhaps; for some it might be impossible, and a study of colours, curves, perfumes, voices – a thousand things – might be substituted for it.

Yet Nature-study is not designed to produce naturalists, any more than music is taught in order to make musicians. If you produce nothing but naturalists you fail, and you will produce very few. The aim of study is to widen the culture of child and man, to do systematically what Mark Pattison tells us in his dry way he did for himself, by walking and outdoor sports, then – at the late age of seventeen – by collecting and reading such books as *The Natural History of Selborne*, and finally by a slow process of transition from natural history into 'the more abstract poetic emotion . . . a conscious and declared poetical sentiment and a devoted reading of the poets'. Geology did not come for another ten years,

> to complete the cycle of thought, and to give that intellectual foundation which is required to make the testimony of the eye, roaming over an undulating surface, fruitful and satisfying. When I came in after years to read *The Prelude* I recognized, as if it were my own history which was being told, the steps by which the love of the country boy for his hills and moors grew into poetical susceptibility for all imaginative presentations of beauty in every direction.

The botany, etc., would naturally be related to the neighbourhood of school or home; for there is no parish or district of which it might not be said, as Jefferies and Thoreau each said of his own, that it is a microcosm. By this means the natural history may easily be linked to a preliminary study of hill and valley and stream, the positions of houses, mills and villages, and the reasons for them, and the food supply, and so on, and this in turn leads on to – nay, involves – all that is most real in geography and history. The landscape retains the most permanent marks of the past, and a wise examination of it should evoke the beginnings of the majestic sentiment of our oneness with the future and the past, just as natural history should help to give the child a sense of oneness with all forms of life. To put it at its lowest, some such cycle of knowledge is needed if a generation that insists more and more on living in the country, or spending many weeks there, is not to be bored or to be compelled to entrench itself behind the imported amusements of the town.

12

Remembering Pan

D. H. LAWRENCE*

AT THE BEGINNING of the Christian era, voices were heard off the coasts of Greece, out to sea, on the Mediterranean, wailing: 'Pan is dead! Great Pan is dead!'

The father of fauns and nymphs, satyrs and dryads and naiads was dead, with only the voices in the air to lament him. Humanity hardly noticed.

But who was he, really? Down the long lanes and overgrown ridings of history we catch odd glimpses of a lurking rustic god with a goat's white lightning in his eyes. A sort of fugitive, hidden among leaves, and laughing with the uncanny derision of one who feels himself defeated by something lesser than himself.

An outlaw, even in the early days of the gods. A sort of Ishmael among the bushes.

Yet always his lingering title: The Great God Pan. As if he was, or had been, the greatest.

Lurking among the leafy recesses, he was almost more demon than god. To be feared, not loved or approached. A man who should see Pan by daylight fell dead, as if blasted by lightning.

Yet you might dimly see him in the night, a dark body within the darkness. And then, it was a vision filling the limbs and the trunk of a man with power, as with new, strong-mounting sap. The Pan-power! You went on your way in the darkness secretly and subtly elated with blind energy, and you could cast a spell, by your mere presence, on women and on men. But particularly on women.

In the woods and the remote places ran the children of Pan, all the nymphs and fauns of the forest and the spring and the river and the rocks. These, too, it was dangerous to see by day. The man who looked up to see the white arms of a nymph flash as she darted behind the thick wild laurels away from him followed helplessly. He was a nympholept. Fascinated by the swift limbs and the wild, fresh sides of the nymph, he followed for ever, for ever, in the endless monotony of his desire. Unless came some wise being who could absolve him from the spell.

But the nymphs, running among the trees and curling to sleep under the bushes, made the myrtles blossom more gaily, and the spring bubble up with greater

*From 'Pan in America', in *Phoenix: The Posthumous Papers of D. H. Lawrence* (ed. Edward D. McDonald), London: William Heinemann, 1936.

urge, and the birds splash with a strength of life. And the lithe flanks of the faun gave life to the oak-groves, the vast trees hummed with energy. And the wheat sprouted like green rain returning out of the ground, in the little fields, and the vine hung its black drops in abundance, urging a secret.

Gradually men moved into cities. And they loved the display of people better than the display of a tree. They liked the glory they got of overpowering one another in war. And, above all, they loved the vainglory of their own words, the pomp of argument and the vanity of ideas.

So Pan became old and grey-bearded and goat-legged, and his passion was degraded with the lust of senility. His power to blast and to brighten dwindled. His nymphs became coarse and vulgar.

Till at last the old Pan died, and was turned into the devil of the Christians. The old god Pan became the Christian devil, with the cloven hoofs and the horns, the tail, and the laugh of derision. Old Nick, the Old Gentleman who is responsible for all our wickednesses, but especially our sensual excesses – this is all that is left of the Great God Pan.

It is strange. It is a most strange ending for a god with such a name. Pan! All! That which is everything has goat's feet and a tail! With a black face!

This really is curious.

Yet this was all that remained of Pan, except that he acquired brimstone and hell-fire, for many, many centuries. The nymphs turned into the nasty-smelling witches of a Walpurgis night, and the fauns that danced became sorcerers riding the air, or fairies no bigger than your thumb.

But Pan keeps on being reborn, in all kinds of strange shapes. There he was, at the Renaissance. And in the eighteenth century he had quite a vogue. He gave rise to an 'ism', and there were many pantheists, Wordsworth one of the first. They worshipped Nature in her sweet-and-pure aspect, her Lucy Gray aspect.

'Oft have I heard of Lucy Gray,' the school-child began to recite, on examination-day.

'So have I,' interrupted the bored inspector.

Lucy Gray, alas, was the form that William Wordsworth thought fit to give to the Great God Pan.

And then he crossed over to the young United States: I mean Pan did. Suddenly he gets a new name. He becomes the Oversoul, the Allness of everything. To this new Lucifer Gray of a Pan Whitman sings the famous *Song of Myself*: 'I am All, and All is Me.' That is: 'I am Pan, and Pan is me.'

The old goat-legged gentleman from Greece thoughtfully strokes his beard, and answers: 'All A is B, but all B is not A.' Aristotle did not live for nothing. All Walt is Pan, but all Pan is not Walt.

This, even to Whitman, is incontrovertible. So the new American pantheism collapses.

Then the poets dress up a few fauns and nymphs, to let them run riskily – oh, would there were any risk! – in their private 'grounds'. But, alas, these tame guinea-pigs soon became boring. Change the game.

We still *pretend* to believe that there is One mysterious Something-or-other

71

back of Everything, ordaining all things for the ultimate good of humanity. It wasn't back of the Germans in 1914, of course, and whether it's back of the bolshevist is still a grave question. But still, it's back of *us*, so that's all right.

Alas, poor Pan! Is this what you've come to? Legless, hornless, faceless, even smileless, you are less than everything or anything, except a lie.

And yet here, in America, the oldest of all, old Pan is still alive. When Pan was greatest, he was not even Pan. He was nameless and unconceived, mentally. Just as a small baby new from the womb may say Mama! Dada! whereas in the womb it said nothing; so humanity, in the womb of Pan, said nought. But when humanity was born into a separate idea of itself, it said *Pan*.

In the days before man got too much separated off from the universe, he *was* Pan, along with all the rest.

As a tree still is. A strong-willed, powerful thing-in-itself, reaching up and reaching down. With a powerful will of its own it thrusts green hands and huge limbs at the light above, and sends huge legs and gripping toes down, down between the earth and rocks, to the earth's middle. . . .

This is the might of Pan, and the power of Pan.

And still, in America, among the Indians, the oldest Pan is alive. But here, also, dying fast.

It is useless to glorify the savage. For he will kill Pan with his own hands, for the sake of a motor-car. And a bored savage, for whom Pan is dead, is the stupefied image of all boredom.

And we cannot return to the primitive life, to live in tepees and hunt with bows and arrows.

Yet live we must. And once life has been conquered, it is pretty difficult to live. What are we going to do, with a conquered universe? The Pan relationship, which the world of man once had with all the world, was better than anything man has now. The savage, today, if you give him the chance, will become more mechanical and unliving than any civilized man. But civilized man, having conquered the universe, may as well leave off bossing it. Because, when all is said and done, life itself consists in a live relatedness between man and his universe: sun, moon, stars, earth, trees, flowers, birds, animals, men, everything – and not in a 'conquest' of anything by anything. Even the conquest of the air makes the world smaller, tighter, and more airless.

And whether we are a store-clerk or a bus-conductor, we can still choose between the living universe of Pan, and the mechanical conquered universe of modern humanity. The machine has no windows. But even the most mechanized human being has only got his windows nailed up, or bricked in.

13

The Organic Community

F. R. LEAVIS AND DENYS THOMPSON*

['PROGRESS']

[GEORGE] STURT SPEAKS of 'the death of Old England and of the replacement of the more primitive nation by an "organized" modern state'. The Old England was the England of the organic community, and in what sense it was more primitive than the England that has replaced it needs pondering. But at the moment what we have to consider is the fact that the organic community has gone; it has so nearly disappeared from memory that to make anyone, however educated, realize what it was is commonly a difficult undertaking. Its destruction (in the West) is the most important fact of recent history – it is very recent indeed. How did this momentous change – this vast and terrifying disintegration – take place in so short a time? The process of the change is that which is commonly described as Progress. This is how George Sturt describes [some specific consequences]:

> ... In what was once the wheelwright's shop, where Englishmen grew friendly with the grain of timber and with sharp tool, nowadays untrained youths wait upon machines, hardly knowing oak from ash or caring for the qualities of either. And this is but one tiny item in the immensity of changes which have overtaken labour throughout the civilised world. The products of work are, to be sure, as important as ever – what is to become of us all if the dockers will not sweat for us or the miners risk their lives? That civilisation may flourish a less civilised working-class must work. Yet others wonder at working-class 'unrest'. But it remains true that in modern conditions work is nothing like so tolerable as it was say thirty years ago; partly because there is more hurry in it, but largely because machinery has separated employers from employed and has robbed the latter of the sustaining delights which materials used to afford to them.

*From *Culture and Environment: The Training of Critical Awareness* (1933), London: Chatto & Windus, 1964.

73

Work is less and less pleasant to do – unless, perhaps, for the engineer or the electrician.

[George Sturt ('George Bourne'), *Change in the Village*]

'That civilization may flourish a less civilized working-class must work.' But it is not merely the working-class that is less civilized and suffers from 'unrest.' We all suffer by the loss of the organic community. 'As a wild animal species to its habitat, so these workmen had fitted themselves to the local conditions of life and death.' The more 'primitive' England represented an animal naturalness, but distinctively human. Sturt's villagers expressed their human nature, they satisfied their human needs, in terms of the natural environment; and the things they made – cottages, barns, ricks and waggons – together with their relations with one another constituted a human environment, and a subtlety of adjustment and adaptation, as right and inevitable. And where England was so predominantly rural the towns themselves were real communities. 'Although Farnham', says Sturt, 'fancied itself a little town, its business was being conducted in the spirit of the village – almost indeed of the mediaeval manor.' They themselves represented an adjustment to the environment; their ways of life reflected the rhythm of the seasons, and they were in close touch with the sources of their sustenance in the neighbouring soil. The modern citizen no more knows how the necessaries of life come to him (he is quite out of touch, we say, with 'primary production') than he can see his own work as a significant part in a human scheme (he is merely earning wages or making profits). . . .

THE LOSS OF THE ORGANIC COMMUNITY

The outward and obvious sign that the loss of the organic community was the loss of a human naturalness or normality may be seen in the building of the industrial era. In their wanton and indifferent ugliness, their utter insensitiveness to humanity and the environment, the towns, suburbs and houses of modern England are unparalleled in history. . . . A brief comparative study of the building of all periods and places would bring out the fact, which should be in any case obvious enough, that the present phase of human history is, in the strictest sense, *abnormal*. And yet, though the destructive process took so short a time, it is so complete, and change still proceeds at such an acceleration, that normality is virtually forgotten and the 'picked experience' of immemorial ages is on the point of being lost. As D. H. Lawrence said, contemplating the industrial Midlands:

There was a gap in the continuity of consciousness almost American, but industrial really. What next?

There are those who think D. H. Lawrence the greatest man of our time, and the reason is that he did more than anyone else to awake and spread a realization of what has happened. He devoted his splendid genius to making it impossible for us to ignore the nature of our loss. After reading him it is impossible to talk easily about a rising 'standard of living':

> The car ploughed uphill through the long squalid straggle of Tevershall, the blackened brick dwellings, the black slate roofs glistening their sharp edges, the mud black with coal-dust, the pavements wet and black. It was as if dismalness had soaked through and through everything. The utter negation of the gladness of life, the utter absence of the instinct for shapely beauty which every bird and beast had, the utter death of the human intuitive faculty was appalling. The stacks of soap in the grocer's shops, the rhubarb and lemons in the greengrocer's! The awful hats in the milliner's! All went by ugly, ugly, ugly, followed by the plaster and gilt horror of the cinema with its wet picture announcements, 'A Woman's Love', and the new big Primitive chapel, primitive enough in its stark brick and big panes of greenish and raspberry glass in the windows. . . .
>
> 'England my England!' But which is *my* England? The stately homes of England make good photographs and create the illusion of a connection with the Elizabethans. The handsome old halls are there, from the days of good Queen Anne and Tom Jones. But smuts fall and blacken on the drab stucco, that has long ceased to be golden. And one by one, like the stately homes, they are abandoned. Now they are being pulled down. As for the cottages of England – there they are – great plasterings of brick dwellings on the hopeless countryside. . . .
>
> This is history. One England blots out another. The mines had made the halls wealthy. Now they were blotting them out, as they had already blotted out the cottages. The industrial England blots out the agricultural England. One meaning blots out another. The new England blots out the old England. And the continuity is not organic, but mechanical.
>
> [from *Lady Chatterley's Lover*]

Lawrence was so sensitive to the ugliness of the environment because he had so vivid a realization of what was lost, and if the positive suggestions of such passages as the following are not in themselves adequate, they convey a spirit without which we shall never attain a new human health and wholeness:

> Now, though perhaps nobody knew it, it was ugliness which really betrayed the spirit of man in the nineteenth century. The great crime which the moneyed classes and promoters of industry committed in the palmy Victorian days was the condemning of the workers to ugliness, ugliness, ugliness: meanness and formless and ugly surroundings, ugly ideals, ugly religion, ugly hope, ugly love, ugly clothes, ugly furniture, ugly houses, ugly relationships between workers and employers. The human soul needs actual beauty even more than bread. The middle-classes jeer at the colliers for buying pianos – but what is the piano often as not but a blind reaching out for beauty? . . .

If the company, instead of building those sordid and hideous squares, then, when they had that lovely site to play with, there on the hill-top: if they had put a tall column there in the middle of the small market-place, and run three parts of a circle of arcade round the pleasant space, where people could stroll or sit, and with handsome houses behind! If they had made big, substantial houses, in apartments of five or six rooms, and with handsome entrances. If, above all, they had encouraged song and dancing – for the miners still sang and danced – and provided hand-some space for these. If only they had given prizes for the handsomest chair or table, the loveliest scarf, the most charming room that the men or women could make! If only they had done this, there would never have been an industrial problem. The industrial problem arises from the base forcing of all human energy into a competition of mere acquisition.

[From *The Architectural Review*, August 1930]

There is an essential truth in what Lawrence says, though *The Wheelwright's Shop* suggests that the 'industrial problem' could not have been staved off as easily as that. And we must beware of simple solutions. We must, for instance, realize that there can be no mere going back: it is useless to think of . . . scrapping the machine in the hope of restoring the old order. Even if agriculture were revived, that would not bring back the organic community. It is important to insist on what has been lost lest it should be forgotten; for the memory of the old order must be the chief incitement towards a new, if ever we are to have one. If we forget the old order we shall not know what kind of thing to strive towards, and in the end there will be no striving, but a surrender to the 'progress' of the machine.

14

The Logic of Domination

Theodor W. Adorno and Max Horkheimer*

... [The] myths which fell victim to the Enlightenment were its own products.
... Myth intends report, naming, the narration of a Beginning; but also presentation, confirmation, explanation: a tendency that grew stronger with the recording
and collecting of myths. Narrative became didactic at an early stage. . . . In place
of the local spirits and demons there appeared heaven and its hierarchy; in place of
the invocations of the magician and the tribe the distinct gradation of sacrifice and
the labor of the unfree mediated through the world of command. The Olympic
deities are no longer directly identical with elements, but signify them. In Homer,
Zeus represents the sky and the weather, Apollo controls the sun, and Helios
nd Eros are already shifting to an allegorical function. The gods are distinguished
from material elements as their quintessential concepts. From now on, being divides
into the *logos* [idea, abstract principle] and into the mass of all things and creatures
without. This single distinction between existence proper and reality engulfs all
others. Without regard to distinctions, the world becomes subject to man. In this
the Jewish creation narrative and the religion of Olympia are at one: '. . . and let
them have dominion over the fish of the sea, and over the fowl of the air, and over
the cattle, and over all the earth, and over every creeping thing that creepeth upon
the face of the earth' [Genesis I.26]. 'O Zeus, Father Zeus, yours is the dominion
of the heavens, and you oversee the works of man . . .' [Homeric hymn]. . . . Man's
likeness to God consists in sovereignty over existence, in the countenance of the lord
and master, and in command.

Myth turns into enlightenment [*sic*], and nature into mere objectivity. Men pay
for the increase of their power with alienation from that over which they exercise
their power. Enlightenment behaves toward things as a dictator toward men. He
knows them in so far as he can manipulate them. The man of science knows things
in so far as he can make them. In this way their potentiality is turned to his own
ends. In the metamorphosis the nature of things, as a substratum of domination, is
revealed as always the same. This identity constitutes the unity of nature. . . .

*From *Dialectic of Enlightenment* (trans. John Cumming), London: Verso, 1972.

The entanglement of myth, domination, and labor is preserved in one of the Homeric naratives. Book XII of the *Odyssey* tells of the encounter with the Sirens. Their allurement is that of losing oneself in the past. But the hero to whom the temptation is offered has reached maturity through suffering. Throughout the many mortal perils he has had to endure, the unity of his own life, the identity of the individual, has been confirmed for him. The regions of time part for him as do water, earth, and air. For him, the flood of that-which-was has retreated from the rock of the present, and the future lies cloudy on the horizon. What Odysseus left behind him entered into the nether world; for the self is still so close to prehistoric myth, from whose womb it tore itself, that its very own experienced past becomes mythic prehistory. And it seeks to encounter that myth through the fixed order of time. The three-fold schema is intended to free the present moment from the power of the past by referring that power behind the absolute barrier of the unrepeatable and placing it at the disposal of the present as practicable knowledge. The compulsion to rescue what is gone as what is living instead of using it as the material of progress was appeased only in art, to which history itself appertains as a presentation of past life. So long as art declines to pass as cognition and is thus separated from practice, social practice tolerates it as it tolerates pleasure. But the Sirens' song has not yet been rendered powerless by reduction to the condition of art. They know 'everything that ever happened on this so fruitful earth', including the events in which Odysseus himself took part, 'all those things that Argos' sons and the Trojans suffered by the will of the gods on the plains of Troy.' While they directly evoke the recent past, with the irresistible promise of pleasure at which their song is heard, they threaten the patriarchal order which renders to each man his life only in return for his full measure of time. Whoever falls for their trickery must perish, whereas only perpetual presence of mind forces an existence from nature. Even though the Sirens know all that has happened, they demand the future as the price of that knowledge, and the promise of the happy return is the deception with which the past ensnares the one who longs for it. Odysseus is warned by Circe, that divinity of reversion to the animal, whom he resisted and who therefore gives him strength to resist other powers of disintegration. But the allurement of the Sirens remains superior; no one who hears their song can escape. Men had to do fearful things to themselves before the self, the identical, purposive, and virile nature of man, was formed, and something of that recurs in every childhood. The strain of holding the I together adheres to the I in all stages; and the temptation to lose it has always been there with the blind determination to maintain it. The narcotic intoxication which permits the atonement of deathlike sleep for the euphoria in which the self is suspended, is one of the oldest social arrangements which mediate between self-preservation and self-destruction – an attempt of the self to survive itself. The dread of losing the self and of abrogating together with the self the barrier between oneself and other life, the fear of death and destruction, is intimately associated with a promise of happiness which threatened civilization in every moment. Its road was that of obedience and labor, over which fulfillent shines forth perpetually – but only as illusive appearance, as devitalized beauty. The mind of Odysseus, inimical both to his own death and to his own happiness, is aware of this. He knows only two possible ways to escape. One of them he prescribes for his men. He plugs their ears with wax, and they must row with all their strength. Whoever would survive must not hear the temptation of that which is unrepeateable, and he is able to survive only by being unable to hear it. Society has always made provision for that. The laborers must be fresh and concentrate as they look ahead, and must ignore whatever lies to one side. They must doggedly sublimate in additional effort the drive that impels to diversion. And so they become practical. – The other possibility Odysseus, the seigneur who allows the others to labor for themselves, reserves to himself. He listens, but while bound impotently to the mast; the greater the temptation the more he has his bonds tightened – just as later the burghers would deny themselves happiness all the more doggedly as it drew closer to them with the growth of their own power. What Odysseus hears is without consequence for him; he is able only to nod his head as a sign to be set free from his bonds; but it is too late; his men, who do not listen, know only the song's danger but nothing of its beauty, and leave him at the mast in order to save him and themselves. They reproduce the oppressor's life together with their own, and the oppressor is no longer able to escape his social role. The bonds with which he has irremediably tied himself to practice, also keep the Sirens away from practice: their temptation is neutralized and becomes a mere object of contemplation – becomes art. The prisoner is present at a concert, an inactive eavesdropper like later concertgoers, and his spirited call for liberation fades like applause. Thus the enjoyment of art and manual labor break apart as the world of prehistory is left behind. The epic already contains the appropriate theory. The cultural material is in exact correlation to work done according to command; and both are grounded in the inescapable compulsion to social domination of nature. . . .

. . . The very spirit that dominates nature repeatedly vindicates the superiority of nature in competition. All bourgeois enlightenment is one in the requirement of sobriety and common sense – a proficient estimate of the ratio of forces. The wish must not be father to the thought. For this reason, however, all power in class society is tied to a nagging consciousness of its own impotence against physical nature and its social descendants – the many. Only consciously contrived adaptation to nature brings nature under the control of the physically weaker. The *ratio* which supplants mimesis is not simply its counterpart. It is itself mimesis: mimesis unto death. The subjective spirit which cancels the animation of nature can master a despiritualized nature only by imitating its rigidity and despiritualizing itself in turn. Imitation enters into the service of domination inasmuch as even man is anthropomorphized for man. The pattern of Odyssean cunning is the mastery of nature through such adaptation. Renunciation, the principle of bourgeois disillusionment, the outward schema for the intensification of sacrifice, is already present *in nuce* [in kernel] in that estimation of the ratio of forces which anticipates survival as so to speak dependent on the concession of one's own defeat, and – virtually – on death. The nimble-witted survives only at the price of his own dream, which he wins only by demystifying himself as well as the powers without. He can never have everything; he has always to wait, to be patient, to do without; he may not taste the lotus or eat the cattle of the Sun-god Hyperion, and when he steers between the rocks he must count on the loss of the men whom Scylla plucks from the boat. He just pulls through; struggle is his survival; and all the fame that he and the others win in the process serves merely to confirm that the title of hero is only gained at the price of the abasement and mortification of the instinct for complete, universal, and undivided happiness.

15

Nature as 'Not Yet'

Theodor W. Adorno*

CONDEMNATION OF NATURAL BEAUTY

SINCE SCHELLING, WHOSE aesthetics is entitled the *Philosophy of Art*, aesthetic interest has centered on artworks. Natural beauty, which was still the occasion of the most penetrating insights in the *Critique of Judgment*, is now scarcely even a topic of theory. The reason for this is not that natural beauty was dialectically transcended, both negated and maintained on a higher plane, as Hegel's theory had propounded, but, rather, that it was repressed. The concept of natural beauty rubs on a wound, and little is needed to prompt one to associate this wound with the violence that the artwork – a pure artifact – inflicts on nature. Wholly artifactual, the artwork seems to be the opposite of what is not made, nature. As pure antitheses, however, each refers to the other: nature to the experience of a mediated and objectified world, the artwork to nature as the mediated plenipotentiary of immediacy. Therefore reflection on natural beauty is irrevocably requisite to the theory of art. Whereas thoughts on it, virtually the topic itself, have, paradoxically, a pedantic, dull, antiquarian quality, great art and the interpretation of it have, by incorporating what the older aesthetics attributed to nature, blocked out reflection on what is located beyond aesthetic immanence and yet is nevertheless its premise. The price of this repression was the transition to the ideological art religion (a name coined by Hegel) of the nineteenth century – the satisfaction in a reconciliation symbolically achieved in the artwork. Natural beauty vanished from aesthetics as a result of the burgeoning domination of the concept of freedom and human dignity, which was inaugurated by Kant and then rigorously transplanted into aesthetics by Schiller and Hegel; in accord with this concept nothing in the world is worthy of attention except that for which the autonomous subject has itself to thank. The truth of such freedom for the subject, however, is at the same time unfreedom: unfreedom for the other. For this reason the turn against natural beauty, in spite of the immeasurable progress it made possible in the comprehending of art as spiritual, does not

*From *Aesthetic Theory* (ed. Gretel Adorno and Rolf Tiedemann; trans. R. Hullot-Kentor), London and Minneapolis, MN: Athlone Press/University of Minnesota Press, 1997.

lack an element of destructiveness, just as the concept of dignity does not lack it in its turn against nature. Schiller's variously interpreted treatise *On Grace and Dignity* marks the new development. . . .

NATURAL BEAUTY AND ART BEAUTY ARE INTERLOCKED

Just how bound up natural beauty is with art beauty is confirmed by the experience of the former. For it, nature is exclusively appearance, never the stuff of labor and the reproduction of life, let alone the substratum of science. Like the experience of art, the aesthetic experience of nature is that of images. Nature, as appearing beauty, is not perceived as an object of action. The sloughing off of the aims of self-preservation – which is emphatic in art – is carried out to the same degree in aesthetic experience of nature. To this extent the difference between the two forms of beauty is hardly evident. Mediation is no less to be inferred from the relation of art to nature than from the inverse relation. Art is not nature, a belief that idealism hoped to inculcate, but art does want to keep nature's promise. It is capable of this only by breaking that promise; by taking it back into itself. This much is true in Hegel's theorem that art is inspired by negativity, specifically by the deficiency of natural beauty, in the sense that so long as nature is defined only through its antithesis to society, it is not yet what it appears to be. What nature strives for in vain, artworks fulfill: They open their eyes. Once it no longer serves as an object of action, appearing nature itself imparts expression, whether that of melancholy, peace, or something else. Art stands in for nature through its abolition in effigy; all naturalistic art is only deceptively close to nature because, analogous to industry, it relegates nature to raw material. . . .

NATURE AS A CIPHER OF THE RECONCILED

Natural beauty is the trace of the nonidentical in things under the spell of universal identity. As long as this spell prevails, the nonidentical has no positive existence. Therefore natural beauty remains as dispersed and uncertain as what it promises, that which surpasses all human immanence. The pain in the face of beauty, nowhere more visceral than in the experience of nature, is as much the longing for what beauty promises but never unveils as it is suffering at the inadequacy of the appearance, which fails beauty while wanting to make itself like it. This pain reappears in the relation to artworks. Involuntarily and unconsciously, the observer enters into a contract with the work, agreeing to submit to it on condition that it speak. In the pledged receptivity of the observer, pure self-abandonment – that moment of free exhalation in nature – survives. Natural beauty shares the weakness of every promise with that promise's inextinguishability. However words may glance off nature and betray its language to one that is qualitatively different from its own, still no critique of natural teleology can dismiss those cloudless days of southern lands that seem to be waiting to be noticed. As they draw to a close with the same radiance and peacefulness with which they began, they emanate that everything is not lost, that things may yet turn out: 'Death, sit down on the bed, and you hearts, listen carefully: / An old man points into the glimmering light / Under the fringe of dawn's first blue: / In the name of God and the unborn, / I promise you: / World, never mind your woes, / All is still yours, for the day starts anew!'[1] The image of what is oldest in nature reverses dialectically into the cipher of the not-yet-existing, the possible: As its appearance this cipher is more than the existing; but already in reflecting on it this almost does it an injustice. Any claim that this is how nature speaks cannot be judged with assurance, for its language does not make judgments; but neither is nature's language merely the deceptive consolation that longing reflects back to itself. In its uncertainty, natural beauty inherits the ambiguity of myth, while at the same time its echo – consolation – distances itself from myth in appearing nature. Contrary to that philosopher of identity, Hegel, natural beauty is close to the truth but veils itself at the moment of greatest proximity. This, too, art learned from natural beauty. The boundary established against fetishism of nature – the pantheistic subterfuge that would amount to nothing but an affirmative mask appended to an endlessly repetitive fate – is drawn by the fact that nature, as it stirs mortally and tenderly in its beauty, does not yet exist. The shame felt in the face of natural beauty stems from the damage implicitly done to what does not yet exist by taking it for existent. The dignity of nature is that of the not-yet-existing; by its expression it repels intentional humanization. This dignity has been transformed into the hermetic character of art, into – as Holderlin taught – art's renunciation of any usefulness whatever, even if it were sublimated by the addition of human meaning. For communication is the adaptation of spirit to utility, with the result that spirit is made one commodity among the rest; and what today is called meaning participates in this disaster. What in artworks is structured, gapless, resting in itself, is an afterimage of the silence that is the single medium through which nature speaks. Vis-a-vis a ruling principle, vis-a-vis a merely diffuse juxtaposition, the beauty of nature is an other; what is reconciled would resemble it.

NOTE

1   Rudolf Borchardt, 'Tagelied'.

16

Shakespeare's Three Natures

JOHN F. DANBY*

[NATURE: FEUDAL AND CAPITALIST]

EDMUND IS A complete Outsider. He is outside Society, he is outside Nature, he is outside Reason. Man, Nature, and God now fall apart. Reason, for Hooker the principle of coherence for all three, dwindles to something regulative rather than constitutive. It is an analyser, a cold calculator. Its knowledge is the knowledge of the watch-maker or engineer, an understanding of cogs and springs and levers, of mining and counter-mining. Nature itself becomes a machine this Reason can have this knowledge of. Descartes' dualism is implicit in Edmund's reasoning on the stars. The New Man is a Mind and a Body. The body belongs to mechanical Lion-headed Nature. The mind stands outside as observer and server of the machine. . . .

For the two Natures and two Reasons imply two societies. Edmund belongs to the new age of scientific inquiry and industrial development, of bureaucratic organization and social regimentation, the age of mining and merchant-venturing, of monopoly and Empire-making, the age of the sixteenth century and after: an age of competition suspicion, glory. He hypostatizes those trends in man which guarantee success under the new conditions – one reason why his soliloquy is so full of what we recognize as common sense. These trends he calls Nature. And with this Nature he identifies Man. Edmund would not agree that any other Nature was thinkable.

Another Nature was being asserted, however, in Edmund's time, because there was another society not yet outgrown. This is the society of the sixteenth century and before. The standards Edmund rejects have come down from the Middle Ages. They assume a co-operative, reasonable decency in man, and respect for the whole as being greater than the part: 'God to be worshipped, parents to be honoured, others to be used by us as we ourselves would be by them.' The medieval procedure was to mutualize conflicting claims by agreeing over limits. Edmund's

*From *Shakespeare's Doctrine of Nature: A Study of 'King Lear'* (1948), London: Faber & Faber, 1975.

instinct is to recognize no limits save those coming from incapacity to get one's way.

Edmund's main significance consists in this. He is not part of a playwright's dream. He is a direct imaging of the times. If we see him in the Shakespearian context of the Natures we can regard him as a symbol. If we think in terms of the historical setting Shakespeare himself belonged to, he is an actuality. . . .

. . . Behind the shift and drift of the meanings of the word 'Nature' there is the shift and drift of humanity in a setting at once historical and spiritual. Behind the word there is Shakespeare certainly. But behind Shakespeare there is the mining engineer breaking into the bowels of the earth; the seeker out of the mysteries of brass, and glass, and salt, and the supplier of the Elizabethan navies; the doctor taking apart the human body to anatomize the mechanism of muscle and bone; the capitalist aware of money as the sinews of war and soon to recognize in it the circulating life-blood of the body politic. All these, too, are vitally concerned to alter the meaning of Nature: to extend the Nature which can be worked, made a tool of, got to produce profits; to minimize the theology which would contend for an aesthetic and moral attitude only to Nature, and which would find no argument in Nature for profit-making. . . .

Thus two societies must be added to the two Natures and two Reasons. Because the play is an allegory of ethical systems and people, it must also be an allegory of community. For according to one of the systems at least we are all members one of another. This society is that of the medieval vision. Its representative is an old King ('Nature in you stands on the very verge of her confine'). It is doting and it falls into error. The other society is that of nascent capitalism. Its representative in chief is the New Man – and a politic machiavel. I have no doubt that if Shakespeare were forced to take sides, he would prefer Lear to Goneril and Regan, Gloster to Edmund. Shakespeare, however, has an alternative to this simple either-or.

The Middle Ages dreamed of the *Civitas Dei* ['City of God']. Here the good man had a ground whereon to base himself, affirming faith in community while standing critically aside from the corrupt society. The sixteenth century, too, had its vision. The orthodox establishment was threatened from one side by the bogey of machiavellism, shaken from the other by the rumour of Anabaptism. Along with most sixteenth century theology the *Ecclesiastical Polity* [of Richard Hooker] controverts the views of Munzer [leader of Peasants' War in Germany in the early sixteenth century] as fervently as those of Rome and Geneva. Anabaptism was kept in mind, like Machiavel's doctrine, by the series of counterblasts against it. (The burnings of Baptists in Elizabeth's reign amounted to about a dozen only. The Baptist community – mainly of Dutch émigrés – was never more than about a hundred until James's reign.) By a profound instinct for the Utopian root of art, Shakespeare saw in the medieval dream and the Anabaptist equalitarianism an alternative to Edmund and a fulfilment of the old King's real Nature. The vision of the new order is given in Lear's prayer and embodied in the King's rejected daughter.

The outline of the allegory still continues clear. – The society with Nature and Reason as its aim can never be utterly lost. At its best, it still admits the constant need for approximation to the absolute pattern. The spirit is not denied for the sake of the letter. Such a society can grow old and dote and commit offence. But it never utterly rejects the possibility of, and therefore it is always open to, regeneration. The Old King in Shakespeare's play is actually launched on a course of regeneration after error and the nemesis of error. The saving fact is that he has a daughter

> Who redeems Nature from the general curse
> Which twain have brought her to.
>
> (IV, vi)

This daughter is Cordelia – threefold like Lear and Edmund: a person, a principle, and a community.

CORDELIA AS NATURE

. . . Cordelia embodies the Nature which Edmund denies to exist, and which Lear – though he believes in it – cannot recognize when it is before him. . . . In so far as there is always a discrepancy between the truth the person aims at and the actual setting which makes it necessary to have that truth for an aim – in so far as the good man is necessarily in relation to a bad society – the ideal community Cordelia implies will be a non-existent one. If we like we can call it a Utopia. If we like we can call it, as the evangelicals and the apocalyptics did, Jerusalem. Art, like ethical action, is utopian in intention. Cordelia expresses the utopian intention of Shakespeare's art.

. . . In Hooker's view Christ's two commandments [love of God and love of neighbour] are approvable by the Light of Nature and Reason. Gerrard Winstanley [leader of the 'Diggers or True Levellers' at the time of the English Revolution] argued from [these] to primitive communism, but otherwise both he and Hooker digged the same intellectual common:

> . . . act righteousness to all fellow creatures; till the ground according to Reason; use the labour of your cattell with Reason; follow your course of trading in righteousness, as Reason requires, do to men and women as you would have them do unto you. . . . But let me tell you, that man whosover he be, that is not careful to look into the light of . . . nature, and follow the rules of this light, to do so he would be done unto, shall never come to see the Spirit, that made and that dwells in nature, which is the father of the whole Creation.
>
> ['Truth Lifting up its Head against Scandals', *Works*,
> ed. G. H. Sabine, p. 137]

. . . [Cordelia] expresses 'the natural virtue' which . . . animated the common men that worked St. George's Heath with Winstanley. Both her sweetness and her strength come from the medieval tradition preserved almost intact by the Eliza-bethan Establishment. . . .

As representing Nature in its communal aspect Cordelia is . . . contrasted with the societies of Edmund and of Lear. Edmund's is the society of the New Man and the New Age: it is a society based on unfettered competition, and the war of all against all. Lear's is the feudal state in decomposition. It is imperfect in its form and operation (Edmund is the product of its imperfection), but it pays nominal allegiance at least to Nature and to Kindness. Of this Nature and Kindness Cordelia is the full realization. She is the norm by which the wrongness of Edmund's world and the imperfection of Lear's is judged. Cordelia fights on her father's behalf, because the medieval world contained at least the seed and recognition of true humanness in society: the advance beyond capitalism will appear in part a return. Cordelia, however, stands for no historically realizable arrangement. Her perfection of truth, justice, charity requires a New Jerusalem. She is in a transcendent rela-tion to the political and the private. She is the norm itself. As such she belongs to the utopian dream of the artist and of the good man.

17

'. . . Poetically Man Dwells . . .'

Martin Heidegger*

THE PHRASE IS taken from a late poem by Hölderlin, which comes to us by a curious route. It begins: 'In lovely blueness blooms the steeple with metal roof.' . . . If we are to hear the phrase 'poetically man dwells' rightly, we must restore it thoughtfully to the poem. For that reason let us give thought to the phrase. Let us clear up the doubts it immediately arouses. For otherwise we should lack the free readiness to respond to the phrase by following it.

'. . . poetically man dwells . . .' If need be, we can imagine that poets do on occasion dwell poetically. But how is 'man' – and this means every man and all the time – supposed to dwell poetically? Does not all dwelling remain incompatible with the poetic? Our dwelling is harassed by the housing shortage. Even if that were not so, our dwelling today is harassed by work, made insecure by the hunt for gain and success, bewitched by the entertainment and recreation industry. But when there is still room left in today's dwelling for the poetic, and time is still set aside, what comes to pass is at best a preoccupation with aestheticizing, whether in writing or on the air. Poetry is either rejected as a frivolous mooning and vaporizing into the unknown, and a flight into dreamland, or is counted as a part of literature. And the validity of literature is assessed by the latest prevailing standard. The prevailing standard, in turn, is made and controlled by the organs for making public civilized opinions. One of its functionaries – at once driver and driven – is the literature industry. In such a setting poetry cannot appear otherwise than as literature. Where it is studied entirely in educational and scientific terms, it is the object of literary history. Western poetry goes under the general heading of 'European literature'.

But if the sole form in which poetry exists is literary to start with, then how can human dwelling be understood as based on the poetic? The phrase, 'man dwells poetically', comes indeed from a mere poet, and in fact from one who, we are told, could not cope with life. It is the way of poets to shut their eyes to actuality. Instead of acting, they dream. What they make is merely imagined. The things

*From '. . . Poetically Man Dwells . . .' (1951), in *Poetry, Language, Thought* (trans. Albert Hofstadter), London and New York: Harper & Row, 1971.

of imagination are merely made. Making is, in Greek, *poiesis*. And man's dwelling is supposed to be poetry and poetic? This can be assumed, surely, only by someone who stands aside from actuality and does not want to see the existent condition of man's historical-social life today – the sociologists call it the collective.

But before we so bluntly pronounce dwelling and poetry incompatible, it may be well to attend soberly to the poet's statement. It speaks of man's dwelling. It does not describe today's dwelling conditions. Above all, it does not assert that to dwell means to occupy a house, a dwelling place. Nor does it say that the poetic exhausts itself in an unreal play of poetic imagination. What thoughtful man, therefore, would presume to declare, unhesitatingly and from a somewhat dubious elevation, that dwelling and the poetic are incompatible? Perhaps the two can bear with each other. This is not all. Perhaps one even bears the other in such a way that dwelling rests on the poetic. If this is indeed what we suppose, then we are required to think of dwelling and poetry in terms of their essential nature. If we do not balk at this demand, we think of what is usually called the existence of man in terms of dwelling. In doing so, we do of course give up the customary notion of dwelling. According to that idea, dwelling remains merely one form of human behaviour alongside many others. We work in the city, but dwell outside it. We travel, and dwell now here, now there. Dwelling so understood is always merely the occupying of a lodging.

When Hölderlin speaks of dwelling, he has before his eyes the basic character of human existence. He sees the 'poetic', moreover, by way of its relation to this dwelling, thus understood essentially.

This does not mean, though, that the poetic is merely an ornament and bonus added to dwelling. Nor does the poetic character of dwelling mean merely that the poetic turns up in some way or other in all dwelling. Rather, the phrase 'poetically man dwells' says: poetry first causes dwelling to be dwelling. Poetry is what really lets us dwell. But through what do we attain to a dwelling place? Through building. Poetic creation, which lets us dwell, is a kind of building.

Thus we confront a double demand: for one thing, we are to think of what is called man's existence by way of the nature of dwelling; for another, we are to think of the nature of poetry as a letting-dwell, as a – perhaps even *the* – distinctive kind of building. If we search out the nature of poetry according to this viewpoint, then we arrive at the nature of dwelling.

But where do we humans get our information about the nature of dwelling and poetry? Where does man generally get the claim to arrive at the nature of something? Man can make such a claim only where he receives it. He receives it from the telling of language. Of course, only when and only as long as he respects language's own nature. Meanwhile, there rages round the earth an unbridled yet clever talking, writing, and broadcasting of spoken words. Man acts as though he were the shaper and master of language, while in fact language remains the master of man. When this relation of dominance gets inverted, man hits upon strange manoeuvres. Language becomes the means of expression. As expression, language can decay into a mere medium for the printed word. That even in such employment of language we retain a concern for care in speaking is all to the good. But this alone will never help us to escape from the inversion of the true relation of dominance between language and man. For, strictly, it is language that speaks. Man first speaks when, and only when, he responds to language by listening to its appeal. Among all the appeals that we human beings, on our part, may help to be voiced, language is the highest and everywhere the first. Language beckons us, at first and then again at the end, towards a thing's nature. But that is not to say, ever, that in any word-meaning picked up at will language supplies us, straight away and definitively, with the transparent nature of the matter as if it were an object ready for use. But the responding in which man authentically listens to the appeal of language is that which speaks in the element of poetry. The more poetic a poet is – the freer (that is, the more open and ready for the unforeseen) his saying – the greater is the purity with which he submits what he says to an ever more painstaking listening, and the further what he says is from the mere prepositional statement that is dealt with solely in regard to its correctness or incorrectness.

'. . . poetically man dwells . . .'

says the poet. We hear Hölderlin's words more clearly when we take them back into the poem in which they belong. First, let us listen only to the two lines from which we have detached and thus clipped the phrase. They run:

Full of merit, yet poetically, man
Dwells on this earth.

The keynote of the lines vibrates in the word 'poetically'. This word is set off in two directions: by what comes before it and by what follows.

Before it are the words: 'Full of merit, yet . . .'. They sound almost as if the next word, 'poetically', introduced a restriction on the profitable, meritorious dwelling of man. But it is just the reverse. The restriction is denoted by the expression 'Full of merit', to which we must add in thought a 'to be sure'. Man, to be sure, merits and earns much in his dwelling. For he cultivates the growing things of the earth and takes care of his increase. Cultivating and caring (*colere*, *cultura*) are a kind of building. But man not only cultivates what produces growth out of itself; he also builds in the sense of *aedificare*, by erecting things that cannot come into being and subsist by growing. Things that are built in this sense include not only buildings but all the works made by man's hands and through his arrangements. Merits due to this building, however, can never fill out the nature of dwelling. On the contrary, they even deny dwelling its own nature when they are pursued and acquired purely for their own sake. For in that case these merits, precisely by their abundance, would everywhere constrain dwelling within the bounds of this kind of building. Such building pursues the fulfilment of the needs of dwelling. Building in the sense of the farmer's cultivation of growing things, and of the erecting of edifices and works and the production of tools, is already a consequence of the nature of dwelling, but it is not its ground, let alone its grounding. This grounding must take place in a different building.

Building of the usual kind, often practiced exclusively and therefore the only one that is familiar, does of course bring an abundance of merits into dwelling. Yet man is capable of dwelling only if he had already built, is building, and remains disposed to build, in another way.

'Full of merit (to be sure), yet poetically, man dwells. . . .' This is followed in the text by the words: 'on this earth.' We might be inclined to think the addition superfluous; for dwelling, after all, already means man's stay on earth – on 'this' earth, to which every mortal knows himself to be entrusted and exposed.

But when Hölderlin ventures to say that the dwelling of mortals is poetic, this statement, as soon as it is made, gives the impression that, on the contrary, 'poetic' dwelling snatches man away from the earth. For the 'poetic', when it is taken as poetry, is supposed to belong to the realm of fantasy. Poetic dwelling flies fantastically above reality. The poet counters this misgiving by saying expressly that poetic dwelling is a dwelling 'on this earth.' Hölderlin thus not only protects the 'poetic' from a likely misinterpretation, but by adding the words 'on this earth' expressly points to the nature of poetry. Poetry does not fly above and surmount the earth in order to escape it and hover over it. Poetry is what first brings man onto the earth, making him belong to it, and thus brings him into dwelling.

> Full of merit, yet poetically, man
> Dwells on this earth.

Do we know now why man dwells poetically? We still do not. We now even run the risk of intruding foreign thoughts into Hölderlin's poetic words. For Hölderlin indeed speaks of man's dwelling and his merit, but still he does not connect dwelling with building, as we have just done. He does not speak of building, either in the sense of cultivating and erecting, or in such a way as even to represent poetry as a special kind of building. Accordingly, Hölderlin does not speak of poetic dwelling as our own thinking does. Despite all this, we are thinking the same thing that Hölderlin is saying poetically.

It is, however, important to take note here of an essential point. A short parenthetical remark is needed. Poetry and thinking meet each other in one and the same only when, and only as long as, they remain distinctly in the distinctness of their nature. The same never coincides with the equal, not even in the empty indifferent oneness of what is merely identical. The equal or identical always moves toward the absence of difference, so that everything may be reduced to a common denominator. The same, by contrast, is the belonging together of what differs, through a gathering by way of the difference. We can only say 'the same' if we think difference. It is in the carrying out and settling of differences that the gathering nature of sameness comes to light. The same banishes all zeal always to level what is different into the equal or identical. The same gathers what is distinct into an original being-at-one. The equal, on the contrary, disperses them into the dull unity of mere uniformity. Hölderlin, in his own way, knew of these relations. In an epigram which bears the title 'Root of All Evil'. . . he says:

Being at one is godlike and good; whence, then,
this craze among men that there should exist only
One, why should all be one?

When we follow in thought Hölderlin's poetic statement about the poetic dwelling
of man, we divine a path by which, through what is thought differently, we come
nearer to thinking the same as what the poet composes in his poem.

But what does Hölderlin say of the poetic dwelling of man? We seek the answer
to the question by listening to lines 24 to 38 of our poem. For the two lines on
which we first commented are spoken from their region. Hölderlin says:

May, if life is sheer toil, a man
Lift his eyes and say: so
I too wish to be? Yes. As long as Kindness,
The Pure, still stays with his heart, man
Not unhappily measures himself
Against the godhead. Is God unknown?
Is he manifest like the sky? I'd sooner
Believe the latter. It's the measure of man.
Full of merit, yet poetically, man
Dwells on this earth. But no purer
Is the shade of the starry night,
If I might put it so, than
Man, who's called an image of the godhead.
Is there a measure on earth? There is
None.

We shall think over only a few points in these lines, and for the sole purpose of
hearing more clearly what Hölderlin means when he calls man's dwelling a 'poetic'
one. The first lines (24 to 26) give us a clue. They are in the form of a question
that is answered confidently in the affirmative. The question is a paraphrase of
what the lines already expounded utter directly: 'Full of merit, yet poetically, man
dwells on this earth.' Hölderlin asks:

May, if life is sheer toil, a man
Lift his eyes and say: so
I too wish to be? Yes.

Only in the realm of sheer toil does man toil for 'merits'. There he obtains them
for himself in abundance. But at the same time, in this realm, man is allowed to
look up, out of it, through it, toward the divinities. The upward glance passes aloft
toward the sky, and yet it remains below on the earth. The upward glance spans
the between of sky and earth. This between is measured out for the dwelling of
man. We now call the span thus meted out the dimension. This dimension does
not arise from the fact that sky and earth are turned toward one another. Rather,

their facing each other itself depends on the dimension. Nor is the dimension a stretch of space as ordinarily understood; for everything spatial, as something for which space is made, is already in need of the dimension, that is, that into which it is admitted.

The nature of the dimension is the meting out – which is lightened and so can be spanned – of the between: the upward to the sky as well as the downward to earth. We leave the nature of the dimension without a name. According to Hölderlin's words, man spans the dimension by measuring himself against the heavenly. Man does not undertake this spanning just now and then; rather, man is man at all only in such spanning. This is why he can indeed block this spanning, trim it, and disfigure it, but he can never evade it. Man, as man, has always measured himself with and against something heavenly. Lucifer, too, is descended from heaven. Therefore we read in the next lines (28 to 29): 'Man measures himself against the godhead.' The godhead is the 'measure' with which man measures out his dwelling, his stay on the earth beneath the sky. Only insofar as man takes the measure of his dwelling in this way is he able to *be* commensurately with his nature. Man's dwelling depends on an upward-looking measure-taking of the dimension, in which the sky belongs just as much as the earth.

This measure-taking not only takes the measure of the earth, *ge*, and accordingly it is no mere geo-metry. Just as little does it ever take the measure of heaven, *ouranos*, for itself. Measure-taking is no science. Measure-taking gauges the between, which brings the two, heaven and earth, to one another. This measure-taking has its own *metron*, and thus its own metric.

Man's taking measure in the dimension dealt out to him brings dwelling into its ground plan. Taking the measure of the dimension is the element within which human dwelling has its security, by which it securely endures. The taking of measure is what is poetic in dwelling. Poetry is a measuring. But what is it to measure? If poetry is to be understood as measuring, then obviously we may not subsume it under just any idea of measuring and measure.

Poetry is presumably a high and special kind of measuring. But there is more. Perhaps we have to pronounce the sentence, 'Poetry is a *measuring*,' with a different stress. '*Poetry* is a measuring.' In poetry there takes place what all measuring is in the ground of its being. Hence it is necessary to pay heed to the basic act of measuring. That consists in man's first of all taking the measure which then is applied in every measuring act. In poetry the taking of measure occurs. To write poetry is measure-taking, understood in the strict sense of the word, by which man first receives the measure for the breadth of his being. Man exists as a mortal. He is called mortal because he can die. To be able to die means: to be capable of death as death. Only man dies – and indeed continually, so long as he stays on this earth, so long as he dwells. His dwelling, however, rests in the poetic. Hölderlin sees the nature of the 'poetic' in the taking of the measure by which the measure-taking of human being is accomplished. . . .

Poetry builds up the very nature of dwelling. Poetry and dwelling not only do not exclude each other; on the contrary, poetry and dwelling belong together, each calling for the other. 'Poetically man dwells.' Do *we* dwell poetically? Presumably we dwell altogether unpoetically. If that is so, does it give the lie to the poet's words; are they untrue? No. The truth of his utterance is confirmed in the most unearthly way. For dwelling can be unpoetic only because it is in essence poetic. For a man to be blind, he must remain a being by nature endowed with sight. A piece of wood can never go blind. But when man goes blind, there always remains the question whether his blindness derives from some defect and loss of lies in an abundance and excess. In the same poem that meditates on the measure for all measuring, Hölderlin says (lines 75–76): 'King Oedipus has perhaps one eye too many.' Thus it might be that our unpoetic dwelling, its incapacity to take the measure, derives from a curious excess of frantic measuring and calculating.

That we dwell unpoetically, and in what way, we can in any case learn only if we know the poetic. Whether, and when, we may come to a turning point in our unpoetic dwelling is something we may expect to happen only if we remain heedful of the poetic. How and to what extent our doings can share in this turn we alone can prove, if we take the poetic seriously.

The poetic is the basic capacity for human dwelling. But man is capable of poetry at any time only to the degree to which his being is appropriate to that which itself has a liking for man and therefore needs his presence. Poetry is authentic or inauthentic according to the degree of this appropriation.

That is why authentic poetry does not come to light appropriately in every period. When and for how long does authentic poetry exist? Hölderlin gives the answer in verses 26–29, already cited. Their explication has been purposely deferred until now. The verses run:

> . . . As long as Kindness,
> The Pure, still stays with his heart, man
> Not unhappily measures himself
> Against the Godhead. . . .

'Kindness – what is it? A harmless word, but described by Hölderlin with the capitalized epithet 'the Pure'. 'Kindness' – this word, if we take it literally, is Hölderlin's magnificent translation for the Greek word *charis*. In his *Ajax*, Sophocles says of *charis* (verse 522):

> *charis charin gar estin he tiktous aei.*
> For kindness it is, that ever calls forth kindness.

'As long as Kindness, the Pure, still stays with his heart. . . .' Hölderlin says in an idiom he liked to use: 'with his heart,' not 'in his heart.' That is, it has come to the dwelling being of man, come as the claim and appeal of the measure to the heart in such a way that the heart turns to give heed to the measure.

As long as this arrival of kindness endures, so long does man succeed in measuring himself not unhappily against the godhead. When this measuring appropriately comes to light, man creates poetry from the very nature of the poetic. When the poetic appropriately comes to light, then man dwells humanly on this earth, and then – as Hölderlin says in his last poem – 'the life of man' is a 'dwelling life'.

Vista

When far the dwelling life of man into the distance goes,
Where, in that far distance, the grapevine's season glows,
There too are summer's fields, emptied of their growing,
And forest looms, its image darkly showing.
That Nature paints the seasons so complete,
That she abides, but they glide by so fleet,
Comes of perfection; then heaven's radiant height
Crowns man, as blossoms crown the trees, with light.

18

*Hyper-Technologism,
Pollution and Satire*

Kenneth Burke*

The unhappy fact is that the subject of my tentatively proposed satire is technological pollution. Obviously, therefore, I'd be at considerable disadvantage if my talk were but special pleading for the virtues of a satire on pollution. Rather, I must place the stress upon the pros and cons of satire in general. Similarly, the treatment of my particular test case must be concerned with the satirist's efforts somehow to be *evasive*.

As a matter of fact, for several years I had been compulsively taking notes on the subject of technological pollution – and I still do compulsively take such notes. But at the same time, I loathe them. I would love to get shut of the whole issue, even to the extent of inattention by dissipation. But it goes on nagging me. Consequently, as I hope to make clear, my thoughts on satire in this connection come to a focus in plans for a literary compromise whereby, thanks to a stylistics of evasion, I both might and might not continue with the vexatiousness of this *idée fixe*, this damned committed nuisance.

HOW SETTLE ON SATIRE?

Possibly, in part at least, because I happened to read George Meredith's essay on comedy when I was quite young and impressionable, I approach my subject, my *idée fixe*, with the assumption that, above all, whenever and wherever possible, one should write comedy. An ideal world would be one for which comedy would be the perfect fit. But to say as much is by the same token to disqualify comedy, since this is so far from being an ideal world.

Tragedy? Though the present developments of technological enterprise, and especially its military resourcefulness, have led to the affliction of much suffering, and raise many threats, the technically experimental attitude behind all such activities is not in spirit tragic. So far as I can see, the technological impulse to keep on perpetually tinkering with things could not be tragic unless or until men became

*From 'Why Satire, with a Plan for Writing One', *Michigan Quarterly Review*, 13(4), 1974.

resigned to the likelihood that they may be fatally and inexorably driven to keep on perpetually tinkering with things. But even so, the chances are that, so long as the present mentality prevails, one would go on tinkering, beguiled by the thought that we might somehow get over the problem by resorting to surgery or giving it a pill. Also, I keep uneasily coming back to the thought that, with the cult of tragedy, maybe you're asking for it. Lamentation is so near to tragedy, it would not figure as an overall mode, though quite relevant to occasional lyric moments.

What, then, of a related, but differently tempered form: the document, the evidence, the indictment? Would that qualify? In one respect, yes. By all means, we should jealously cherish the Cult of the Records. But precisely there is where the trouble came in. For years I had worked valiantly to uphold what I thought of as a 'Comic Perspective'. And I still won't quite relinquish it. Then, on working with socio-psychological problems to do with the nature of human congregation, I became convinced that the establishing of an Order in human affairs involves a *sacrificial* principle. With such thoughts in mind, I studied the modes of victimage in tragedy, and in highly developed theological structures.

I am not here being inconsistent. For though the principle of victimage is obviously central to tragedy, it itself is not exclusively tragic. Tragedy enters with the principle of sympathetic resignation, but Hitlerism is evidence enough that the principle of victimage can be viciously polemical. For instance, consider Hitler's use of it as a rhetorical and administrative device for unifying his party. It was an example of what I would call 'congregation by segregation', unifying a people by antithesis, in terms of a common enemy. Though tragedy would well befit an account of Hitler's victims as such, the situation with which we are concerned would be of a different sort, with a relation to technology that ultimately involved us all, though I shall try to show how this fact might be stylistically denied, in a fiction that reaffirmed our problem by offering a satirically absurd 'solution', as with Swift's 'solution' to the problem of hunger in Ireland.

A treatment of 'the evidence', 'the documents', in the accents of invective would be even more wearisome than unrelieved accumulation of the data, though as with lamentation an occasional sally in that mode would be justified.

Thoughts on Greek tragedy and its implied theology had got me particularly interested in ideas and images of *ritual* pollution. But later, I found myself taking notes on pollution in the most pragmatic, literal, scientific sense; namely: pollution as the 'unwanted by-products', or 'side effects', of advances in modern industry. In my accumulation of clippings, here indeed were the documents, the records, the factual data, the *indictment*. But, as I have said, a mighty boredom beset me, even while I kept plunging on, compulsively adding to this unsightly pile. And that brings us to satire, but not too directly; rather by a somewhat roundabout route.

In essays and reviews that I wrote during the Thirties I got to thinking of what I called projects that 'go to the end of the line'. James Joyce's later work would be a prime example. Certain artists, or purely speculative minds, glimpse certain ultimate possibilities in their view of things, and there is no rest until they have tracked down the implications of their insight, by transforming its potentialities into total actualization.

Eventually, I came to think of this tendency as a third creative motive, not quite reducible to either self-expression or communication, and even at times running counter to communication. I began to think of it as implicit in termi-nology as such. Each specialized nomenclature, for instance, suggests further possi-bilities in that direction – and the person who glimpses them is 'called', thus being under a kind of compulsion to track down the implications of his terministically goaded vision. Utopias are obvious examples of this goad. And in this purely formal, or logical sense. Marxism would be an example of such thoroughness, regardless of the distinction that some partisans might want to introduce here between an outright Utopia and the socialist future that Marx held to be implicit in the nature of capitalism's birth, growth, and decay.

Later I began to ask myself whether I could round out this notion of a purely formal motive (or goad, implicit in our nomenclatures) by adapting for my purposes the Aristotelian concept of the 'entelechy'. Aristotle applied the term in a quite broad sense. For instance, a stone would actualize its potentials as a stone, a tree would actualize its potentials as a tree, and man might (not so successfully) actualize his potentials as a rational animal. But I would settle for less. I would apply the term simply to the realm of symbolism, with verbal structures as different as the Marxist view of history. Bellamy's *Looking Backward*, and Lewis Carroll's *Through the Looking Glass*, all illustrative, in their different ways, of the 'entelechial' principle, tracking down the implications of a position, going to the end of the line.

We're now ready for the one further step that brings us to satire. To this end I will quote a quatrain that I have used elsewhere, when discussing the principle of entelechy as I would adopt it and adapt it. The lines have a title borrowed from Henley's 'Invictus' (the poem that rings out so challengingly, 'I am the master of my fate, the captain of my soul'):

> If things are bad, and I can't make them better,
> then all the more I'll be mine own begetter.
> Adversity shall be my universe,
> making me free to act to make things worse.

It is thus that satire can embody the entelechial principle. But it does so perversely, by tracking down possibilities or implications to the point where the result is a kind of Utopia-in-reverse. Is the world quite imperfect? If but some particular aspect of its imperfection happens to engage you, demanding despite yourself that you treat of it, you still have a fighting chance. Change the rules, resort to the ways of satire – and lo! once more there opens up for you the most delightful of all promises, the opportunity to fare freely forth in pursuit of perfection, and thus under the aegis of perfection. In brief, the prospect of dwelling in the keen exhilaration of No-Place (that is, Utopia) beckons to you – with but the one minor proviso that, by the rules of perfection peculiar to satire, you depict your ideal realm as a species of Utopia-in-reverse.

Think of the situation thus: Technology is in its very essence rational. Yet the accumulation of its instruments, with their unwanted by-products, has in effect transformed the fruits of our rationality into a prodigious problem, thereby giving rise to many compensatory cults of irrationality. On the other hand, as I shall try to show, the satirizing of technology can be as rational as technology itself. And thereby, once again, we glimpse the possibility of a compromise. For the satire can be as rational as the 'technological psychosis' out of which it arises; yet at the same time in its way it can manifest great sympathy with the trends embodied in the irrationality of current anti-technologic trends. And even though conditions that once seemed absurd (the implicit and even explicit equating of 'culture' with a cult of commodities) now seem ominous, the task of the satirist is to set up a fiction whereby our difficulties can be treated in the accents of the promissory. Whitman, in his accents of gladness, had given us the clue:

> I know not where they go,
> But I know that they go toward the best – toward
>   something great.

The satirist's quasi-solution should track that down, not just leaving it *en route* as with Whitman's words, but to the end of the line.

The turn involves certain implications in such poems of Whitman's as 'The Song of Occupations', 'The Song of the Open Road', 'The Song of the Broad-Axe', and 'O Pioneers'. But they are to be seen satirically in the light of subsequent developments. Considered thus, they are reducible to a proposition of this sort. Since they were celebrating almost an orgy of construction, and since there is no construction without destruction, it is now clear that those poems were joyously ushering in the very era of care-free destruction now nearing its care-worn culmination in environmentalist problems due to technologically caused pollution.

Whitman's poems of that sort were in effect (or at least for purposes of satire they could be viewed as) utterances by a great prophetic bard of real estate promotion. Of course there was much more to Whitman than that, and I am among those who have said so. But for reasons that will become apparent my project needs him badly, in the role I have assigned him. And now that all the territory within our borders has become the transformation of nature into real estate of one kind or another, we need but ask ourselves how, by putting satire in place of his easy idealism, we can reclaim and thus enjoy once more the accents of the exultantly promissory.

There are further tangles, still to be considered. But for the moment let us be content with what opens up before us: a post-Whitman, neo-Whitman vision, carrying the ambiguities of construction and destruction into areas of pioneering and colonization unthinkable to the technology of Whitman's times. Thus was born the project of HELHAVEN, a scientifically designed culture-bubble on the moon, and also involving a high degree of technical *organization*, whereas Walt was but content to loaf and invite his soul.

HELHAVEN, the expertly planned and guided enterprise of Lunar Paradisiacs, Incorporated. A womb-heaven, thus in the most basic sense Edenic, yet made possible only by the highest flights of technologic progress – hence, Eden and the

Tower [of Babel] in one. A true eschatology, bringing first and last things together – the union of Alpha and Omega. And so, soon now, TOWARDS HELHAVEN.

For quite a long time, I had been content to abide by a theory of satire that I had offered in a book, *Attitudes Towards History*, published in the Thirties. Approaching satire from the standpoint of the distinction between 'acceptance' and 'rejection' (yea-saying and nay-saying, which are attitudinally tinged variants of Yes and No) I put satire on the negative side of the equation. In contrast, for instance, I thought of epic, tragedy, and comedy as on the 'acceptance' side.

Later, along those lines, I noticed the shrewdness of Homer who did not 'suppress' a critique of epic war. The poet, or poets, so thoroughly poetic as the sources behind the two Homeric epics, would not, like political bureaucrats in office, seek to *suppress* a critique of the poems' assumptions. No, you'll find in the *Iliad* itself an attack upon the heroism of epic war. And who was entrusted with the job of voicing such an opposition? None other than Thersites, so loathsome an excuse for a human being that Hegel expanded him into the concept of 'Thersitism', a term he would doubtless have applied to much that Marx was to say of Hegelianism.

As a way of moving on by adding further considerations for present purposes, let me quote this much from my earlier comments on satire as a 'poetic category':

> The satirist attacks *in others* the weaknesses and temptations that are really *within himself*. . . . One cannot read great satirists like Swift or Juvenal without feeling this strategic ambiguity. We sense in them the Savanarola, who would exorcize his own vanities by building a fire of other people's vanities. Swift's aptitude at 'projection' invited him to beat himself unmercifully.

When I began plans for the satire I wanted to build up, I had in mind that principle. I mean: If I am to write a satire, when all the returns are in it mustn't turn out that I am holier than thou. I must be among my victims. That is to say: I take it that my satire on the 'technological psychosis' will be an offspring of that same psychosis.

But to my earlier notion that we are all, including the satirist, tarred by the same brush, there are added the sophistications whereby we can get the curative *accents* of assertion and perfection by calling for a Utopia-in-reverse. . . .

TOWARDS HELHAVEN

About the edges of satire, obviously, hover related modes of expression: humor, comedy, irony, burlesque, the grotesque (which might be defined as a kind of comic incongruity without the laughter). But whereas the incongruousness of the grotesque is 'gargoyle-thinking', perhaps the major resource of satiric amplification is an *excess of consistency*. Taking conditions that are here already, the satirist perversely, twistedly, carries them 'to the end of the line.'

... For instance, we are told that Buckminster Fuller centers his energy 'in a single drive: to promote *the total use of total technology for total population* at the maximum feasible rate of acceleration.' There surely lies the material for satire. In that formula, surely, is implicit the incentive for satiric exaggeration. Yet who among us is not affected and infected at least to some degree by technological ways of thinking and living ... which might be called 'Hyper-Technologism'? ...

Thus, I can envision such ideal future circumstances as when Helhaven, our transcendent culture-bubble, has a Luna-Hilton Hotel, in every way indistinguishable from its uniform counterparts in the hotel-chains you find now all over the world. The main difference between the Luna-Hilton and its opposite numbers on the terrestrial globe is that the guest will have a simulated outlook from each imitation window. For but a small fee, he can, as it were, gaze upon a beautiful lake, or upon a distant, snow-capped mountain, or a tropical beach – or if he gets homesick for urban things back here, by but pressing a different button, he can watch, squirming beneath him, a typical tangle of traffic, simulated even with the same noises, plus the stench (yet though the smell will be like on Earth, it will be scientifically free of all the poisons that actually accompany such conditions here). I assure you that there will be a far greater range of such Perspectivos, if I may call these outlooks by their future trade name – but since I am not good at science fiction, I cannot imagine whether there'll also be views of muggings, pick-ups, and riots. Such decisions will be at the discretion of the management, when the time comes. ...

The lay-out of the place would be in general simply things here over again, except that technological artificiality would be complete. This is an important point to keep in mind. For underneath the satire must be the fact that *in principle* the Helhaven situation is 'morally' here already. For instance, you're already in Helhaven insofar as you are, directly or indirectly (and who is not?) deriving a profit from some enterprise that is responsible for the polluting of some area, but your share in such revenues enables you to live in an area not thus beplagued. Or think of the many places in our country where the local drinking water is on the swill side, distastefully chlorinated, with traces of various industrial contaminants. If, instead of putting up with that, you invest in bottled spring-water, to that extent and by the same token you are already infused with the spirit of Helhaven. Even now, the kingdom of Helhaven is within you. ...

THE PLOT THICKENS

How, proceed, in keeping with the thesis that a satire on so tiresome though perhaps fatal a subject as technological pollution must contrive to hang on even while dodging? That compromise, I thought, might best be contrived if things were so set up that, in keeping with the nature of the fiction, and 'indictment' of technology's excesses could be welcomed as a momentous positive step towards the ideal future (or, I should say, the parody of such a step).

In keeping with our entelechial ideal of going to the end of the line, we needed some twists whereby the 'logical conclusion' (which is to say, the reduction to absurdity) of Hyper-Technologistic energy-consumption could attain 'perfect' fulfillment in the total pollution of our once handsome planet. And reasons should be welcomed, as mankind's final attaining and transcending of our earthly aims after long and arduous effort. By a twist of that sort one might recapture the stylistics of assertiveness so greatly needed for our time, and so imperative, if we were to keep on confronting, without the nausea of boredom, the basic problem that persisted in platitudinously pursuing us.

When we are confronting so fundamental a problem of sociology, precisely then, in keeping with the methodology of logology the first principle of axiology advises us to look for some analogy of morphology in the realm of theology. And there it was, as though made to order, in the last book of the New Testament, the Apocalypse, that is a summing up if there ever was one, hence manifesting to perfection the kind of drive I would call entelechial, despite its divergence from the technological variety we have been considering.

As in both Revelation and *The Divine Comedy*, all should come to a focus in a crucial distinction between The Chosen and the Reprobates, except that in the fictive technological fulfillment, the counterpart of those not among The Chosen would not be sinners, but simply out of luck.

It became clear that the design called for the ironic version of an exalted promissory attitude, such as would befit the 'Vision' of an ultimate peaceful existence in a perfectly air-conditioned culture-bubble on the Moon, a transcendent step beyond the radical polluting of the Earth. And 'perfection', as thus perversely defined, would in turn be perfected if, by the conditions of the fiction, things were so set up that those among The Chosen had been largely responsible for the very conditions on Earth they were escaping. . . .

THE SEVEN STEPS

[Burke explains how Helhaven would be ruled by the 'Master' or 'Prime Personalist', a follower of Whitman, and would be administrated by the 'Vice Personalist'.] The pattern as a whole might be summed up in these seven steps:

(1) The growing evidence of pollution as the fatal cost of technology had first caused The Master, the Personalist Supreme, to lose his faith in the Whitmanite ideal of conquering a continent by Ecstatic, headlong, anti-conservationist upheaval.

(2) But The Master turned from the threat of a breakdown to a breakthrough, once he found his principle of transformation, the Vision of Division (with its 'entelechial' principle, 'the worse the better') whereby all could again become confident, forward-looking, eschatologically ultimate, a perfect road to perfection.

(3) His administrative assistant, the Vice-Personalist, would introduce coarser elements into the Vision; but never for one moment would he lose the Affirmative Spirit of the ultimate ideal, as salvaged by following through with the logic of the distinction between The Chosen and the Regrettably Unfortunate for whom there is no escape from the increasing ecological disasters.

102

(4) The pattern gets its ultimate refinement in the Ad Interim principle whereby those very persons who are among The Chosen can accelerate the pace of the decay by temporarily investing in the stocks of whatever corporations are secretly contributing to the project with funds derived from enterprises that further the ecological deterioration.

(5) Thereby is fulfilled the development that, in *The Education of Henry Adams*, is called the 'law of the acceleration of history', as per what is now called an 'exponential curve' (involving a machine ecology as distinct from a biological ecology).

(6) Having attained an Apocalyptic understanding of dialectical principles in their role as The Chosen who are to transcend conditions here on Earth, the Lunar Paradisiacs can smile (not maliciously, but hopefully) at the evidences that, if but technology continues to proliferate as it is now doing, things can end, not in a reactionary rejection of technology (which is the essence of human rationality), but in a super-technology that can rise out of the very decay it is producing.

(7) To back their thesis that, human nature being what it is, the entelechial lure of technology has already developed to the point where it is irreversible, they cite as an authority the views of that blithe Dymaxion spirit, Buckminster Fuller, though he might with some justice object to their interpretation of his views, as Whitman, if he were still among us, might object to my discussing certain poems of his in terms of vatic real estate promotion.

19

The Machine in the Garden

Leo Marx*

SLEEPY HOLLOW, 1844

ON THE MORNING of July 27, 1844, Nathaniel Hawthorne sat down in the woods near Concord, Massachusetts, to await (as he puts it) 'such little events as may happen'. His purpose, so far as we can tell, was chiefly literary. Though he had no reason to believe that anything memorable would happen, he sat there in solitude and silence and tried to record his every impression as precisely as possible. The whole enterprise is reminiscent of the painstaking literary exercises of his neighbour, Henry Thoreau. . . .[1]

Without any perceptible change of mood or tone, he shifts from images of nature to images of man and society. He insists that 'these sounds of labour' do not 'disturb the repose of the scene' or 'break our sabbath; for like a sabbath seems this place, and the more so on account of the cornfield rustling at our feet.' He is describing a state of being in which there is no tension either within the self or between the self and its environment. Much of this harmonious effect is evoked by the delicate interlacing of sounds that seem to unify society, landscape, and mind. What lends most interest, however, to this sense of all-encompassing harmony and peace is a vivid contrast:

> But, hark! There is the whistle of the locomotive – the long shriek, harsh, above all other harshness, for the space of a mile cannot mollify it into harmony. It tells a story of busy men, citizens, from the hot street, who have come to spend a day in a country village, men of business; in short of all unquietness; and no wonder that it gives such a startling shriek, since it brings the noisy world into the midst of our slumbrous peace. As our thoughts repose again, after this interruption, we find ourselves gazing up at the levels, and comparing their different aspect, the beautiful diversity of green. . . .

*From *The Machine in the Garden: Technology and the Pastoral Ideal in America*, London and New York: Oxford University Press, 1964.

THE PASTORAL DESIGN

... By *design* I refer to the larger structure of thought and feeling of which the *ideal* is a part. The distinction is a vital one. Much of the obscurity that surrounds the subject stems from the fact that we use the same word to refer to a wish-image of happiness and to literary compositions in their entirety – pastoral dreams and pastoral poems. Then, too, we sometimes confuse matters even more by taking the word completely out of its literary context to describe our experience of the real world. We say of a pleasing stretch of country that it is a 'pastoral scene', or that it gives us a 'pastoral feeling'. But our reactions to literature seldom are that simple. (The confusion arises, as it so often does, in crossing the borderland between life and literature.) Most literary works called pastorals – at least those substantial enough to retain our interest – do not finally permit us to come away with anything like the simple, affirmative attitude we adopt toward pleasing rural scenery. In one way or another, if only by virtue of the unmistakable sophistication with which they are composed, these works manage to qualify, or call into question, or bring irony to bear against the illusion of peace and harmony in a green pasture. ...

In addition to the ideal, then, the pastoral design in question (it is one among many) embraces some token of a larger, more complicated order of experience. Whether presented by the plight of a dispossessed herdsman or by the sound of a locomotive in the woods, this feature of the design brings a world which is more 'real' into juxtaposition with an idyll vision. It may be called the *counterforce*. Admittedly, the portentous, melodramatic connotations of this term make it inappropriate for the discussion of many bland, pre-industrial versions of pastoral. ... Nevertheless, the term *counterforce* is applicable to a good deal of modern American writing. The anti-pastoral forces at work in our literature seem indeed to become increasingly violent as we approach our own time. For it is industrialization, represented by images of machine technology, that provides the counterforce in the American archetype of the pastoral design.

Since Jefferson's time the forces of industrialism have been the chief threat to the bucolic image of America. The tension between the two systems of value had the greatest literary impact in the period between 1840 and 1860, when the nation reached that decisive stage in its economic development which W. W. Rostow calls the 'take-off'. In his study of the more or less universal stages of industrial growth, Rostow defines the take-off as the 'great water-shed in the life of modern societies' when the old blocks and resistances to steady development are overcome and the forces of economic progress expand and come to dominate the society. In America, according to Rostow, the take-off began about 1844 – the year of the Sleepy Hollow episode – just at the time our first significant literary generation was coming to maturity. Much of the singular quality of this era is conveyed by the trope of the interrupted idyll. The locomotive, associated with fire, smoke, speed, iron, and noise, is the leading symbol of the new industrial power. It appears in the woods, suddenly shattering the harmony of the green hollow, like a presentiment of history bearing down on the American asylum. The noise of the train, as Hawthorne describes it, is a cause of alienation in the root sense of the word: it makes inaudible the pleasing sounds to which he had been attending, and so it estranges him from the immediate source of meaning and value in Sleepy Hollow. In truth, the 'little event' is a miniature of a great – in many ways the greatest – event in our history.[2]

That Hawthorne was fully aware of the symbolic properties of the railroad is beyond question. Only the year before he had published 'The Celestial Railroad', a wonderfully compact satire on the prevailing faith in progress. In the popular culture of the period the railroad was a favorite emblem of progress – not merely technological progress, but the overall progress of the race. Hawthorne's sketch turns upon the idea of the new machine as a vehicle for an illusory voyage of salvation whose darkest meanings are reserved for readers of Bunyan. Like the hero of *The Pilgrim's Progress*, the American pilgrim thinks he is on his way to the Heavenly City. As it turns out, however, the same road can lead to hell, the partly concealed point being that the American protagonist is not a Christian at all; he has much more in common with the other traveler in Bunyan's Calvinist allegory Ignorance.

Nevertheless, it would be wrong to suppose that the primary subject of the Sleepy Hollow notes is the transition from an agrarian to an industrial society. Plausible on its face, such a reading confuses literary ends and means. The whole tenor of the notes indicates that Hawthorne is not interested in directing attention from himself to what is happening 'out there' in the great world of political and institutional change. Nor can it be said, incidentally, that any of the works that embody variants of the motif are, in the usual sense, *about* the great transformation. The point may seem a niggling one, but it is crucial if we are to define the precise relation between literature and that flow of unique, irreversible events called history. Although Hawthorne's account includes an element of representation – he draws upon actual objects and events – his chief concern is the landscape of the psyche. The inner, not the outer world, is what interests him most as he sits there in the woods, attempting to connect words and sense perceptions. His aim, as he says, is to represent the broad tide of dim emotions, ideas, and images coursing through his mind. When he seizes upon the auditory image of the train it is because it serves this purpose.

The primary subject of the Sleepy Hollow notes, then, is the contrast between two conditions of consciousness. Until he hears the train's whistle Hawthorne enjoys a serenity close to euphoria. The lay of the land represents a singular insulation from disturbance, and so enhances the feeling of security and repose. The hollow is a virtual cocoon of freedom from anxiety, guilt, and conflict – a shrine of the pleasure principle. To describe the situation in the language of Freud, particularly when we have only one example in view, no doubt seems farfetched. But the striking fact is that again and again our writers have introduced the same overtones, depicting the machine as invading the peace of an enclosed space, a world set apart, or an area somehow made to evoke a feeling of encircled felicity. The setting may be an island, or a hut beside a pond, or a raft floating down a river, or a secluded valley in the mountains, or a clearing between impenetrable walls of forest, or the beached skeleton of a whale – but whatever the specific details, certain general features of the pattern recur too often to be fortuitous. Most important is the sense of the machine as a sudden, shocking intruder upon a fantasy

106

of idyllic satisfaction. It invariably is associated with crude, masculine aggressive-
ness in contrast with the tender, feminine, and submissive attitudes traditionally
attached to the landscape.

But there is no need, actually, to choose between the public and private, political and psychic, meanings of this event. Even in these offhand notes, Hawthorne's
first concern – he is, after all, a writer of fiction – is the emotional power of his
material, and that power unquestionably is heightened by the larger, political implications of the machine image. Emerson makes the point this way: the serious artist,
he says, 'must employ the symbols in use in his day and nation to convey his
enlarged sense to his fellow-men'. The ideas and emotions linked to the fact of
industrialization provide Hawthorne with just such an enlargement of meaning.
Their function is like that of the secondary subject, or 'vehicle', of a grand metaphor.
To say this is not to imply that the topical significance of the machine is 'extrinsic'
to the literary process, or that it may be treated as a merely illustrative appendage.
As with any well-chosen figure, the subsidiary subject is an integral part of the
metaphor. Thought and feeling flow both ways. The radical change in the character of society and the sharp swing between two states of feeling, between an
Arcadian vision and an anxious awareness of reality, are closely related: they illu-
minate each other. All of which is another way of accounting for the symbolic
power of the motif: it brings the political and the psychic dissonance associated
with the onset of industrialism into a single pattern of meaning. Once generated,
of course, that dissonance demands to be resolved.

At the end of [the ancient Roman poet] Virgil's first eclogue [pastoral poem]
the resolution is effected by a series of homely images. Tityrus invites Meliboeus
to postpone his journey into exile. 'Yet surely,' he says, 'you could sleep here as my
guest for this one night, with green leaves for your bed?' This symbolic gesture
may be interpreted as an offer of a 'momentary stay against confusion' – Robert
Frost's way of defining the emotional end-product of a poem. 'It begins in delight,'
says Frost, 'and ends in wisdom . . . in a clarification of life – not necessarily a
great clarification, such as sects or cults are founded on, but in a momentary stay
against confusion.' To objectify this state of equilibrium Virgil closes the gap
between hope and fear. In the last lines of the poem Tityrus blends the two emotions
in a picture of the landscape at twilight:

> I have got ripe apples, and some mealy chestnuts and a good supply of
> cheese. See over there – the rooftops of the farms are already putting up
> their evening smoke and shadows of the mountain crests are falling farther
> out.[3]

So ends the first eclogue. As far as the narrative is concerned, nothing has been
solved. The poem offers no hint of a 'way out' for Meliboeus or those who inhabit
the ravaged countryside. All that he gets for solace is one night's postponement of
his exile – one night of comfort and companionship. Yet this twilight mood, a
blend of sadness and repose, succeeds aesthetically. It is a virtual resolution. Like
the middle landscape, or the ritual marriage at the end of a pastoral romance, this

consolatory prospect figuratively joins what had been apart. At the end of the Sleepy Hollow notes, similarly the train moves off and a sad tranquillity comes over Hawthorne. Although he manages to regain some of his earlier sense of peace, the encroaching forces of history have compelled him to recognize its evanescence. Just as Virgil ends with the image of falling shadows, so Hawthorne ends with the thought of a 'dreamer's Utopia' in ruins. In each case the conflict aroused by the counterforce is mitigated. These highly stylized resolutions are effective partly because the writers succeed in maintaining an unruffled, contemplative, Augustan tone. This tone, characteristic of Virgilian pastoral, is a way of saying that the episode belongs to a timeless, recurrent pattern of human affairs. It falls easily into a conventional design because it has occurred often before.

But the fact is that nothing quite like the event announced by the train in the woods had occurred before. A sense of history as an unpredictable, irreversible sequence of unique events makes itself felt even in Hawthorne's notes. In spite of the resemblance between the train and the archetypal city of Western literature, the 'little event' creates an unprecedented situation. For in the stock contrast between city and country each had been assumed to occupy a more or less fixed location in space: the country here, the city there. But in 1844 the sound of a train in the Concord woods implies a radical change in the conventional pattern. Now the great world is invading the land, transforming the sensory texture of rural life – the way it looks and sounds – and threatening, in fact, to impose a new and more complete dominion over it. True, it may be said that agents of urban power had been ravaging the countryside throughout recorded history. After they had withdrawn, however, the character of rural life had remained essentially unchanged. But here the case is different: the distinctive attribute of the new order is its technological power, a power that does not remain confined to the traditional boundaries of the city. It is a centrifugal force that threatens to break down, once and for all, the conventional contrast between these two styles of life. The Sleepy Hollow episode prefigures the emergence, after 1844, of a new, distinctively American, post-romantic, industrial version of the pastoral design.

NOTES

1   *The American Notebooks by Nathaniel Hawthorne* (ed. Randall Stewart), New Haven, CT: Yale University Press, 1932, pp. 102–5.

2   W. W. Rostow, *The Stages of Economic Growth: A Non-Communist Manifesto*, Cambridge: Cambridge University Press, 1960, p. 7, and chart, p. xii.

3   *Virgil: The Pastoral Poems* (trans. E. V. Rieu), Harmondsworth: Penguin, 1949; Robert Frost, 'The Figure a Poem Makes', in *Complete Poems*, New York: Henry Holt, 1949, p. vi.

20

Against Single Vision

THEODORE ROSZAK*

[BLAKE'S STRUGGLE]

SAD TO SAY: Blake did not love nature. It remained for him the Shadowy Female, the seductive Vala. 'Satan's Wife. The Goddess Nature.' 'Natural Objects,' he confesses in his notes on Wordsworth, 'always did & now do weaken, deaden & obliterate Imagination in me.' And elsewhere: 'Nature Teaches nothing of Spiritual Life but only Natural Life.' Love of nature, Blake felt, had to be purchased at the cost of divine love: 'Everything is atheism which assumes the reality of the natural and unspiritual world.' Finally, at his Gnostic darkest: 'Nature is the work of the Devil.'

Blake's anti-naturalism cuts him off sharply from the other Romantics. But why the hostility? Because nature had become, since Newton, the province of the single-visioned scientists. They laid claim to 'saving the appearances' and Blake (mistakenly) surrendered to the claim – then reacted against the loss by bitterly abandoning all poetic interest in 'natural objets'. They survive as symbols to him, but as nothing in their own right.

Blake was too naively too crudely the disciple of Berkeley. 'Mental Things are alone Real.' Accepting that the world was 'really' in the mind, he could not then make much of the fact that it is also 'really' in the senses and there to be enjoyed.

To be sure, in the *Marriage*, Blake pleads for 'an improvement of sensual enjoyment.' The *notion* is there; Blake is nothing if not rich and various. But the idea never makes its way into his poetry. He discusses it, but does not *express* it.

What he failed to grasp is that the scientist's sense-world (Ulro) is *not* the sense-world *as it really is*. It *claims* to be 'empirical', but is in fact a materialist-theoretical model designed for the sake of power-knowledge. It corresponds to nature as a map does to a landscape: as a useful reduction of reality. It is painters and poets who *really* look at the world – and look at it, and look at it, until they lovingly gaze it into their art; no explaining, no theorizing, no generalizing, no analyzing . . . only the pure pleasure of seeing (or hearing, or smelling, or feeling). The 'Newtonian Phantasm' is exactly that: a phantasm, a gray ghost of the immediate sensory environment.

*From *Where the Wasteland Ends: Politics and Transcendence in Post-Industrial Society*, New York: Doubleday, 1972.

So to grow drunk on the sensory delights of nature – birdsong, flowersmell, skycolor, herbtaste – is as much a way of undermining 'Satan's Mathematic Holiness' as to pierce through to the visionary correspondences. Here was an element of Hermeticism which Blake lost along the way. For alchemy is a science of just those 'secondary qualities' that Galileo, Descartes, Locke had banished: the feel and odor, hue and texture of the world's sensible stuff.

But then, Blake could not do the whole job. His task was to save the other aspect of Hermetic science: the transcendent symbolism.

> I rest not from my great task!
> To open the Eternal Worlds, to open the immortal Eyes
> Of man inwards into the Worlds of thought, into Eternity
> Ever expanding in the Bosom of God, the Human Imagination.

[WORDSWORTH'S REVOLUTION OF PERCEPTION]

. . . Blake's eye had to pierce nature as if it were a delusive veil; Wordsworth could let the natural aspect rest easy in his eye and there become the simple wonder it is. *Both these are way and means of transcendence. Both transcend single vision.* But Blake beneath his Gnostic burden sweats at the job; he must climb home to heaven hand over hand, hauling himself free of the 'vegetable universe'. Wordsworth relaxes into the visionary mood, moves submissively (with 'a feminine softness') along the grain of things, finding himself already at home *within* the 'outward creation'. He is not afraid to enjoy Vala's beauties; he does not close out the 'pure organic pleasure', but delicately unfolds its secret.

> I held unconscious intercourse with beauty
> Old as creation, drinking in a pure
> Organic pleasure from the silver wreaths
> Of curling mist, or from the level plain
> Of waters colored by impending clouds . . .

> To every natural form, rock, fruit, or flower,
> Even the loose stones that cover the highway,
> I gave a moral life: I saw them feel,
> Or linked them to some feeling: the great mass
> Lay bedded in a quickening soul, and all
> That I beheld respired with inward meaning.

Wordsworth's tone: always one of stillness, of pregnant calm. But beneath the placid surface, there is a revolutionary current strongly running. Not political revolution (which Wordsworth embraced in youth, rebuffed with age) but a revolution of perception – in fact, that very apocalypse-promising 'improvement of sensual enjoyment' Blake himself demanded.

In Wordsworth, in all the Romantic nature lovers, the secret idolatry of Judeo-Christian tradition finds its most militant opposition. The natural objects cease to be idols; they are resurrected and pulse with life. Their 'inward meaning' returns. They glow, they breathe, they speak. ('My mind hath looked / Upon the speaking face of earth . . .') Wordsworth talks to mountains . . . to trees, seas, clouds, birds, stones, stars – *person to person*. It is no poetic convention but true conversation.

Here is indeed natural philosophy – but nothing of our science. For Wordsworth does not probe, prod, dissect ('We *murder* to dissect'). No research, no theory. He but attends and converses. And *then* it happens: the *power* breaks through . . . 'gleams like the flashing of a shield.'

> . . . and I would stand,
> If the night blackened with a coming storm,
> Beneath some rock, listening to notes that are
> The ghostly language of the ancient earth
> Or make their dim abode in distant winds.
> *Thence did I drink the visionary power . . .*

A 'wise passiveness' does the trick. There is much here of the Tao: the illuminated commonplace:

> . . . in life's everyday appearances
> I seemed about this time to gain clear sight
> Of a new world . . .
> Whence spiritual dignity originates.

Wait, watch, be still, be open: even the humblest objects may allow 'fit discourse with the spiritual world.'

'The spiritual world.' Yet the spirit must always be a palpable, sensible presence: seen, touched, smelled, heard, tasted. Wordsworth is pre-eminently the psychologist of the visionary senses. A mystic sentiency. . . .

Wordsworth's ecstasies of the sense are real; so too the natural world that excites them. He never lets us doubt for a moment the reality of sense-life or its objects. His study of nature is through and through empirical. And yet (here is where the prophetic lightning strikes) nature lovingly embraced by the senses becomes suddenly 'a new world' – in fact, 'the spiritual world'. Magically . . . it becomes more than it is . . . *no!* it becomes all that it *really* is, but is rarely seen to be.

And *then*, Wordsworth tells us, we pass gracefully beyond 'the bodily eye', 'the fleshly ear'. But 'beyond' is only reached '*through*'. *The spirit is in the thing* and must be, can *only* be, palpably known therein. Again: this is Adam's 'knowledge' of Eve: the person *in* the flesh.

Blake protested: 'Wordsworth must know that what he Writes Valuable is Not to be found in Nature.' But Wordsworth's reply would be: the vision can be found *noplace else but* in the mind's marriage to living nature. . . .

[THE VISIONARY WHOLE]

. . . Here and now, as we restore the orders of reality, we are in the stage of closing up all the traditional dichotomies of western culture which have served as the bulwarks of the old Reality Principle. Spirit–flesh, reason–passion, mad–sane, objective–subjective, fact–value, natural–supernatural, intellect–intuition, human–non-human . . . all these familiar dualisms which have divided the spectrum of consciousness vanish as we create the higher sanity. The dichotomies are healing over like old wounds. Even science, in its awkward single-visioned way, has been led to continuities that baffle traditional assumptions. It can no longer draw hard lines between matter and energy, organic and inorganic, man and lower animal, law and the indeterminate, mind and body. What is this but a final cold reflection of the visionary Whole, the Tao, the One, at last appearing in the alienated mind where it reaches the end of its tether?

In the society generally, this closure of the dichotomies appears as a ransacking of all the excluded human traditions. It is as if the repressed collective unconscious of our culture were being turned inside out before our very eyes. Everything once forbidden and outcast now makes its way into paperback editions, comic books, poster art, pop music. A dizzying spectacle. A necessary stage. Easy enough to ridicule the excesses. They are apt to be with us for some time to come. Perhaps there will always be people undergoing at some interval in their lives the same ungainly traumas of liberation, desperately trying this and that. There will surely always be fourteen-year-olds coming along the way, absolute beginners. But the fair questions to ask are: how did the traumas resolve themselves . . . where are the fourteen-year-olds ten years later . . . what was learned by the failed experiments? These exotic samplings and improvisations – even where they abandon caution – are essential to the personal and cultural search for wholeness. Though of course the whole, as a disciplined creation, must finally become more than a chaos of possibilities. Just as the finished painting must be more than the well-heaped palette.

Only one dichotomy will remain, the inevitable distinction between more and less. There must always be this tension between those who would have sanity be less than the whole, and those who would have the whole. Where this book, for example, has taken issue with single vision, it has been with the *exclusiveness* of 'Satan's mathematic holiness'. Not, in turn, to exclude it, but to find it its proper place in a science of rhapsodic intellect. Between those who are still locked in the box of the Reality Principle and those who have escaped it, there will always be the tension of disagreement. For Jack In-the-Box will insist there is nowhere to be but where he is. Jack Out-of-the-Box will know otherwise. It is the inevitable contrast of sensibilities between the free and the imprisoned mind – and only the *experience* of more will ever overcome anyone's allegiance to less.

To argue as I do that urban-industrialism is a failed cultural experiment and that the time is at hand to replace it with the visionary commonwealth amounts to a strict denial of the secularized myth of progress as we have learned it from our forebears of the Enlightenment. That is a bitter pill. It declares many generations of hardship and effort to have been a catastrophic mistake. For those who are not in touch with other, more fulfilling realities, such an admission is bound to seem an intolerable humiliation. But I hope I have made clear that I am not, as has become so much the morbid fashion among western intellectuals since the *fin de siècle*, rejecting the pursuit of secular progress in favor of wholesale cynicism. Such cynicism, being legitimately unacceptable to society at large as a basis for life, has only increased the desperation with which the millions cling to that myth despite their inadmissible misgivings. We must remember Blake's warning.

> Man must & will have Some Religion: if he has not the Religion of Jesus, he will have the Religion of Satan & will erect the Synagogue of Satan, calling the Prince of the World, God, and destroying all who do not worship Satan under the name of God.

True enough, no one who is not lying himself blind to the obvious can help but despair of the well-being that a reductionist science and power-ridden technology can bring. Nothing humanly worthwhile can be achieved within the diminished reality of such as science and technics; nothing whatever. On that level, we 'progress' only toward technocratic elitism, affluent alienation, environmental blight, nuclear suicide. Not an iota of the promise of industrialism will then be realized but it will be vastly outweighed by the 'necessary evils' attending.

But there is another progress that is not a cheat and a folly; the progress that has always been possible at every moment in time. It goes by many names. St. Bonaventura called it 'the journey of the mind to God'; the Buddha called it the eightfold path; Lao Tzu called it finding 'the Way'. The way *back*. To the source from which the adventure of human culture takes its beginning. It is *this* progress which the good society exists to facilitate for all its members.

The higher sanity will find its proper politics when we come to realize in our very bones that we have nothing to add to the splendor of the Old Gnosis and can make no progress 'beyond it'. We can do no more than return to it, borrow from it, reshape it to suit the times. This is to recognize that all the resources of the spirit human beings have ever needed to work out their destiny have always been with them . . . *in* them . . . provided; all they have needed to be beautiful and dignified, graceful and good. *In this sense*, there is nothing to do, nowhere to get. We need only 'stand still in the light.' This is something that must be emphasized not only to the technocrats with their ingrained contempt for traditional wisdom, but also to the young media-freaks and acid heads with their bizarre passion for an electrochemical epiphany. For they seem not to realize how pleased Westinghouse, Du Pont, and RCA would be to wire them up for skull-flicks and throw the switches. Anything to keep the public grateful and distracted.

Technologically speaking, there is indeed a course of history, obviously linear and cumulative. Its measure is increase of material power and, within a discipline of the sacred, that historical potentiality must also be unfolded. But the Old Gnosis needs no history; it is whole in every moment of time. The Romantics, in their struggle against single vision, thought they saw such a timeless self-fulfillment in

113

the delights of infancy. Certainly they, with most artists, found it in their work, in the stasis that comes of capturing a symbol's transcendent meaning.

But such symbols are with all of us everywhere and at all times; not only in the language and imagery of our cultural making, but in every most ordinary moment, every least scrap of the world around us, in the rhythms of our own body, in the lights and airs that fill the sky, in the things and creatures with which we share the earth. It is the presence of transcendent symbols instructing, nurturing, brightening life at every turn that makes the world at large a magical object and human culture a whole from its most technologically primitive origins to the present time. Here we find what can alone give meaning to our historical project: the eternity that seeks its reflection in the mirrors of time.

SECTION TWO

Green Theory

PART III

Nature/Culture/Gender

Part III

Nature, Culture and Gender

Introduction

While the writers represented here do not strictly belong to the school of ecocriticism, they certainly are crucial to what I have called 'the ecocritical age'. They each of them address the most fundamental question of all for green studies – that of the relationship between the non-human and the human. Perhaps we ought to begin by addressing the philosophical theme to which our question will inevitably be referred, namely dualism.

Val Plumwood, in an important work called *Feminism and the Mastery of Nature* (1993), argues that to see two entities or categories dualistically is not the same as merely asserting that they differ. Dualism may be defined as 'an alienated form of differentiation, in which power construes and constructs differences in terms of an inferior and alien realm.'[1] Let us consider what this involves. According to Plumwood, nature has, since at least the time of Plato, been systematically subordinated to 'the master subject', the hero of 'the master story'. This story privileges male over female just as it privileges reason over nature: indeed, it identifies rationality with masculinity, and justifies the absolute rights of both. We will not be able to repudiate 'the master subject' until we have gone beyond dualism. Dualism sets up a contrast between, for example, higher and lower, or ruler and ruled, according to its own tyrannous and dubious logic. Thus, in the following list, the former are always maintained to be superior to the latter:

culture	/	nature
reason	/	nature
male	/	female
mind	/	body (nature)
master	/	slave
reason	/	matter (physicality)
rationality	/	animality (nature)
reason	/	emotion (nature)
mind, spirit	/	nature
freedom	/	necessity (nature)
universal	/	particular
human	/	nature (non-human)
civilised	/	primitive (nature)

production   /   reproduction (nature)
public   /   private
subject   /   object
self   /   other.[2]

Plumwood traces the history of western philosophy in terms of this dualism, demonstrating how a 'female' nature has been systematically degraded, dominated and exploited. The logical culmination, which now seems imminent, will be the destruction of the planet by 'the master subject' in the name of 'rational economy' and global profit, unless 'reason' can be remade. This cannot simply involve privileging 'female' nature instead of subordinating it, for that is simply to invert the logic of patriarchy. The answer is to develop 'the rationality of the mutual self', which would ensure 'the incomparable riches of diversity in the world's cultural and biological life' and encourage participatation in 'the community of life'.[3]

The central dualistic constructs are those of culture and nature and of male reason and female nature. They are not just parallel oppositions but intricately connected modes of oppression. However, it is implicit in Plumwood's thesis that it is not enough for green studies simply to reject the distinction between the human and the non-human world because of the logic of dualism. Kate Soper would agree, and in the two extracts from *What is Nature?* that are included here she argues that there is something called 'nature' that exists independently of our cultural constructions, to which we are responsible, even though it is always necessarily experienced in a mediated form. That last reservation will indicate that Soper is by no means indifferent to the 'culturalist' argument. Indeed, in our first extract she usefully demonstrates how the term 'nature' shifts its meaning, and she reminds us to be conscious of, and careful in, our usage. Her distinction between three 'ecological discourses of nature' might usefully be considered alongside Hochman's differentiation between the terms 'nature' and 'Nature', already discussed. In our second extract, Soper explores the history of the female-nature connection and, along grounds similar to Plumwood's, encourages scepticism about a feminism that would unproblematically identify earth and woman. (An added bonus of this extract is a challenging comparison between the aggressive language of colonial settlement and a poem by Wordsworth: this is a timely reminder, perhaps, that even the tradition of green romanticism demands revising as well as reviving.) Taken as a whole, Soper's contribution to the reader is a spirited defence of philosophical realism, as distinguished from dualism: she affirms difference but denies superiority; she sees human beings as answerable to nature even as they define themselves as separate from it. But of course, it should be stressed that in making her case she is conscious of opting for a particular 'ecological discourse' which might not be shared by others working in green studies. Her work, careful and circumspect, is a reminder of the complexity of the relationship between nature and culture, and between nature and gender.

Another approach to the debate is offered by Gary Snyder, a leading ecological poet who takes his cue from the wisdom of Zen. Maintaining the Buddhist emphasis on meditation, Zen also benefits from the ancient Taoist principle of 'the Way', a never-ending force which is expressed through nature itself. Zen is about waking up to the natural world and being prepared to learn from it: one can become enlightened by contemplating a sparrow on a tree more effectively than by poring over commentaries on scriptures. As we saw in the General Introduction, Wordsworth expresses a similar idea to Zen when he invites the reader to 'Come forth into the light of things'. Such an attitude is a denial of dualism, but it also casts doubt on conventional realism: ultimately, difference itself is as illusory as is hierarchical contrast. In his essay Snyder seeks to refute the nature–culture split. In particular, he argues that it is mistaken to assume that language is uniquely human and primarily cultural, organising and civilising an otherwise 'chaotic' world. Invoking Thoreau's notion of 'tawny grammar', he asserts that language is above all biological, becoming genuinely cultural in the articulation of the complexity of 'the wild'. Thus, dualism is overcome when humanity finds a properly local, humble place on the planet.

Interestingly, Snyder's case for 'the practice of the wild' is not that remote from Claude Lévi-Strauss's reflections on the relation between myth and the environment. Lévi-Strauss has usually been associated with an arid rationalism and with a rigid distinction between culture and nature. But here he explicitly repudiates that association, and proposes that his structuralist anthropology is a way of putting 'Man' in his place: what he has learnt from his study of 'the savage mind' is that nature and humanity form a living harmony, and that the aesthetic response to plants and animals is the beginning of wisdom. This decentring of the human subject anticipates the postmodernist speculations of Jean-François Lyotard. For him the question of ecology cannot be separated from the arrogant treatment by the 'civilised' of the 'primitive' and the exploitation of the rich 'First World' of the poor 'Third World'. If we are to affirm the importance of the 'oikos' or 'world household', we must resist globalisation and all oppressive totalities. Indeed, in the extract from his essay which has been provided here, he wishes to affirm the importance of private and secluded experience, over against public and systematised expenditure. The child is not a mere computer. Nature here becomes the hidden life that must be defended against excessive culturalisation.

If Lyotard wishes to refuse dualism yet affirm difference, the scientist Donna Haraway has become celebrated for her attempt to subvert the categories of culture and nature, male and female, human and animal, person and machine. In her 'Cyborg Manifesto' she argues that it is in the creative play along the border of such categories that the hope for feminism lies.[4] In the extract from *Primate Visions* she offers a useful reflection on the analogies between 'orientalism' and primatology, as equally expressive of the western, male imagination. When she declares that primatology has been about 'the construction of the self from the raw material of the other, the appropriation of nature in the production of culture ... [and] the issue of man from the body of woman', she goes right to the heart of the debate which we are conducting in this part of the reader. More particularly, her own anti-patriarchal position is worth comparing with that of Hélène Cixous. Much closer to what we call 'ecofeminism' in her positive identity of woman with nature, Cixous's achievement is discussed here by Verena Andermatt Conley in an extract from her book *Ecopolitics*. Conley demonstrates that Cixous' affirmation of a female language that precedes the severance from nature made by male language, while being rhetorically effective in inspiring women to refuse their subordination and inferior identity, yet suffers from a 'blind spot'. In agreement with Plumwood, Conley suggests that it is not enough to assert woman's proximity to nature, given the immense task ahead of countering dualism itself. Thus, Part III ends with a reminder that the nature/culture/gender debate has only just begun.

NOTES

1   Val Plumwood, *Feminism and the Mastery of Nature*, London and New York: Routledge, 1993, p. 42.
2   Ibid., p. 43.
3   Ibid., pp. 195–6.
4   See Donna J. Haraway, 'A Cyborg Manifesto: Science, Technology, and Socialist-Feminism in the Late Twentieth Century', in *Simians, Cyborgs, and Women: The Reinvention of Nature*, New York and London: Routledge, 1991, pp. 149–82.

21

The Idea of Nature

KATE SOPER*

[THE 'TEXTUALITY' OF NATURE?]

GIVEN HOW LARGELY the appeal to the preservation of a 'natural' order of intrinsic worth has figured in the discourse of social conservatism, an uncritical ecological naturalism is always at risk of lending ideological support to those systems of domination that have played a major role in generating ecological crisis. This may seem an obvious point to make. But ecological critics of the atomizing and destructive effects of instrumental rationality need to be careful in redeploying the organicist imagery that has been such a mainstay of right-wing rhetoric. Romantic and aestheticizing approaches to nature have as readily lent themselves to the expression of reactionary sentiment as sustained the radical critique of industrialism,[1] and this means that left-wing ecologists, however understandably keen they may be to re-seize this tradition of romanticism for their own purposes, are dealing with a problematic legacy.

We have also to be wary of the ways in which romantic ideology may serve as the cover for the continued exploitation of nature. However accurate it may be to portray our engagement with nature as 'anthropocentric', 'arrogant' and 'instrumental', it is the work of a culture that has constantly professed its esteem for nature. The societies that have most abused nature have also perennially applauded its ways over those of 'artifice', have long valued its health and integrity over the decadence of human contrivance, and today employ pastoral imagery as the most successful of conventions to enhance the profits on everything from margarine to motor-cars.

At the same time, ecological politics needs to be ever alert to the multiple dimensions and repercussions of its own social impact. Today, we are building 'virtual reality' zoos to preserve wildlife from the miseries of captivity, and eschewing nature's fur and flesh in favour of synthetic fibres and factory-made proteins; Japanese businessmen are seeking relief from the pressures of catering to a booming leisure industry in 'refresh capsules' where they can revel in the sounds and scents

* From *What is Nature?* London: Blackwell, 1995.

of 'nature';[2] heritage and nature conservancy have become themselves big business; green products are the latest capitalist growth area; the interests of thousands of human offspring are daily discounted as we monitor the habitats of other animal species. Meanwhile public support for any radically corrective logical programme remains vanishingly small. These developments speak to complex and contradictory attitudes to 'nature' and our place within it, and indicate that we may be contributing to its destruction and pollution in the very name of its preservation. In an overall way, I suggest that an eco-politics will prove that much more incisive the more prepared it is to question its own discourse on 'nature'.

It is, however, one thing to argue that eco-politics must rid culturalist criticisms of naturalist rhetoric; it is another to suppose that everything has been said about nature once we have remarked on its 'textuality' and its continually shifting signifier. It is true that we can make no distinction between the 'reality' of nature and its cultural representation that is not itself conceptual, but it does not justify the conclusion that there is no ontological distinction between the ideas we have of nature and that which the ideas are about: that since nature is only signified in human discourse, inverted commas 'nature' *is* nature, and we should therefore remove the inverted commas.

In short, it is not language that has a hole in its ozone layer; and the 'real' thing continues to be polluted and degraded even as we refine our deconstructive insights at the level of the signifier. Hence the inclination to respond to the insistence on the 'textuality' of nature as Johnson did to Berkeleyan idealism, by claiming to refute it with straightforward realist kick, by pointing to the latest oil spill or figures on species extinction and saying, 'there's nature fouled and destroyed by human industry, and I refute your anti-naturalism thus'. This is an understandable response to those who would have us focus only on the play of the 'sign' of nature. But the straightforward realist kick is not only insensitive to the ideological representations of nature already discussed, but also fails to register the fact that an adequate response to anti-realism can only be conducted from a position which recognizes how difficult it is to refer to the landscape one is seeking to conserve simply as 'nature'. For if nature is conceptualized and valued, as it sometimes is in environmental philosophy, as that which is independent of human culture, then rather little of the environment corresponds to the concept: hardly anything we refer to as natural landscape *is* natural in this sense, and its supposed value might therefore be seen to be put in question. Even Cicero distinguished between an inherited non-human nature and a nature constructed through human activity, and concluded his survey of the forms taken by the latter by remarking that 'one may say that we seek with our human hands to create a second nature in the natural world'.[3] In our own time the human impact on the environment has been so extensive that there is an important sense in which it is correct to speak of 'nature' as itself a cultural product or construction.[4]

Yet there is, of course, all the difference in the world between recognizing the truth of this and refusing to recognize the independent existence of the reality itself or the causal role played in its creation by processes that are not humanly created. It is one thing to recognize that much that is referred to as 'nature' takes the form it does only in virtue of human activity, another to suppose that this has no extra-discursive reality, or that there are no discriminations to be drawn between that which is and that which is not an effect of culture. . . .

ECOLOGICAL DISCOURSES OF NATURE

[It] would seem important to recognize the multiple roles which 'nature' can be called upon to play in ecological discussion, and notably to distinguish between three very differing concepts it may be drawing upon. . . . I shall refer to these as the 'metaphysical', the 'realist' and the 'lay' (or 'surface') ideas of nature.

1   Employed as a metaphysical concept, which it mainly is in the argument of philosophy, 'nature' is the concept through which humanity thinks its difference and specificity. It is the concept of the non-human, even if, as we have seen, the absoluteness of the humanity–nature demarcation has been disputed, and our ideas about what falls to the side of 'nature' have been continuously revised in the light of changing perceptions of what counts as 'human'. But in a formal sense, the logic of 'nature' as that which is opposed to the 'human' or the 'cultural' is presupposed to any debates about the interpretations to be placed on the distinction and the content to be given to the ideas. One is invoking the metaphysical concept in the very posing of the question of humanity's relation to nature.

2   Employed as a realist concept, 'nature' refers to the structures, processes and causal powers that are constantly operative within the physical world, that provide the objects of study of the natural sciences, and condition the possible forms of human intervention in biology or interaction with the environment. It is the nature to whose laws we are always subject, even as we harness them to human purposes, and whose processes we can neither escape nor destroy.

3   Employed as a 'lay' or 'surface' concept, as it is in much everyday, literary and theoretical discourse, 'nature' is used in reference to ordinarily observable features of the world: the 'natural' as opposed to the urban or industrial environment ('landscape', 'wilderness', 'countryside', 'rurality'), animals, domestic and wild, the physical body in space and raw materials. This is the nature of immediate experience and aesthetic appreciation; the nature we have destroyed and polluted and are asked to conserve and preserve.

I submit that when the Green Movement speaks of nature, it is most commonly in this third 'lay' or 'surface' sense: it is referring to nature as wildlife, raw materials, the non-urban environment, and thus to a 'nature' that has been affected in certain respects by human occupancy of the planet, and in some cases acquired its form only in virtue of human cultural activity. But when it appeals to humanity to preserve nature or make use of it in sustainable ways, it is also of course employing the idea in a metaphysical sense to designate an object in relation to a subject (humanity), with the presumption being that subject and object are clearly differentiable and logically distinct. At the same time, by drawing attention to human transformation (destruction, wastage, pollution, manipulation, instrumental use) of nature, it is, at least implicitly, invoking the realist idea of nature, and referring us to structures and processes that are common to all organic and inorganic entities, human beings included. Through the metaphysical concept, then, it refers to that realm of being that is differentiated from and opposed to the being of humanity, through the realist concept to nature as causal process and through the lay concept to nature as a directly experienced set of phenomena. I shall not, however, attempt to expound these concepts any further in isolation from each other, since they are interlocking, and getting clear about the one will necessarily depend on establishing the meaning of the other.

NOTES

1   Cf. Raymond Williams, *Culture and Society*, London: Hogarth, 1987, pp. 229f; Terry Eagleton, *The Ideology of the Aesthetic*, Oxford: Blackwell, 1990, pp. 60–1.
2   See Gavin McCormack, 'The Price of Affluence: The Political Economy of Japanese Leisure', *New Left Review*, 188 (July–August), 1991, pp. 121–34.
3   Cicero, *De Natura Deorum*, II, 151–2.
4   See Neil Smith, *Uneven Development: Nature, Capital and the Production of Space*, Oxford: Blackwell, 1984, ch. 5.

22

Language Goes Two Ways

Gary Snyder*

LANGUAGE HAS BEEN popularly described, in the Occident, as that by which humans bring order to the 'chaos of the world'. In this view, human intelligence flowers through the supposedly unique faculty of language, and with it imposes a net of categories on an untidy universe. The more objective and rational the language, it is thought, the more accurate this exercise in giving order to the world will be. Language is considered by some to be a flawed mathematics, and the idea that mathematics might even supplant language has been flirted with. This idea still colors the commonplace thinking of many engineer types and possibly some mathematicians and scientists.

But the world – ordered according to its own inscrutable mode (indeed a sort of chaos) – is so complex and vast on both macro and micro scales that it remains forever unpredictable. The weather, for hoary example. And take the very mind that ponders these thoughts: in spite of years of personhood, we remain unpredictable even to our own selves. Often we wouldn't be able to guess what our next thought will be. But that clearly does not mean we are living in hopeless confusion; it only means that we live in a realm in which many patterns remain mysterious or inaccessible to us.

Yet we can affirm that the natural world (which includes human languages) is mannerly, shapely, coherent, and patterned *according to its own devices*. Each of the four thousand or so languages of the world models reality in its own way, with patterns and syntaxes that were not devised by anyone. Languages were not the intellectual inventions of archaic schoolteachers, but are naturally evolved wild systems whose complexity eludes the descriptive attempts of the rational mind.

'Wild' alludes to a process of self-organization that generates systems and organisms, all of which are within the constraints of – and constitute components of – larger systems that again are wild, such as major ecosystems or the water cycle in the biosphere. Wildness can be said to be the essential nature of nature. As reflected in consciousness, it can be seen as a kind of open awareness – full of

*From *A Place in Space: Ethics, Aesthetics, and Watersheds*, Washington, DC: Counterpoint, 1995.

imagination but also the source of alert survival intelligence. The workings of the human mind at its very richest reflect this self-organizing wildness. So language does not impose order on a chaotic universe, but reflects its own wildness back.

In doing so it goes two ways: it enables us to have a small window onto an independently existing world, but it also shapes – via its very structures and vocabularies – how we see that world. It may be argued that what language does to our seeing of reality is restrictive, narrowing, limiting, and possibly misleading. 'The menu is not the meal.' But rather than dismiss language from a spiritual position, speaking vaguely of Unsayable Truths, we must instead turn right back to language. The way to see *with* language, to be free with it and to find it a vehicle of self-transcending insight, is to know both mind and language extremely well and to play with their many possibilities without any special attachment. In doing this, a language yields up surprises and angles that amaze us and that can lead back to unmediated direct experience.

Natural Language, with its self-generated grammars and vocabularies constructed through the confusion of social history, expresses itself in the vernacular. Daily usage has many striking, clear, specific usages and figures of speech that come through (traditionally) in riddles, proverbs, stories, and such – and nowadays in jokes, raps, wildly fluid slang, and constant experiment with playful expressions (the dozens, the snaps). Children on the playground chant rhymes and enjoy fooling with language. Maybe some people are born with a talent for language, just as some people are born with a talent for math or music. And some natural geniuses go beyond being street singers, mythographers, and raconteurs to become the fully engaged poets and writers of multicultural America.

The world is constantly in flux and totally mixed and compounded. Nothing is really new. Creativity itself is a matter of seeing afresh what is already there and reading its implications and omens. (Stephen Owen's *Traditional Chinese Poetry and Poetics: Omen of the World* speaks to this point.) There are poems, novels, and paintings that roll onward through history, perennially redefining our places in the cosmos, that were initiated by such seeing. But creativity is not a unique, singular, godlike act of 'making something'. It is born of being deeply immersed in what is – and then seeing the overlooked connections, tensions, resonances, shadows, reversals, retellings. What comes forth is 'new'. This way of thinking about language is a world away from the usual ideas of education, however.

The standards of 'Good Language Usage' until recently were based on the speech of people of power and position, whose language was that of the capital (London or Washington), and these standards were tied to the recognition of the social and economic advantages that accrue to their use. Another kind of standard involves a technical sort of writing that is dedicated to clarity and organization and is rightly perceived as an essential element in the tool kit of a person hoping for success in the modern world. This last sort of writing is intrinsically boring, but it has the usefulness of a tractor that will go straight and steady up one row and down another. Like a tractor, it is expected to produce a yield: scholarly essays and dissertations, grant proposals, charges or countercharges in legalistic disputes, final reports, longrange scenarios, strategic plans.

Truly Excellent Writing, however, comes to those who have learned, mastered, and passed through conventional Good Usage and Good Writing, and then loop back to the enjoyment and unencumbered playfulness of Natural Language. Ordinary Good Writing is like a garden that is producing exactly what you want, by virtue of lots of weeding and cultivating. What you get is what you plant, like a row of beans. But really good writing is both inside and outside the garden fence. It can be a few beans, but also some wild poppies, vetches, mariposa lilies, ceanothus, and some juncos and yellow jackets thrown in. It is more diverse, more interesting, more unpredictable, and engages with a much broader, deeper kind of intelligence. Its connection to the wildness of language and imagination helps give it power.

This is what Thoreau meant by the term 'Tawny Grammar', as he wrote (in the essay 'Walking') of 'this vast, savage, howling mother of ours, Nature, lying all around, with such beauty, and such affection for her children, as the leopard; and yet we are so early weaned from her breast to society. . . . The Spaniards have a good term to express this wild and dusky knowledge, *Grammatica parda*, tawny grammar, a kind of mother-wit derived from that same leopard to which I have referred.' The grammar not only of language, but of culture and civilization itself, comes from this vast mother of ours, nature. 'Savage, howling' is another way of describing 'graceful dancer' and 'fine writer'. (A linguist friend once commented, 'Language is like a Mother Nature of feeling: it's so powerfully ordered there's room to be 99 percent wild.')

We can and must teach our young people to master the expected standard writing procedures, in preparation for the demands of multinational economies and of information overload. They will need these skills not only to advance in our postindustrial precollapse world, but also to critique and transform it. Those young learners with charming naive writing talents may suffer from the destructive effect of this discipline, because they will be brought to doubt their own ear and wit. They need to be assured that their unique personal visions will survive. They can take a deep breath and leap into the current formalities and rules, learn the game, and still come home to the language of heart and 'hood. We must continually remind people that language and its powers are far vaster than the territory deemed 'proper usage' at any given time and place, and that there have always been geniuses of language who have created without formal education. Homer was a singer-story-teller, not a writer.

So, the more familiar view of language is:

1   Language is uniquely human and primarily cultural.
2   Intelligence is framed and developed by language.
3   The world is chaotic, but language organizes and civilizes it.
4   The more cultivated the language – the more educated and precise and clear
     – the better it will tame the unruly world of nature and feeling.
5   Good writing is 'civilized' language.

But one can turn this around to say:

1   Language is basically biological; it becomes semicultural as it is learned and practiced.
2   Intelligence is framed and developed by all kinds of interactions with the world, including human communication, both linguistic and nonlinguistic; thus, language plays a strong – but not the only – role in the refinement of thinking.
3   The world (and mind) is orderly in its own fashion, and linguistic order reflects and condenses that order.
4   The more completely the world is allowed to come forward and instruct us (without the interference of ego and opinion), the better we can see our place in the interconnected world of nature.
5   Good writing is 'wild' language.

The twelfth-century Zen Buddhist philosopher Dogen put it this way: 'To advance your own experience onto the world of phenomena is delusion. When the world of phenomena comes forth and experiences itself, it is enlightenment.' To see a wren in a bush, call it 'wren', and go on walking is to have (self-importantly) seen nothing. To see a bird and stop, watch, feel, forget yourself for a moment, be in the bushy shadows, maybe then feel 'wren' – that is to have joined in a larger moment with the world.

In the same way, when we are in the act of playful writing, the mind's eye is roaming, seeing sights and scenes, reliving events, hearing and dreaming at the same time. The mind may be reliving a past moment entirely in this moment, so that it is hard to say if the mind is in the past or in some other present. We move mentally as in a great landscape, and return from it with a few bones, nuts, or drupes, which we keep as language. We write to deeply heard but distant rhythms, out of a fruitful darkness, out of a moment without judgment or object. Language is a part of our body and woven into the seeing, feeling, touching, and dreaming of the whole mind as much as it comes from some localized 'language center'. Full of the senses, as

> Sabrina fair
>   Listen where thou art sitting
> Under the glassy, cool translucent wave,
>   In twisted braids of lilies knitting
> The loose train of thy amber-dropping hair;
>   Listen for dear honor's sake,
>   Goddess of the silver lake,
>   Listen and save.
>
>   (Milton, *Comus*)

Chill clarity, fluid goddess, silvery waves, and silvery flowers.

The faintly visible traces of the world are to be trusted. We do not need to organize so-called chaos. Discipline and freedom are not opposed to each other. We are made free by the training that enables us to master necessity, and we are made disciplined by our free choice to undertake mastery. We go beyond being a 'master' of a situation by becoming a friend of 'necessity' and thus – as Camus would have put it – neither victim nor executioner. Just a person playing in the field of the world.

23

The Environment of Myth

CLAUDE LÉVI-STRAUSS*

FOR THE PEOPLES of the Algonkian linguistic family who lived in the Canadian ecological zone, the porcupine was a real animal. They hunted it assiduously for its flesh, which they relished, and for its quills, which the women used in embroidery. The porcupine also played a conspicuous part in mythology. One myth speaks of two girls who, while traveling on foot to a distant village, find a porcupine nested in a fallen tree. One of the girls pulls out the poor animal's quills and throws them away. The tormented porcupine conjures up a snowstorm, and the girls perish of cold. Another myth has two lonely sisters for heroines. One day, while wandering far from their home, they find a porcupine nested in a fallen tree, and one of the girls is fool enough to sit on the rodent's back so that all its quills get stuck in her rump. It takes her a long time to recover from her wounds.

Now, the Arapaho, also members of the Algonkian linguistic stock, make the porcupine the hero of a quite different tale. According to them, the brothers Sun and Moon quarrel about the kind of wife each would like to marry: which would be better – a frog or a human girl? Moon, who prefers the latter, transforms himself into a porcupine in order to entice an Indian girl. So covetous is she of the quills that she climbs higher and higher up the tree in which the porcupine is pretending to take refuge. The porcupine succeeds by this ruse in luring her to the sky world, where Moon resumes his human form and marries her.

How are we to account for the differences between stories that, apart from the presence of the porcupine in both, seem to have nothing in common? Although widespread in the Canadian ecological zone, the porcupine was rare in, if not absent from, the Plains where the Arapaho moved a few centuries ago. In their new environment, they could not hunt the porcupine; and to get quills, they had to trade with northern tribes or undertake hunting expeditions of their own in foreign territory. These two conditions seem to have had an effect both on the technological and economic levels and on the mythological one. The Arapaho quill-work ranks among the best in North America, and their art was profoundly imbued

*From Claude Lévi-Strauss, 'Structuralism and Ecology', in *The View from Afar* (trans. Joachim Neugroschel and Phoebe Hoss), Oxford: Blackwell, 1985.

with a mysticism that can scarcely be matched elsewhere. To the Arapaho, quill-work was a ritual activity; their women undertook no work of this kind without fasting and praying, in the hope of supernatural help which they deemed essential for the success of their work. As for Arapaho mythology, we have just seen that it radically modifies the characteristics of the porcupine. From a magical land-dwelling animal, master of the cold and the snow, it becomes – as in neighboring tribes – the animal disguise of a supernatural being in human form, a sky dweller responsible for a biological periodicity instead of a meteorological and physical one. The myth specifies, indeed, that Moon's wife becomes the first of her sex to have regular menses every month and, when pregnant, to be delivered after a fixed time span.

Therefore when we shift from the northern Algonkian to the Arapaho, the empirical axis–horizontal, uniting the near and the far – shifts to an imaginary axis – vertical, uniting the sky and the earth. This . . . transformation . . . occurs when an animal, important both technologically and economically, is lacking in a particular geographical situation. Also . . . there follow other transformations, which are inwardly, not outwardly, determined. Once it is understood that, despite their different origins, all these transformations are related, that they are structurally part of the same set, it is clear that the two stories are actually one and the same; and that coherent rules permit the conversion of one to the other.

In one case, the two women are sisters; in the other, they belong to different zoological species – human and amphibian. The sisters move on a horizontal plane from near to far, while the two other females move on a vertical plane from low to high. Instead of pulling out the porcupine's quills like the first heroine, the second is pulled out of her village, so to speak, by the quills she covets. One girl recklessly throws away the quills; the other girl desires them as precious objects. In the first group of stories, the porcupine nests in a dead tree that has fallen to the ground, while the same animal in the second group climbs up an endlessly growing tree. And if the first porcupine slows down the traveling sisters, the second lures the heroine into climbing up faster and faster. One girl crouches down on the porcupine's back; the other girl stretches out to grab it. The first porcupine is aggressive; the second is a seducer. While the former lacerates the girl from behind, the latter deflowers – that is, 'pierces' her – in her foreparts.

Considered separately, none of these changes is attributable to environmental peculiarities; they result together from a logical necessity which links each to the other in a series of operations. Should an animal as important as the porcupine for the technology and the economy be lacking in a new environment, it could keep its role only in another world. As a result, low becomes high, horizontal swings to vertical, the internal becomes external, and so on. All these shifts proceed from an obscure wish: to maintain the coherent relationships conceived by men in a previous environment. So strong does the need for coherence appear to be that, to preserve the unvarying structure of relationships, people prefer to falsify the image of the environment rather than to acknowledge that the relationships with the actual environment have changed. . . .

. . . Vulgar materialism and sensual empiricism put man in direct confrontation with nature, but without seeing that the latter has structural properties that, while undoubtedly richer, do not differ essentially from the codes by which the nervous system deciphers them or from the categories elaborated by the understanding to return to reality's original structure. It is not being mentalist or idealist to acknowledge that the mind is able to understand the world only because the mind is itself part and product of this world. It is verified a little more each day that, in trying to understand the world, the mind operates in ways that do not differ in kind from those that have unfolded in the world since the beginning of time.

Structuralists have often been accused of playing with abstractions having no bearing upon reality. I have tried to show that, far from being an amusement for sophisticated intellectuals, structural analysis gets going in the mind only because its model already exists in the body. From the very start, visual perception rests on binary oppositions; and neurologists would probably agree that this statement is also true of other areas of cerebral activity. By following a path that is sometimes wrongly accused of being overly intellectual, structuralism recovers and brings to awareness deeper truths that have already been dimly announced in the body itself; it reconciles the physical and the moral, nature and man, the mind and the world, and tends toward the only kind of materialism consistent with the actual development of scientific knowledge. Nothing could be farther from Hegel – and even from Descartes, whose dualism we try to overcome while adhering to his rationalist faith.

The misunderstanding is related to the fact that only those who practice structural analysis every day can clearly conceive the direction and range of their undertaking: that is, to unify perspectives that the narrow scientific outlook of the last few centuries has believed to be incompatible – sensibility and intellect, quality and quantity, the concrete and the geometrical. . . . Even ideological works whose structure is very abstract (everything that can be included under the label *mythology*), and that the mind seems to elaborate without unduly submitting to the constraints of the techno-economic infrastructure, remain rebellious to both description and analysis if minute attention is not paid to ecological conditions and to the different ways each culture reacts to its natural environment. Only an almost slavish respect for the most concrete reality can inspire in us confidence that mind and body have not lost their ancient unity.

Structuralism knows of other less theoretical and more practical justifications. The so-called primitive cultures that anthropologists study teach that reality can be meaningful on the levels of both scientific knowledge and sensory perception. These cultures encourage us to reject the divorce between the intelligible and the sensible declared by an outmoded empiricism and mechanism, and to discover a secret harmony between humanity's everlasting quest for meaning and the world in which we appeared and where we continue to live – a world made of shapes, colors, textures, flavors, and odors. Structuralism teaches us better to love and respect nature and the living beings who people it, by understanding that vegetables and animals, however humble they may be, did not supply man with sustenance only but were, from the very beginning, the source of his most intense esthetic feelings and, in the intellectual and moral order, of his first and even then profound speculations.

24

Ecology as Discourse of the Secluded

Jean-François Lyotard*

I WOULD LIKE to interrogate the word *ecology*, a word made up of *oikos* and *logos*. Do we speak of the *oikos*, or is it the *oikos* that speaks? Do we describe the *oikos* as an object, or is it rather that we listen to it, to what it wants? In Greek, there is a very clear opposition between *oikeion* and *politikon*. The *Oikeion* is the women, whose sex is *oikeion*; the children, whose generation is also *oikeion*; the servants, everything that can be called 'domesticity' in the old Latin sense, that which is in the *domus*, like the dogs, for example. In the final analysis, *oikeion* is everything that is not [public]. And the opposition between the *oikeion* and the *politikon* exactly matches up to that between the secluded on one side and the public on the other. The political is the public sphere, while the *oikeion* is the space we call 'private', an awful word that I'm trying to avoid in saying 'secluded'. It is the shadowy space of all that escapes the light of public speech, and it is precisely in this darkness that tragedy occurs.

SUPPLEMENTARITY AND THE SECLUDED

We need something like a way to express that *oikeion*, which is not an environment at all, but a relation with something that is inscribed at the origin in all minds, souls, or psychic apparatuses. We are not prepared (and that is our difference from computers, the fact that we are unarmed or undefended, in being born), not prepared to speak, not prepared to control the environment, and so on. In this sense we are born too soon.

But at the same time we are born too late because a lot of meanings or stories have already been narrated about our birth. In this sense we are already the object of a lot of meanings, and we have to conquer these meanings afterward and probably we try all our lives to understand what was expected of us. It is too late, because these expectations are already part of our lives. That is to say that this

*From 'Oikos', *Political Writings* (trans. B. Readings and K. P. Geiman), London: UCL Press, 1993.

belatedness (this paradoxical relationship with time) probably characterizes what I called the secluded. Any communication strives to resolve this paradoxical situation with regard to time. In this respect I do not agree at all with the parallel . . . drawn between our minds and computers precisely because no computer has ever been a child. . . .

WRITING AS ANAMNESIS AND WORKING THROUGH

Insofar as we are concerned with the task of thinking or writing, we have to fight the heritage of meaning implicit in words and phrases in order to make words and phrases appropriate to what we need to say. We also have to deconstruct, to dismember, to criticize the defenses that are already built into our psyche, impeding us from hearing original fundamental questions. I imagine the filter also as a sound filter, as a sort of noise that allows us not to hear the real questions. The task – I call it 'anamnesis' – involves . . . a working through the filter or the screen preserving our quietness.

CHILDLIKE FEAR OF THE GIVEN

Thus, the task implies that one admits a large element of childish anxiety that is a result of the fact that something is given, has been given, and will have been given to us before we are able to receive it, before we are in the condition of agreeing to it, before becoming aware of it. And this something is merely that there is something, more than nothing. This 'there is' is necessarily linked with questions of birth, death, and sexual difference.

I think that when Freud speaks of a 'psychic economy', he would have done better to speak of a 'psychic ecology', for the term 'libidinal economy' (in the Freudian sense, not mine), presupposes that something necessarily escapes publicity, that something resists openness and hence communication. Call it what you will, the 'unconscious' or whatever. One can only describe this something as contradiction, tension (physical operation), repression, deferral (physical operations), displacement (physical operation), and in general distortion. All these concepts are terms of transport, of the modification of forces, masses, and volumes. Precisely the order of passion or pathos, and this pathos is described in physical terms.

Today . . . what we call the economy is precisely part of the public sphere. I would even say that the economy is the very substance of the public sphere, because it is simply the regulation, the *nomos*, of goods, values, and services. When *oikos* gives rise to *oikonomikos* or *oikonomikon*, a complex transformation of the word *oikos* occurs. If 'economic' means the public sphere, it implies that the *oikos* itself has slipped away elsewhere. It would certainly be wrong to believe that it has disappeared. I mean simply that, for me, 'ecology' means the discourse of the secluded, of the thing that has not become public, that has not become communicational, that has not become systemic, and that can never become any of these things. This

136

presupposes that there is a relation of language with the logos, which is not centered on optimal performance and which is not obsessed by it, but which is preoccupied, in the full sense of 'pre-occupied', with listening to and seeking for what is secluded, *oikeion*. This discourse is called 'literature', 'art', or 'writing' in general.

WRITING AND PRESENCE

I am describing a situation of distress, of suffering, that is at the same time the mere condition of thinking and writing. And especially when we question the property of words, it is obvious that the answer to the question of what is proper in the realm of words lies in our ability to pay attention to a feeling, the feeling that the question we try to ask is of this or that kind. This feeling is what leads us in search of the proper word or the proper phrase, but feeling is not a phrase, it is only the sketch of possible phrases. It implies uncertainty about meaning, as if meaning were present before being present. That is to say, I am obliged to admit a sort of presence different from the explicit linguistic and communicable present.

MANY BODIES

There are a lot of 'bodies' that form the subject matter of various sciences or practices. The body can be dealt with under different rubrics: growing up and coming of age (health), developing fitness (sports), cultivating intensity (eroticism, using drugs, etc.), exploring resistance and flexibility (life in space, underwater, underground, in freezing conditions), challenging artificial conditions (surgery, prosthesis).

Thus nobody can be said to be the owner of this body as a whole. Bodies are shared according to various rubrics among various claims and practices. . . .

SURVIVAL AFTER THE EXPLOSION OF THE SUN –
CREATIVITY AND CHILDHOOD

. . . The sun is due to explode quite soon, in four and a half billion years, which is not very long. And probably genetic manipulation and the development of electronics are ways of challenging this catastrophe; that is to say, ways to permit what will be called humankind at that time (probably just meaning computers, very intelligent computers) to be saved and to emigrate from this dead cosmological system. I have the idea that under these conditions so-called evolution or development will have erased the question of birth, the question of childhood, the question of a certain anxiety concerning the internal rather than the external situation. In this case we have to take into account that the relation that we can have with this internal stranger, this uncanny familiarity, is the source of every invention, creation, and writing – even in science, let me add, even in science. That is the big difference between an everyday scientist and somebody like Einstein. Unquestionably, Einstein has been a child and has remained a child, and we have to be children if we are to be capable of the most minimal creative activity. If we are sent to space after the explosion of the sun (I don't even know if it will be us), if something is sent to space without this extraordinary complexity that is precisely the paradox of childhood, I am afraid that this complexity is not complex enough. In this case, we could call this by the terrible name of mere survival, which is not very interesting. I am not interested in surviving, not interested at all.

I am interested in remaining a child.

25

Naturalized Woman and Feminized Nature

KATE SOPER*

WOMAN AS 'NATURE'

[THE] ASSOCIATION OF femininity with naturality represents a more specific instance of the mind–body dualism brought to conceptions of nature, since it goes together with the assumption that the female, in virtue of her role in reproduction, is a more corporeal being than the male. If we ask, that is, what accounts for this coding of nature as feminine – which is deeply entrenched in Western thought, but has also been said by anthropologists to be crosscultural and well-nigh universal[1] – then the answer, it would seem, lies in the double association of women with reproductive activities and of these in turn with nature. As feminists from de Beauvoir onwards have argued, it is woman's biology, or more precisely the dominance of it in her life as a consequence of her role in procreation, that has been responsible for her allocation to the side of nature, and hence for her being subject to the devaluation and de-historization of the natural relative to the cultural and its 'productivity'. The female, de Beauvoir tells us, is 'more enslaved to the species than the male, her animality is more manifest'.[2] Others have pointed out that in virtue of their role in the gratification of physiological needs, reproductive activities are viewed as directly linked with the human body, and hence as natural. As Olivia Harris puts it, 'since the human body is ideologically presented as a natural given, outside history, it is easy to slide into treating domestic labour as a natural activity, also outside the scope of historical analysis'.[3] In the argument of Sherry Ortner, woman's

> 'natural' association with the domestic context (motivated by her natural lactation functions) tends to compound her potential for being viewed as closer to nature because of the animal-like nature of children, and because of the infra-social connotation of the domestic group as against the rest of society. Yet at the same time, her socializing and cooking functions within the domestic context show her to be a powerful agent of the

*From *What is Nature?*, London: Blackwell, 1995.

cultural process constantly transforming raw material resources into cultural products. Belonging to culture, yet appearing to have stronger and more direct connotations with nature, she is seen as situated between the two.[4]

In the view of Ortner, then, and other anthropologists, what is at issue here is not so much a simple conflation of woman with nature, as an alignment of the two that derives from the female role in child-birth and her consequent activities as initial mediator between the natural and the cultural.[5] As those responsible for the nursing and early socialization of children, women are 'go betweens' who stay closer to nature because of their limited and merely preparatory functions as 'producers' of the cultural. . . .

We might also note, in this connection, the extent to which the presumption that 'art' is a distinctively male preserve has influenced the reception of female cultural production. As Griselda Pollock and Rozsika Parker have pointed out, certain subject matters and art forms (the painting of flowers, for example) were typically viewed as appropriate to women in virtue of their similarity to their own nature, so that 'fused into the prevailing notion of femininity, the painting becomes solely an extension of womanliness, and the artist becomes a woman only fulfilling her nature.'[6] At the same time, for needlework, quilt work and other forms of craft traditionally produced by women to be perceived as 'art', their origins as craft had to be overlooked. They cite (adding their own italics) the deliberate amnesia of the critic, Ralph Pomeroy:

> I am going to forget, *in order really to see them*, that a group of Navajo blankets are only that. In order to consider them as I feel they ought to be considered as Art with a capital 'A' – I am going to look at them as paintings – created with dye instead of pigment, in unstretched fabric instead of canvas – *by several nameless masters of abstract art*.[7]

What is interesting about this remark, we may add, is not only its blindness to the chauvinism of its patronage of female 'art', but its failure to appreciate that the abstract pattern of a Navajo blanket could be viewed as 'art' only *after* (male) 'high art' had come to encompass and value abstraction. In this sense, female cultural production was actually in advance of 'masculine' aesthetic conceptions.

More generally, it must be said that the antithetical equivalence: woman = reproduction = nature versus man = production = culture offers a doubly distorting picture: firstly, in that it invites us to suppose that 'production' proceeds without reliance on nature, when in fact any form of human creativity involves a utilization and transformation of natural resources; and secondly because it presents 'reproduction' as if it were unaffected by cultural mediation and innured against the impact of socio-economic conditions. Production, however, can no more be regarded as independent of biological and physical process than reproduction can be viewed as reducible to an unmediated matter of biology outside the cultural-symbolic order. This does not mean that there are no distinctions to be drawn between the production of human beings and the production of armaments, or between the different kinds of work and activity involved when human beings transform natural materials. Feminists, for example, have pointed to the ways in which any economic theory (that of Marx, for example) that conceives of 'production' as essentially a matter of producing objects or commodities will tend to overlook the productivity of domestic labour and skew perceptions of its contribution accordingly. The adequacy of the 'object' model of production for thinking about agricultural production has also been justly questioned. Equally there is no denying that insofar as human reproduction is a biological process, the sexes are differently involved in it, and have tended to assume distinctive social roles as a result of that. The point is only that a simple mapping of the culture–nature opposition onto these various differences obscures rather than assists the discriminations necessary to thinking clearly about them.

NATURE AS 'WOMAN'

If women have been devalued and denied cultural participation through their naturalization, the downgrading of nature has equally been perpetuated through its representation as 'female'. Looked at from this optic, too, the symbolization testifies to considerable confusion of thought, and its very complexity indicates some profound ambiguities about 'man's' place within and relations to the natural world.

Nature has been represented as a woman in two rather differing senses: 'she' is identified with the body of laws, principles and processes that is the object of scientific scrutiny and experimentation. But 'she' is also nature conceived as spatial territory, as the land or earth which is tamed and tilled in agriculture (and with this we may associate a tendency to feminize nature viewed simply as landscape – trees, woodland, hills, rivers, streams, etc. are frequently personified as female or figure in similes comparing them to parts of the female body). In both these conceptions, nature is allegorized as either a powerful maternal force, the womb of all human production, or as the site of sexual enticement and ultimate seduction. Nature is both the generative source, but also the potential spouse of science, to be wooed, won, and if necessary forced to submit to intercourse. The Aristotelian philosophy, claimed Bacon, in arguing for an experimental science based on sensory observation, has 'left Nature herself untouched and inviolate'; those working under its influence had done no more than 'catch and grasp' at her, when the point was 'to seize and detain her';[8] and the image of nature as the object of the eventually 'fully carnal' knowing of science is frequently encountered in Enlightenment thinking and famously pictured in Louis Ernest Barrias's statue of *La Nature devoilant devant la science*, a copy of which stood in the Paris Medical Faculty in the nineteenth century.

Nature as physical territory is also presented as a source of erotic delight, and sometimes of overwhelming provocation to her masculine voyeur-violator. Describing the confluence of the Potomac and Shenandoah rivers, Thomas Jefferson writes:

For the mountain being cloven asunder, she presents to your eye, through the cleft, a small catch of smooth blue horizon, at an infinite distance in the plain country, inviting you, as it were, from the riot and tumult roaring around, to pass through the breach and participate of the calm below.[9]

Wordsworth's poem, *Nutting*, offers one of the most powerfully voluptuous descriptions of the 'virgin scene' of nature, and one of the most disturbed accounts of the ravishment it provokes:

> Then up I rose,
> And dragged to earth both branch and bough, with crash
> And merciless ravage; and the shady nook
> Of hazels, and the green and mossy bower,
> Deformed and sullied, patiently gave up
> Their quiet being; and, unless I now
> Confound my present feelings with the past,
> Even then, when from the bower I turned away
> Exulting, rich beyond the wealth of kings,
> I felt a sense of pain when I beheld
> The silent trees and the intruding sky.[10]

. . . But it is in the perception of the colonizer, for whom nature is both a nurturant force – a replenished bosom or womb of renewal – and a 'virgin' terrain ripe for penetration, that the metaphor of the land as female is most insistent; and also most equivocal – for it is one thing to cajole – or force – a virgin to surrender to her lover (rapist), another for the son to direct his sexual attentions towards his mother. Incestuous desires, or acts, (which constitute, indeed, a crime against nature) are of an altogether different order from those of a suitor overwhelmed by a natural interest in possessing the rightful object of his desire. . . .

Many have remarked on the analogies between the domination of nature and the oppression of women. Fewer have noted the equivocation in the mother-virgin-lover imagery, which is surely expressive of the conflicting feelings that 'real' nature has induced in 'men'. If Nature is, after all, both mother and maid, this surely reflects a genuine tension between the impulse to dominate and the impulse to be nurtured. The urge to feminize nature contains within it, that is, something of the contrariness of attitude that is inspired by the interaction with it; or, as Annette Kolodny has put it in her study of the 'pastoral impulse' in American art and letters, it combines both a 'phallic' and a 'foetal' aspect, the conflict between them testifying to deep-seated ambiguities about the use of nature. For the American colonizer, suggests Kolodny, who was 'beginning again', nature was a site of rebirth, 'but only on condition of its settlement and taming – a 'violating' intervention by the phallic pioneer upon the nurturing womb, which was bound to prove a source of guilt. The mother's body as the first ambience experienced by the infant becomes a kind of 'archetypal primary landscape' to which subsequent perceptual configurations of space are related. As such, moreover, it is expressive of a nostalgia for a mother–child unity, this unity itself being a figure of a desired harmony and 'at oneness' of man and nature.[11]

To pursue this idea further is to suggest that there is a parallel mapping of the regrettable but inevitable mother–child separation onto the relation to nature as inevitable object of 'phallic' intervention. The Oedipal drama, whereby the child acquires masculine subjectivity in 'giving up' incestuous desires for the mother in exchange for eventual possession of another female, is here inscribed in the 'body' of nature itself as both protective mother to be shielded from ravishment, and (as Thomas Morton described New England) the 'faire virgin, longing to be sped / And meete her lover in a Nuptiall bed.'[12] If viewed in this light, nature's retributions on those who would force her to yield her secrets or submit to 'husbandry' can readily appear to be maternal punishments; or the desire to be overwhelmed by nature indicate a remorse felt for her violation.

Femininized nature is not therefore emblematic simply of mastered nature, but also of regrets and guilts over the mastering itself; of nostalgias felt for what is lost or defiled in the very act of possession; and of the emasculating fears inspired by her awesome resistance to seduction.

NOTES

1   Its universality is stressed by Sherry B. Ortner in 'Is Female to Male as Nature is to Culture?', in Michelle Zimbalist Rosaldo and Louise Lamphere (eds) *Woman, Culture, Society*, Stanford, CA: Stanford University Press, 1974, pp. 67–87.

2   Simone de Beauvoir, *The Second Sex* (trans. H. B. Parshley), Harmondsworth: Penguin, 1953, p. 239.

3   Olivia Harris, 'Households as Natural Units', in Veronica Beechey and James Donald (eds) *Subjectivity and Social Relations*, Milton Keynes: Open University Press, 1985, p. 129.

4   Ortner, 'Is Female to Male?', p. 80.

5   Ibid., pp. 85–6.

6   Griselda Pollock and Rozsika Parker, *Old Mistresses*, London: Routledge & Kegan Paul, 1981, p. 58.

7   Ibid., p. 68.

8   Francis Bacon, *Thoughts and Conclusions*, in B. Farrington, *The Philosophy of Frances Bacon: An Essay on its Development from 1603 to 1609 with New Translations of Fundamental Texts*, Liverpool: Liverpool University Press, 1964, sec. 13, p. 83; and *Novum Organum* I, aphorism CXXI, in *The Physical and Metaphysical Works of Lord Bacon* (ed. J. Devey), London: George Bell, 1901, p. 441.

9   Cit. Annette Kolodny, *The Lay of the Land*, Chapel Hill, NC: University of North Carolina Press, 1975, p. 28.

10 William Wordsworth and Samuel Coleridge, *The Lyrical Ballads* (ed. Derek Roper), London: Collins, 1968, pp. 206–7.

11 Kolodny, *Lay of the Land*, pp. 127–8, 148–60.

12 Ibid., p. 12.

26

The Dualism of Primatology

DONNA HARAWAY*

THERE ARE MANY subjects in the history of biology and anthropology that could sustain the themes discussed in this introduction, so why has this book chosen to explore primate sciences in particular? The principal reason is that monkeys and apes, and human beings as their taxonomic kin, exist on the boundaries of so many struggles to determine what will count as knowledge. . . .

The argument of this book is that primatology is about an Order, a taxonomic and *therefore* political order that works by the negotiation of boundaries achieved through ordering differences. These boundaries mark off important social territories, like the norm for a proper family, and are established by social practice, like curriculum development, mental health policy, conservation politics, film making, and book publishing. The two major axes structuring the potent scientific stories of primatology that are elaborated in these practices are defined by the interacting dualisms, *sex/gender* and *nature/culture*. Sex and the west are axiomatic in biology and anthropology. Under the guiding logic of these complex dualisms, western primatology is simian orientalism.

Edward Said (*Orientalism*, London: Routledge, 1978) argued that western (European and American) scholars have had a long history of coming to terms with countries, peoples, and cultures in the Near and Far East that is based on the Orient's special place in western history – the scene of origins of language and civilization, of rich markets and colonial possession and penetration, and of imaginative projection. The Orient has been a troubling resource for the production of the Occident, the 'East's' other and periphery that became materially its dominant. The West is positioned outside the Orient, and this exteriority is part of the Occident's practice of representation. Said quotes Marx, 'They cannot represent themselves; they must be represented' (xiii). These representations are complex mirrors for western selves in specific historical moments. The West has also been positioned mobilely; westerners could be *there* with relatively little resistance from the other. The difference has been one of power. The structure has been limiting,

*From 'Introduction', in *Primate Visions: Gender, Race, and Nature in the World of Modern Science*, New York and London: Routledge, 1989.

of course, but more importantly, it has been *productive*. That productivity occurred within the structured practices and discourses of orientalism; the structures were a condition of having anything to say. There never is any question of having anything truly original to say about origins. Part of the authority of the practices of telling origin stories resides precisely in their intertextual relations.

Without stretching the comparison too far, the signs of orientalist discourse mark primatology. But here, the scene of origins is not the cradle of civilization, but the cradle of culture, of human being distinct from animal existence. If orientalism concerns the western imagination of the origin of the city, primatology displays the western imagination of the origin of sociality itself, especially in the densely meaning-laden icon of 'the family'. Origins are in principle inaccessible to direct testimony; any voice from the time of origins is structurally the voice of the other who generates the self. That is why both realist and postmodernist aesthetics in primate representations and simulations have been modes of production of complex illusions that function as fruitful generators of scientific facts and theories. 'Illusion' is not to be despised when it grounds such powerful truths. Simian orientalism means that western primatology has been about the construction of the self from the raw material of the other, the appropriation of nature in the production of culture, the ripening of the human from the soil of the animal, the clarity of white from the obscurity of color, the issue of man from the body of woman, the elaboration of gender from the resource of sex, the emergence of mind by the activation of body. To effect these transformative operations, simian 'orientalist' discourse must first construct the terms: animal, nature, body, primitive, female. Traditionally associated with lewd meanings, sexual lust, and the unrestrained body, monkeys and apes mirror humans in a complex play of distortions over centuries of western commentary on these troubling doubles. Primatology is western discourse, and it is sexualized discourse. It is about potential and its actualization. Nature/culture and sex/gender are not loosely related pairs of terms; their specific form of relation is hierarchical appropriation, connected as Aristotle taught by the logic of active/ passive, form/matter, achieved form/resource, man/animal, final/material cause. Symbolically, nature and culture, as well as sex and gender, mutually (but not equally) construct each other; one pole of a dualism cannot exist without the other.

Said's critique of orientalism should alert us to another important point: neither sex nor nature is the truth underlying gender and culture, any more than the 'East' is really the origin and distorting mirror of the 'West'. Nature and sex are as crafted as their dominant 'others'. But their functions and powers are different. The task of this book is to participate in showing how the whole dualism is built, what the stakes might be in the architectures, and how the building might be redesigned. It matters to know precisely how sex and nature become natural-technical objects of knowledge, as much as it matters to explain their doubles, gender and culture. It is not the case that no story could be told without these dualisms or that they are part of the structure of the mind or language. For one thing, alternative stories within primatology exist. But these binarisms have been especially *productive* and especially *problematic* for constructions of female and race-marked bodies; it is crucial to see how the binarisms may be deconstructed and maybe redeployed.

It seems nearly impossible for those who produce natural sciences and comment on them for a living really to believe that there is no *given* reality beneath the inscriptions of science, no untouchable sacred center to ground and authorize an innocent and progressive order of knowledge. Maybe in the humanities there is no recourse from representation, mediation, story-telling, and social saturation. But the sciences succeed that other faulty order of knowledge; the proof is in their power to convince and reorder the whole world, not just one local culture. The natural sciences are the 'other' to the human sciences, with their tragic orientalisms. But these pleas do not survive scrutiny.

The pleas of natural scientists do not convince because they are set up as the 'other'. The claims are predictable and seem plausible to those who make them because they are built into the taxonomies of western knowledge and because social and psychological needs are met by the persistent voices of the divided knowledge of natural and human sciences, by this division of labor and authority in the production of discourses. But these observations about predictable claims and social needs do not reduce natural sciences to a cynical 'relativism' with no standards beyond arbitrary power. Nor does my argument claim there is no world for which people struggle to give an account, no referent in the system of signs and productions of meanings, no progress in building better accounts within traditions of practice. That would be to reduce a complex field to one pole of precisely the dualisms under analysis, the one designated as ideal to some impossible material, appearance to some forbidden real.

The point of my argument is rather that natural sciences, like human sciences, are inextricably *within* the processes that give them birth. And so, like the human sciences, the natural sciences are culturally and historically specific, modified, involved. They matter to real people. It makes sense to ask what stakes, methods, and kinds of authority are involved in natural scientific accounts, how they differ, for example, from religion or ethnography. It does not make sense to ask for a form of authority that escapes the web of the highly productive cultural fields that make the accounts possible in the first place. The detached eye of objective science is an ideological fiction, and a powerful one. But it is a fiction that hides – and is designed to hide – how the powerful discourses of the natural sciences really work. Again, the limits are *productive*, not reductive and invalidating.

One grating consequence of my argument is that the natural sciences are legitimately subject to criticism on the level of 'values', not just 'facts'. They are subject to cultural and political evaluation 'internally', not just 'externally'. But the evaluation is also implicated, bound, full of interests and stakes, part of the field of practices that make meanings for real people accounting for situated lives, including highly structured things called scientific observations. The evaluations and critiques cannot leap over the crafted standards for producing credible accounts in the natural sciences because neither the critiques nor the objects of their discourse have any place to stand 'outside' to legitimate such an arrogant overview. To insist on value and story-ladenness at the heart of the production of scientific knowledge is not equivalent to standing nowhere talking about nothing but one's biases – quite the opposite. Only the pose of disinterested objectivity makes 'concrete objectivity' impossible.

Part of the difficulty of approaching the embedded, interested, passionate constructions of science non-reductively derives from an inherited analytical tradition, deeply indebted to Aristotle and to the transformative history of 'White Capitalist Patriarchy' (how may we name this scandalous Thing?) that turns everything into a resource for appropriation. As 'resource' an object of knowledge is finally only matter for the seminal power, the act, of the knower. Here, the object both guarantees and refreshes the power of the knower, but any status as *agent* in the productions of knowledge must be denied the object. It – the world – must, in short, be objectified as thing, not agent; it must be matter for the self-formation of the only social being in the productions of knowledge, the human knower. Nature is only the raw material of culture, appropriated, preserved, enslaved, exalted, or otherwise made flexible for disposal by culture in the logic of capitalist colonialism. Similarly, sex is only the matter to the act of gender; the productionist logic seems inescapable in traditions of western binarisms. This analytical and historical narrative logic accounts for my nervousness about the sex/gender distinction in the recent history of feminist theory as a way to approach reconstructions of what may count as female and as nature in primatology – and why those reconstructions matter beyond the boundaries of primate studies. It has seemed all but impossible to avoid the trap of an appropriationist logic of domination built into the nature/culture binarism and its generative lineage, including the sex/gender distinction.

27

Hélène Cixous: The Language of Flowers

VERENA ANDERMATT CONLEY*

ALL OF HÉLÈNE CIXOUS'S voluminous, prolific work – fiction, 'theory' and theater alike – consists in rewriting oppositions that she then turns into differences. Despite the apparent 'essentialism' of her attachment to the causes of women, she makes it clear that in all areas of life there are no essences, only relations between terms that can be perceived in historical configurations. Presently in the Occident, she notes, differences are turned by reigning ideologies into oppositions and hierarchies (Cixous and Clement 1975). These she sets out to expose and undo through a medium that privileges writing 'as' metaphor and 'more than' metaphor since it replaces nothing. In the wake of structuralism she puts in question the division between nature and culture elaborated since the early Middle Ages. A phallocratic culture is founded on the exclusion of nature and of women. In at least two distinct moments, Cixous rewrites nature, an inherited term of an opposition, into differ-ence by associating it with women. She begins with a damning critique of the Hegelian dialectic that had spelled death for women and nature. The second, more constructive if not equally dialectical, moment in her work, is part of a shift to Heidegger. In her affinity for the German philosophy she develops new modes of being that live in accord with nature.

In the beginning of 'Sorties', her part of *The Newly Born Woman* (co-authored with Catherine Clement, 1975), Cixous notes that binary oppositions underlie most of Western thought. Woman is always on the side of nature, outside of culture, and thus relegated to passivity. Thought is structured by binary opposi-tions that are ordered hierarchically. A vertical order becomes law and organizes everything that is intelligible at a given moment into oppositions: dual, irrecon-cilable, sublatable, dialectical. These oppositions extend into Nature/History, Nature/Art, Nature/Mind, Passion/Action. Theory of culture, theory of society, the whole of symbolic systems, art, religion, family, language, are all elaborated along the lines of the same schemata. And the movement through which each opposi-tion is constituted is the same as that through which the couple is being destroyed.

*From *Ecopolitics: The Environment in Post-Structuralist Thought*, London and New York: Routledge, 1997.

148

We are confronted with a generalized battlefield. Each time a war is being waged, death is always at work in the constitution of logical categories (Cixous and Clement 1975: 115–17).

Cixous approaches the problem of nature from a perspective of philosophy and writing. A semiotic chain is established:

| **High:** | Culture | Mind | Speech | Man |
| **Low:** | Nature | Body | Writing | Woman |

The elaboration of culture in the Occident is directly proportional to a repression of nature. Culture privileges mind and represses the body. It favors full speech and presence to oneself and devalorizes writing based on absence, representation, and a *techné* or supplement. Man elaborates culture; woman is part of nature. Cixous revalorizes the woman by exposing the locus of her exclusion from a symbolic system. A transformation of hierarchies and oppositions into mere differences serves to disinter the repressed terms. Reasoning in dialectics that requires the death of one term so that the other can live is thus, in a strong sense, deconstructed, its genesis exposed. Masculine culture spells the death of woman and nature. Cixous's program consists of rewriting the opposition so that woman and nature can come back to life. Yet body and woman are always 'cultural', 'always already' written or ciphered, in the sense of both genetics (inhering in DNA) and cultural process in general (a result of imprinting). No life is possible without writing, without some kind of an inscription. Writing – or *techné* – is now believed to be anterior to speech, indeed to all forms of life. This information is in the flesh transmitted along neurons or pathways.

It has been said that, in a given culture, affective relations are linked to economic relations. Hegelian dialectics deal with property, sameness, and refusal or denial of difference; in such a political climate, men accumulate women and goods and put nature at their service; in order to be identical to himself, man appropriates woman whose role it is to admire him. He derives his identity from an appositional either/or logic that puts everything under the sign of unity, narcissism, and death. Women die so that men can live. Cixous extends this deadly logic to Freudian psychoanalysis, the founding science of subjectivity, where oppositions are produced and repression sets in when a male order cuts the child from the mother's body and forces him or her to enter into an abstract symbolic realm. The masculine subject asserts himself through negation of the other. He spirals toward the spirit and leaves the body (that is, nature) behind. The world of 'natural' language, closer to body and affect, is lost. From there on, a phallocentric, martial culture puts everything under the sign of grammar and repression, hence a condition that furthers war. In her nascent vision of a cultural ecology, Cixous outlines modes of exchange that would be different from those ordered by the masculine tradition and closer to the gift. Subjects are urged to approach each other through tact, to give themselves to each other, freely, without seeking obligatory returns on their investments.

In a second step, important for the rethinking of woman and nature and for the creation of mental ecology, Cixous invents a language before any decisively

149

originary cut can be imagined as that which is constitutive of subjectivity. Emphasizing the mother's (ciphered) body, she searches for a relation with the world that would be 'harmonious'. There, a masculine language that divides the subject from the mother's body, and teaches him or her through grammar and rules to speak of things from a distance, is replaced with a poetic idiom of proximity. Technologies of application that repress the body have given way to a *techné* as *poiesis* in the wake of a terminology that is drawn from the work of Martin Heidegger. This *techné* is located inside the body. Writing in the sense of 'instrumentality' is but secondary and derivative. It opens to a 'poetic approach' of the other, by means of which both terms are altered but not annulled. The other is not idealized. A space is opened that welcomes the arrival of the unknown. To loosen the grid, to de-dialectize, is to de-alienate. The process is tantamount to bringing into harmony a relation established through poetic language that reveals being. In this apparent collapse of dialectics, women have a conscious and unconscious memory of their childhood as a paradise garden. They carry their childhood in them like a spring to which they not so much actively return as – somewhat passively – let rise in them. The nature-garden functions as a metaphor, as a paradise of sorts, before the fall, before symbolic separation, before the loss of nature or of the maternal body. The new feminine 'subject' will not be cut from the language of nature. It has to listen to things, speak to them:

> I have an Oranian childhood that remembers the plants at the foot of the hills inside the *Jardin d'Essai*. What I can still understand of what the plants are saying, I learned from there. It was a childhood absolutely faithful to the world: natural. . . . We have been taught a language that speaks from above, from afar, that listens to itself, that has ears only for itself, the dead language of deafening, that speaks to us in advance. We have been taught a language that translates everything in itself, understands nothing except in translation; speaks only in its language, listens only to its grammar, and we separated from the things under its orders. . . .
>
> But I have a childhood that knew. It dwells in the *Jardin d'Essai*. It still knows what I alone no longer know. What it knows, I have so much to unlearn, to know it again. Language distracts us. We let ourselves be led aside by grammar, we let ourselves be distanced from objects by sentences, we let language double us, let it throw itself surreptitiously in front of objects just before we can attain them.
>
> (Cixous 1980: 135–7)

In an idealizing gesture, Cixous urges women to return to a condition before the moment of exclusion, that is, before a language conceived as translation grounds all communication, at a time when they communicated and were in communion with nature through bodily immediacy. She condemns any language that separates and that by being imagined as preceding things smothers them.

In this view, identity means fixity, a condition deprived of becoming. It interrupts harmonious flows of giving and receiving. Imposed by society, from the outside, it is always related to arrestation and to death. The language of translation immobilizes, enframes, and kills life. The feminine 'subject', by contrast, is attuned to the language of things, to feeling, or pathos, as a range of affect that precedes any kind of translation. Cixous repeatedly emphasizes bodily communication along vibrations in 'language' of the flesh without words. Women communicate with the body, through vibrations that go from blood to blood, through musical vibrations, and cosmic harmony. In contrast to knowledge – and power – born from the fall and separation, Cixous proposes another type of knowing, an active condition, where the divisions between body and intellect (language) and between nature and culture are not clearly drawn. The separation between subject and object – here the maternal body and nature – hinges on language. Historically, this loss, beginning with the advent of modern science, is fancied to come about with writing and the printing press, with the shift that in communication depended on voice and the body to mental abstraction involved with the decipherment of fixed symbolic characters. A haptic experience is lost. The subject no longer walks in the world among things that freely give themselves to be seen but wills to apprehend and dominate the globe. The planimetric flattening of the world evidenced in both cartography and science is related to technology and the control of nature. The nature that is conveyed through especially oral or ostensibly prelapsarian writings is, by contrast, a *friendly* nature, benevolent, maternal, a French trellis garden, with English outcroppings, that ramify a bit like the branches of German philosophy. Writes Cixous:

> To enjoy blissfully a walk from the path of the summit ridge to the ground of *the Jardin d'Essai*, to make the trip faithfully, in accord with life, the body, we have to exit softly, leave all phrases of recommendation, and now live, simply live, live entirely there where we live, begin the way it begins, to let things happen according to their mode, let the rose be felt in a rose way, to descend toward the garden attracted, led by the appeal of its freshness, to descend trusting the body, the way my childhood descended, before I knew the names of the streets, but the senses know their ways, before the proper noun and the common nouns, along the perfumes, walking with feet in sandals in the heavy perfumes, in the movement of the marketplace.
>
> (Cixous 1980: 139)

Contrary to the ascending movement proposed by men, Cixous writes a path into nature. Things are felt more by being caressed with discourse than being classified and named. They are felt in their essence. But such an essence depends on a *techné* which, paradoxically, remains as 'natural' as possible. She makes full use of her poetic license so that she can slip and slide between *techné* and poetic plenitude. For her purposes it is important that nature not be dominated or subjected to accelerated control, but that each thing possess its own intrinsic time. Nature for Cixous is harmonious and peaceful, the way it can be found anywhere but in 'life itself'. 'Naturalness' – inspired by Heidegger's philosophy of language – privileges the anti-technological and anti-scientific. It rebukes *instrumental* technology and its application of distinctions of gender in favor of another *techné, in* the body through which the 'naturalness of woman' is reinserted in a friendly, forever revalorized nature. Woman is in the role of both mother and daughter and now lives naturally, in this harmonious, unchanging nature set far away from a dominant, repressive discourse of grammar and logic that tries to master the world and that, by imposing the order of abstract logic upon it, would reduce nature, woman, and other cultures to silence.

Nature here is in movement. It flows as opposed to being cut off, congealed, retained, dammed up. Consequently, it does not allow for framing, arresting, or neat delimiting of a subject and an object at the level of language. Oppositions are spaced into a play of differences where one is in the other. It privileges 'humanness' and subjective *Dasein*. Nature is born under the sign of birth, fertility, song, vibration, proximity, and an absence of symbolic language that separates subject from object. Nature consists of flora and fauna; it is a discursive herbarium and a bestiary, part of an archaic, unchanging world of immanence.

. . . By looking – via Heidegger – for a poetics of being in the world, Cixous wants to invent a writing that brings its author as close as possible to the living thing. Such a poetic view of nature is meant to empower women and, by criticizing the moment of separation between nature and culture, to rehabilitate the mother–daughter rapport. It shows that each thing has its own time to disclose and to reveal itself. Cixous's position remains staunchly anti-scientific and anti-technological, the rhetoric resonating with a willfully archaic ring. Nature is lyrical poetry, it is the age of Greek mythology and immanence that sparkles on the horizon of the Aegean archipelago and conveys pure sensation. Can it be said that the ancient is the most modern? Can we reconnect with Greek myth where a lapsarian event initiated the process of history? Can we go back to an origin, to a fantasy of attunement in a generalized, unmarked eros in which men are absent? Even metaphors have a life and the equation of a peaceful, fertile nature and woman are among those that barely exist outside of feminist fictions, where they serve as devices to empower women. . . .

In an ecofeminist politics, writing has to work tirelessly in dialogue with specific issues that are not just human-centered but that mobilize both a vision of, and an attention to, specifically interconnected elements in given environments. At the risk of reducing it to a set of contents, we discover in the French work of Cixous . . . the celebration of a discovery of ecological awareness, but rarely a *mobilization* of the heightened consciousness that would move in the direction of praxis. Paul Virilio stated, it is worth repeating, that the ecological battle is the *only one* worth fighting for: meaning that no loops, no rhetorical embroideries, no filibustering, no plea bargains, no attenuations, no damage controls, etc., can be allowed. Unlike any that we have known in history, no single battle has ever been so marvelously simple, rudimentary, indelibly clear, or so threatening. It would not be apocalyptic to say that the world is collapsing under the effects of the history of the last four centuries, but what recent history has produced can serve to change the future in a way that makes the destiny of the planet something not only worth thinking about in a mental ecology or celebrating in *écriture féminine*, but ultimately worth fighting for.

In this light Cixous . . . seem[s] mired in an egocentric politics seen when we glance at the history of [her] affiliation with women's writing. Her most effective politics emerged from *The Newly Born Woman* (1975), a work coauthored with the Lévi-Straussian critic and journalist Catherine Clement. . . . But since 1975 the production of a monument or of a great pyramid of prose, the effect of the neurosis of 'production' that defines the *homo faber* of modern times . . . seems to inspire part of Cixous's work. Thirty or more plays and novels have appeared, and in such febrile frenzy, it would be impossible for any ecologist or feminist to divide attention between activism and careful assimilation of Cixous's writing.

Ironically though, the *critical* writings of Cixous . . . stand among the most potent for the pragmatics of ecofeminism. When [she] disengage[s] from classical texts their tacit relations with nature, a high degree of consciousness is awoken. In the studies of Clarice Lispector, for example, Cixous melds with her artist and becomes the very language of flowers, cockroaches, eggs, chickens, and homunculi in the Brazilian writer's universe. But when Cixous is left to the devices of her own *écriture féminine*, the consciousness gets attenuated. . . .

In this chapter I have argued that Cixous's writings and its conceptual ground . . . display what ecofeminists would discern as a 'blind spot', what Val Plumwood calls 'understandings which deny dependency and community' (Plumwood 1993: 194). There is in the work a 'colonizing perspective', which claims authority despite what it says to the contrary, which seeks the assurance of its being that of a 'master culture' that, 'because it has not fully come to terms with earthian existence . . . clings to illusions of identity outside nature' (ibid.). We see in the work, at least in Cixous's fictions, a 'denial of dependency' and even a 'self-deception with respect to the conditions of its own life' (ibid., 195). It may be that a gap is opened between what is said and what is done. As we have remarked, Cixous denounces the effects of advanced technology, celebrates the woman whom she places 'closer' to nature, and so forth, but she makes no effort at engaging or inventing an 'ecological democracy' that would enable women and ecology to make gains in the struggle against the degradation of the planet. . . .

WORKS CITED

Cixous, Hélène (1980) *Illa*, Paris: Des Femmes.

Cixous, Hélène and Clement, Catherine ([1975] 1986) *The Newly Born Woman* (trans. Betsy Wing), Minneapolis, MN: University of Minnesota Press.

Plumwood, Val (1993) *Feminism and the Mastery of Nature*, New York and London: Routledge.

PART IV

Ecocritical Principles

Introduction

'On Tuesday, December 29, 1988,' according to Michael Branch of the University of Nevada in the USA, 'ecocriticism officially arrived at the Modern Language Association.'[1] After six years of campaigning Cheryll Glotfelty, former president of ASLE (the Assocation for the Study of Literature and Environment), had managed to gain approval for staging two sessions at each MLA conference devoted to environmental literary criticism. One of the first two sessions was entitled 'Ecocroticism: Trajectories in Theory and Practice', and one of the speakers was Scott Slovic, editor of the journal ISLE (*Interdisciplinary Studies in Literature and Environment*) and author of *Seeking Awareness in American Nature Writing* (Salt Lake City, UT: University of Utah Press, 1992). His statement makes a useful introduction to this part of the reader, as it opens up important issues in ecocriticism in a succinct and accessible manner. A more elaborate, but no less readable, summation of the issues at stake in green theorising is offered by William Howarth, in an extract from his definitive 'Some Principles of Ecocriticism'. In the early part of the essay, not reprinted here, Howarth reminds his readers that ecology is inseparable from ethics: *oikos*, the world household, needs to be inhabited in a spirit of humility and cooperation, a proper *ethos*. In the section extracted here, he argues that an ethical sense will want to engage with science, with language theory, with history and with feminist scholarship: if we are concerned with the mutual influence of culture and nature, we need to be fully conversant with the way the relationship between human and nonhuman life is variously understood. Howarth provides a useful overview of current scholarship.

Despite the difficulties experienced by Cheryll Glotfelty, it remains true that the North American academy has been the most receptive to green studies. By contrast, an English ecocriticism is only now beginning to be defined (leaving aside the possibility of a Scottish, an Irish or, indeed, a European equivalent). There can be no doubt that the most decisive case for the subject has been made by Jonathan Bate. His favoured term is 'ecopoetics', but there is no doubt that his revaluation of 'the ecological tradition' has been crucial in making environmental literary criticism possible in England. His *Romantic Ecology* is represented here. It should be understood from the start that Bate is setting out to repudiate the conventional Marxist and new historicist views of nature as cultural/social/political construct, and their implication that romantic poets who enthuse about it are guilty of foisting class-interested illusion on their readers. Bate categorically defends the 'romantic ecology' thesis against what he sees as the bogus 'romantic ideology' thesis. Complementing his case is Terry Gifford's reflection on 'social construction'. While sympathetic to the notion that human beings cannot experience the non-human world other than in 'mediated' form, Gifford calmly reaffirms that nature itself must precede the word 'nature'. His article is an early declaration of ecocritical principles from an English point of view.

In the USA, there is more than one book which might be compared to Bate's *Romantic Ecology* in terms of controversy, impact and significance. One such is Karl Kroeber's *Ecological Literary Criticism: Romantic Imagining and the Biology of Mind* (New York: Columbia University Press, 1994). It is not represented here because, though it is a distinguished ecocritical work, it is chiefly a confirmation and consolidation of Bate's challenge to 'cold war criticism', that is, to the polarity between left and right, 'red' and reactionary, which no longer seem appropriate in the ecocritical age. More significant still is Lawrence Buell's *The Environmental Imagination*, which is probably the most ambitious single work of ecocriticism written to date. In the extract provided in this part of our reader, Buell defends the mimetic dimension of literature, its capacity for referring to natural reality. Beyond culture, he affirms, there is nature; the latter can and must be represented. However, he does not simply argue for a revival of interest in descriptive prose: rather, 'nature writing', like any literature which addresses the natural environment, should acknowledge its 'dual accountability' – that is, to both outer and inner landscapes. Thus, nature is best represented, not through a flat 'naturalism' but rather though a creative play of language which alerts the reader to the delicate poise between the non-human world and the human mind. In thus incorporating the claims of formalism – that literature is as much about literariness as it is about extra-literary reality, that the 'intertextual' context is as important as the environmental – Buell endorses ecocriticism as an inclusive, progressive development of literary theory. In this enterprise he would seem to be supported from an English perspective by Greg Garrard in his article 'Radical Pastoral?' Like Buell, he does not accept that the pastoral mode of writing can simply be dismissed as reactionary on the grounds that its appeal to natural beauty tends to support the established human order. The historicist approach, which places 'nature' firmly in political 'quotes', itself needs historicising and its politics queried. Garrard counters the claim that pastoral underpins the equation of nature with fixity and essence by reminding us that romanticism at its best demonstrates open-ness and expansiveness: thus, pastoral might come to be seen as the most radical of literary forms.

The necessity for green studies to distinguish itself from conventional, Marxist-oriented criticism if it is to demonstrate its radicalism is addressed also by Jhan Hochman. His book *Green Cultural Studies* has had a major impact in the United States, but remains comparatively unknown in the UK. Here we reprint part of his early draft of the introduction to that volume, which first appeared in the journal *Mosaic*. Its general importance is that he makes his pioneering case for 'worldnature' as a category worthy to be placed at the centre of cultural studies, being equally important as class, race, gender and age/generation. Its specific importance is that he offers his challenge to Donna Haraway's reading of culture as nature, which he sees as potentially disastrous for the latter.

Complementing it, our two final extracts articulate a radical, non-Marxist position which is known as 'ecofeminism'. Patrick Murphy sees the future of green studies as anti-essentialist: identifying postmodernism positively with posthumanism, he repudiates anthropocentrism in favour of a 'dialogics' exemplified by the work of the Russian critic Mikhail Bakhtin. Murphy wants the human self to be related to the natural 'other', that relationship being one of 'heterarchy' rather than 'hierarchy'. We must replace the sterile opposition of humanity as 'one-for-oneself' and nature as 'things-for-us' with the principle of 'anotherness', by which culture opens itself up to 'interanimation' with nature. Feminism has the potential to realise this principle because it has learnt the lessons of the oppressive construction of the natural and the female. Karla Armbruster elaborates further on the ecofeminist promise, but this time by drawing on the contribution of Haraway: it is worth comparing her approach to critical theory with that of Hochman, for she sees the 'blurring of boundaries' as a positive challenge to the deadly dualism charted by Val Plumwood. Appropriately, her article is no arid pronouncement of principles but a demonstration, by a subtle reading of a short story of Ursula Le Guin's, that it is possible to write, read and live as a 'trickster' occupying a creative borderland between culture and nature. Thus, once again, the last extract of the section takes us back to the issues raised at the beginning.

NOTE

1   Michael P. Branch, 'Introductory Remarks' to 'Ecocriticism at the MLA: A Roundtable', *ASLE News*, 11(1), 1999, p. 4.

28

Ecocriticism: Containing Multitudes, Practising Doctrine

Scott Slovic*

EACH OF US has only a few minutes to speak at today's session, so I suppose I'd like to use my time to make two central points about the field of ecocriticism.

I'll anchor each of my points in a well-known quotation. The first is a parenthetical statement from the end of a famous American poem: 'I am large, I contain multitudes.' This is one of my favourite lines from Whitman's 'Song of Myself'. I use it whenever someone tells me of strange goings-on in the organization ASLE, such as fracases on the e-mail list or odd presentations at a conference of one kind or another. Well, I say, 'ASLE is large and it contains multitudes' – it's my way of saying, 'It takes all kinds of people . . .'. The same is true of ecocriticism as a scholarly perspective, as an academic 'movement'. There is no single, dominant world-view guiding ecocritical practice – no single strategy at work from example to example of ecocritical writing or teaching. Cheryll Glotfelty neatly defines 'ecocriticism' as 'the study of the relationship between literature and the physical environment' (Glotfelty and Fromm, *Ecocriticism Reader*, University of Georgia Press, 1996, xviii). My own definition, when asked for a broad description of the field, is 'the study of explicit environmental texts by way of any scholarly approach or, conversely, the scrutiny of ecological implications and human–nature relationships in any literary text, even texts that seem, at first glance, oblivious of the nonhuman world.' In other words, any conceivable style of scholarship becomes a form of ecocriticism if it's applied to certain kinds of literary works; and, on the other hand, there is not a single literary work anywhere that utterly defies ecocritical interpretation, that is 'off limits' to green reading. How's that for an encompassing definition?

This is actually an important point, because I often find that, despite my best efforts and the efforts of colleagues like those sitting up here with me this afternoon, many people continue to have a rather narrow and dismissive attitude toward ecocriticism and environmental literature, as if we somehow represent merely a nostalgic, millennialist fad, a yearning to resurrect and re-explain a limited tradition of hackneyed pastoral or wilderness texts. In the fall of 1997, I proposed a special issue of the journal *PMLA* devoted to ecocriticism and environmental

*From 'Ecocriticism at the MLA: A Roundtable', *ASLE News*, 11(1), 1999.

literature, taking great pains to indicate that ecocriticism does not merely mean studying a narrow body of nineteenth- and twentieth-century American literature. In February of 1998, I heard that the proposal had been turned down by the *PMLA* board, in part because, as editor Martha Banta put it in her sympathetic letter, 'Environmental literature is generally deemed to be almost entirely an "Americanist" issue, and the Board feared being taken one more time around the track. with a flood of essays about Emerson, Thoreau, etc. MLA members still need to be educated to the realization that this is a global concern, not tied to the American situation' (Banta, letter, 4 Feb. 1998). Hence my ceaseless effort, as the editor of *ISLE*, to recruit studies of international environmental literature and to solicit submissions from proposing environmental writers throughout the world; hence the importance of such recent books as John Elder and Hertha Wong's *Family of Earth and Sky: Indigenous Tales of Nature from Around the World* (Beacon, 1994), Robert M. Torrance's *Encompassing Nature: A Sourcebook* (Counterpoint, 1998), and Patrick D. Murphy's *Literature of Nature: An International Sourcebook* (Fitzroy Dearborn, 1998); and hence my reiteration that both ecocriticism and environmental literature 'are large and contain multitudes'.

My second point, if I have time, is that ecocriticism has no central, dominant doctrine or theoretical apparatus – rather, ecocritical theory, such as it is, is being re-defined daily by the actual practice of thousands of literary scholars around the world. The quotation that always surfaces when someone asks me about the 'theory of ecocriticism' comes from Edward Abbey's 1975 novel *The Monkey Wrench Gang* in which a brief dialogue near the beginning of this narrative of eco-sabotage goes as follows:

> 'Do we know what we're doing and why?'
> 'No.'
> 'Do we care?'
> 'We'll work it all out as we go along. Let our practice form our doctrine, thus assuring precise theoretical coherence.'
>
> (Abbey, 65)

Another routine way of dismissing ecocriticism is to claim the field has no 'theory', no substance. In her letter to me about the proposed special issue of *PMLA*, Professor Banta's second key point about the board's response was as follows: 'However unfair this may be, another general perception is that environmental studies is "soft". As several members put it (although they themselves know better), it is characterized as "hug-the-tree stuff"' (Banta, letter, 4 Feb. 1998). Of course, all of us actually working in the field can point to any number of examples of lucid, practical 'ecocritical theory', ranging from Larry Buell's far-reaching perceptions of American culture to the insights of Molly Westling, Annette Kolodny, Patrick Murphy, Greta Gaard, and many others regarding the gendered understanding of landscape. We have many ecocritics helping to demonstrate a new theory and praxis of 'narrative scholarship'. Still others are finding ways of applying rhetorical theory, geographical discourse of 'place', and concepts from ecology and conservation biology to the study of literature. Perhaps the overriding feature of ecocritical theory, though, is it is nearly always attached to an accessible, helpful application, sometimes making it almost unrecognizable as theory. We do not (yet) have any Lacans or Foucaults in our ranks (although we certainty have our share of colleagues and students applying Lacanian and Foucaultian perspectives to green texts). If you're looking for ecocritical theory, look for it in our practice.

29

Ecocriticism in Context

WILLIAM HOWARTH*

ECOCRITICISM IS A name that implies more ecological literacy than its advocates now possess, unless they know what an embattled course ecology has run during its history. *Eco* and *critic* both derive from Greek, *oikos* and *kritis*, and in tandem they mean 'house judge', which may surprise many lovers of green, outdoor writing. A long-winded gloss on *ecocritic* might run as follows: 'a person who judges the merits and faults of writings that depict the effects of culture upon nature, with a view toward celebrating nature, berating its despoilers, and reversing their harm through political action.' So the *oikos* is nature, a place Edward Hoagland calls 'our widest home', and the *kritos* is an arbiter of taste who wants the house kept in good order, no boots or dishes strewn about to ruin the original decor.

I am toying with words, in the hope they will raise some questions about ecocriticism and its future. If its political agenda insists on an Us–Them dichotomy, then ecocriticism cannot be self-scrutinizing, only adversarial. Since ecology studies the relations between species and habitats, ecocriticism must see its complicity in what it attacks. All writers and their critics are stuck with language, and although we cast *nature* and *culture* as opposites, in fact they constantly mingle, like water and soil in a flowing stream. . . .

. . . We know nature through images and words, a process that makes the question of truth in science or literature inescapable, and whether we find validity through data or metaphor, the two modes of analysis are parallel. Ecocriticism observes in nature and culture the ubiquity of signs, indicators of value that shape form and meaning. Ecology leads us to recognize that life speaks, communing through encoded streams of information that have direction and purpose, if we learn to translate the messages with fidelity.

To see how far these values dwell from current humanism, we may turn to a Modern Language Association guide, *Redrawing the Boundaries: The Transformation of Literary Studies* (1992). As its title implies, this survey proposes a sweeping act

*From 'Some Principles of Ecocriticism', in Cheryll Glotfelty and Harold Fromm (eds) *The Ecocriticism Reader: Landmarks in Literary Ecology*, Athens, GA and London: University of Georgia Press, 1996.

of land reform in all literary *fields*, medieval to postcolonial, by using bold spatial imagery: ideas *intersect at odd angles*, disciplinary *maps* raise questions of *boundaries* (national, racial, sexual, political), *frontiers* project beliefs that shape imagined *spaces*. Yet this geography is only rhetorical, according to its mappers, because literature dwells Nowhere: 'The odd thing, in fact, about literature as an imagined territory is that there are apparently no natural limits – and hence, it would seem, there are apparently no natural limits to the field of literary criticism' (Greenblatt and Gunn 6).

The dogma that culture will always master nature has long directed Western progress, inspiring the wars, invasions, and other forms of conquest that have crowded the earth and strained its carrying capacity. Humanists still bristle with tribal aggression, warring for dominion even though they spurn all forms of hegemony. The boldest new scholars have focused on 1500–1900, four centuries of global dominion, with such revisionist ferocity as to sustain what Leah S. Marcus astutely calls 'a set of geographic metaphors ... that suggest our continuing engagement on one level with a cast of mind we have rejected on another' (Greenblatt and Gunn 61). Many recent works of critical theory chart *borders*, *boundaries*, *frontiers*, *horizons*, *margins*, but these tropes also have no natural or geographical reference (Marshall). Yet if current literary maps are devoid of content, postmodern geographers are not: several have used contemporary theory to re-examine the spatial, perceptual, and textual conventions of maps and land (Entrikin, Monmonier).

Ecocriticism seeks to redirect humanistic ideology, not spurning the natural sciences but using their ideas to sustain viable readings. Literature and science trace their roots to the hermeneutics of religion and law, the sources for early ideas of time and space, or history and property. Concepts of property and authority are central directives in science; hence its long service to Western expansion (Bowler). Today science is evolving beyond Cartesian dualism toward quantum mechanics and chaos theory, where volatile, ceaseless exchange is the norm. While some forms of postmodern criticism are following this lead, many humanists still cling to a rationalist bias that ignores recent science. . . .

Throughout the twentieth century, literary theory has often challenged the scale and verity of science. The 'human sciences' of Dilthey asserted differences between scientific knowledge and human understanding, laying emphasis on consciousness and sympathetic insight as traits cultivated by civilization. War and genocide dimmed this optimism, yet among humanists the conviction endures that experience is mind-centered and free of reference to actualities of space and time. Literary critics still place an expansive trust in poetry and dreams, states they see as providing alternative relations to material substance. Hence the persistence of psychoanalytic criticism, despite recent advances in medicine that provide chemical aids for mental disease. As philosophers of mood and ego, humanists are inclined to trust 'the talking cure' above pharmacology, finding lithium or Prozac less reliable than Freud and Kristeva.

Cultural critics share an attachment to ideology and a distrust of physical experience. Marxist theory has influenced environmental history, often by ignoring natural science. In Marxist readings, economics determines social history; hence capitalism becomes the source for all conflict, oppression, and environmental abuse (Crosby). Such views ignore many inconvenient facts: that disturbance is common-place in nature; that aborigines and socialists often commit ecocide. Revolutionary theories tend to ignore natural constraints on production: as farmers have long known, floods and locusts can destroy years of rational planning. A more consis-tent approach examines how social systems change as rural agrarian life evolves toward urban industry (Benjamin, Williams). This emphasis on the interaction of place and work agrees with ecology, which charts how physical conditions may affect beliefs. Historians who accept such a teleology are anticipating ecocriticism, which shares the hope that flawed social conditions may be improved. . . .

Ecocritics may detect more parity between literary and scientific writing than other postmodernists, but that view is not eccentric or unprecedented. The early formalists present systematic studies of language, so regular in Jakobson as to resemble genetic code. New Critics used close readings to explore the intricate diver-sity of words, insisting that they share an organic coherence (Krieger). Structuralism and semiotics focused on descriptive language, offering precise descriptions of the signs and signifying that form culture (Blanchard). . . . Also anticipating ecocriti-cism were structuralist critics of myth and anthropology who examined symbols, often from agricultural fertility rites, that explain natural conditions or try to prevent disasters, such as famine and flood (Blumenberg). Ethnic and postcolonial studies have a strong regional emphasis, but they dwell on political or cultural spaces rather than their physical environs. In time, ecocriticism may provide critics of race and ethnicity with a view of how those social constructions relate to larger histories of land use and abuse. As land is traded, people are degraded, moved to and from regions as mere chattel in an invidious property system (Dixon).

Ecocriticism finds its strongest advocates today in feminist and gender critics, who focus on the idea of place as defining social status. Of particular interest is 'a woman's place', often described as an attic or closet, that contains yet sustains indi-viduals until they locate a congenial environs (Gilbert and Gubar). Some feminists equate anatomy with geography, envisioning the female body/text as a 'no man's land' aligned against a hostile masculine world, the patriarchal settlement (Gilbert and Gubar, Kolodny). But in this work most ideas of sexual difference still derive from Freudian theory, rather than recent biogenetics. Ecocriticism urges the study of gender to examine evolutionary biology, where communities are not just cultural spaces.

WORKS CITED

Benjamin, Walter (1968) *Illuminations*, New York: Harcourt.
Blanchard, Marc E. (1979) *Description, Sign, Self, Desire: Critical Theory in the Wake of Semiotics*, The Hague: Mouton.
Blumenberg, Hans (1985) *Work on Myth*, Cambridge, MA: MIT Press.
Bowler, Peter J. (1993) *The Norton History of the Environmental Sciences*, New York: Norton.

Crosby, Alfred (1993) 'Ecological Imperialism', in Carolyn Merchant (ed.) *Major Problems in American Environmental History*, Lexington, MA: D. C. Heath.

Dixon, Melvin (1987) *Ride Out the Wilderness: Geography and Identity in Afro-American Literature*, Urbana, IL: University of Illinois Press.

Entrikin, Nicholas (1991) *The Betweenness of Place: Towards a Geography of Modernity*, Baltimore, MD: Johns Hopkins University Press.

Gilbert, Sandra and Susan Gubar (1979) *The Madwoman in the Attic: The Woman Writer and the Nineteenth-Century Literary Imagination*, New Haven, CT: Yale University Press.

Greenblatt, Stephen and Giles Gunn (1992) *Redrawing the Boundaries: The Transformation of English and American Studies*, New York: MLA (Modern Language Association of America).

Kolodny, Annette (1979) *The Lay of the Land: Metaphor as Experience and History in American Life and Letters*, Chapel Hill, NC: University of North Carolina Press.

Krieger, Murray (1989) *A Reopening of Closure: Organicism against Itself*, New York: Columbia University Press.

Marshall, Donald (1993) *Contemporary Critical Theory: A Selected Bibliography*, New York: MLA.

Monmonier, Mark (1993) *Mapping it Out: Expository Cartography for the Humanities and Social Sciences*, Chicago: University of Chicago Press.

Williams, Raymond (1976) *Keywords*, Oxford: Oxford University Press, 1976.

30

From 'Red' to 'Green'

Jonathan Bate*

[ROMANTIC IDEOLOGY?]

The air pollution, more than the existence of the Iron Curtain, brought about the revolution in Czechoslovakia.
    Lubos Beniak, *Mlady Svet*, Prague, December 1989

LITERARY CRITICISM HAS never been a pure discipline. Ever since Plato and Aristotle argued over whether poets are harmful or beneficial to the state, political and moral concerns have borne in upon the discussion of literature. Inevitably and properly this will be the case so long as poetry continues to have any effect on how we understand ourselves, how we think about the ways in which we live our lives. As political and moral visions change, so literary criticism will change too. I began writing this introduction on a fairly typical day early in 1990 when the three leading stories on the evening television news were: the Central Committee of the Communist Party of the Soviet Union voted to abolish article six of the constitution, thus bringing to an end the formal guarantee of the Party's sole right to power; the announcement of a move towards a unified German currency; and the appearance of a scientific report supporting the hypothesis that there are links between freak weather conditions and global warming.

[The year] 1989 was more of an 1848 than a 1789, but it may well take its place in history beside the original revolutionary year as a moment when an old order finally died. One could well imagine a citizen of Czechoslovakia who had seen the Prague Spring of 1968 nipped in the bud finding in the events of 1989 'the shoots / And hopeful blossoms of a second spring'. The phrase is Wordsworth's. He used it when he opened the eleventh book of the 1850 text of his autobiographical epic, *The Prelude*, at the moment after the execution of Maximilien Robespierre: 'From that time forth, Authority in France / Put on a milder face; Terror had ceased.' The resonances with 1989 do not need spelling out. But in

*From *Romantic Ecology: Wordsworth and the Environmental Tradition*, London and New York: Routledge, 1991.

167

making a contemporary application it is worth pausing for a moment on the metaphorical appeal to spring. The 'Prague Spring' has remained a powerful image because of its seasonal propriety: it makes us think of the end of a long winter of tyranny or perhaps of flowers sprouting from an iron curtain. As with Wordsworth's 'second spring', a transformation in the volatile political order is dramatized by means of comparison with a familiar process in the cyclical order of external nature. The force of the image depends on the stability of the notion of 'spring', the knowledge that every winter will be followed by a spring which will bring warmth and new life. This notion in turn depends on a set of assumptions about meteorological certainty: it assumes that, in Europe at least, winter will always be cold. A phrase like Wordsworth's 'It is the first mild day of March' only makes sense after a cold January and February.[1] Suddenly that third news item is seen to be relevant not only to politics but also to poetry. One effect of global warming will be (is already?) a powerful increase in the severity of winds in northern Europe; the swallow has great difficulty in coping with wind, so there is a genuine possibility that within the lifetime of today's students Britain will cease to be a country to which this bird migrates. Keats's ode 'To Autumn' is predicated upon the certainty of the following spring's return; the poem will look very different if there is soon an autumn when 'gathering swallows twitter in the skies' for the last time.

The 1980s witnessed something of a return to history, a move away from ahistorical formalisms, among practitioners of literary criticism. In the area of English Romantic poetry, the foundation for the most characteristic work of the decade was laid by Jerome J. McGann in a series of essays and a small but provocative book called *The Romantic Ideology*.[2] The capstone of the decade's criticism, published in 1989, was a very large book by Alan Liu called *Wordsworth: The Sense of History*.[3] The conceptions of 'ideology' and 'history' underlying these books are in the broad sense Marxist; indeed, McGann's title is a very conscious echo of Marx's *The German Ideology*. If we reduce the thesis of these critics to its bare bones, we find that it is essentially a sophisticated revision of a very old accusation:

> In honoured poverty thy voice did weave
> Songs consecrate to truth and liberty, -
> Deserting these, thou leavest me to grieve,
> Thus having been, that thou shouldst cease to be.
>
> (Shelley, 'To Wordsworth')

> Just for a handful of silver he left us,
>   Just for a riband to stick in his coat . . .
> He alone breaks from the van and the freemen,
>   He alone sinks to the rear and the slaves!
>
> (Browning, 'The Lost Leader')

Wordsworth developed a creed of the all-powerful, redeeming poetic Imagination, it is proposed, as a kind of compensation for his political disillusionment or even apostasy. Romanticism gives up on its original revolutionary impulses and finds what it supposes is 'A paradise within, happier far'. Wordsworth's great autobiographical epic ends not with the blissful dawn of the early days of the French Revolution, but with the Restoration of Imagination:

> the mind of man becomes
> A thousand times more beautiful than the earth
> On which he dwells, above this frame of things
> (Which, 'mid all revolutions in the hopes
> And fears of men, doth still remain unchanged)
> In beauty exalted, as it is itself
> Of substance and of fabric more divine.
>
> (*The Prelude*, xiii, 446–52)[4]

Imagination is seen as a way of transcending 'this frame of things', the earth in which we dwell, where revolutions go sour; imagination remains 'unchanged', it is 'exalted', 'divine'. The most remarkable *tour de force* in Alan Liu's book is an excavation of the 'history' – in this instance the Napoleonic matter – that is buried beneath Wordsworth's most powerful apostrophe to the Imagination, the crossing of the Alps section of *The Prelude*, book six. Implicitly, Wordsworth is upbraided for suppressing history and for 'privileging' the individual imagination. After all, 'individualism' is a bourgeois fetish.

The arguments are extremely subtle, at times brilliant, but the underlying vision is the crude old model of Left and Right. This is understandable: after all, those terms themselves are derived from the seating plan of the National Assembly in the revolutionary France which Wordsworth visited. But it is precisely this old model that is beginning to look redundant as Marxist-Leninism collapses in Eastern Europe. Furthermore, if the quotation at the beginning of my introduction is to be believed, this collapse cannot be constructed as anything so simple as a triumph of the Right, let alone of international capitalism. It is not difficult to assimilate nationalism and religion, two of the driving forces of the 1989 revolutions, into a Left-Right model, but the political significance of air pollution demands a rethinking of the categories. The political map has been redrawn and it is time for literary criticism to politicize itself in a new way. . . .

[THE GREAT PASTORAL CON-TRICK?]

. . . In Romantic poetics, poetry is to be found not only in language but in nature; it is not only a means of verbal expression, it is also a means of emotional communication between man and the natural world. John Clare's poem 'Pastoral Poesy' begins with a manifesto remarkably similar to Hazlitt's [in the first of his *Lectures on the English Poets*]. . . . [He speaks of] 'A language that is ever green'.[5] . . . For Clare, himself a farm-labourer, not a 'gentleman' like Wordsworth, 'pastoral poesy' is the life and the beauty in nature. It is available to give joy unto all, to elevate even the 'simplest hearts'; when the shepherd's heart lifts with joy at the sight of a wild flower, that is poetry. Pastoral poetry has a permanent, enduring power – it is an *ever*green language.

For modern criticism, however, pastoral poetry is historically and socially specific. *Pace* Clare, it is not really written by shepherds, it is a comforting aristocratic fantasy that covers up the real conditions of oppression and exploitation in feudal and neo-feudal agrarian economies. Raymond Williams writes with honest indignation: 'It is not easy to forget that Sidney's Arcadia, which gives a continuing title to English neo-pastoral, was written in a park which had been made by enclosing a whole village and evicting the tenants.'[6] Roger Sales lashes out with less measure: 'Pastoralism covers a multitude of economic sins. Literary criticism ought, therefore, to take the form of a brutal strip-tease. Pastoralism should be divested of its silver-tongued language and myths of the golden age.'[7] A major count in the critical indictment of Wordsworth is that he was among the many conspirators in the Great Pastoral Con Trick. . . .

What, then, are the politics of our relationship to nature? For a poet, pastoral is the traditional mode in which that relationship is explored. Pastoral has not done well in recent neo-Marxist criticism, but if there is to be an ecological criticism the 'language that is ever green' must be reclaimed. . . . I would suggest . . . that Wordsworth built an account of the pastoral into the pivotal retrospective eighth book of *The Prelude* in order to forge a link between the holistic values of his native vales and the 'social meliorism' that underlay the French Revolution. If this is so, then we must abandon the model of Wordsworth the young radical with his 'outraged' social and political instincts sooner or later . . . becoming Wordsworth the 'counter-revolutionary' promoting a conservative ideology. An 'ideology' based on a harmonious relationship with nature goes beyond, in many ways goes deeper than, the political model we have become used to thinking with. By recuperating the Wordsworthian pastoral, we may begin to reconfigure the model.

Book eight of *The Prelude*, 'Retrospect: Love of Nature leading to Love of Mankind', was written before book seven, but in the structure of the completed poem it is crucial that it comes after it. . . . For Wordsworth, the distinction between being in the city and being in nature is cardinal; so it is that the move from book seven to book eight is from negative types to positive ones. As 'Residence in London' ends with [the competitive chaos of] Bartholomew Fair, so 'Retrospect' begins with Grasmere Fair. In contrast to the unknown faces in the city, the community gathered in Grasmere for the annual fair is a 'little family'. The only patriarch is the mountain itself. The Vale of Grasmere is imagined as a visionary republic; as Wordsworth put it in his *Guide to the Lakes*, it is a 'pure Commonwealth; the members of which existed in the midst of a powerful empire like an ideal society or an organized community, whose constitution had been imposed and regulated by the mountains which protected it'.[8] The language here – 'Commonwealth', 'ideal society', 'organized community' – is from a tradition of radical republicanism that goes back to the English civil war. To summon up English republicanism was to declare allegiance to the French Revolution; it therefore follows that, by associating Grasmere Vale with republicanism, Wordsworth was retrospectively finding a seedbed for his own revolutionary enthusiasm in the rural communities that he had known since his earliest years.

[THERE IS NO NATURE?]

Whatever our class, nature can do something for us. Alan Liu writes that 'nature is the name under which we use the nonhuman to validate the human, to interpose a mediation able to make humanity more easy with itself'.[9] This seems to me to describe accurately what nature does for Wordsworth, for Hazlitt, for Clare, for Morris, for the factory-labourer who contributed to the Derwentwater appeal. However, Liu links this statement to the claim that '*There is no nature*', in other words that 'nature' is nothing more than an anthropomorphic construct created by Wordsworth and the rest for their own purposes. The polemical desire to reject any casual recourse to 'nature' as panacea for social ills has the unfortunate consequence of occluding any consideration of the whole question of human society's stewardship of 'the features and products of the earth itself, as contrasted with those of human civilization' (OED's thirteenth sense of the word). 'Nature' is a term that needs to be contested, not rejected. It is profoundly unhelpful to say 'There is no nature' at a time when our most urgent need is to address and redress the consequences of human civilization's insatiable desire to consume the products of the earth. We are confronted for the first time in history with the possibility of there being no part of the earth left untouched by man. 'Human civilization' has always been in the business of altering the land, whether through deforestation or urbanization or mining or enclosure or even the artificial reimposition of 'nature' through landscaping in the manner of William Kent and Capability Brown. But until now there have always been domains into which 'human civilization' does not extend; there has always been a 'state of nature'. Enclosure and landscape gardening have had no effect on the higher fellsides and tarns of Westmorland. Chernobyl, however, has. There is a difference not merely in degree but in kind between local changes to the surface configuration of the land and the profound transformations of the economy of nature that take place when the land is rendered radioactive or the ozone layer is depleted. When there have been a few more accidents at nuclear power stations, when there are no more rainforests, and when every wilderness has been ravaged for its mineral resources, then let us say '*There is no nature*'.

NOTES

1   The opening of 'Lines written at a distance from my House', in *Lyrical Ballads* (1798).
2   J. J. McGann, *The Romantic Ideology: A Critical Investigation*, Chicago, 1983, and the essays collected in *The Beauty of Inflections: Literary Investigations in Historical Method and Theory*, Oxford, 1988.
3   A. Liu, *Wordsworth: The Sense of History*, Stanford, CA, 1989.

4   *The Prelude 1799, 1805, 1850* (ed. Jonathan Wordsworth, M. H. Abrams, and Stephen Gill), New York, 1979. All quotations are from this edition in the 1805 text, unless otherwise stated.

5   J. Clare, *Selected Poetry* (ed. Geoffrey Summerfield), London, 1990, p. 163.

6   R. Williams, *The Country and the City*, London, 1973, repr. 1975, p. 33.

7   R. Sales, *English Literature in History 1700–1830: Pastoral and Politics*, London, 1983, p. 77.

8   *Wordsworth's Guide to the Lakes: The Fifth Edition (1835)* (ed. Ernest de Selincourt) Oxford, 1906, repr. 1977, p. 68.

9   Liu, *Wordsworth*, p. 38.

31

The Social Construction of Nature

Terry Gifford*

I AM WRITING this at my home in Sheffield. If I turn my head a little away from the frame of the screen on which I am writing, I look through the frame of a window. This frame is filled by two things: tree and sky. Both are constantly changing, although at different rates. The Japanese cherry has just finished its two weeks of flowering. Now as I look out into the top of the tree I see branches and leaves. In the winter I shall look through the branches to the top of a terrace of houses dipping away to miles of industrial buildings and housing estates. Above the tree the blue sky is filling with clouds. It has started to rain. The newly arrived swifts have disappeared. The rain gets heavier. I see it and hear it.

Do you? I have not described it, so what has the word rain signified to you here? Presumably you have imagined water falling past my window and not custard, or cats and dogs? (Perhaps not.) Your own direct experiences of rain will have been framed by your contexts, but you will know what it generally looks, sounds, and feels like so that the word rain works in a broad sense. [The signified thus still has a primacy over the signifier](I am relieved to discover). However, as soon as I communicate in words my own context or frames, I am mediating 'rain' for a reader. To convey more of what it has meant to me would require the suggestibility of poetry, which in turn would require in the reader some degrees of experience of rain for the signifiers to make distinctions. The Amhara people of Ethiopia have only one word for all rain. A German correspondent recently sent me sixty-four German expressions for rain. Rain can be a concept, such as fertility or pollution, but the feel of rain, snow, or sun is a direct contact with external nature that we lose touch with at our peril. If we lose direct experience of seasonal changes, how are we to understand growth and decay in ourselves?

But from this material world in which we live we have become strangely alienated. There is much evidence to show that those of us living in large industrial cities (and in Britain that is most of us) still need to have unmediated contact with nature. A study of the therapeutic value of trees for hospital patients found that, compared with patients whose windows looked out onto brick walls, those whose windows

*From 'The Social Construction of Nature', *ISLE*, 3(2), 1996.

gave them a view of trees required fewer painkillers and were discharged earlier. The frame here is a healing one. We not only need this sort of contact, we need to communicate it, examine it, and share its meaning through our symbolic sign systems. Our semiology of nature keeps us sane by reminding us that we are animals.

Our semiology also communicates conceptions and attitudes toward things in the very act of naming them. In *Keywords* Williams distinguishes between Nature – 'the inherent force that directs either the world or human beings or both' – and nature – 'the material world itself, taken as including or not including human beings' (184). This is the reason Wordsworth writes about Nature and I have been writing about nature. There are, of course, overlapping usages, and Williams gives a brilliant illustration of six examples from *King Lear* (186–7). But at the heart of his six pages of definition is the statement that 'any full history of the uses of "nature" would be a large part of the history of human thought' (186). Here Williams is sharing the theoretical position of the Americans Roderick Nash and Max Oelschlaeger that 'nature' is a way of thinking. Notions of nature are, of course, socially constructed and determine our perception of our direct experiences, which, in turn, determine our communications about them. I see and hear the rain through my window, but already its meaning for me will be framed by my socialized perception of it. It may signify the source of life, or the pollution of life. Similarly my poem about it may be perceived by readers as a nature poem, or an ecological protest. Williams himself never formulated the phrase 'the social construction of nature' and it has not been formulated by the few writers who have, in fact, been deploying the concept of 'nature' as a cultural construct.

Like Neil Evernden, I am indebted to two writers on the sociology of knowledge who, in 1967, published an influential book with a challenging title; Peter L. Berger and Thomas Luckmann's *The Social Construction of Reality* elaborated a theory of language that can now be seen to be poststructuralist and to have much in common with Mikhail Bakhtin's theory of dialogics. For Berger and Luckmann, 'language is capable of becoming the objective repository of vast accumulations of meaning and experience' (52) by which subjective experience is given shared cultural meaning. But 'since socialization is never complete' (166), these meanings are continuously being qualified at an individual and at a social level: 'the relationship between man, the producer, and the social world, his product, is and remains a dialectical one' (78). Of course, poetry is one form of this dialectic, although the poet may choose the degree to which he or she challenges or qualifies or endorses this unstable shared meaning. Indeed, the poet may be aware that there is a diversity of conflicting categories of shared meanings in different social groups, and one of those categories can be the expected poet's view. Thus the World War I poet Edward Thomas can ask, 'And as for seeing things as in themselves they really are . . . what is a fine summer's day as in itself it really is? Is the meteorological office to decide? or the poet? or the farmer?' (Smith 105). One does not think of Edward Thomas as a deconstructionist, but here he is deconstructing some significations of 'a fine summer's day'.

One development from the 1960s sociology of knowledge has been the 1980s study of 'cultural politics'. In a recent series of books from Manchester University

Press under this general title, two by Simon Pugh deal directly with notions of nature. (The second of them, *Reading Landscape: Country-city-capital*, edited by Pugh, is dedicated to Raymond Williams.) It is in *Garden-nature-language* that Pugh, who is not a writer on literature but on garden history, makes the next generation's restatement of Williams's pioneering six-page definition of 'nature' in *Keywords*:

> The 'natural' is the cultural meaning read into nature, meaning determined by those with the power and the money to use nature instrumentally, as a disguise, as a subterfuge, as a pretence that things were always thus, unchangeable and inevitable, which they never were. . . . The garden is a better remade nature, but in respecting the inherent goodness of nature, what is unpleasant in the real world becomes 'unnatural'. In both cases 'nature' is a recipient of social values and becomes a social construct. What nature really is is not in question. The implications of this for a world fast on the way to destroying its environment is [*sic*] self-evident.
>
> (Pugh 2)

The last part of this is less than convincing. A concern for an environment under threat needs to be underpinned by some sense of 'what nature really is.' The problem with the deconstructionists of the 'cultural studies' school is that their purely intellectual awareness of 'nature' seems to prevent them from communicating a direct experience of nature from any perspective whatever. There are no smells in Pugh's garden. There is only the problem of 'the pleasure of the capital wealth that it represents' (114). Raymond Williams, for all his tendency toward abstractions like 'structure of feeling' (*Country*, 22), does take his starting point from 'the heavy smell, on still evenings, of the silage ricks' outside his window (12).

The American Wordsworth scholar Alan Liu would deny that these sensuous realities are nature at all: they are simply themselves. When he says, 'There is no nature', he is pointing out that the word is a human construct: 'Nature is the name under which we use the nonhuman to validate the human, to interpose a mediation able to make humanity more easy with itself' (38). While Liu is right to identify the word *nature* as 'a mediation', he is wrong to deny the general physical presence that is one side of that mediation. There has to be a nature to be called 'nature'. While he is correct in pointing out that our *use* of the term *nature* is an abstraction he is wrong to suggest that it makes humanity 'more easy with itself'. This may hold true for pastoral poets, but for many contemporary poets their exploration of their relationship with nature is a matter of unease. As Jonathan Bate says in discussing Liu's proposition, '"Nature" is a term that needs to be contested, not rejected' (56). If we contest these notions as Bate suggests, we can at least choose which conception of nature we can provisionally live with and explore in our poetry about nature. Ultimately this should lead to a debate about which notions are most useful to our survival and that of the planet.

The problem with those poststructuralists who contest everything at once and are therefore only able to answer a question with another question is the pretense that they are not using provisional assumptions in order to communicate. Choosing provisional notions of nature is crucial to considered action. And whether we like it or not we act upon the environment every day. A similar pretense is perpetrated by the fashionable postmodernist construct of the complete fragmentation of experience. When my students say, 'But there are no "grand narratives" possible any more,' I say, 'We are living them. We call them "growth and decay", "the seasons", "a river".' I point to my balding head as a not-so-grand narrative, in flux, capable of many representations and demanding constant questioning, but following a natural narrative of decay. Daily, postmodernists have to use an active, if tentative, concept of ageing, or of justice, or of environmentalism, however these concepts have been socially constructed.

So what I have termed, following Berger and Luckmann, 'the social construction of nature' represents the view that there can be no 'innocent' reference to nature in a poem. Any reference will implicitly or explicitly express a notion of nature that relates to culturally developed assumptions about metaphysics, aesthetics, politics, and status – that is, in many cases, ideologies. In other words, in literature nature is culture. In poetry, with its particularly self-conscious discourse, culture is nature. . . .

A personal notion of nature will always be in dialectical relation to socially constructed notions of nature. The poem is a site where writer and reader negotiate that dialectic of personal and social meanings. Literary criticism is, of course, the exchange of reports from that imaginative encounter. It is an articulation of what has been provisionally taken for granted and what has been provisionally taken as suspect in the text. To put it another way, 'Consciousness, mind, imagination and language are fundamentally wild. "Wild" as in wild ecosystems-richly interconnected, interdependent, and incredibly complex. Diverse, ancient, and full of information' (Snyder 29). Here Gary Snyder is implying that in articulating and evaluating that 'information', literary criticism is one way of nature itself thinking. Through the elaboration and questioning of notions of nature in poetry the human species is learning, still, how to live on the earth now.

WORKS CITED

Bate, Jonathan (1991) *Romantic Ecology*, London: Routledge.

Berger, Peter L. and Thomas Luckmann (1967) *The Social Construction of Reality*, Harmondsworth: Penguin.

Evernden, Neil (1992) *The Social Creation of Nature*, Baltimore, MD: Johns Hopkins University Press.

Liu, Alan (1989) *Wordsworth: The Sense of History*, Stanford, CA: Stanford University Press.

Pugh, Simon (1988) *Garden-nature-language*, Manchester: Manchester University Press.

Smith, Stan (1986) *Edward Thomas*, London: Faber & Faber.

Snyder, Gary (1994) 'Nature Writing', *Resurgence*, 163 (March/April): 29.

Williams, Raymond (1973) *The Country and the City*, London: Chatto & Windus.

—— (1976) *Keywords*, London: Fontana.

32

Representing the Environment

LAWRENCE BUELL*

[THE REFERENTIAL DIMENSION]

TO MOST LAY readers, nothing seems more obvious than the proposition that literature of a descriptive cast, be it 'fictional' or 'nonfictional', portrays 'reality', even if imperfectly. John Stuart Mill, who found solace in Wordsworth's compelling rendition of physical nature, would have been astonished by the stinginess of the modern argument that Wordsworth reckoned nature as at best a convenience and at worst an impediment to the imagination. Most amateur Thoreauvians would find equally strange the claim that in Thoreau's *Journal* 'when the mind sees nature what it sees is its difference from nature', a million-word paper trail of unfulfilled desire.[1] In contemporary literary theory, however, the capacity of literary writers to render a faithful mimesis of the object world is reckoned indifferent at best, and their interest in doing so is thought to be a secondary concern.

One basis for this divergence between commonsensical and specialized wisdom may be that the modern understanding of how environmental representation works has been derived from the study of the fictive genres rather than nonfiction. The consequence of this is suggested by the common omnibus term used for designating the sphere of the nonhuman environment in literary works: setting. It deprecates what it denotes, implying that the physical environment serves for artistic purposes merely as backdrop, ancillary to the main event. The most ambitious monograph on place in literature criticizes Thomas Hardy's evocation of Egdon heath (which 'almost puts his work into the kind of place-saturated fiction which is expressly devoted to the assault upon a mountain') and commends by contrast the Parisian chapters of Henry James's *Ambassadors* as containing 'the barest minimum of detail and the maximum of personal reflection on these details.'[2] In 'good' writing, then, it would seem that the biota has only a bit part. If we map literary history from this angle of vision, we reinforce the impression that attentive representation of environmental detail is of minor importance even in writing

*From *The Environmental Imagination: Thoreau, Nature Writing, and the Formation of American Culture*, Cambridge, MA: Harvard University Press, 1995.

where the environment figures importantly as an issue. In American literature, the main canonical forms of environmental writing are the wilderness romance and the lyric meditation on the luminous natural image or scene. Cooper's *Deerslayer*, Faulkner's 'Bear', Bryant's poem 'To the Fringed Gentian', Whitman's 'Out of the Cradle', Robert Frost's 'Design' – of such is the core of these traditions comprised. It is easy to persuade oneself on the basis of the average critical discussion of these works that the literary naturescape exists for its formal or symbolic or ideological properties rather than as a place of literal reference or as an object of retrieval or contemplation for its own sake. It is unthinkable that Bryant could have sought to immerse himself in the natural history of the gentian, or Frost in observing spiders. And so professors of literature, whatever their behavior in ordinary life, easily become antienvironmentalists in their professional practice.

Yet the explanation cannot simply be that literature specialists mostly study novels and poems, for during the past two decades we have ranged freely across the human sciences, subjecting ethnography and phenomenology and even scientific monographs to literary analysis almost as readily as sonnets and short stories. Today, as Carolyn Porter has said, 'we confront a virtually horizonless discursive field in which . . . the traditional boundaries between the literary and the extraliterary have faded.'[3] No doubt we have derived our critical skepticism or disdain for the notion that literature does or can represent physical reality from the idea of writing as construct, whether this idea takes the form of the old-fashioned formalist theory of the literary work as artifact or the contemporary theory of writing as discourse. Thus, during the very half-century since Aldo Leopold, as environmental writing in America has unprecedentedly thriven, literary theory has been making the idea of a literature devoted to recuperating the tactical environment seem quaintly untheoretical. All major strains of contemporary literary theory have marginalized literature's referential dimension by privileging structure, text(uality), ideology, or some other conceptual matrix that defines the space discourse occupies apart from tactical 'reality', as . . . Foucault imagines having been done once and for all during the classical era. New critical formalism did so by insisting that the artifact was its own world, a heterocosm. Structualism and poststructualism broke down the barrier between literary and nonliterary, not however to rejoin literary discourse to the world but to conflate all verbal artifacts within a more spacious domain of textuality. Quarreling with this unworldliness, Marxist and Marxoid (for example, Foucaultian) models of analysis during the 1980s combined with poststructualism in Anglo-America to generate the so-called new historicism, which set text within context. But it did so in terms of the text's status as a species of cultural production or ideological work. In this type of formulation, literature's appropriation of the world in the service of some social allegiance or commitment seemed to render merely epiphenomenal the responsiveness of literature to the natural world either in its self-existence as an assemblage or plenum or in the form of a gestalt that can impress itself on the mind or text in [a] fundamental and binding way. . . . It seems that literature is simply not thought to have the power to do this, that such power it might have is thought to have been overridden by the power of imagination, textuality, and culture over the malleable, plastic world

178

that it bends to its will. Whitman, in 'Song of Myself', may insist that 'I lean and loafe at my ease observing a spear of summer grass', but there is no grass, no summer, no loafer (despite the title-page illustration done from a photograph of Whitman himself). No, there is only an image, a symbol, a projection, a persona, a vestige or democratic deformation of aristocratic pastoral (compare Thomas Gray's 'disporting on the margent green'), a contortion of heptameter.

The historicist movement that succeeded poststructuralism as the dominant theoretical paradigm of literary studies during the 1980s attached greater impor-tance than its formalist and structuralist predecessors to art's mimetic function and might thus seem to be more environment-responsive. Yet it turns out to interpose obstacles no less daunting to making the case for representation in the affirmative sense. The recent dismantling of nineteenth-century realism is instructive here. Within a decade it has become almost hackneyed to point out that so-called realism, far from being a transparent rendering, is a highly stylized ideological or psychohis-torical artifact that we have sloppily agreed to call realistic. The powerful rereading by art historian Michael Fried of the high point of realism in American painting, Thomas Eakins's *Gross Clinic*, is a striking example of the new orthodoxy in forma-tion. Although Fried by no means denies the painting's graphic fidelity to docu-mentary detail (the wincing observers, the blood on the scalpel, the almost violent dominance of the surgeon over the patient and the operating room), he argues that the painting is much more fundamentally shaped by intertextual and psychobio-graphical forces. The referent, the text–clinic correspondence itself, seems almost epiphenomenal.[4]

Ironically, during the same period that 'realism' has been deconstructed, histo-rians and social scientists have often drawn on realistic fiction for evidentiary support. One cultural geographer, for example, praises John Steinbeck's *Grapes of Wrath* as providing 'focus for instruction in migration, settlement forms, economic systems, cultural dualism, agricultural land use patterns, transportation technology and social change'; as well as 'a window on geographic phenomena broadly ranging from mental maps to economic infrastructures'.[5]

And why not? I am not the first to wonder whether the discrediting of realism as an attempted transparency has gone too far. George Levine, for one, urges that 'the dominant distaste for anything that smacks of the empirical' within the human sciences 'needs to be overcome, just as the scientists' tendency to dismiss theory and antirealism must be'. Levine contends that 'the discriminations that have been obliterated between objectivity and subjectivity, scientific and literary discourse, history and fiction, are in effect, still operative' and that they 'need to be recuper-ated, if modified'.[6] His statement about differences in representational mode between disciplines I would apply to the literary field itself. There is a mimetic difference hard to specify but uncontroversial to posit between the Chicago of Theodore Dreiser's *Sister Carrie* and the places of Italo Calvino's *Invisible Cities*, a difference also between Calvino's cities and the cities of Marco Polo's original *Travels*. There is a difference between the relatively 'uncomposed' western photographs of Timothy O'Sullivan and nineteenth-century landscape photographs of a more 'luminist' persuasion like those by Thomas Moran. In the theory – or countermyth

– of representation that I [am proposing], these differences are not just symptoms of Dreiser's petit-bourgeois romance of commodities or Calvino's avant-gardist critique (or perhaps reflection) of the more abstract commodifications of contemporary globalized capitalism. My account of the reality of these fictional realities does not deny that they can profitably be so read but focuses on the recuperation of natural objects and the relation between outer and inner landscapes as primary projects.

[THE AESTHETICS OF DUAL ACCOUNTABILITY]

... The capacity of the stylized image to put the reader or viewer in touch with the environment is precisely what needs stressing as a counter to the assumptions that stylization must somehow work against outer mimesis or take precedence over it. We need to recognize stylization's capacity for what the poet-critic Francis Ponge calls *adequation*: verbalizations that are not replicas but equivalents of the world of objects, such that writing in some measure bridges the abyss that inevitably yawns between language and the object-world.[7]

It should come as no surprise to find the aesthetics of dual accountability applicable beyond the expository, in the realm of fictive poesis as well. Indeed, in poets like Whitman and Gerard Manley Hopkins, inwardness produces outwardness, exuberance produces catalog.

> Glory be to God for dappled things, –
>   For skies of couple-colour as a brindled cow;
>   For rose-moles all in stipple upon trout that swim;
> Fresh-firecoal chestnut-falls; finches' wings;
>   Landscape plotted and pieced – fold, fallow, and plough;
>   And all trades, their gear, and tackle and trim.[8]

What makes Hopkins's exquisite responsiveness to environmental stimuli especially striking is the unlikeliness of it. He views landscape in a mood of prayerful exaltation that could easily have thrust him upward after glancing briefly outward. Indeed, properly speaking this is not a landscape at all. Hopkins creates a collage by darting in all directions at once in search of pied images. His fondness for collecting perceptual bits bespeaks a detachment of the aesthetic specialist from the ordinary landscapes and rhythms of country life. But how delicately responsive the poem is to the stimuli it registers! Who would have thought to see trout's 'rose-moles all in stipple'? In this way, aestheticism produces environmental bonding. Literally, the poet sees a painted fish; effectively, the aestheticist distortion animates the trout and makes its body palpable. There can be no question that this is a live trout shimmering for an instant in Hopkins's imaginary pool. With another glance, Hopkins evokes the feel and look of chestnutfalls, with another the mottled look of the agricultural landscape. So the poem is after all not just a 'space of accumulation' but a tiny energizer that disperses the reader's attention, in imitation of the poet's own, out to various points of environmental contact. Activating this process is an idiosyncratic blend of old-fashioned natural theology and new-fashioned delight in the materiality of natural *things*.

The symbiosis of object-responsiveness and imaginative shaping that we have seen in the series of examples from Lopez to Hopkins, as well as in the theories of Burroughs and Ruskin, calls into question the charges of epistemological naivete and ideological tyranny that have been leveled against 'classic realism' by proponents of the theory of representation. 'The strategies of the classic realist text,' alleges Catherine Belsey, 'divert the reader from what is contradictory within it to the renewed recognition (misrecognition) of what he or she already "knows", knows because the myths and signifying systems of the classic realist text re-present experience in the ways in which it is conventionally articulated in our society.'[9] Clearly this need not be so. Representational projects that aspire to render the object-world need not be monologic, may indeed be founded on self-division about the possibilities of such a project, may even make these self-divisions explicit to the reader, and are as likely to dislocate the reader as to placate her. Indeed it might be quite difficult to find among the realist classics a clear case of classic realism as Belsey defines it.

NOTES

1   Sharon Cameron, *Writing Nature: Henry Thoreau's Journal*, New York: Oxford University Press, 1985, p. 44.

2   Leonard Lutwack, *The Role of Place in Literature*, Syracuse, NY: Syracuse University Press, 1985, p. 24.

3   Carolyn Porter, 'History and Literature: "After the New Historicism"', *New Literary History*, 21, 1990: 257.

4   Michael Fried, *Realism, Writing, Disfiguration*, Chicago: University of Chicago Press, 1987.

5   Christopher Salter, 'John Steinbeck's *The Grapes of Wrath* as a Primer for Cultural Geography', in C.D. Pocock (ed.) *Humanistic Geography and Literature: Essays on Experience of Place*, London: Croom Helm, 1981, pp. 156–7.

6   George Levine, 'Scientific Realism and Literary Representation', *Raritan*, 10(4), 1991: 23, 21.

7   For exemplification, see Francis Ponge's collection of prose-poems, *The Voice of Things* (ed. and trans. Beth Archer), New York: McGraw Hill, 1974.

8   *Gerald Manley Hopkins: A Selection of his Poems and Prose* (ed. Helen Gardner) Harmondsworth: Penguin, 1953, 'Pied Beauty', p. 30.

9   Catherine Belsey, *Critical Practice*, London: Methuen, 1980, p. 128.

33

Radical Pastoral?

GREG GARRARD*

RADICAL PASTORAL: IN literary-critical circles in the 1980s, the phrase had come to appear as oxymoronic as 'military intelligence' or 'humane slaughter', and for certain specific theoretical reasons. In the 1990s, however, driven by a powerful sense of anxiety regarding the state of our natural environment, a new group of literary critics has started to reinterpret the literary canon in order to make sense of this conjunction. They have found English and American romanticism congenial surroundings from which to launch a coherent attack on the critical orthodoxies of today. It is important to clarify some of the matters of literary theory that this recuperative project involves. . . .

THE NEWER HISTORICISM

Looking for the meaning of 'radical pastoral', it is first necessary to examine the critical hegemony that would most object to the phrase, that is most hostile to ecocriticism, and that nevertheless seems its *sine qua non*: historicism. In romantic studies it is Jerome McGann who is credited with developing the modern critique of romantic ideology, and thus takes most of the flak from ecocritics like Jonathan Bate or Karl Kroeber. Raymond Williams' *The Country and the City* anticipates his demand for Wordsworth, for example, to be read with an eye on the real social and political history which the poetry only partly addresses, but McGann is indebted far more than Williams to the 'hermeneutic of suspicion', characterized by Kroeber as an '[extension of] Cold War psychology into literary scholarship' (Kroeber 39). The genealogy of this practice is complex, but the axiomatic form is that provided by Walter Benjamin:

> There is no document of civilization which is not at the same time a document of barbarism. And just as such a document is not free of barbarism, barbarism taints also the manner in which it was transferred

*From 'Radical Pastoral?', *Studies in Romanticism*, 35(3), 1996.

from one owner to another. A historical materialist therefore dissociates himself from it as far as possible. He regards it as his task to brush history against the grain.

(Benjamin 248)

Several things are clear from this quote, not least of which is the superiority of the critic over the artist which it implies and endorses. Interpretation is about the discovery of 'barbarism' in the monuments of magnificence which were happily (and barbarically) reproduced through generations of ideological complicity. The aseptic critic has the job of finding the signs of the repression of 'history' (as the absolute *locus* of truth) in the faint-hearted artist and his or her genetic descendants, and exposing the disreputable truth. Thus Antony Easthope can describe a kind of criticism that accepts 'at face value' Wordsworth's intentions as a poet as 'collaborationist', with all the cruel connotations that this term brings with it (Easthope 129). For McGann, the job of historicist critics is to show how an artistic production 'historicizes the ideological materials, gives a local habitation and a name to various kinds of abstractions,' and to trace the ensuing process of reiification by critics anxious to deny their status as 'alien creatures' relative to the deeply *archaic* works they study (McGann 11, 2).

At least this approach has the advantage of accepting a notion of the 'independently real', which is more than can be said for the radical textualism of the deconstructive formalism that preceded it – it is this shift which seems to have given positive opportunities to ecocriticism. However, the admirable attempt to contrast real social and economic conditions with their representations in romantic poetry carries with it the anthropocentric bias of a certain distinctive *construction* of history. We can therefore historicize historicism, and suggest that a preoccupation with non-human nature is not *per se* an evasion of any kind. Indeed, the idea that it might be is itself founded on another, related mistake: that 'politics' is finally only about social relations between humans. In other words, that famous *zoon politikon* has only its own affairs to study, as indeed the etymological relationship between *polis* and 'politics' suggests. Thus McGann praises Heine (with no apparent sense of irony) for his ability to situate artworks critically in their 'concrete and human environment', although it is only recently that the environment has come to seem predominantly 'human' or 'concrete' (McGann 13). The new criticism would counter that sincere interest in the economy of nature is not *necessarily* a 'compensation' for anything but the political and historical *Ding an sich.*

This reduction of politics to the business of human society is looking increasingly untenable, just as the Marxist ideology that drives the historicist project is looking increasingly marginal even in terms of this reduced definition. Thus Bate describes the left–right confrontation that structures their anthropocentric politics as 'crude' and 'redundant', while Kroeber's 'Cold War' appellation suggests that a merely destructive anachronism is at stake here (Bate 3, Kroeber 5). Insofar as both capitalism and historically-instantiated Marxism subscribe to a notion of continuous economic growth at odds with the limited resources and capacities of the earth, these claims seem justified. However, they should be qualified by an historical awareness of both the 'left entryism' that characterizes and moulds modern 'Green' movements, and the appropriation of ecologism by Nazism. Perhaps 'ecologism', as a complex cultural formation, represents an 'excess' over conventional political categories – it can neither be subsumed within them, nor assumed to have simply superseded them. Perhaps the term 'post-political' would be useful, if by 'post' we understand the kind of ambiguous, contested and partial entail that it suggests in 'postmodern', for example. In any case, there is little question that ecopolitics represent, even for socialists, an important *political* force in contemporary society, far outstripping Marxism and rivalled only by feminist and ethnic movements in terms of counterhegemonic potential. Where Marxism survives, it does so in Maoist forms that appeal to the rural poor rather than Marx's proletariat, and even here there may be admixtures of ecologism.

Thus the new readings of romanticism have arisen asserting the centrality of nature in Wordsworth and Shelley, building on a far earlier critical tradition but assigning a new political significance to their impassioned, contradictory writing. Ironically, Williams (a progenitor of historicism) had seen the genuine importance of the new poetry that was launched with the *Lyrical Ballads*:

> [Wordsworth's] active sympathy is the real change of mind, the new consciousness if only in a minority, in the very period in which the willed transformation of nature, not only of the land and water but of its raw materials and its essential elements, was to enter a new phase, in the processes we now call industrial.
>
> (Williams 127)

Where Easthope, responding to the 'Boy of Winander' scene in Book V of *The Prelude,* doubts parenthetically 'whether you really can mimic owls in this way' (Easthope 2) (you can, and you can even attract them by this means), Williams is able to see in Wordsworth a real 'confidence in nature, in its own workings, which at least in the beginning was also a broader, a more humane confidence in men' (Williams 127). These remarkable new forms of 'sympathy' and 'confidence' do not sound like mere delusions, but the central elements in a new, perhaps radical, form of pastoral. . . .

CIVIC IRONY AND PATHETIC FALLACY

Our feeling for nature is like the feeling of an invalid for health.

Schiller could not have known, writing in 1795–6, the resonances this phrase would have for us now, in a time of terrible sickness. We feel, as Wordsworth does in 'The world is too much with us', an alienation that seems less inevitable than historical – for these as well as for Puskin and Nietzsche, 'the Greeks' are posited as a site of a certain *health*. In our idealizations of aboriginal peoples, especially indigenous Americans, we reiterate this logic of nostalgia as the loss of the hypostatized Other. As a result, ecophilosophers call for an ethical relinquishment or 'ecocentrism' that finds an echo, for example, in Lawrence Buell's fruitless search for an 'aesthetics of relinquishment' of subjectivity in the American lyric, 'imaging human selves as unstable constellations of matter occupying one among innumerable niches in an interactive biota' (Buell 167). Yet here alarm bells ring – 'unstable' in what sense exactly? Just one amongst others, yet also the writers of poetry? Indeed, the recognition of an *historical* loss is precisely an account of an alienation prescribed by *temporality*, a state shared by [the native North American] Lakota, archaic Athenians and modern Welshmen. Robert Harrison has pointed that *material* interdependence, and the obvious myopia of atomistic humanism, cannot elide *ontological* difference that has language as its ultimate ground: 'Language is a differential, a standing-outside of nature, an *ecstasis* that opens a space of intelligibility within nature's closure' (Harrison 200). But there again, we know that we are evolved, that absolute difference must be impossible, that we are consubstantial and kin with animals.

This problem, which I suspect is *undecidable,* is also the problem of pathetic fallacy and hence a critical issue for romantic poets and for us. Bate assumes that Wordsworth envisaged a 'marriage of humankind to the natural world – "the very world which is the world / Of all of us, the place in which, in the end, / We find our happiness, or not at all"' (Bate 33; Wordsworth, *The Prelude* 10.725–7). This is to naturalize and resolve what was *a real choice* – longing, or belonging?

Kroeber attempts the ecophilosophical sleight-of-hand clumsily: 'The romantics . . . believed that humankind *belonged* in, could and should be at home within, the world of natural processes' (Kroeber 5). The space between the prescriptive and descriptive here marks a real *aporia*. Yet this view is belied by his sensitive reading of 'I heard a thousand blended notes,' which finds Wordsworth quite uncertain, and in that sense modern. Thus, 'the poet finds himself *constrained* to entertain the notion of the twig's pleasure' (Kroeber 45) while simultaneously qualifying his feeling almost out of existence. It is this undecided quality that allows Harrison to read the same poem as a 'testimony of civic irony' (Harrison 164) that bears witness to the poet's temporal alienation (as 'man') even as it asserts that his 'human soul' is linked to nature. We might note also the second half of the third stanza: 'faith' attaches to 'enjoys' in a tentative natural pleasure principle, while 'breathes' reminds us of the natural science that does not need to be questioned as 'creed'.

It is this puzzlement, not its resolutions, which mark romanticism as proto-ecological. Human/nature is posed as a question, just as today it is. Ruskin's account, although situated within an historically-nostalgic history, highlights something of our confusion whilst clearly addressing Wordsworth's:

And then, puzzled, and yet happy; pleased, and yet ashamed of being so; accepting sympathy from nature, which we do not believe it gives and giving sympathy to nature, which we do not believe it receives . . . we necessarily fall into the curious web of hesitating sentiment, pathetic fallacy, and wandering fancy, which form a great part of our modern view of nature.

(Ruskin, *Modern Painters* III.IV.xiii)

185

The radicalism of pastoral is not given, because the meanings of both terms are always at stake. Shelley represents a quasi-pastoral Utopianism – politically radical but strongly humanistic – while in Wordsworth the problematic of pastoral is central but unresolved, in a conflicting play of spiritual and material fidelities.

We are less sure than Marxists what would *count* as 'radicalism': Advocacy or idealization; pathetic fallacy or naturalism; social ecology or the dream of relinquishment. Thus the radical problem of pastoral: It may cloud our social vision, or open out a human ecological one; it may help in the marginalization of nature into 'pretty ghettoes' (Buell 4) or engender a genuine counter-hegemonic ideology. If pastoral can be radical, if it has been so, it is not as a finished model, exhortation or ideology, but as a questioning, as itself a question. With a new appreciation of the literal, and a theory of the pathetic fallacy as ontological problematic, and a recognition of the special power of poetry to hold in suspension the undecidable, 'radical pastoral?' appears as the political, poetical question of be/longing, of the root of human being on this earth.

WORKS CITED

Bate, Jonathan (1991) *Romantic Ecology: Wordsworth and the Environmental Tradition*, London and New York: Routledge.

Benjamin, Walter (1973) *Illuminations* (ed. Hannah Arendt), London: Fontana.

Buell, Lawrence (1995) *The Environmental Imagination: Thoreau, Nature Writing and the Formation of American Culture*, Cambridge, MA: Harvard University Press.

Easthope, Antony (1993) *Wordsworth Now and Then*, Buckingham: Open University Press.

Harrison, Robert Pogue (1992) *Forests: The Shadow of Civilization*, Chicago: University of Chicago Press.

Kroeber, Karl (1994) *Ecological Literary Criticism: Romantic Imagining and the Biology of Mind*, New York: Columbia University Press.

McGann, Jerome (1983) *The Romantic Ideology: A Critical Investigation*, Chicago: University of Chicago Press.

Williams, Raymond ([1973] 1993) *The Country and the City*, London: Hogarth Press.

34

Green Cultural Studies

Jhan Hochman*

[THE CATEGORY OF 'WORLDNATURE']

A SATELLITE TOPOGRAPHY of the English literary tradition since the Industrial Revolution might show nature as a spiritual-imaginative object in the Romantic climes, as a religious or scientific object in the Victorian domain, and as a symbolic/formal object in the Modern realm. In the territory of Postmodernity, nature, probably due to its rapid decimation, emerges as a politico-cultural object, one which is no longer restricted to literature, 'fine' art, and formalist cinema and video, but also has starring roles in commercials, photos, and movies, and is at the center of heated public debates about 'ecocide', 'ecoterrorism', 'ecopornography', 'greenwashing' and 'animal rights'. Responding to these concerns, academia has itself developed a variety of subdisciplines – 'ecopsychology', 'ecological economics', 'ecofeminism', 'ecosophy' – as well as the many orientations named by adding the adjective *environmental:* science, law, ethics, history. In the humanities, the academic response has primarily taken the form of 'ecocriticism', a literature-based approach within a still loosely federated but emerging field generally designated as 'green cultural studies'.

As the term suggests, green cultural studies has major affinities with cultural studies, whose prevalent concern has been the impact that texts and social practices have upon ethnicity/color, gender, sexuality, economic class, and age (particularly youth subcultures). The origins of green cultural studies could in this sense be located in the admission of a newcomer into this nexus of concerns: namely, nature (plants, animals, elements, or what I have frequently called 'worldnature' or the 'fifth world'). . . . Within this context . . . the project of green cultural studies is the examination of nature through words, image, and model for the purpose of foregrounding potential effects representation might have on cultural attitudes and social practices which, in turn, affect nature itself. What this also means, however, is that green cultural studies must be equally cautious of the impact that it – like other forms of representation – can have on nature. . . .

*From 'Green Cultural Studies: An Introductory Critique of an Emerging Discipline', *Mosaic* 30(1), 1997.

What seems to have been overlooked or ignored [in the critique of the use of the word 'nature' by proponents of conventional cultural studies] is that to assert an ontological worldnature is not necessarily to claim an epistemological Nature as the realm of Truth or knowable referent(s) recognized through the heroism of Human Thought. Cannot one aver nature's existence without claiming to know the particular Framework to which that existence must conform? While existence and essence may not be ultimately separate at thought's vanishing point, distinguishing them is hardly avoidable. It is, of course, paramount to cultivate suspicion of claims of 'common sense', 'common knowledge', and of Truth, but it seems puerile centrism or regressive religiosity (ourselves as gods) to render all existence dependent on human senses, language, culture. . . .

[CULTURE AS NATURE?]

Perhaps the confusion about the cultural construction of nature is the word, *construction*: *to construct* a house, an artifact, means 'to cause to exist', as well as 'to fashion'. The cultural *construction* of nature, however, must clearly be restricted to the latter sense, if not to sound like nonsense. Conversely, that culture fashions and manipulates worldnature, that it has invented the word *nature* with its multiple meanings, hardly needs arguing.

One could, perhaps, optimistically argue that worldnature has not yet been swallowed up by culture, or that the trend of nature's destruction by intellectual and industrial culture is reversing since nature is now dubbed – supposedly indicating a new awareness of nature – *environment*. This term, however, runs another risk related to chronic, excessive anthropocentrism. *Environment* is not inclusive of all plants, animals, and elements, and furthermore the term has increasingly come to mean a nature tangibly important only to human health or livelihood. We thereby cease to pay as much attention when nature is destroyed by manipulation, development, consumerism, and dumping as long as *our* environment stays intact. This merely anthropocentric brand of environmentalism would be fine if nature were not simultaneously precluded as important in itself, for itself, outside human considerations.

More shrapnel against nature issues from an unrestrained blurring of the nature/culture boundary: the idea that technology is nature, is an aid to 'reinventing' nature. Here, I have Donna Haraway in mind, formidable critic of the biological sciences but problematic advocate of nature:

> In the belly of the local/global monster in which I am gestating, often called the postmodern world, global technology appears to *denature* everything, to make everything a malleable matter of strategic decisions and mobile production and reproduction processes. Technological decontextualization is ordinary experience for hundreds of millions if not billions of human beings, as well as other organisms. I suggest that this is not a *denaturing* so much as a *particular production* of nature.
>
> ('Promises' 297)

Unlike the previous instance of boundary blurring, where concrete nature was vulnerable to absorption by culture, Haraway's suggestion that technology is a 'particular production of nature' is a sub-set of the argument that everything, including culture and technology, is n/Nature.

The contention that everything is nature is surely difficult to dispute. But what might result from such a statement? Haraway's suggestion seems already to have been co-opted by developers, scientists, and technophiles who argue that they and their products are part of nature. Already we have a car commercial in which a slowly panning shot of a dashboard in close-up reveals its gradual metamorphosis into a rocky landscape. Other commercials portray cars as revered hunting animals, superior to wolves who admire and envy the particular car's speed and traction. Haraway's assertion that technology is nature also seems to be a veiled attempt to call upon nature to justify technology, to naturalize technology as intrinsic to humanity, as good. As cultural studies has long noted, the naturalization argument is extremely faulty and dangerous: by such reasoning, for example, circumcision and clitoridectomy can also be called natural – not a genital mutilation which 'denatures' the human body as much as a 'particular production' of nature, producing merely 'altered' or 'fixed' bodies (terms already used to refer to the mutilated bodies of pets). If one employs even some amateur psychology it is not too difficult to see why technoculture gets naturalized, even promoted, by the environmentally-minded: technology's out-of-sight and out-of-mind processes of extraction, production, consumption and disposal make damage to nature seem non-existent or minimal. Even dropping bombs on unseen 'targets' better connects cause to effect.

Maintaining that technology is a particular production of nature is probably one thing Haraway meant by *The Reinvention of Nature*, the subtitle of her *Simians, Cyborgs, and Women* (presumably she means the *concept of* nature or the *cultural construction* of nature, not worldnature itself). Yet Haraway should have been more careful with the phrase, 'reinvention of nature', and more attentive to the consequences of not putting 'nature' within quotation marks. Imagine the indignation if heterosexuals, men, and whites called for the reinvention of gays and lesbians, women, people of color, respectively. Would it not be more accurate to call for the 'reinvention of culture', or even the less catchy and dramatic, 'reinvention of cultural concepts of nature'? One such possible re-invention is of culture as a technological weapon of mass destruction unleashed on nature. . . .

[WHO SPEAKS FOR NATURE?]

Finally, I want to address what I hope is not a tired issue when it comes to green concerns – that of who speaks for nature. . . . Haraway complains against [the notion of] environmentalist as 'ventriloquist' ('Promises' 313). Haraway is irritated by the question, 'Who speaks for the jaguar?' asked by Joe Kane in his review of Susanna Hecht's *The Fate of the Forest* (26). Why? Because, Haraway says, the question 'was precisely like that asked by some pro-life groups in the abortion debates:

Who speaks for the fetus?' (311). Both questions irritate Haraway because they complicate her resolute pro-choice position. Though I do not doubt Haraway's 'care about the survival of the jaguar', I believe that she tries to disembowel a difficult environmental issue by relying too comfortably on a more easily discredited abortion argument.

I believe or at least hope that most environmentalists and animal-rights advocates . . . do not think of themselves as ventriloquists putting words into the mouths of (dumb) animals. Environmentalists and animal-rights advocates might be better characterized as *representing* jaguars or speaking, as Andrew Ross says, *in the name* of jaguars ('Interview' 58); for this, as I see it, means speaking for *the survival and the continued well-being* of the jaguar, which, with or without a jaguar's sanction, is less problematic than not representing them at all. For instance, in June 1994, a US federal appeals court ruled that those who denounce laboratory torture of birds and rodents were not legal plaintiffs. Legal plaintiffs would only be animals who spoke out for themselves! Increasingly, however, not even *human* plaintiffs speak out for themselves. Their lawyers do. Yet what is so interesting about this criticism of 'ventriloquism' by those like Haraway and Ross who seek a blurred line between nature and culture is a call for separation of animal and human, nature and culture when it comes to speaking (out) for animals. If, as Haraway mentions, there is no longer any convincing boundary between human and animals, why should animals not be represented by people, just as people are represented by people. It could even be convincingly argued that animals, like people who cannot or do not represent themselves, are the ones most in need of representation.

Yet Haraway . . . would still complain about the phrase, 'speaking in the name of', since it addresses jaguars as if they were not connected to the larger picture of forests with indigenous peoples, just as speaking for fetuses seems to imply that they are not connected to the larger picture, mothers ('Promises' 312). Though these connections of individual with environment are different, Haraway's complaint is worth entertaining. It is part and parcel of that more quotidian argument that demanding the preservation of nature usually involves callousness toward people. This argument resembles one conservative response to identity politics: that marginalized groups 'singled out' for what some cultural conservatives call 'special treatment' will lead to conservatives, themselves, being marginalized by 'reverse discrimination', that attention to the rights of women, people of color, gays and lesbians will turn white heterosexual men into the Other.

When it comes to the rights of nature, even a certain Leftist element boards this 'special treatment' bandwagon, claiming that focus on nature hurts jobs, ignores third- and fourth-world peoples, is anti-human. Within the ranks of environmentalists, some Earth-First members and deep ecologists maintain that animal rights calls for the special treatment of animals. By and large, these are flawed arguments; 'special treatment' is much more about getting decent, equal, or appropriate treatment, about avoiding the worse kinds of treatment.

The problem, then, is this: how can plants, animals, and elements, even disparaged people, gain decent, equal treatment, within and outside cultural studies? The recourse to the argument that 'we're all connected, people to people and people to nature', is of too limited appeal for the following reason: mother and fetus can be disconnected; people's bodies are increasingly disconnected from each other; animals (even those with emotions and intelligence) are routinely sacrificed; plants (even those with value when alive) are cut down without a second thought. In cases like these, a plea to 'only connect' appears futile. 'Connection', regretfully, is ignored or scoffed at by people increasingly cut off from each other and nature. Besides, why should connection be a precondition for care? Can care not be directed at those deemed different or unconnected? Maybe it is time to argue for life and liberty without the tedious rationales of difference or similarity, rationales often rooted in intelligence or consciousness.

One could argue that Deleuze and Guattari – though far more concerned with breaking down than reasserting the culture/nature, animal/human boundary – offer a more promising scenario than Haraway, one dialectically careful not to abandon the advantages accruing to borders and boundaries, to separations in terms of 'molar individuals' and 'subjects' on 'planes of organization'. Their view of 'becoming-in-the-world' (in contrast to a more fixed, being-in-the-world) incorporates structuralism (boundaries, limits, identities) with post-structuralism (transgressions, joyous confusions, protean fluctuations) into a shape-shifting multiplicitous postmodernism. After pages of lexical spawning, of darting and diving in fluid non-separation – where 'molecular multiplicities' are 'haeccities' 'deterritorializing', 'involuting', becoming 'bodies without organs' on a 'plane of consistency', in short, where the human can, at least, 'become animal' – Deleuze and Guattari slow down to counsel sobriety:

> But once again so much caution is needed to prevent the plane of consistency from becoming a pure plane of abolition or death, to prevent the involution from turning into a regression to the undifferentiated. Is it not necessary to retain a minimum of strata, a minimum of forms and functions, a minimal subject from which to extract materials, affects, and assemblages?
>
> (278)

And when or where are these minimal strata, subjects, etc., to be retained, even if temporarily? Their answer is, in the realm of politics:

> It is, of course, indispensable for women to conduct a molar politics, with a view to winning back their own organism, their own history, their own subjectivity: 'we as women . . .' makes its appearance as a subject of enunciation. But it is dangerous to confine oneself to such a subject, which does not function without drying up a spring or stopping a flow. . . . It is thus necessary to conceive of a molecular women's politics that slips into molar confrontations, and passes under or through them.
>
> (276)

Deleuze and Guattari's sense of movement is their strength: first, their advocacy of 'becoming-other' along a 'plane of consistency' (an improvement over 'imitation' or 'identification'); and second, their move from the plane of consistency – where no impervious boundaries exist between nature and culture, animal and human, that plane of *temporary and strategic* becomings – to a 'plane of organization', that realm of subjects and individuals, of *temporary and strategic* fixities.

If green cultural studies is to be an effective politico-cultural tool in the service of nature and culture, it will need to study not only how to 'become' nature, how to attempt a merging with the real or imagined subjectivity of a plant, animal, or mineral, of air, water, earth and fire; it will also need to pull back and grant these beings and entities unromanticized difference, an autonomy apart from humans, a kind of privacy and regard heretofore granted almost exclusively only to those considered human. Nature and culture cannot be willed together by glibly naturalizing culture, by culture simplistically proclaiming itself part of nature, or by stupidly making worldnature into an appendage of culture, worldnature into a culturally constructed product. Any substantial (reciprocal) merging of nature and culture will take generations of internal cultural struggle. Green cultural studies and human culture would do well to ensure that plants and animals are granted separateness, independence, and liberation (an apartness distinct from excusing and advocating separation because of superiority) before mucking about too much with forced fusions and coalescences. Otherwise it is nature who/that will suffer most by this shotgun marriage with culture(s) made monstrous by thousands of years of naturalized atrocities against plants, animals, and elements.

WORKS CITED

Deleuze, Gilles, and Felix Guattari (1987) A *Thousand Plateaus: Capitalism and Schizophrenia* (trans. Brian Massumi), Minneapolis, MN: Minnesota University Press.

Haraway, Donna (1992) *Simians, Cyborgs, and Women: The Reinvention of Nature*, New York: Routledge.

—— (1992) 'The Promises of Monsters: A Regenerative Politics for Inappropriate/d Others', in Lawrence Grossberg, Cary Nelson and Paula Treichler (eds) *Cultural Studies*, New York: Routledge.

Kane, Joe (1990) Review of *Fate of the Forest*, by Susanna Hecht and Alexander Cockburn, *Voice Literary Supplement*, February: 26.

Ross, Andrew (1994) 'Interview: "Green Ideas Sleep Furiously"', *Lingua Franca*, December: 57–65.

35

Ecofeminist Dialogics

Patrick D. Murphy*

I

PLURALISTIC HUMANISM HAS run its course. What may have once encouraged individual growth and intellectual diversity for some components of the culture is now producing a *laissez-faire* attitude that truncates the debate over cultural values through nonjudgmental or 'undecidability' postures. As Gerald Graff has trenchantly suggested, 'real disagreement has become rare, for the multiplicity of tongues leads not to confrontation but to incommensurability and talking at cross-purposes' (*Literature* 190). The various cataclysms of the twentieth century that dethroned the idealist humanism that posited the linear progression of western civilization did not dethrone the anthropocentrism of religious and secular humanism, nor did they disrupt the androcentrism that arises from the patriarchal base of western culture. Similarly, the theoretical projects that arose to challenge humanism have produced an energetic scepticism and a shifting of foci of theoretical and critical attention, but they have promoted neither a world view that enables any kind of affirmation of new values nor a praxis that enables the application of such values in the physical world. In marked contrast to the critical maladies of enervated humanism, solipsistic scepticism, and paralytic undecidability, a triad of (re)perceptions has appeared, which, if integrated, can lead toward an affirmative praxis: the Bakhtinian dialogical method, ecology, and feminisms.

Dialogics enables the differential unification of ecology and feminisms, which is to say a conjoining that does not conflate particularities or subordinate one to the other. Such an integration can produce a new perception of the relationship of humanity and world, and a praxis that works toward the decentering dealienation of andro/anthropocentric humanism and the reintegrative, affirmative dissolution of the intellectual isolation of radical scepticism. Dialogics encompasses Marxist dialectics by emphasizing the unity of opposites and their interanimating dynamic tension. At the same time, it reveals that the most fundamental relationships are

*From *Literature, Nature, and Other: Ecofeminist Critiques*, Albany, NY: State University of New York Press, 1995.

not resolvable through dialectical synthesis: humanity/nature, ignorance/knowledge, male/female, emotion/intellect, conscious/unconscious. And these paired terms are not even actually dichotomous or dyadic but only indicate idealized polarities within a multiplicitous field, such as that of planet, thought, sex/gender, perception, and mind. Bakhtin's conception of centripetal/centrifugal tension provides a means of countering totalization, so that any totality is continuously recognized as already a relativized, temporal centripetal entity in need of centrifugal destabilizing. While human forces are always at work centralizing, quantifying, and coding phenomena, other human forces are always challenging and breaking up such reductions and constructions in order to sustain themselves.

II

Ecology and feminisms provide the groundings necessary to turn the dialogical method into a livable critical theory, rather than a merely usable one applicable only to literature, language, and thought. As Gayatri Chakravorty Spivak candidly observes, 'one must fill the vision of literary form with its connections to what is being read: history, political economy – the world. And questioning the separation between the world of action and the world of the disciplines. There is a great deal in the way' (95). And one of the 'deals' in the way consists of critical theories that can be represented as critical discourses in the classroom but cannot be implemented as transformative pedagogics or applied in the rest of our interpretive behavior, by means of which we act in the world.

Ecology as a discipline means, fundamentally, the study of the environment in its interanimating relationships, its change and conservation, with humanity recognized as a part of the planetary ecosystem. Ecology, then, is not a study of the 'external' environment which we enter, or a management system for the raw materials at our command, although some misperceive it in these ways; it is a study of interrelationship, place, and function, with its bedrock the recognition of the distinction between things-in-themselves and things-for-us. The latter entities result from intervention, manipulation, and transformation. And, as a corollary, if we can render other entities things-for-us, the reverse also exists: other entities can render us things-for-them. Ecology can be a means for learning how to live appropriately in a particular place and time, so as to preserve, contribute to, and recycle the ecosystem. As Adrienne Rich expresses it, 'I need to understand how a place on the map is also a place in history, within which as a woman, a Jew, a lesbian, a feminist, I am created and trying to create' (8).

In a very basic way, the recognition of the difference between things-in-themselves and things-for-us, and the corollary of us-as-things-for-others leads directly into feminisms, particularly in their interrogations of gender. Only by recognizing the existence of the 'other' as a self-existent entity can we begin to comprehend a gender heterarchical continuum in which difference exists without binary opposition and hierarchical valorization. And the 'male' and 'female' that constitute the dyad are not absolute gender categories but species generative distinctions in reproduction carried over into conceptualizations of the cultural formation of gender. Those feminisms committed to exposing, critiquing, and ending the oppression of women, overthrowing patriarchy and phallocentrism, demand male recognition of the other as not only different in more ways than binary configurations can recognize, but also of equal ontological status. And this would mean recognizing the concepts of both self and other as interdependent, mutually determinable, constructs; it would also mean female recognition of a woman not only as an other but also as a self. As the poet Sharon Doubiago dramatically states it, 'because of sexism, because of the psychotic avoidance of the issue at all costs, ecologists have failed to grasp the fact that at the core of our suicidal mission is the psychological issue of gender, the oldest war, the war of the sexes' (4).

But that first recognition of the other as self-existent entity is just that, a first step. It enables the further recognition of interrelationship and interanimation, but on a heterarchical basis rather than on a hierarchical use-value or exchange-value basis, both of which would define autonomy from the perspective of individualism as a strength, rather than as a lack. Barbara Johnson notes that only a romantic androcentrism can phallaciously raise autonomy over all other relationships: 'Clearly, for Thoreau, pregnancy was not an essential fact of life. Yet for him as well as for every human being that has yet existed, someone else's pregnancy is the very *first* fact of life. How might the plot of human subjectivity be reconceived (so to speak) if pregnancy rather than autonomy is what raises the question of deliberateness?' (190). Such a question arises only as a result of feminist interrogation. It not only interrogates autonomy but also affirms relationship, and privileges nurturing over engendering to the degree that these two wholly interrelated phases of the parent/offspring relationship have been separated in Western culture since the time of the Greeks, with engendering having more status than nurturing. Thus, while slaves have always been thought capable of nurturing, they have never been officially delegated to engendering the wealthy classes. Johnson's privileging provides a necessary corrective to the androcentric-based difference between the definitions of 'fathering' and 'mothering', which in themselves have significant ecological implications, the former of begetting and unlimited expansion and the latter of sustaining and cultivating, as Annette Kolodny discusses at some length in *The Lay of the Land*. . . .

III

If, indeed, psychoanalysis and self-analysis involve a dialogue of the conscious and unconscious, which together constitute the life of the mind, then conscious/unconscious form an unsynthesizable dialogical relationship. Freud, recognizing that the unconscious could not be abolished, attempted to keep it in check through the Superego. Others before Freud attempted a similar manoeuver in the realm of the intellect/emotion dichotomy construct, believing that rationality and reason, products of enlightenment, would enable one to overcome the emotions. Emotions, of course, were the province of the feminine. Suprisingly enough, despite the obviously oppressive character of this hierarchical assignation of reason and emotion to the differing genders, we see its repetition in the attempted Lacanian identification of the unconscious with the female (see Jardine, 'Gynesis', for a critique of this position). And yet again, we have both within each of us, emotion and intellect, conscious and unconscious, and at various times one serves us better than the other in our worldly encounters. Dialogics lets us recognize the mutually constitutive character of these dyads, with each aspect at specific times constituting a center of mental activity and requiring the other to act as centrifugal force to prevent the solidification of that center into dogma. If emotion and instinct arise from historical natural influences upon the evolution of the species, then their impact on our behavior, their entry into consciousness, are a form by which the nonhuman world speaks to us through signs that our conscious renders verbally. To deny emotion as feminine and/or instinct as primitive nature is to reserve the role of speaking subject only for the ego and to deny a voice to the other, which is in reality a part of ourselves.

The dialogical relationships of intellect/emotion and humanity/nature, conceptualized as complementary dyads rather than dichotomies, can be ascertained only by attempting to facilitate the coming into verbal being of both sides of the slash (/). And here one of the limitations of Bakhtin's formulations reveals itself, in his restricting the conception of the other to participants in human society. Ecology must be brought to bear, to break dialogics out of the anthropocentrism in which Bakhtin performs it (see, for example, 'Discourse in Life' 95). The limitation he imposes renders it impossible for any aspect of the nonhuman to be rendered as a speaking subject, whether in artistic texts, other texts, or human behavior. Although he does argue that the object of the utterance is a living participant, a third constitutive factor of the utterance, which can be the external/nonverbal world to which the speech act is oriented, it remains an object ('Discourse' 101–2). And yet, does not instinct itself, which arises from outside of or prior to society, become a speaking subject through the unconscious and the emotions, which themselves create electrochemical changes in the human body?

Numerous authors and artists have attempted to render nature as a speaking subject, not in the romantic mode of rendering nature an object for the self-constitution of the poet as speaking subject, but as a character within texts with its own existence. I think here of the efforts of such writers as Dorothy Wordsworth, Robinson Jeffers, Mary Oliver, John Haines, Ursula Le Guin, Gary Snyder, and Linda Hogan. I think these attempts are most successful when they include human characters as well, enabling the differential comparison of self and other. An ecofeminist dialogics requires this effort to render the other, primarily constituted by androcentrism as women and nature (and actually as the two intertwined: nature-as-woman and woman-as-nature), as speaking subjects within patriarchy in order to subvert that patriarchy not only by decentering it but also by proposing other centers. . . .

IV

Not long before his death Bakhtin wrote that 'there is neither a first nor a last word and there are no limits to the dialogic context' (*Speech Genres* 170). The dialogic method is a way to incorporate that decentering recognition of a permanent *in media res* of human life and a constantly widening context for human interaction and interanimation within the biosphere and beyond. Coupled with the two basic pivots outlined here, ecology and feminisms, dialogics provides a method by which we may yet effect one of the paradigm shifts necessary to break down the dualistic thinking of patriarchy that perpetuates the exploitation and oppression of nature in general and women in particular. At the same time, it warns us that once we do succeed in dismantling patriarchy and its socioeconomic systems, a new host of problems and contradictions will arise, as yet unenvisioned, that will require new debates, new answers, and new pivots. Ecofeminist dialogics provides a place and method by which to step and dance, but not to stand.

WORKS CITED

Bakhtin, Mikhail (1981) *The Dialogic Imagination: Four Essays by M.M. Bakhtin* (trans. Michael Holquist and Caryl Emerson; ed. Holquist), Austin, TX: University of Texas Press.

[Bakhtin] / V.N. Volosinov (1976) 'Discourse in Life and Discourse in Art', in [Bakhtin]/ Volosinov, *Freudianism: A Marxist Critique* (trans. I.R. Titunik; ed. Titunik and Neil H. Bruss), New York: Academic Press.

—— (1986) *Speech Genres & Other Late Essays* (trans. Vern W. McGee; ed. Caryl Emerson and Michael Holquist), Austin, TX: University of Texas Press.

Doubiago, Sharon (1988) 'From Mama Coyote Talks to the Boys', *Upriver/Downriver*, 11: 1–5.

Graff, Gerald (1979) *Literature Against Itself: Literary Ideas in Modern Society*, Chicago: University of Chicago Press.

Jardine, Alice A. (1986) 'Gynesis', in Hazard Adams and Leroy Searle (eds) *Critical Theory since 1965*, Tallahassee, FL: Florida State University Press, 560–70.

Johnson, Barbara (1987) *A World of Difference*, Baltimore, MD: Johns Hopkins University Press.

Rich, Adrienne (1985) 'Notes towards a Politics of Location', in Miriam Diaz-Diocaretz and Iris M. Zavala (eds) *Women, Feminist Identity and Society in the 1980s: Selected Papers*, Philadelphia, PA: John Benjamins, 7–22.

Spivak, Gayatari Chakravorty (1987) *In Other Worlds: Essays in Cultural Politics*, New York: Methuen.

36

A Poststructuralist Approach to Ecofeminist Criticism

KARLA ARMBRUSTER*

I BELIEVE . . . THAT creative, complex ecofeminist interpretations of literary texts should be able to enhance the growth of ecofeminist theory rather than wait for its development. In order for the project of ecofeminist literary criticism to flourish, though, it must become more responsive to its position at the intersection of two broad fields – ecofeminism and literary theory and criticism – and simultaneously draw from and contribute to both of these fields. Currently, ecofeminist literary criticism is very dependent on ecofeminist theory, a condition that limits its capacity to meaningfully contribute to literary theory and criticism; in particular, it is limited by certain trends of thought in ecofeminist theory that are difficult to apply to the interpretation of literature in ways that result in complex and ideologically subversive readings. The trends I refer to are allegorically described by Val Plumwood in *Feminism and the Mastery of Nature*: as she explains, it is all too easy for the ecofeminist theorist 'pilgrim' to 'fall into the Ocean of Continuity on the one side or stray into the waterless and alien Desert of Difference on the other, there to perish' (3). As she suggests, there is a tendency within ecofeminist theory to emphasize the connections or continuity between women and nature at the expense of recognizing important differences between the two groups. While seeing the connections and potential for communion between humans and nonhuman nature is an important step toward overcoming the dualisms that structure our culture's thinking, relying only on connection can collapse the self/other dualism into an undifferentiated whole. Such holism risks simply incorporating the other into the self, a move that Jim Cheney warns leaves no room for 'respecting the other *as* other' (124). Other tendencies within current ecofeminist theory go to the opposite extreme and emphasize differences based on aspects of identity such as gender, race, or species in ways that can isolate people from each other and from nonhuman nature.

The path between continuity and difference that ecofeminist theorists must walk is so narrow and difficult, not because of inadequacies in the theorists or the

---

*From 'Blurring Boundaries in Ursula Le Guin's "Buffalo Gals, Won't You Come Out Tonight": A Poststructuralist Approach to Ecofeminist Criticism', *ISLE*, 3(1), 1996.

theories, but because of the complexity of their task. Ecofeminism explicitly works to challenge dominant ideologies of dualism and hierarchy within Western culture that construct nature as separate from and inferior to human culture (and women as inferior to men). While many ecofeminists identify such ideologies primarily as masculine, such a characterization is oversimplistic; as Plumwood explains, 'It is not a masculine identity pure and simple, but the multiple, complex cultural identity of the master formed in the context of class, race, species and gender domination, which is at issue' (5). The dualism and hierarchy that ground all these forms of domination are such pervasive forces within our culture that even a movement with the most subversive motives and discourse cannot help but reflect their influence. Within ecofeminism, an unproblematized focus on women's connection with nature can actually reinforce dualism and hierarchy by constructing yet another dualism: an uncomplicated opposition between women's perceived unity with nature and male-associated culture's alienation from it. On the other hand, an unbalanced emphasis on differences in gender, race, species, or other aspects of identity can deny the complexity of human and natural identities and lead to the hierarchical ranking of oppressions on the basis of importance or causality.

Although many ecofeminist theorists are keenly aware of the pervasiveness of dualism and hierarchy in dominant ideologies, they are far more likely to note the ways that other fields manifest the influence of such forces than to search for their traces in ecofeminist discourse itself. Thus, they risk unconsciously reinforcing the very cultural beliefs and attitudes that they wish to transform. In order to help fulfill the political potential of ecofeminism, ecofeminist literary criticism must become more conscious of the ways that ecofeminist theory can be subtly diverted into the traps of continuity or difference, and thus recontained by the pervasive force of dualistic and hierarchical thinking. And in order to make a significant impact on literary criticism and theory, ecofeminist literary criticism must offer a perspective that complicates cultural conceptions of human identity and human relationships with nonhuman nature rather than relying on unproblematized visions of continuity or difference. . . .

[BLURRING BOUNDARIES: AN ECOFEMINIST READING OF URSULA LE GUIN'S 'BUFFALO GALS, WON'T YOU COME OUT TONIGHT?']

Le Guin's story begins when a little girl, injured in a plane crash somewhere in a desert landscape in the American West, is discovered by a coyote, who tells the girl, 'You fell out of the sky' (7). The coyote's unexplained command of human language creates the sense that this story will blur the boundary between humans and other animal species, a sense that grows as the little girl, Myra, follows the coyote back to her home. In the process, Myra's perception of the coyote is suddenly, inexplicably transformed from that of an animal 'gnawing at the half-dried carcass of a crow, black feathers sticking to the black lips and narrow jaw' to that of a 'tawny-skinned woman with yellow and grey hair and bare, hard-soled feet' (21).

Once Myra arrives at Coyote's village, she meets more characters who, despite predominantly human appearances, also possess qualities that identify them with particular species of nonhuman animals: Doe, for instance, could be identified as a deer simply by her walk – 'a severely elegant walk, small steps, like a woman in high heels, quick, precise, very light' (33) – and the Chipmunk family lives in a dark, burrowlike house. In addition, these people possess characteristics that are distinctly supernatural: Blue Jay replaces Myra's eye, damaged in the plane wreck, with a new eye made out of pine pitch, and after a few healing licks from Coyote's tongue, it works quite well.

In creating such characters, Le Guin is drawing on Native American legends of the First People, whom anthropological linguist William Bright describes as 'members of a race of mythic prototypes who lived before humans existed' (xi). . . . Ultimately, Le Guin's complex First People represent a world view that resists definite boundaries and dualisms, neither choosing one side over the other or collapsing difference. Nevertheless, this world is separated from the world of Myra's origin, a world inhabited by what the First People call the New People. This separation represents, not an inevitable opposition between the two peoples, but the dualism that human culture has constructed not only between itself and nonhuman nature but also between its dualistic way of perceiving reality and a perceptual mode that refuses such boundaries. While the First People thus cannot be labeled 'nonhuman' in the sense that they have no human aspects, they do represent the nonhuman to Myra in the sense that they offer an alternative to the dominant, dualistic human culture that she comes from. On this level, the story is about the process of Myra adapting to, learning about, and coming to love the nonhuman, and to love Coyote in particular as their representative.

. . . In representing the First People as she does, Le Guin . . . renders the natural world in the form of speaking, active subjects, thus questioning the idea of impermeable boundaries between human and animal (especially the boundary that excludes the nonhuman from discourse). Importantly, Coyote is portrayed as especially active in seeking connections with Myra. In the legends of Native American cultures, particularly those native to the American Southwest, the figure of Coyote has links with human culture beyond the human aspect all First People share. Bright characterizes the legendary Coyote as 'a Levi-Straussian "mediator" who links the world of humanity, with all of its curiosity, self-awareness, and resultant "cultural" baggage, to the "natural" world of animals' (22). The legendary Coyote's affinity for humanity is paralleled to some degree by the relationship of the biological coyote to dominant human culture: it has shown an impressive ability to adapt to the changes human cultures have imposed upon its environment, often expanding its range to include areas where wolves have been eliminated or adapting to life in close proximity to human beings. Even more incredibly, the species thrives in North America today despite persistent and brutal campaigns intended to eliminate it.

True to this biological and legendary relationship with human culture, Le Guin's Coyote represents such an openness to interconnection, even when connecting means crossing hostile boundaries erected by human culture. As Myra figures out, 'That was Coyote's craziness, what they called her craziness. She wasn't afraid. She went between the two kinds of people, she crossed over' (39). Eventually, Myra realizes that although some of the other People accept her, it is only with 'the generosity of big families' (39). Coyote alone consciously chose to take care of her, a choice growing out of Coyote's 'crazy' ability and desire to cross over and make connections with human culture. In response to Coyote's attitude and actions, Myra chooses to connect across the boundaries as well. She decides to stay with Coyote rather than Chipmunk or Rabbit, even though Coyote's house is filthy and her bed is smelly and full of fleas. Ultimately, as Myra lies listening to Coyote singing 'one of the endless tuneless songs that wove the roots of trees and bushes and ferns and grass in the web that held the stream in the streambed and the rock in the rock's place and the earth together', she tells Coyote, 'I love you' (56). . . .

Significantly, 'Buffalo Gals' begins with Myra's displacement across a boundary, into a realm where she is asked to take a drastically different view of identity and community than that held in dominant human culture. Le Guin represents this boundary quite vividly by the change in Coyote's appearance from unambiguously animal – Myra first notes that the coyote is 'a big one, in good condition, its coat silvery and thick. The dark tear-line from its long yellow eye was as clearly marked as a tabby cat's' (17) – to ambiguously human, animal, and supernatural. Near the end of the story, when Myra decides to try to reapproach the world of the New People, her experience suggests that the boundary between the two worlds extends beyond physical appearance to the way the people on either side of it perceive and name reality. As Myra draws near,

> it did seem there was a line, a straight, jerky line drawn across the sage-brush plain, and on the far side of it – nothing? was it mist?
> 'It's a ranch,' the child said. 'That's a fence. There's a lot of Herefords.' The words tasted like iron, like salt in her mouth. The things she named wavered in her sight and faded, leaving nothing – a hole in the world, a burned place like a cigarette burn.
>
> (46)

Because she has crossed this boundary, at Coyote's invitation, Myra is confronted with confusions and inconsistencies, with multiple interpretations of reality and of her own identity. Throughout the course of the story, she learns to negotiate these multiple interpretations in a way that allows her consciously to step beyond her culturally constructed human perception and, at least temporarily, perceive as the nonhuman. For example, at one point Myra wonders why Coyote sleeps in the night and wakes in the day like humans rather than the other way around, but 'when she framed the question in her mind she saw at once that night is when you sleep and day when you're awake' (34–5). While the readers of Le Guin's story may never be physically displaced across a boundary in the way Myra is, her experience can lead us to imagine situations that would encourage us to take the perspectives of identities and positions different than those we are accustomed to. . . .

In the end, Myra's experience demonstrates a way that human beings can forge a relationship with nonhuman nature for political ends without positing essential or static connections that erase difference and reinscribe dualism or hierarchy. In 'A Cyborg Manifesto', one of her essays in *Simians, Cyborgs, and Women: The Reinvention of Nature*, [Donna] Haraway turns to appositional consciousness, a model of political identity formulated by Chela Sandoval: a kind of postmodernist identity constructed out of 'otherness, difference, and specificity' (155). Importantly, 'this identity marks out a selfconsciously constructed space that cannot affirm the capacity to act on the basis of natural identification, but only on the basis of conscious coalition, of affinity, of political kinship' (157). Ultimately, Le Guin's story provides us with a sense in which we can each act as conscious agents of political change. Through an openness to viewpoints and communities outside dominant human cultural experience, Myra becomes, and accepts the necessity of remaining, what Haraway would call a 'split and contradictory self'. Such a self holds potential for subverting dominant ideologies because her divisions and contradictions allow her to connect without oversimplifying her identity in ways that reinscribe those ideologies in new forms. Haraway describes such a self later in the volume, in 'Situated Knowledges', as 'the one who can interrogate positionings and be accountable, the one who can construct and join rational conversations and fantastic imaginings that change history' (193).

[IMPLICATIONS FOR ECOFEMINIST LITERARY CRITICISM]

In this way, the work of poststructuralist feminists can complement and complicate the ideas most commonly associated with ecofeminism by providing an approach to identity that encourages neither the erasure of difference by representing women and nature as a homogeneous, continuous whole nor its overemphasis, which can lead to alienation and the dominations of humans and nature. Such a sense of identity destabilizes views of both human subjectivity and nature, refusing static, definite boundaries between nature and culture, myth and reality, or any other traditionally constructed dualisms. Given this transformed vision of identity, differences between humans and the rest of nature, as well as the differences among humans, including gender, race, ethnicity, and sexual orientation, need not be the roots of conflict; instead, they can be the potential source of new and more sustainable relationships both within human culture and between culture and nonhuman nature. Thus, by going beyond the boundaries of self-defined ecofeminist theory, ecofeminist literary criticism can strengthen its potential to offer us models of human identity and human relationships with nonhuman nature that can disrupt and challenge dominant ideologies, both through literary interpretations and through the politicized perceptions and actions that texts and interpretations can inspire.

Currently, ecofeminist literary criticism exists primarily in potential form, and the potential it holds for contributing to ecofeminism's agenda of political change as well as for expanding and complicating literary criticism's scope and methodology is significant. However, critics must work not only to apply the principles of ecofeminist theorists, but also to put them into dialogue with other theories and critical approaches as well as with the literary texts themselves. By opening ourselves up to a variety of approaches and viewpoints, ecofeminist literary critics can engage in a process of constant self-interrogation and transformation. In this way, by exploiting our position at the intersection of ecofeminism and literary theory and criticism, we can encourage theorists, critics, and readers alike to cross boundaries, building on our connections with each other while using our differences to expand the range of what we can imagine for our future.

WORKS CITED

Bright, William (1993) *A Coyote Reader,* Berkeley, CA: University of California Press.

Cheney, Jim (1897) 'Ecofeminism and Deep Ecology', *Environmental Ethics*, 9: 115–45.

Haraway, Donna (1991) *Simians, Cyborgs, and Women: The Reinvention of Nature*, New York: Routledge.

Le Guin, Ursula (1987) 'Buffalo Gals, Won't You Come Out Tonight', in *Buffalo Gals and Other Animal Presences*, New York: Penguin, 17–60.

Plumwood, Val (1993) *Feminism and the Mastery of Nature*, London: Routledge.

SECTION THREE

Green Reading

PART V

Environmental Literary History

Introduction

Our third section demonstrates the potential of ecocritical interpretation. Its first part provides a selection of environmental perspectives on literary history. We have already noted the existence of a rich and varied 'green tradition'; now we consider comparative, generalising evaluations by contemporary green critics of the literary past. We begin with two paired extracts from *Forests* by Robert Pogue Harrison. Though the first of these deals with a single text, and so might seem more appropriate to the final part of the reader, it very much depends upon our being aware of the significance of the book's subtitle, 'The Shadow of Civilization', in relation to the process which the book itself traces. Harrison argues that in pagan antiquity the forest was known as a substantial reality, preceding human institutions and having its own power and authority. Urban civilisation involved the partial destruction of the forest, attended by an awareness of offence: culture defined itself against nature in an act which was fully understood to be a tragic transgression. With the rise of Christianity, however, the sense of tragedy was replaced by the comic faith in salvation, regardless of the cost to nature. Indeed, it was then that the forest became the 'shadow' or 'other' of civilisation, culminating in Dante's vision of the 'dark wood' where sinners lost their way, existing as a demonic counterpart to the approved 'earthly paradise' of Eden. In the first of our extracts, Harrison sees Shakespeare as beginning to problematise the Christian 'divine comedy'. With actual forests being destroyed at an astonishing rate to satisfy human greed, the tragedy of *Macbeth* shows the savagery and sinfulness associated with the 'dark wood' becoming internalised. Indeed, this process is seen as going so far that eventually 'natural law' reacts against 'the moral wasteland of Macbeth's nature'. Harrison's thesis does not end there, however: in our paired extract, he moves into our own era, which has been obliged to construct a postmortem on modernity. With the demise of the Enlightenment project, a pervasive sense of irony has taken over: the modern world itself becomes a 'wasteland', as indicated by writers as diverse as Eliot, Pound and Beckett. But their disillusionment with the narrative of 'progress' may yet turn out to be a prelude to a new sense of environmental responsibility. We have no space to include Harrison's Heideggerian hypothesis on the possibility of a new mode of 'dwelling' on the earth, a new 'ecology of finitude'; but I am

209

sure that anyone who has read the material given here will want to read his whole book. In scope and significance it ranks very close to Lawrence Buell's *The Environmental Imagintion*.

Selections from overviews of literary history run the risk of misleading readers as to the general argument of the critic concerned. This is a particular danger in the case of Terry Gifford's *Pastoral*. It is true that he considers this literary convention under three aspects, 'pastoral', 'anti-pastoral' and 'post-pastoral'; but the sequence is not meant to indicate a triumphant Hegelian dialectic. Rather, the three modes of writing may exist simultaneously at any given period of literary history, and may even coexist in the same writer's mind. Nor should we deduce that an 'anti-pastoral' text is a simple repudiation of reverence for nature: rather, it seeks to purge sentimental pastoral of its fantasy element and address the question of how we might live in real harmony with nature. Again, to have entered into a 'post-pastoral' relation with the earth is not to have jettisoned the first two perspectives. Gifford is recovering a tradition – here represented by Shakespeare, Blake and Hughes – in order to refine, revise, or even redeem it. On the other hand, Betty and Theodore Roszak's celebration of our debt to romantic poetry is a persuasive plea for modernity to redeem itself from its external, mechanical world view: if we could respond with humility to the 'deep form' which the romantics discovered in literature and landscape alike, we might be able to develop a genuinely ecological art for our time. The range of references, even in the abbreviated form in which their article appears here, reminds us of the contribution made earlier in his career by one of its two authors (see Chapter 20). We get yet another perspective on tradition, on the relation between past and present, and between imagination and landscape, from John Elder in our extract from his *Imagining the Earth*. Relating the visions of T. S. Eliot and Gary Snyder, he argues that their common assumption is that 'culture' may be best seen, given the etymology of the term, as an organic or 'bacteriological' process. 'Decay', therefore, may be viewed positively as well as negatively: Eliot and Snyder find hope as well as despair in the breaking down of traditions, for such a decomposition may form the basis of new life. This radically new comparative approach, by which a modernist poet normally associated with a decidedly grey formalism and a green poet who could be aligned with 'reconstructive' postmodernism turn out to be speaking the same language, certainly makes Elder's chapter a stimulating read.

Turning to the fictional tradition, our two last contributors to this part cover, respectively, the challenge of relating green theory to the history and conventions of the novel, and the way in which contemporary narratives are incorporating the possibility of ecocatastrophe. Dominic Head addresses the fact that fiction seems intrinsically anthropocentric rather than ecocentric: the answer is not to advocate greater commitment to describing landscapes, but to work within the context of cultural mediation towards a more critical sense of the relationship between human and non-human worlds –

as some postmodernist fiction is doing, and as ecocriticism itself is seeking to do. Richard Kerridge, in his article on contemporary ecothrillers, sees them as at least offering an example of how to address the larger environmental themes, rather than use them as background material, as in realist texts; but he has no illusions about their sensational distortion of those themes in the interests of a good plot. Kerridge's article is particularly useful as a closing overview because it includes a comparison between fiction's use of fact and the way the facts of the BSE scare in Britain have taken narrative shape in a mode analogous to the ecothriller itself. The link between literature and environment could not, I think, be more effectively made.

37

The Forest of Literature

ROBERT POGUE HARRISON*

MACBETH'S CONCLUSION

FORESTS RECEDE FROM the civic horizon, appear through the pathos of distance, lengthen their shadows in the cultural imagination. Even John Manwood's treatise on forest laws, composed in 1592, was a work of nostalgia. The royal forests were by that time in a state of degradation, infractions all too often going unpunished. Manwood hoped that by defining its origin and purpose he could reinvigorate the old corpus of laws which had once preserved the forests' integrity, if not sanctity. In his country the problem was more severe than elsewhere. England had already been heavily deforested by the time William arrived in the eleventh century, but the clearing of woodlands (not royal forests) continued indiscriminately during Tudor and Stuart times. It was not until the seventeenth century, thanks largely to the publication of John Evelyn's *Silva* (1664), that the problem of timber shortage for Navy ships forced a new awareness on the administration about the vital economic and national importance of woodlands. Until then the English had generally congratulated themselves on their razing efforts, considering woodlands obstacles to progress or havens for thieves and other degenerates.

The changing landscape accounts at least in part for the remarkable topical inversion that we find in the work of Shakespeare: the savagery that once traditionally belonged to the forests now lurks in the hearts of men – civic men. The dangers lie within, not without. As the city becomes sinister, forests become innocent, pastoral, diversionary, *comic*. The Shakespearean comedies that take place in the forests – *A Midsummer Night's Dream* and *As You Like It*, for example – follow the [same] comic patterns [as we find in Boccaccio's *Decameron*]: disguise, reversals, and a general confusion of the laws, categories, and principles of identity that govern ordinary reality. In this respect there is nothing new in Shakespeare's forests with regard to the underlying logic of comedy (which in no way means that his comedies bring nothing new to the genre). The same cannot be said, however, of

*From *Forests: The Shadow of Civilization*, Chicago and London: University of Chicago Press, 1992.

212

his dramas about civic barbarism. Those dramas are unique for the way they bring the shadow of natural law to bear on the religious, moral, and social crises that were shaking the traditional foundations of society.

We [have] claimed . . . that the Christian era puts an end to tragedy as the highest form of wisdom, subverting its ideological basis. If we assume – and it is a questionable assumption – that tragedy, not merely as a genre but above all as an *insight*, becomes possible once again with Shakespeare, we must look in effect to the end of the Christian era for an explanation. This end is in many ways the enduring drama of Shakespeare's tragedies. Historically speaking the end of the Christian era is a prolonged and indefinite event – it represents an era in itself – and Shakespeare certainly did not see the end of it himself. What he did see, however, was the shadow of its dissolution lurking in the hearts of civic heroes.

He did not portray the dissolution so much in Christian terms as in terms of gross violations of natural law. Natural law lies at the basis of positive law; it is not the law of nature as such but rather the transcendent foundations of human social law. The depraved Shakespearean characters – Iago, Edmund, Macbeth, etc. – violate the most sacred natural bonds, and once such bonds lose their binding power Shakespeare's characters degenerate into a savagery of spirit which recalls Vico's words about those treacherous human-aged men [as opposed to those of the earlier ages of gods and of heroes] who have been 'made more inhuman by the barbarism of reflection than the first men had been made by the barbarism of sense. For the latter displayed a generous savagery, against which one could defend oneself or take flight or be on one's guard; but the former, with a base savagery, under soft words and embraces, plots against the life and fortune of friends and intimates' (*New Science*, section 1106). For Vico such barbarism signaled the beginning of the end of the human age and the imminent metamorphosis of cities into forests – a return, as it were, to the lawless state of nature. In Shakespeare's work it is portrayed as an ungodly upheaval in the natural order of things, that is to say, the *lawful* order of things. It is here that the term 'nature' becomes an ambiguous word. On the one hand it means the presocial or prelawful state of anarchy; on the other it means the 'natural', that is, nonconventional basis of human law itself.

In a famous soliloquy of *King Lear*, the bastard Edmund declares his allegiance to nature, not to custom. He speaks of the 'plague of custom' as if custom were a disease of nature; he speaks of the 'curiosity of nations' as if the so-called law of nations were no more than a deviation from nature's law; and finally he speaks of 'legitimacy' as if it were an artificial contrivance that has nothing to do with the 'law' of his goddess (I. ii. 1–22). But we know from *King Lear* as a whole that Edmund's notion of nature as sheer will to power offends nature herself. The storm scene of act 3 appears as a cosmic response to the moral confusion that follows upon the corruptions of natural law on the part of Edmund and Lear's daughters.

Perhaps the most corrupt Shakespearean character in this sense is Lady Macbeth. Unlike Edmund, however, Lady Macbeth avows that human law has its basis in nature. Thus, in one of her speeches, she expresses her desire to be denatured, so that she might successfully, and without remorse, carry out her murderous plot against the king of Scotland:

213

> . . . Come, you spirits
> That tend on mortal thoughts, unsex me here,
> And fill me, from the crown to the toe, top-full
> Of direst cruelty! Make thick my blood;
> Stop up th' access and passage to remorse,
> That no *compunctious visitings of nature*
> Shake my fell purpose nor keep peace between
> Th' effect and it! Come to my woman's breast
> And take my milk for gall, you murd'ring ministers,
> Wherever in your sightless substances
> You wait on *nature's mischief!* Come, thick night,
> And pall thee in the dunnest smoke of hell,
> That my keen knife see not the wound it makes,
> Nor heaven peep through the blanket of the dark
> To cry 'Hold, hold!'

(I.v.41–55)

Lady Macbeth's defiance of nature has its cause in something more than a depraved will to power; it comes, in effect, from a spirit of vengeance. Nature itself has wronged her, for we know that Macbeth and his wife have no children. They are afflicted with sterility. Life is a tale full of sound and fury, signifying nothing, but this is a fact of some significance. In her speech Lady Macbeth reappropriates her own barrenness when she asks to be 'unsexed'. It is in this unsexed womb that she conceives all her plots and schemes. For that very reason, perhaps, they are destined to abort.

The barrenness in question has its symbolic counterpart in a natural land-scape. This landscape is the heath, or waste place, where the three witches commu-nicate their prophecies to Macbeth. This barren wasteland remains the place of origin for all the crimes that Macbeth will commit against his fellow man (crimes which, significantly enough, involve the destruction of family lineages). But the prophecies uttered there, which foreshadow Macbeth's abortive schemes and doom, ironically come to fruition. One of those prophesies has to do with a forest:

> Macbeth shall never vanquish'd be, until
> Great Birnam wood to high Dunsinane Hill
> Shall come against him.

(IV.i.92–4)

It is typical that Macbeth should misunderstand the prophecy, his blindness to prophetic intent being the counterpart of his corrupted nature. There is consider-able irony in his reaction to the witch's utterance:

> That will never be.
> Who can impress the forest, bid the tree
> Unfix his earth-bound root? Sweet bodements, good!
> Rebellious dead, rise never, till the Wood

Of Birnam rise, and our high-placed Macbeth
Shall live the lease of nature, pay his breath
To time and moral custom. Yet my heart
Throbs to know one thing, Tell me, if your art
Can tell so much: shall Banquo's issue ever
Reign in this kingdom?

(IV.i.94–103)

Who can impress the forest? The word 'impress' here means, among other things, to conscript – impress into military service – which is exactly what occurs when Birnam Wood moves against Macbeth. But Macbeth's question contains other connotations as well, namely, who can put his impress on the forest? Who can impose a human or political will upon the will of nature? Who can force the forest into one's service? These are questions that have been with us from the beginning of this chapter. Humankind is always 'impressing' the forest in one way or another, stripping it, conquering it, cultivating it, conscripting it. Likewise the forest is always impressing those who lose their way in its labyrinth. The relation between forests and civilization during the Christian era is largely one of impression – what we have called also the law's shadow.

The irony of this prophecy about Birnam Wood is that it refers to the visual impression of a moving forest, but Macbeth – who is impressed by visions and hallucinations throughout the play – literalizes its intent. He is the victim, in short, of his own impressions – the forest's shadow, as it were, which is peopled by the ghosts of the 'rebellious dead'.

In the final act of the play, as Macbeth's destiny closes in on him, the rebellious dead move against Macbeth in the impression of Birnam Wood. The soldiers of the opposing army advance toward the castle camouflaged behind boughs cut from the trees of this forest. As the forest moves against Macbeth, the play concludes in what appears to be a denouement of poetic justice. The lawlessness that Vico associated with the 'nefarious forests' has here found haven in Macbeth's civic barbarism, but by the end of the play the moving forest of Birnam comes to symbolize the forces of natural law mobilizing its justice against the moral waste-land of Macbeth's nature. In this powerful image the law appears in its natural basis. As the army hides behind the boughs, they employ the same ruses of deception by which Macbeth carried out his crimes, only now the camouflage reverses the order of evil. This forest is impressed by 'Banquo's issue'. We see in the image of Birnam Wood the law of genealogy – the family tree, as it were – vanquishing its sterile enemy. We see the law of kinship and kingship avenging itself. We see the law of the *land* in a strangely literalistic guise.

The comic conclusion of *Macbeth* gives us a final image of the law and its own shadow – an image with which to conclude. . . . From one point of view *Macbeth* is clearly a tragedy, but its comic, if not happy, ending recalls us to the logic we have been following all along. If *Macbeth* is tragic it is not so in the pre-Christian sense. This is not because of its comic ending. Several Greek tragedies end comically, with the triumph of justice, but justice in their case meant the

215

reconciliation of opposing laws, each of which had their legitimate claim. When Orestes murdered his mother he was avenging his father's death, obeying the dictates of an ancient law; when the furies began to persecute him they too were avenging a law that his matricide had violated. The ending of Aeschylus's trilogy represents a triumphant reconciling of these two laws, but in *Macbeth* it is not a case of two legitimate laws striving against one another; the drama involves the law and its own corruption, the law and its own negation, the law and its own *shadow*. In this case the 'walking shadow' is Macbeth himself, but as Birnam Wood moves against him, his hour on the stage is over. . . .

WASTELANDS

Sooner or later we will have to come up with a less ironic name than 'greenhouse effect' for the choking of the atmosphere with carbon dioxide. Green is the wrong color. The color is ashen. One-tenth of the carbon dioxide emitted into the atmosphere comes from the fires of deforestation in Brazil alone. That is a lot of green rising in smoke. The earth is on fire; it has a fever. Perhaps we should call it the 'fever effect' rather than greenhouse effect. But beyond its name, this 'effect' is part of a worldwide phenomenon that will mark the ecological legacy of the twentieth century: desertification. Roquentin's nightmare [in Jean-Paul Sarte's novel *Nausea*] – his vision of vegetation crawling toward the cities waiting to place its 'green paws' over everything – is strangely out of touch with the times, for it is the desert that is extending its domain over the realm vegetation.

'The wasteland grows,' wrote Nietzsche over a century ago, 'Woe to him who harbors wastelands within.' But as we remarked earlier in another context, such things are as mirrors: if a monkey looks in no apostle will look out. If desertification occurs within, the forests cannot survive without. Soul and habitat – we are finally in a position to know this – are correlates of one another. It is not by accident, then, that the 'wasteland' figures as one of the dominant emblems, or landscapes, of modernist literature, from Eliot's poem by that same name to Dino Buzzatti's *Deserto dei Tartari*. T. S. Eliot's poem 'Gerontion', originally part of *The Waste Land* and separated out in later revision, ends with the verse: 'Thoughts of a dry brain in a dry season.' The season in question is the epoch under critique in *The Waste Land*, which opens with the famous verses:

> April is the cruelest month, breeding
> lilacs out of the dead land, mixing
> memory and desire, stirring
> dull roots with spring rain.

We have been taught, among others by Eliot himself, to read *The Waste Land* as a testimony of despair over a civilization in spiritual decay. But that is only one aspect of the testimony. Poetry does not only monitor spiritual states of being, or what one used to call the 'spirit' of an age; it also registers the spiritual effects

of a changing climate and habitat. As the external environment undergoes transformations, poets often announce them in advance with the clairvoyance of seers,
for poets have an altogether sixth sense that enables them to forecast trends in the
weather, so to speak. Like oracles, they may couch their message in the language
of enigma. And like oracles, the meaning of their message becomes fully manifest
only after the events it foretells have unfolded. Modern poetry at its best is a kind
of spiritual ecology. The wasteland grows within and without and with no essential distinction between them, so much so that we might now say that a poem like
Eliot's *The Waste Land* is in some ways a harbinger of the greenhouse effect. Or
better, we can, say that the greenhouse effect, or desertification of habitat in general,
is the true 'objective correlative' of the poem.

But poets are not always reliable in this regard. In retrospect it seems clear
that a modernist writer like James Joyce, whose literature exploited the almost limit-
less resources of the sayable, never really heeded the 'nature' of the times. His luxuriant forest of prose does not grow in the desiccated ground of the modern habitat
but rather in some garden of nostalgia. His work thrives on the illusion of plenitude – the plenitude of nature, of the vigorous body, of meaningfulness in every
dimension of being. On the other hand the bleak essentialist literature of a writer
like Samuel Beckett seems truly to reflect, or preannounce, the changing climate
of the times. In his case the ecology of the sayable is reduced to an authentic
poverty. The failure of his word to flourish in any grand sense reveals, in its minimal
flower, the depleted resources of the ground that lies outside the writer's window.
This window of the soul, so to speak, appears in one of Beckett's plays as one of
the bleakest mirrors in modernist literature. In *Endgame*, Hamm periodically asks
Clov to go look out of the window of their room, and each time he does so Clov
reports that nothing has changed: the habitat lies wasted, devoid of trees or signs
of life. At one point during the play Hamm fails asleep and his mind drifts back
in thought to some mysterious recollection or fantasy. When he wakes up he mutters
to himself: 'Those forests!' These two words, left uncommented, refer to some
impossible space beyond the world, beyond the wasteland that exists both inside
and outside of the room. Hamm's cryptic utterance as he awakens from the dream
of some other world rarely intrudes into the action of play, yet it may well hold
the secret of the drama as a whole: 'Those forests!' Which forests? The forests of
Vico's giants? The forests of pre-Cartesian 'prejudices'? Or the forests that are disap-
pearing as this sentence is being read?

As for Ezra Pound, since we are speaking of modernist writers, it would seem
at times that he tried to defy the growing wasteland in a mad attempt at cultural
and historical reforestation. In his *Cantos* he created a true wilderness of beauty,
but one that dried up and exhausted its sources almost as quickly as it flourished.
Pound struggled to the death against the inhospitable climate of the times, and
those same times reduced his efforts to ashes. In the fragments that end the *Cantos*
he offers his most intimate confession of all:

> M'amour, m'amour
> what do I love and

where are you?
That I lost my center
fighting the world.
The dreams clash
and are shattered –
and that I tried to make a paradiso
terrestre.

(Pound, 802)

Like 'those forests' in Hamm's dream, the green dream of an earthly paradise pertains to other times and climates than those which suffer from greenhouse effects. Meanwhile Pound lost his center fighting the world – the desiccated land outside Hamm's window – attesting in his failures that green is not the color of the age.

WORKS CITED

Beckett, Samuel (1988) *Endgame*, New York: Chelsea House.
Eliot, T. S. (1963) *Collected Poems 1909–1962*, London: Faber & Faber.
Pound, Ezra (1983) *The Cantos of Ezra Pound*, New York: New Directions.
Shakespeare, William (1951) *Macbeth* (ed. Kenneth Muir), London: Methuen.
Vico, Giambattista (1968) *The New Science* (trans. T. G. Bergin and M. H. Fisch), Ithaca, NY: Cornell University Press.

38

Pastoral, Anti-Pastoral, Post-Pastoral

Terry Gifford*

[PASTORAL: SHAKESPEARE]

[IN *AS YOU LIKE IT*] Shakespeare is using a real pastoral setting as the context for a very different Arden that is, in effect, a court in exile based upon alternative values to that from which Duke Senior, Orlando and Rosalind have been exiled. That these values can heal and transform is evidenced by Orlando's action in the dilemma of saving from the lioness the brother responsible for his exile and Oliver's subsequent transformation, shown in the language with which he describes Orlando's moral choice:

> Twice did he turn back, and purpos'd so.
> But kindness, nobler ever than revenge,
> And nature, stronger than his just occasion,
> Made him give battle to the lioness.
>
> (IV.iii.127)

Nature in Arden is associated with kindness rather than revenge, which drives the court in its supposedly noble behaviour. Duke Frederick cannot even penetrate Arden. The extremity of his bitterness against his brother Duke Senior requires the extreme antidote of becoming a religious recluse. Arden is the platform from which Jaques can launch his humbling satires on the human condition, which, in their high Renaissance rhetoric, are clearly aimed at both delighting and deflating a court audience.

But the function of Arden in this play is not directly to challenge with an alternative pastoral social, as it is in *The Winter's Tale*. It is to provide a border-land space in which the nature of declarations of love and gender can be tested. In this process each of the distinctive characters finds out who they are and returns to court married not only to their 'true' lovers, but to their better selves. Their

*From *Pastoral*, London and New York: Routledge, 1999.

219

distinctiveness is what gives depth to their simple dramatic declarations at the end of the play that together make a voice poem of a diverse, if tangled, society:

> *Silvius*: And so am I for Phebe.
> *Phebe*: And so am I for Ganymede.
> *Orlando*: And so am I for Rosalind.
> *Rosalind*: And so am I for no woman.

> (V.ii.98)

In Rosalind's ability to untangle these misplaced and inappropriate attachments to each individual's satisfaction she is able to bring harmony to the society of Arden by revealing to each of them their true desires.

Marriage is Shakespeare's dramatic motif for natural harmony, generosity, humility and justice that is taken back into the court. The dance is his dramatic celebration of it. The extent to which an audience feels these qualities have been earned through the process of retreat will determine the extent to which they are convinced these qualities will persist upon the return. . . .

[ANTI-PASTORAL: BLAKE]

The difficulty for the anti-pastoral writer in finding a voice that can be celebratory whilst corrective, that does not adopt the very vices it is criticising, that avoids over-stating its case whilst accepting that its case is inevitably a counter one, was solved by Blake in *Songs of Innocence and Experience* (1794) by accepting the dialectic as the mode of writing. He was thus able to celebrate the lamb whilst recognising the 'fearful symmetry' of the need for a celebration of the tiger. By adopting the form of Sunday School homilies, Blake was able both to show the way the sentimentalising pastoral worked and to undercut it to expose the hypocrisy upon which it was based. He was able to give true innocence its importance, whilst indicating the experience required to recognise it. In 'The Garden of Love' from *Experience*, 'A Chapel was built in the midst / Where I used to play on the green.' The 'Thou shalt not, writ over the door' has the effect of 'binding with briars my joys and desires' which, in 'The Echoing Green' in *Experience*, can now be appreciated as communal joys responding to the seasons with desires that are as natural as the flowers. Blake's dialectic demands a return to the *Songs of Innocence* after reading *The Songs of Experience* in order to value the depth of the innocent vision which transcends the sentimental pastoral of their formal origins. The journey through Hell was the way to achieve a perception of Heaven that was not an idealised Arcadia.

Blake's *The Marriage of Heaven and Hell* (*c.* 1793) is his great anti-pastoral work. In it he exposes pastorally-comforting images of Heaven as self-deceiving constructs, what he calls in the poem 'London' from *Experience*, 'the mind-forg'd manacles'. For Blake this is a matter of perception and human choice. As an engraver making his own book in the manner of an artist, Blake again takes his form as the metaphor for his content:

But first the notion that man has a body distinct from his soul is to be expunged. This I shall do by printing in the infernal method by corrosives, which in Hell are salutary and medicinal, melting apparent surfaces away, and displaying the infinite which was hid.

If the doors of perception were cleansed everything would appear to man as it is – infinite.

For man has closed himself up, till he sees all things through narrow chinks of his cavern.

Blake's emphasis is on the self-imprisonment of selective perception. A self-protective tendency has led people to retreat behind the narrow chinks of a cavern of their own making. They are in manacles of their own making that in *Songs of Experience* are 'binding with briars my joys and desires' to such an extent that in the final line of 'London', the evident distortion of desires that leads to the need for the 'harlot', 'blights with plagues the Marriage hearse'. . . .

POST-PASTORAL: HUGHES

Fundamental to post-pastoral literature [are]: [1] an awe in attention to the natural world; [2] the recognition of a creative-destructive universe equally in balance in a continuous momentum of birth and death, death and rebirth, growth and decay, ecstasy and dissolution; [3] the recognition that the inner is also the workings of the outer, that our inner nature can be understood in relation to external nature; [4] an awareness of both nature as culture and culture as nature; [5] [the recognition that] with consciousness comes conscience; [6] the ecofeminists' realisation that the exploitation of the planet is of the same mind-set as the exploitation of women and minorities. . . .

By way of summary of the six qualities of post-pastoral it might be helpful to illustrate their presence in a single book. This could be chosen from any one of a range of post-pastoral authors whose work has been touched upon so far: Blake, Wordsworth, Muir, Thoreau, Lawrence, Le Guin, MacLean, Heaney, Clarke and Rich. But perhaps the major achievement of contemporary post-pastoral to date is Ted Hughes's mythic sequence of poems *Cave Birds* (1978). It is an interesting case because it begins and ends with a critique of the pastoral. The cockerel protagonist is put on trial for the neglect of his inner self and his alienation from the forces of nature in himself and outside himself. 'The hero's cockerel innocence, it turns out, becomes his guilt,' Hughes said in the original 1975 radio broadcast. 'His own self, finally, the innate nature of his flesh and blood, brings him to court.' The choice of a cockerel, the archetypal image of arrogance, to represent a human hero, hints at the lack of humility derived from awe at natural processes (first post-pastoral element) that is immediately displayed in the complacently pastoral way the hero responds to death in the first poem. His facing and accepting his own death in the poem 'The Knight' marks his recognition of a creative-destructive universe of which he is a part (second post-pastoral element). The endorsement of this in showing him the role of the worm in 'A Green Mother' [may be] referred to. . . . The way inner nature is 'exquisitely fitted' to outer nature, and the fact that processes of outer nature are taking place in human inner nature (third post-pastoral element), is subtly suggested by the poem 'Bride and Groom Lie Hidden for Three Days'.

In this poem Hughes boldly uses images of fitting pieces of machinery together with a sense of wonder that becomes erotic when one realises that these pieces are parts of the body that 'she' gives to 'him' and 'he' gives to 'her'. This mechanical imagery prevents sentimentality or idealisation whilst biologically endorsing the symbolism of a marriage of the inner to the outer, of the self to nature. At the sexual climax of this poem 'they bring each other to perfection'. Their ecstatic completeness is compared to that of 'two gods of mud', an image that implies the vision of a god, but not one that is transcendentally above the mud of the marvellous material world. In *Cave Birds* Hughes is making a myth about the essence of material nature with an awareness that nature is mediated by culture. He is also using this myth to reconnect us to the nature in ourselves, knowing that culture is nature, in that his myth, his imaginative act, is an act of our natural capacity to heal our alienation from nature and from ourselves (fourth post-pastoral element).

In the final poem, 'The Risen', the cockerel is reborn as a falcon, an image of self-possession and predatory power. The regaining of full consciousness in this poem is also to find a renewal of conscience (fifth post-pastoral element): 'His each wingbeat – a convict's release. / What he brings will be plenty.' The final lines of the whole sequence are the two-line coda: 'At the end of the ritual / up comes a goblin', as though self-knowledge is never complete, nor free, as we shall see, from the goblin tempting a reversion to complacency. The last lines of 'The Risen' are, 'But when will he land / on a man's wrist.' This is curious in several senses: it is a statement not a question; 'a man' has not been present in the sequence; and what is its meaning in terms of the allegory? That it is a statement suggests an ironic inevitability to the human tendency to want to control nature again. The image is from the human activity of falconry, suggesting that, although the cockerel protagonist may have achieved the wholeness of this falcon, readers may now step outside the allegory and may typically want to ask this question. So these lines are the goblin raising the old hubris of human desire to control and exploit the wild energy of nature. At an allegorical level these lines represent that hubris as a fascist 'will to power', the complacent, unquestioning macho desire to exploit both social groups and natural 'resources' (sixth post-pastoral element). The male protagonist of this 'ritual' poem sequence had found that, as Hughes put it, 'the innate nature of his flesh and blood brings him to court'. This goblin suggests that he may not have learned all there is to learn about the consequences of his hubris. The cockerel of the narrative may have done, but the human he represents may not be able to resist a reversion to the complacency of the pastoral attitude expressed in the first poem of the sequence.

39

Deep Form in Art and Nature

BETTY AND THEODORE ROSZAK*

THE SPIRITUAL CRISIS of the modern world has been described in many ways. From the viewpoint of the arts, Herbert Read's diagnosis is among the most incisive. Read believed a serious loss of aesthetic sensitivity has paralleled our progressive estrangement from nature. We suffer, he said, from an 'atrophy of sensibility'. Art as well as science and technology harbours the illusion that we *live outside or above* the natural world, and so may treat it as we please, turning it into an object of exploitation for the exclusive benefit of our species.

Over the past century whole philosophical and aesthetic movements have been predicated upon and even dedicated to our alienation from nature as if it were the inevitable human condition.

The essence of modernism has been a deepening immersion in extremes of despair, anxiety, or outright cynicism. Few would dispute that it is the role of art to reflect its times. But 'reflection' should include what art itself has to offer to the soul in need; it must look beyond the contemporary wasteland to find life-enhancing possibilities.

Settling for the fashionably anguished or fashionably cynical, mainstream art stops at the city limits of a culture that has lost or forgotten its ecological roots. In a time when so many artists have learned to confabulate with extremes of horror and alienation, the most daring thing an artist can do is to fill a book, a gallery or a theatre with joy, hope and beauty. This is more than a matter of calling for a new 'movement' or 'style'. As the degradation of the planetary environment worsens, we are being forced to recognize that a culture divorced from the biological foundations of life is simply not sustainable. Both environmental ignorance and aesthetic atrophy are rapidly approaching terminal status. To refuse despair has become an ecological imperative.

In her provocative survey of the outer limits of modernism, the art critic Suzi Gablik asks: 'After the avant garde, what?' Her answer can be found in the title of her book: *The Re-Enchantment of Art*. There she writes hopefully of a new art

*From 'Deep Form in Art and Nature', *Resurgence*, 176 (May–June), 1996.

'ushered in by twentieth-century physics, ecology and general systems theory, with its call for integrative and holistic modes of thinking'. The terminology Gablik uses is drawn from modern science, but the re-enchanted sensibility she calls for takes us back to the shamanic roots of art.

On the far side of modernism artists may find they have a great deal to 'learn from Lascaux'. This is not a matter of scavenging the 'primitive'. There has been enough of that in the twentieth century. Too often the effort to salvage ancestral images has been animated by a domineering consciousness, one that insensitively ransacks or even plunders the tribal cultures. Lately, spokespeople for traditional societies have taken issue with such invasive practices. Jerome Rothenberg's 'ethno-poetics' is a better approach. It seeks to redress this essentially colonialist attitude by preserving and enhancing the human values that connect us with primary people. Our goal should not be to borrow from elsewhere, but to search among our own cultural resources, perhaps even in modern science and industrialism, for ways to restore art to the status it has always held among primary people as a form of knowledge.

In the modern Western world, the Romantics were the last major cultural movement to assert the 'truth of the imagination', defending art as a way of knowing the world that equalled or surpassed scientific reason. In their. resistance to what Blake called 'Satan's Mathematik Holiness', their goal was not to reject science but to enlarge it. Newtonian science sought to understand the world by a process of reductionism. The method may be legitimate enough, but it can carry over into reducing in value. Phenomena deprived of their dignity and vitality become 'nothing but . . . nothing but'. They are cheapened by the very act of knowing.

In contrast, the Romantics sought to understand by augmentation. In Blake's terms, they sought 'fourfold vision' rather than 'single vision'. From the Romantic perspective, a landscape by Constable makes our knowledge of nature bigger; art adds to what we learn from any combination of physics, biology, geology and chemistry. It tells us the world is (to offer a poor verbal translation) magnificent, perhaps sacred, therefore deserving of reverence. At its highest level, it transforms our consciousness by uniting us with Deep Form in the natural world.

By 'Deep Form' we mean the correspondence between formative processes of mind and formative processes in nature. As Coleridge put it, 'the rules of the imagination are themselves the very powers of growth and production.' For the Romantics, recognizing this congruency between creativity in art and in nature was not a mere subjective reflex; it was as much a fact as anything a botanist tells us about photosynthesis or a geologist about continental drift. Deep Form offers us the knowledge that an authentically deep ecology requires in order to place us in a respectful, sustainable relationship with nature.

'Great works of art', Goethe believed, 'are works of nature just as truly as mountains, streams and plains.' The oneness of art and nature has not been wholly beyond the reach of scientists themselves. Even as tough-minded a Darwinian as Thomas Huxley once admitted to the fact that 'in travelling from one end to the other of the scale of life, we are taught one lesson, that living nature is not a mechanism, but a poem.' Georg Groddeck, Freud's most eccentric follower, was among the few psychotherapists who granted art an epistemological status of its own. An admirer of Goethe, Groddeck regarded art as the key criterion of sanity. Healthy art creates a healthy soul; sick art creates neurosis. Groddeck believed that, since the Renaissance, the art of Western society has been corrupted by an excessive humanism. He warned that when we turn away from nature we lose 'the chance of cultural development, cease to recognize our dependence upon the universal whole, and direct our love, fear and reverence only upon the strivings and sulferings of our fellow men.' This degenerates into a narrow psychologism especially as our lives come to be bounded by what the neo-Romantic poet Robinson Jeffers called 'the incestuous life of the cities'.

It is heartening to see how the sense of Deep Form has managed to survive in the arts despite all that urban industrial society has done to shatter the natural continuum. We can find celebrations of Deep Form among some of the masters of modernism, a small, gallant contingent who never lost their nourishing connection with the Earth beneath the pavement. While their style is distinctly of our time and place, their sensibility allies them to the dawn of human culture. Paul Klee is a leading example. He once gave this advice to a fellow art teacher:

> Lead your students to Nature, into Nature! Let them learn by experience how a bud is formed, how a tree grows, how a butterfly opens its wings, so that they will become as rich, as variable, as capricious, as Nature herself. Follow the ways of natural creation, the becoming, the functioning of forms. That is the best school.

According to Werner Haftmann, Klee collected skeletons of small animals, mosses, bark and lichen, shells and stones, beetles and butterflies. 'They were most carefully selected, for if one can see through them and master the laws governing their existence and their form, nature itself becomes transparent, the spirit moves and the artist feels compelled to attempt similar acts of formal creation.'

Similarly, Emil Nolde subscribed to a deeply organic aesthetic. He too sensed the forces of nature that work within the artist, bringing us the knowledge of an *animated* universe. 'My aim', he said, 'was that colours should be transmitted to the canvas, through myself as the painter, with the same inevitability as when Nature herself is creating forms, just as minerals and crystals are formed, just as moss and seaweed grow.'

One can name many others whose work is an expression of Deep Form. They are not the dominant movement in twentieth-century art, but they appear here and there like upstart springs that flow from the distant shamanic sources of their vocation. The voice of the Earth sounds throughout Walt Whitman and his major disciple Pablo Neruda. Georgia O'Keeffe must be numbered among the company; and so too Emily Carr, who so vividly recalls in her diaries the unitive experience that comes with the discovery of Deep Form:

> I woke up this morning with 'unity of movement' in a picture strong in my mind. For long I have been trying to get the movement of the parts.

Now I see there is only *one* movement. It sways and ripples. It may be slow or fast but it is only one movement sweeping out into space but always keeping going – rocks, sky, one continuous movement.

The artist, like a tree, drinks up nourishment from the depths and from the heights, from the roots and from the air, to bring forth a crown of leaves. The organic metaphor is essential here to the concept of Deep Form. Nature is reborn through artistic vision. 'Think what it would be like, [Italo Calvino once wrote] to create a work outside the limited perspective of the individual ego, not only to enter into selves like our own, but to give speech to that which has no language, to the bird perching on the edge of the gutter, to the tree in spring.'

Yes, and to the stones, clouds, and stars.

Deep Form reveals the web of vital relationships embedded in all things; its vision of the universe is what Read called 'a prodigious animism'. It reminds us that the great drama of our time is the discovery that all things and creatures on Earth share a common destiny. We are linked to one another in what the poet Robert Duncan once called a 'symposium of the whole'.

Duncan's poetry is among the most eloquent appeals for the creation of what the Deep Ecologists have called an 'ecocentric community'. He writes:

to compose such a symposium of the whole, such a totality, all the old excluded orders must be included. The female, the proletariat, the foreign; the animal and vegetative; the unconscious and the unknown, the criminal and failure – all that has been outcast and vagabond must return to be admitted in the creation of what we consider we are.

The words echo Klee's profession: 'I sink myself beforehand in the universe and then stand in a brotherly relationship to my neighbours, to everything on this Earth.' . . .

Deep Form offers the artist a new repertory of gestures: instead of grasping, seizing, mastering, struggling, it attempts a tender touching, a noninterfering gaze, a receptive bonding with Earth and the other. The dark, submerged feminine reappears as image and informing spirit, a new *anima mundi* with her rich welter of sensuous experience in colour, scent and sound. Wherever Deep Form wells up among the poets, the painters, the architects, the performers, life is made whole again and the universe is re-animated. The creative imagination returns us to an aesthetic both old and new, to a mode of knowing the natural world which can be the ally of science. The human again becomes an integral part of nature; life and mind become part of a vital matrix as vast and as old as the universe. This primary ecological insight views human art not as anomaly or arbitrarily fashionable decoration, but as integral to the natural order, the common root being inherent formative processes at work at every level of reality from the structure of atoms to the formation of galactic clusters.

40

Culture as Decay: Arnold, Eliot, Snyder

John Elder*

I BELIEVE THAT behind America's flourishing poetry of nature lies a reinterpretation of culture, and that through the work of numerous poets this new culture is now being further developed and exemplified. By way of introducing the major elements of this vision, I would like to juxtapose passages of prose from T. S. Eliot and Gary Snyder. Their similarities indicate a significant continuity between contemporary poetry and the cultural and poetic ambitions of writers at the beginning of the century. The points of divergence are equally important, however, revealing characteristic values held both by Snyder and by others among today's outstanding poets of nature.

The passage from Eliot is a well-known one from his essay on 'Tradition and the Individual Talent':

> Tradition . . . cannot be inherited, and if you want it you must obtain it by great labour. It involves, in the first place, the historical sense, which we may call nearly indispensable to anyone who would continue to be a poet beyond his twenty-fifth year; and the historical sense involves a perception, not only of the pastness of the past, but of its presence; the historical sense compels a man to write not merely with his own generation in his bones, but with a feeling that the whole of the literature of Europe from Homer and within it the whole of the literature of his own country has a simultaneous existence and composes a simultaneous order. This historical sense, which is a sense of the timeless as well as of the temporal and of the timeless and temporal together, is what makes a writer traditional. And it is at the same time what makes a writer most acutely conscious of his place in time, of his contemporancity.
>
> No poet, no artist of any art, has his complete meaning alone. His significance, his appreciation is the appreciation of his relation to the dead poets and artists. You cannot value him alone; you must set him, for

*From *Imagining the Earth: Poetry and the Vision of Nature*, Urbana and Chicago, IL: University of Illinois Press, 1985.

contrast and comparison, among the dead. I mean this as a principle of aesthetic, not merely historical, criticism. The necessity that he shall conform, that he shall cohere, is not one-sided; what happens when a new work of art is created is something that happens simultaneously to all the works of art which preceded it. The existing monuments form an ideal order among themselves, which is modified by the introduction of the new (the really new) work of art among them. The existing order is complete before the new work arrives; for order to persist after the supervention of novelty, the *whole* existing order must be, if ever so slightly, altered; and so the relations, proportions, values of each work of art toward the whole are readjusted; and this is conformity between the old and the new.[1]

Snyder's statement, corresponding in its broad cultural perspective, though differing significantly in its terms, was originally part of a talk at Brown University:

The communities of creatures in forests, ponds, oceans, or grasslands seem to tend toward a condition called climax, 'virgin forest' – many species, old bones, lots of rotten leaves, complex energy pathways, woodpeckers living in snags, and conies harvesting tiny piles of grass. This condition has considerable stability and holds much energy in its web – energy that in simpler systems (a field of weeds just after a bulldozer) is lost back into the sky or down the drain. All of evolution may have been as much shaped by this pull toward climax as it has by simple competition between individuals or species. If human beings have any place in this scheme it might well have to do with their most striking characteristic – a large brain, and language. And a consciousness of a peculiarly self-conscious order. Our human awareness and eager poking, probing, and studying is our beginning contribution to planet-system energy-conserving; another level of climax.

In a climax situation a high percentage of the energy is derived not from grazing off the annual production of biomass, but from recycling dead biomass, the stuff of the forest floor, the trees that have fallen, the bodies of dead animals. Recycled. Detritus cycle energy is liberated by fungi and lots of insects. I would then suggest: as climax forest is to biome, and fungus is to the recycling of energy, so 'enlightened mind' is to the daily ego mind, and art to the recycling of neglected inner potential. When we deepen or enrich ourselves, looking within, understanding ourselves, we come closer to being like a climax system. Turning away from grazing on the 'immediate biomass' of perception, sensation, and thrill; and re-viewing memory, internalized perception, blocks of inner energies, dreams, the leaffall of day-to-day consciousness, liberates the energy of our own sense-detritus. Art is an assimilator of unfelt experience, perception, sensation, and memory for the whole society. When all that compost of feeling and thinking comes back to us then, it comes not as a flower, but – to complete the metaphor – as a mushroom; the fruiting body of the buried threads of mycelia that run widely through the soil, and are intricately married to the root hairs of all the trees. 'Fruiting' – at that point – is the completion of the work of the poet, and the point where the artist or mystic reenters the cycle: gives what she or he has done as nourishment, and as spore or seed spreads the 'thought of enlightenment', reaching into personal depths for nutrients hidden there, back to the community. The community and its poetry are not two.[2]

The crucial principle affirmed by each of these extended statements is that culture must be understood in terms of dynamic continuity. The thunder's three commands at the end of *The Waste Land* – give, sympathize, control – were likewise all verbs of process rather than of possession, definitive action, or perception. Both of these quotations also define culture as something one does, within which one lives, rather than as a good that one simply receives or holds. One enters into continuity with the past precisely through the relation of one's *efforts* to those of his ancestors. A crucial point to note here is that Eliot's and Snyder's emphasis is itself in continuity with an older, English tradition of writing about culture. Matthew Arnold, no less than Eliot and Snyder, sought to distinguish between true, life-giving culture and the fastidiousness of connoisseurship:

Culture has got its name touched, in the fancies of men, with a sort of air of bookishness and pedantry, cast upon it from the follies of the many bookmen who forget the end in the means, and use their books with no real aim at perfection. . . . But what we are concerned for is the thing, not the name; and the thing, call it by what name we will, is simply the enabling ourselves, whether by reading, observing, or thinking, to come as near as we can to the firm intelligible law of things, and thus to get a basis for a less confused action and a more complete perfection than we have at present.[3]

Arnold's concern for perfection is, like Eliot's and Snyder's cultural thought, a social value rather than one directed primarily toward the cultivation of the individual:

Not a having and a resting, but a growing and a becoming, is the character of perfection as culture conceives it; and here, too, it coincides with religion.

And because men are all members of one great whole, and the sympathy which is in human nature will not allow one member to be indifferent to the rest or to have a perfect welfare independent of the rest, the expansion of our humanity, to suit the idea of perfection which culture forms, must be a *general* expansion. Perfection, as culture conceives it, is not possible while the individual remains isolated.[4]

A recognition of Arnold's connection with modern cultural thought is important, because other elements of his writing have led him, and the literary tradition he represents, to be discounted by many twentieth-century authors. Unfortunately, Arnold's emphasis on the 'sweetness and light'of Hellenism can suggest a *static* value as the goal of cultural striving. Raymond Williams has written, 'Perfection is a "becoming", culture is a process, but part of the effect of Arnold's argument is to create around them a suggestion that they are known absolutes'.[5] And Arnold's assumption of cultural *standards* frequently leads him, just where his intention seems most playful, to reveal a fearful snobbery. He discourses pleasantly on the necessary cultural impoverishment of Nonconformists, as opposed to those nurtured, like Arnold himself, in the Church of England. His complacency also bubbles out characteristically when he asks, of the Phillistines, 'consider these, people, then . . . would any amount of wealth be worth having with the condition that one was to become just like these people?'[6]

In their common divergence from Arnold's particular values, Eliot and Snyder perpetuate his *central* contribution – the understanding of culture as a dynamic continuity. Where Arnold sees the individual and the group striving back toward a classical ideal, Eliot and Snyder point to the tradition itself as a working, continually re-forming mass. An individual does not need to move *toward* culture, but rather to find a way of participating *in* culture. Such a shift of emphasis makes it harder to be ensnared in the assumption that one's own caste, as defined by classical education or inherited wealth, is at the apex of a cultural hierarchy. It also leads automatically to a more *inclusive* sense of culture and history. While for Arnold history is implicitly the attenuation and retreat of true culture, Snyder, in particular, understands it as a widening circle, an enrichment analogous to the work of yeast in dough, or of microorganisms in the soil. Such a dynamic sense of continuity accords more fully with the experience of a century that has seen the dissolution of empire, the collapse of culture's proudest towers. It also harmonizes with a shift in scientific understanding, as we have moved from the precision of Newton's mechanism to a world comprehensible only in terms of relativity, of uncertainty, of progressive variation. Culture, in an era like ours, makes sense only as a medium through which the past and the present mutually absorb and inform one another. Instead of Arnold's ironic distinction between the past and the present, Eliot emphasizes the present's perpetual groundedness in the past. At one point in 'Tradition and the Individual Talent', Eliot writes, 'Some one has said: "The dead writers are remote from us because we *know* so much more than they did." Precisely, and they are that which we know.'[7]

Snyder has, in turn, remarked, 'What's really fun about Eliot is his intelligence and his highly selective and charming use of Occidental symbols which point you in a certain direction. . . . He had the sense of roots.'[8] Both poets are alert to a living tradition beyond that of Christian Europe. Whatever coherence the conclusion of *The Waste Land* achieves may be related to Eliot's use of ancient Sanskrit mythology and language. Even in *Four Quartets*, with its Dantesque vision of the mystic rose, the wisdom and symbolism of Buddhism are essential to Eliot's design. Snyder's debt to Buddhist insight, in particular, is even more pervasive than Eliot's.

In the initial long quotation from Snyder, his reference to 'the thought of enlightenment' and his final anti-dualistic admonishment both reveal the harmony between his understanding and that of traditional Zen Buddhism.

Gary Snyder's governing metaphor of the growth of soil clarifies an important implication also present in *The Waste Land*: the past and the dead only become accessible for recombination in the present because of their decay. 'Poets are more like mushrooms or fungus', as Snyder says in a related statement from *The Real Work*: 'They can digest the symbol-detritus.'[9] The fact that he and Eliot, living in the Western cultural sphere, bring Eastern elements into their syntheses reflects decay in this positive sense. Separate cultures, as they break down, create new life in a composting, fermentive pattern. The extreme fragmentation of society in *The Waste Land* thus offers simultaneously the grounds for despair and the basis for hope. A bacteriological sense of culture allows Snyder to value decay as a crucial part of life's nutrient cycle. 'That's really what we mean by being cultured – that the time process really does enrich and deepen what you have at hand at any time.'[10]

Such an engagement with culture as a process of decay is simultaneously empowering and humbling, even annihilating. Artistic memory thus becomes a means to self-transcendence – becoming a part of larger realities by giving up one's own hermetic integrity, in what Thomas Mann has called 'the warmth of decay'. Eliot addresses this process when he writes:

> The emotion of art is impersonal. And the poet cannot reach this impersonality without surrendering himself wholly to the work to be done. And he is not likely to know what is to be done unless he lives in what is not merely the present, but the present moment of the past, unless he is conscious, not of what is dead, but of what is already living.'[11]

A sense of impersonal surrender to a process comprehending present and past also underlies Snyder's affirmation that

> poetry is a social and traditional art that is linked to its past and particularly its language, that *loops* and draws on its past and that serves as a vehicle for contact with the depths of our own unconscious – and that it gets better by practicing. And that the expression of self, although it's a nice kind of energy to start with, would not make any expression of poetry per se.[12] . . .

The main way in which Snyder extends Eliot's sense of culture is by his attentiveness to an even wider range of elements than were comprehended in *The Waste Land*. Eliot looks to the East for wisdom to address Western culture's decay. But his synthesis of European and Western symbolism still depends largely on the traditions of 'high' culture and on the formal expressions of religion. Though equally respectful of the *sutras* and of traditional Oriental practices, Snyder places them within a continuum of cultural values which also includes 'primitive', non-book-centered cultures. *Turtle Island*, in particular, explores Native American life and practice as a fulfillment of many Eastern values, and one which is especially suited to the topography and history of this continent. In his lengthy quotation at the beginning of this chapter, Snyder speaks of the natural world's tendency 'toward a condition called climax, "virgin forest".' Only through the fulfillment of its cycles of growth and decay may a forest be *renewed*. Snyder finds the same principle of wholeness in traditional Native American cultures: because of their harmonious adjustment to particular regions, 'the only societies that are mature are primitive societies.'[13] . . .

[There is a] comprehensive view of culture in the writing of Gary Snyder. Poetry is the perfect medium for such a reconciliation. It belongs, on one hand, to the culture of the book, achieving formal and thematic resonance with the West's tradition of 'high' poetic expression. But poetry also makes possible, especially for a writer as alert to its incantatory powers as Snyder, a connection with oral traditions of mythology and ritual. Snyder has been associated with the revival of poetry readings as an American cultural form, and such readings have made poetry's reverberation both with European and with Native American models more audible. University teachers and scholars of literature also need, in Snyder's view, a more '*tribal* sense of their own work'. 'Looping backward' to establish the tradition, they would benefit from 'an anthropological or prehistoric perspective.'[14]

As Snyder says, quoting Lévi-Strauss, arts do have a special cultural status: they are the 'national parks of the mind'.[15] But they therefore only make sense within a larger awareness of culture's landscape. To understand the geology or ecology of the largest park, one must still understand something of the region in which it is located, and of the earth on whose surface it rests. To protect such a wild preserve one must be concerned with the world beyond its boundaries, with the legislation keeping it out of private hands, and with the factors influencing the quality of air, groundwater, and rain which it must share with the cities and farms of a continent. Conversely, the broader culture depends upon the high definition of art just as our store of natural diversity and standards of environmental purity depend upon the reservoir of remaining wilderness. Art, human community, and the all-embracing physical cycles of the earth must be understood as mutually expressive and sustaining. To live in an urban world, cut off from tradition and nature alike, is to experience a life-threatening wasteland. But the inward withdrawal of a distanced tradition, without regard for current necessities of the tribe, becomes absurd; flight into the wilderness, accompanied by a denunciation of all human civilization, arrives finally at the utterance of self-cancellation. Art and the earth are poles around which culture must raise the double arc of its gravitational field.

The initial quotations from Eliot and Snyder differ most obviously in Snyder's scientific terminology and perspective. Anthropology approaches culture as a universal human phenomenon, and one which operates by a genetic principle rather than a mechanical absolute. But it still maintains the limits of a *human* sphere. Kroeber and Kluckhohn, in their most concise definition, state that 'culture is the special and exclusive product of men, and is their distinctive quality in the cosmos.'[16] Snyder goes beyond this aspect of the anthropological view, asserting that the cycles of human life only achieve health and wholeness in a community which also includes the earth's nonhuman processes and entities. One immediate advantage of such inclusiveness is that it amplifies an organic metaphor implicit throughout modern cultural thought. Snyder's biochemical analogy extends Eliot's definition of poetry as 'a more finely perfected medium in which special, or very varied, feelings are at liberty to enter into new combinations.'[17] Even 'sweetness and light', Arnold's most ridiculed phrase, becomes more meaningful within this understanding of poetry as breaking down an anaerobic mass, making available to oxygen and sunshine the materials for new growth. Such a parallel holds up surprisingly well as one reads over Arnold's interpretation of Hellenism's function in a densely compacted 'Hebraic' culture like that of the Anglo-Saxons.

Modern science has illuminated nature's creative cycles in ways that make the organic metaphor of culture even more helpful. Genetic information is retained and exchanged with a precision worthy of comparison with human memory, both that of the individual and that – which we call culture – of the species. In his essay on 'The Wilderness', from *Turtle Island*, Gary Snyder writes:

> If we can tentatively accommodate the possibility that nature has a degree of authenticity and intelligence that requires that we look at it more sensitively, then we can move to the next step. 'Intelligence' is not really the right word. The ecologist Eugene Odum suggests the term 'biomass' . . . stored information in the cells and in the genes.[18]

An understanding that nonhuman life transmits precise information without recourse to human languages allows human culture, paradoxically, to reassert its own necessary connection with nature. Because nature is demonstrably there in its own terms, it becomes available once more for integration with the human cycle of life. It is neither inert nor a fabric of poetic conventions: earth's culture and human culture include and nourish one another. . . .

NOTES

1   T. S. Eliot, *The Sacred Wood: Essays on Poetry and Criticism*, London: Methuen, 1960, p. 49.
2   From Gary Snyder, *The Real Work: Interviews and Talks, 1964–1979* (ed. W. Scott McLean), New York: New Directions, 1980, pp. 173–4.
3   Matthew Arnold, *Culture and Anarchy*, Cambridge: Cambridge University Press, 1960, pp. 162, 48.
4   Ibid., p. 48.
5   Raymond Williams, *Culture and Society*, New York: Harper & Row, 1966, p. 125.
6   Arnold, *Culture and Anarchy*, p. 52.
7   Eliot, *The Sacred Wood*, p. 52.
8   Snyder, *The Real Work*, pp. 56, 57.
9   Ibid., pp. 71, 62.
10 Ibid., p. 62
11 Eliot, *The Sacred Wood*, p. 59.

12 Snyder, *The Real Work*, p. 65.
13 Ibid., p. 116.
14 Ibid., pp. 63, 64.
15 Ibid., p. 132.
16 A. L. Kroeber and Clyde Kluckhohn, *Culture: A Critical Review of Concepts and Definitions*, New York: Vintage, 1963, p. 84.
17 Eliot, *The Sacred Wood*, pp. 53–4.
18 From Gary Snyder, *Turtle Island*, New York: New Directions, 1974, p. 107.

41

Ecocriticism and the Novel

Dominic Head*

[ECOCRITICISM]

THERE ARE . . . GROUNDS for expecting a more extensive area of commonality between literary theory and the ecocritical agenda. Arguably, the broader Green movement is predicated on a typically postmodernist depriviling of the human subject. This phenomenon is in tune with a wider cultural decentring drive, and it is a depriviling which can lead to a possible grass-roots micropolitics. Such a process itself is characterized by a paradoxical combination of decentring and *re-centring*: traditional given hierarchies are overturned – the assumptions on which they are based decentred – and a new, provisional platform of judgement is installed in a qualified recentring.

One construction of ecological thinking can be shown to be based on this same paradoxical combination, and here there is a direct parallel with elements of postcolonial theory, where the colonizer and his discourses are decentred in relation to the colonized (now no longer seen to be at the margin). In some postcolonial texts (including critical works) there is a transitional dynamic in which decolonization is process. This, in a sense, is a qualified recentring where the Other is unable (yet) to reclaim its history.

Superficially, it might seem that ecocriticism could build on this transitional dynamic in approaching the problem of giving 'voice' to the nonhuman Other. Indeed, there is a tendency within ecocriticism to follow the lead of critics recouping marginalized voices. However, this also involves a deliberate act of prestidigitation, a problematic process in which an identity is projected onto nature.

[Lawrence] Buell's 'aesthetic of relinquishment' actually involves the need to imagine 'nonhuman agents as bona fide partners', and in his discussion of 'Nature's Personhood' Buell considers how, in environmental law, an identity can be assigned to nature 'to engineer a change in the legal and ethical status quo by a discursive innovation frankly announced as fictive.' The larger claim is that a cultivated emphasis on the kinship between human and non-human is a powerful ideological tool, that 'to change discourse is to change society.'[1] . . .

*From 'Problems in Ecocriticism and the Novel', *Key Words*, 1, 1998.

[THE NOVEL]

The greatest challenge may be to make the novel relevant to this new critical field. The difficulty of the challenge is considerable, given the emphasis on 'textuality' in both novelistic and critical discourse, and the suspicion voiced by some ecocritics that this emphasis might lead readers away from an engagement with representations of the natural. The tendency of the novel to focus on personal development, and on social rather than environmental matters (and on time rather than place) is sometimes said to create an impression of alienation from the natural. A simple solution would be to detach a consideration of content from form: we might then find much to say about the regional novel, or about narrative fictions written in the utopian and dystopian traditions. But if ecocriticism is to realize its full potential, it will need to find a way of appropriating novelistic form. The focus, here, is our perceived crisis of disconnection from the non-human Other.

A representative ecocritical solution for this crisis of disconnection is offered by Glen A. Love, for whom there may be something redemptive in the literature of place, especially in nature writing which celebrates the natural world as Other. A problem emerges when Love blurs the literature of place from different traditions in his prescriptive cure for our 'communal neurosis'. . . . The indisputable natural otherness of Arizona, a touchstone for Love, may indeed inspire the kind of celebratory nature writing of which there is a strong tradition in the US, and which is directly linked to North American ecocriticism. Yet we must surely baulk at his invocation of Hardy and Lawrence in the same connection: the resonant 'nature' imagery of these novelists has the reverse impetus to that North American wilderness writing which offers a poetic and contemplative elsewhere.[2] Whether we think of Ursula Brangwen's vision of the rainbow above the colliers' houses of Beldover, or of Eustacia Vye atop Rainbarrow, or Tess entering the vale of the Great Dairies like a fly on a billiard table, we are confronted with 'natural' images in which questions of social history and sexual politics are inscribed in the scene or in the landscape. This *inscription*, of course, is directly material in the worlds of these novels, and not only a matter of poetic affinity or correlation. To understand this kind of 'nature novel' one must not forget, in Raymond Williams' words, that 'a considerable part of what we call natural landscape . . . is the product of human design and human labour, and in admiring it as natural it matters very much whether we suppress that fact of labour or acknowledge it.'[3] Following the trained critical archaeology this implies, the represented landscape becomes a text in which human interaction with the environment is indelibly recorded: it follows that a Green materialist reading of this inner text cannot divorce the social from the natural, or, indeed, the question of form from content.

This last point is crucial because it places emphasis on 'textuality' in a way which is sensitive to an organic perception of literary form, and which may allay the fears of some ecologically-minded critics concerning a perceived widening gap between world and text in literary studies. . . . Hardy and Lawrence both consciously employ a pointed textuality – the encodings and inscriptions of the represented landscapes – as an integral part of their designs. The simple point is that a textualizing process, for the novel, belongs to the creative as much as the critical sphere, and that, far from producing alienation, it may indicate the necessary route to an invigorated Green materialism.

Yet this reasoning may be redundant, if the novel is peculiarly resistant to the operations of ecocritical enquiry. Here there are grounds for pessimism about the dominance of the novel in twentieth-century literature, since this is a mode of discourse which speaks to an increasingly urbanized population whose concerns appear to have no immediate connection with the non-human environment. A Green reading of the genre, baldly summarized in this way, would seem to demand a vulgar ecocritical exposure of what is left out – of the genre's environmental bad faith. Lawrence Buell's solution to the problems involved in the dominance of fictive literary modes (and the effects of this dominance on literary theorists) is to turn to environmental nonfiction – nature writing. . . .

Buell's checklist of the ingredients of 'an environmentally oriented work' is instructive. The first (and most evidently ecocentric) of his four requirements is that '*the nonhuman environment is present not merely as a framing device but as a presence that begins to suggest that human history is implicated in natural history*'.[4] One can think of very few novels in which this principle is sustained throughout, and the logic of this requirement may contradict the way in which the novel's role as a social medium is usually articulated. Raymond Williams' unfinished trilogy *People of the Black Mountains* (in which narrative continuity is supplied by place rather than character) could be read as a major experiment in support of this ecocentric principle, but it is hard to conceive of the novel as a genre reinventing itself in this way. . . .

From an ecocritical perspective, the advantage of non-fictional nature writing is that it simplifies the processes of discursive mediation in putting readers in touch with the outer reality that is represented. Buell shows how environmental nonfiction can cultivate a new kind of realism – or outer mimesis – which can palliate the over-textualizing tendency of literary analysis which is presented, in this argument, as complicitous with our crisis of disconnection. . . . This alternative kind of outer mimesis . . . is not mimesis as imitation. . . . The apparent paradox of a representation which is stylized yet referential at the same time is aptly illustrated by those field guides containing paintings or drawings which, for example, emphasize only certain markings on a bird or a butterfly. Such representations contain a level of abstraction, yet assist the identification of species in the field more effectively than a photographic representation. It is the stylized image which has the greater capacity to put the reader or viewer in touch with the environment.[5]

There are affinities, at a technical level, between this celebration of environmental representation and Paul Ricoeur's tripartite explanation of mimesis in narrative fiction, as representation rather than imitation.[6] Mimesis 1 is the stage of preunderstanding of action and the need for it to be mediated in articulation, and a preunderstanding of Being in time. Mimesis 2 is the configuration of action in the emplotment of the work itself. Crucially important to this level is how the fictive present in a work of narrative fiction supplies a framework for conjoining recollection and anticipation, a framework which emulates our authentic experience of Being in time. The reading process supplies a bridge to mimesis 3. This is the stage of refiguration, which marks the intersection of two worlds: the world of the text and the world of the reader. For Ricoeur, narrative has its full meaning when it is restored to the time of action and suffering in mimesis 3. And an essential part of this restoration is a quest for personal identity in the act of reading and interpretation – in our assuming responsibility for a story.

This three-stage mimesis begins with our worldly experience of time and action, traces how these elements of preunderstanding are drawn on in the composition of a text, and stresses a return to the world of the reader in the active process of reception and interpretation. And the more self-conscious and artificial the text is, the more effort is required in its interpretation, and so (if it is successful) the greater its impact will be at the level of mimesis 3. As in the field guides, and in nature writing, where stylization produces recognition, the novelistic effect is produced by a complex stylization as an integral part of a substantive mimesis.

If there are affinities, technically, between the novel and environmental non-fiction in their mimetic procedures, what is distinctive about the novel in this connection is its dual stress on Being in time and personal growth as structural components. The answer to the question 'how Green is the novel?' may depend on how these components are viewed. Ostensibly, the stresses on personal time and personal growth might seem catastrophically anthropocentric. Yet . . . these features need not be seen as indices of an unregenerated anthropocentrism, but rather a literary route for changing consciousness, part of that necessary transitional process of bringing things to a crisis. This does not mean, of course, that all novels will treat environmental topics; even so we may have progressed beyond a simple dichotomy between form and content, with the novel retaining the capacity to treat environmental themes in a manner to create an impact on consciousness at the level of mimesis 3.

This notion of bridging world and text – in which a formal capacity is available for the treatment of an apposite content – may also tap into an innate human process of cognition. The possibility of an habitual environmental sensitivity is suggested by the emergent field of literary analysis combined with biological science. If biological science can definitively break down the separation between the human individual and his or her environment – since even our own bodies play host to apparently independent micro-organisms – then the implications for our modes of perception appear to be enormous. Arnold Berleant's aesthetics of environment registers the enormity here. His argument, beginning with the premise that 'person and environment are continuous', necessitates a new understanding of perception in which an aesthetic response is always already a material engagement rather than merely a contemplative one: 'If every *thing* has an aesthetic dimension, then so does every *experience* of every thing . . . an aesthetic dimension is inherent in all experience.'[7]

The beauty of this conception of aesthetic experience is that it undercuts the binary opposition between anthropocentrism and ecocentrism, since human perception is continuous with the material world. However, the dismantling of this opposition may be potentially irresponsible if, for example, all human activity is seen as 'natural'. Nevertheless, it appears to offer a way of mitigating the distancing effects of literary mediation, since an aesthetic response is common not just to the refiguration of a literary effect, but to all sensory processing.

It seems to me that an idealistic ecocriticism, in a thorough-going ecocentric form, would need to establish an aesthetic which is very much like this, and which demolishes the self–Other dualism. . . . The projection of a prelapsarian oneness of Being is also strangely abstract, removed from social processes. More important, for my purposes, is the difficulty in making this kind of aesthetic response relevant to novelistic discourse, and here the dream begins to fade. The close reading of novels, after all, trades on the discrepancy and interaction between different ontological (and epistemological) levels, and does so not because it follows an arcane agenda of its own, but because novelistic representations always install these different levels. The literary effect, in general, I am tempted to say, is generated by a kind of self-consciousness which a thoroughly ecocentric criticism might need to extirpate. . . .

Can we, then, imagine a novel which incorporates contemporary environmental concerns; which traces the intersection of time and space; which shows how personal time and personal identity are implicated in both social and environmental history; and does all of this – not *despite* – but *because* of its self-consciousness about textuality? I would argue that this is an accurate summary of what makes Graham Swift's *Waterland* the important novel it is.[8]

[*WATERLAND*]

Waterland is a novel constructed through a combination of different narratives: public, national histories; the history of the Fens; private, 'dynastic' histories (focused on the human interaction with the environment down the centuries); superstition and the supernatural form another element, and equally important is the natural history of the eel. The configuration of these different strands demonstrates a process of siltation in History teacher Tom Crick's quest for personal identity. The quest is conducted through the uncovering of layers of personal guilt – guilt by historical association as well as the guilt rooted in personal actions.

Even if there is no *overtly* ecological message in this novel, the motif of siltation – as both structure and theme – insists on certain connections in the construction of human identity: the necessary coexistence of private feeling and public event, but also the interdependence of time, place and politics. If the discovery of human siltation brings the past vitally into the present, it does so by insisting on Being in an environment: this has to do not simply with matters of subsistence, but also with environment as a limit to consciousness (there are repeated references to how the flat Fenland landscape may affect the psyche, and adversely so). My point, of course (drawing on the simplified model of Ricoeur's mimesis) is that Swift makes special use of the formal capacities of the novel in making these connections, most especially a bringing to crisis of personal consciousness through complex configuration. At the level of refiguration the novel forces our analytical hand in a way which redeems much of the negative emphasis.

When Dick – Tom's brain-damaged half-brother – discovers his personal history – the novel's tragic denouement unfolds. He is the product of an incestuous relationship between his mother and his unbalanced grandfather, who has inter-pellated Dick as 'Saviour of the World'. But the irony of this designation is effaced by Dick's suicide: he dives off the dredger that is his place of work (his business is the control of siltation) and is imagined by narrator Tom Crick swimming out to sea like the eel, the mystical creature with which he has been closely associated. The dive installs Dick as a scapegoat figure, sacrificed in expiation of society's sins. He is the product of a multitude of sins by blood or by association: industrial exploitation; imperialism; sexual jealousy; incest; murder and a lost political vision. Here Dick swims symbolically away from the developed West – the setting sun behind him – to return to his mythic origins. Subtly the focus on Tom Crick is displaced by this ending, which recentres the sense of tragedy on Dick. The personal guilt of Tom Crick has the same components as the collective guilt projected onto Dick as scapegoat for a society's sins. By this correspondence the sense of personal time / personal history becomes necessarily linked to collective goals, which implic-itly emerge, through the realization that a disastrous banishing of the natural is the product of modern social and industrial history.

Graham Swift manages to make the *form* of his novel carry this larger agenda, and the effect is by no means unique: it is not difficult to think immediately of a handful of novels which would lend themselves to this kind of analysis – my list would include: Ian McEwan's *The Child in Time*, J. M. Coetzee's *Life and Times of Michael K*, Gabriel Garcia Marquez's *Love in the Time of Cholera*, and Nadine Gordimer's *The Conservationist*. Of course, the choice is selective, but the point is merely that it is possible to list several novelists to support the projected princi-ples. And this is without having recourse to writers consciously writing in the tradi-tion of the 'regional' novel; or drawing on the fertile traditions of wilderness and utopian/dystopian writing. My modest – and perhaps rather obvious – suggestion is just this: that the modern novel, with its emphasis on private feeling as the source of public action, can be an appropriate vehicle for a Green agenda, whether creative or critical. . . .

My larger – and perhaps more contentious – suggestion is that if the novelist and the critic have no place in a Green Utopia, they do function properly in the transitional context of bringing things to a crisis. If we permit the use of the term ecocriticism to designate the cultural work of this interim, we can do so only by acknowledging that it is underpinned by the kind of 'weak anthropocentrism' that Andrew Dobson sees as essential to the politics of ecology, or ecologism.[9] My worry is that if a transitional dynamic is not cultivated within ecocriticism, together with an acknowledged anthropocentrism, this is a critical practice which will get precisely nowhere, confining itself to an unrealized utopia.

NOTES

1   Lawrence Buell, *The Environmental Imagination: Thoreau, Nature Writing, and the Formation of American Culture*, Cambridge, MA: Harvard University Press, 1995, pp. 179, 203, 204.

2   Glen A. Love, 'Revaluing Nature: Toward an Ecological Criticism', in *Old West, New West: Centennial Essays* (ed. Barbara Howard Meldrum) Moscow, ID: University of Idaho Press, 1993, pp. 283–99 (p. 292). Love refers to John Alcorn's *The Nature Novel from Hardy to Lawrence*, London: Macmillan, 1977.

3   Raymond Williams, 'Ideas of Nature', in *Problems in Materialism and Culture*, London: Verso, 1989, pp. 67–85 (p. 78).

4   Buell, pp. 7–8, 168.

5   Buell, pp. 110–11, 99, 97–98.

6   See Paul Ricoeur, *Time and Narrative*, 3 vols (trans. Kathleen McLaughlin and David Pellauer), Chicago: University of Chicago Press, 1984–8.

7   Arnold Berleant, *The Aesthetics of Environment*, Philadelphia, PA: Temple University Press, 1992, pp. 4, 10–11.

8   Graham Swift, *Waterland* (1983), London: Picador, 1984.

9   Andrew Dobson, *Green Political Thought*, London: Unwin Hyman, 1990, pp. 53–67.

42

Ecothrillers: Environmental Cliffhangers

RICHARD KERRIDGE*

WHY HAS LITERATURE – the realist novel in particular – been so slow to respond to environmentalism? In public debate, environmental issues have been a conspicuous presence for at least three decades. Environmentalism asks new questions (as well as some old ones) about consumerist assumptions and habits. It asks us to re-examine pleasure, desire, ambition. It intrudes into personal lives and demands inclusion in many areas of political and moral debate. It throws into sharp focus the question of what rich and poor nations should expect of each other. Since ecology is concerned with the interdependencies of different life forms which inhabit and constitute the same environment, an ecological approach to culture will search for the hidden interdependencies between areas of life usually seen as opposites: nature and artifice, pastoral and urban, leisure and work, fantasy and reality.

One would expect a cultural development of this magnitude to register strongly in literature. Feminism, for example, has found expression across the range of literary genres. We might expect to see by now a flow of novels, plays and poems exploring the conflicts aroused by environmentalism and producing new environmentalist literary forms. In Britain, at least, this has been slow to happen. Some versions of environmentalist sensibility have begun to emerge in poetry; Terry Gifford discusses a number of these in *Green Voices* (1995). But in literary fiction environmental preoccupations have not yet made a very noticeable appearance.

There are some exceptions. Graham Swift's *Waterland* (1983) continues a tradition of novels in which landscape dominates both as setting and metaphor. Jenny Diski's *Rainforest* (1987) takes as its main character a woman ecologist working on a species-survey; this minutely detailed work tightens around the heroine, as she is besieged by formless anxieties. Ian McEwan's *The Child in Time* (1987) draws on recent scientific ideas to suggest that non-linear patterns of time, to be found in nature and childhood, can counter the oppressive values of the Thatcherite period.

*Adapted by the author from the following two articles: 'Ecothrillers: Environmentalism in Popular Culture', *English Review*, 8(3), 1998; 'BSE Stories', *Key Words: A Journal of Cultural Materialism*, 2, 1999.

Julian Barnes's book of short stories *A History of the World in 10½ Chapters* (1989) repeatedly teases its reader with the undecidability of environmental fears. A.S. Byatt's novella *Angels and Insects* (1992) visits Victorian nature-writing to explore the different economies and vulnerabilities of masculine and feminine versions of 'nature', in a tense fable of sexual selection. But these books do not approach environmentalism directly, or engage with its strongest desires and anxieties, its eroticism, its politics. They tend to subordinate it, treating it as background or period-colour, or as subsidiary to the main concerns of each work.

Why does the realist novel have such difficulty in involving itself with environmental issues? One reason may be hinted at in a recent comment by the postmodernist geographer David Harvey. What makes the ecological movement 'so special and so interesting', he says, is 'the variety of conceptions of time and space which it brings to bear' (Harvey 230). To an unsettling degree, environmentalism asks us to take into account the possible long-term results of present actions. Consequences such as global warming do not register as immediate changes in life around us, but must be projected, uncertainly, onto the world fifty years hence.

An example of special concern in Britain is the continuing story of Bovine Spongiform Encephalopathy, or 'mad cow disease'. BSE is a calamity which may produce lasting changes or none. Two contradictory narratives appear to be unfolding together. One tells of a return to normality, as, step by step, the disease disappears from cattle herds, consumers are persuaded to eat British beef again and old assumptions and habits, temporarily thrown into confusion, are able to return. But the other reveals an intractable crisis, in which every piece of good news seems to be followed by a twist back into fear. Reassurance is given and then snatched back. Are these the last spasms of a fading anxiety, or will the problem flare up again? Will the disease prove only to have reached a small number of victims, or will there be a large epidemic? Is the story ending or beginning?

This indeterminacy is typical of environmental narratives. Chernobyl was another event that, as its drama unfolded, seemed likely to be a great turning-point. If we could only get out of this one safely, things would *surely* have to change. Now Chernobyl appears to have made strangely little difference. It has not functioned – and could not function – as the event which changed everything.

Barbara Adam argues that in order to take environmental problems seriously, we need what she calls a 'timescape perspective', in which the timespans of ordinary life, onto which we map our personal hopes and plans, are viewed alongside drastically longer and shorter distances (the instantaneous reception of an infection as well as the drawn-out process of its incubation). Such a perspective would enable us to 'see the invisible' (Adam 19), and begin to take some account of the concealed hazards of industrial life. Timespans would momentarily contract, enabling us to imagine the distant and uncertain consequences of an action. Events too large and slow for the scale of ordinary human perception (such as climate-change), or too small and quick (the activities of micro-organisms, or of the nervous-system) could begin to register.

These stretches of time are outside the span normally used by realist novels, whose seriousness is achieved through committed absorption in the details and cadences of individual perception. This is the genre's limitation in dealing with environmental issues. It is also, however, a threshold which environmentalism neeeds to cross; a discipline it needs to accept. To explain why, I want to look at some of the problems raised by the treatment of environmental concerns in another genre, the popular thriller.

For readers in the West, environmental issues are much more the stuff of potentiality than of actuality: tomorrow rather than now, elsewhere rather than here, a crisis building rather than a crisis reached. Because of their intangibility, such matters can always be postponed; set aside, for now, in the face of more pressingly immediate and familiar demands. Their very reality is constantly in question. Their elusiveness poses problems of representation which the realistic novel has scarcely begun to address.

They therefore become prime material for the popular thriller which brings fears to artificial climax and release. The thriller allows its audiences to be voyeuristic spectators of calamity. In disaster-movies, for example, environmental dangers cease to be elusive. Catastrophes strike individuals with dramatic suddenness, usually because glaring signs have been ignored. Such violent events produce rapid action rather than subtle reflection and development of character. This genre stands in stark contrast to the realist novel, traditionally valued for the leisure it seems to have; the humaneness of the care with which it can watch people and acknowledge their complexities. This is its liberalism, and its capacity to resist the imposition of abrupt, evasive closure.

Environmentalists frequently feel that time is running out. They feel panic in the face of the world's indifference. Sometimes this fear finds expression in fantasies of apocalypse – or rather of apocalypse excitingly and heroically averted, the escape narrow and frightening enough to stop industrial capitalism in its tracks. This is the ecological disaster as warning: the shock we needed, the lesson administered by providence to open our eyes just in time.

Environmentalism here is in a position full of traps. Sometimes environmentalists are accused of *wanting* such disasters to be worse: of cherishing fantasies of apocalypse. Tom Athanasiou gives a useful discussion of this in *Slow Reckoning* (73–82). The accusation is often cheaply made, but it does ask serious questions of environmentalists, who may feel frustrated at the ease with which normality returns after a disaster. Their frustration arises from a perception that the underlying conditions which led to the disaster have not been addressed. Yet in showing this feeling, environmentalists can appear reluctant to relinquish an emergency which carried the possibility of change as well as calamity.

There is a temptation, therefore, to prophesy disaster with a hint of relish. This is a particularly damaging form of bad faith for environmentalists, suggesting that they too, deep down, do not take the threat wholly seriously. Fantasies of apocalypse which compensate for a sense of powerlessness arise in the face of a normality felt to be permanent: the very presence of such fantasies can be read as evidence of an underlying assumption that things will not change. One of the most important tasks for the new ecocriticism is to make explicit the precise function of apocalyptic fantasy; which means acknowledging and describing the pleasures of this genre.

Hollywood ecothrillers such as *Jurassic Park* (1993) and *Waterworld* (1995) depict the ecological catastrophe as a result of capitalist *hubris*, but also as an opportunity for heroism and Edenic rebirth. A significant variation on the redemption theme is provided by Paul Watkins's novel *Archangel* (1995), a thriller about a logging company and an eco-saboteur in an American old-growth forest. The novel ends with an unlikely change of heart by an industrialist finally appalled by the violence his policies have produced. This ending expresses a timid, conservative wish that everything may be solved by *hearts* changing, so that *systems* will not need to change. It also touches on a central environmentalist hope: that capitalism can somehow be shocked into changing before it is too late. Thus, ecological threats can be deployed for their scariness without ecological *solutions* being considered or given literary form.

Such novels manage to exploit environmentalism's topicality, and genuinely acknowledge some of its concerns, without sacrificing their allegience to industrial capitalism. They express, finally, a belief that capitalism is subject not to the full range of political and economic forces but to the free consciences of individuals at the top. These, the consciences of secretly tormented industrialists, are the chink in the system's armour, through which environmentalism can penetrate to the human, responsive, emotional core of an apparently hard and impersonal system. The struggle of the environmentalist thus becomes an effort to reach that centre, to fight through the outer layers and touch the system's heart. Sometimes this narrative turns into that most masculine of narratives, the story of two strong men engaged in a personal struggle which is also a form of intimacy.

Catastrophes unleashed by accidents in military laboratories, or by other over-confident uses of technology, have long been part of repertoire of horror fiction, as in James Herbert's *The Fog* (1975), or Stephen King's *The Stand* (1978). A standard pattern is that the disaster, and the horrors it releases, come both as nemesis to human greed and presumption, and also as a test which rouses latent qualities in the characters who eventually defeat the horror: qualities they would not otherwise have discovered. This is a reassuring message, borrowing from Christian narratives of ordeal and redemption. It is linked to the notion, persistent among American survivalist militias and elsewhere, that modern civilisation constrains and buries 'natural' abilities which need a crisis to release them (I have colluded with this in using words like 'unleashed'). This belief is quite close to a common environmentalist fantasy: that the crisis is a necessary ultimatum to modern culture to change its ways and rediscover its real – that is, its 'natural' – self. Such fantasies are beguiling because they seem to promise a dramatic reversal of the powerlessness many environmentalists feel. They are dangerous because they presume a successful outcome; their rhetoric suggests that, as in *The Stand*, some sort of providence is controlling the experiment and will not permit the wrong ending.

These ecothrillers have a predictable ambivalence about the disasters they summon up, the same ambivalence a crime thriller has about violent crime. The disaster is a warning, something ostensibly there to frighten us into changing our ways, but it is also a source of pleasure. The excitement the thriller generates depends on the eruption of danger. This danger has to be genuinely appalling, but has also to be under the plot's control, so that closure can take place and survival be guaranteed.

This ambivalence, flirting with catastrophe while remaining sure of security, sets a pattern for our responses to real ecological crisis. Styles and structures continually cross from fiction to non-fiction. Television documentaries about health hazards or environmental threats now routinely employ stylistic features from horror films: creepy tinkling music to make us feel nervous, sudden explosive chords to make us jump. Tom Jagtenburg and David McKie have recently analysed television news as 'a branch of show business' (65) which borrows many narrative devices from thrillers and other genres. They describe how in news reports the arousal of fear takes place within a frame of reassurance:

> Night after night the bulletins intone habitual responses to predominantly negative happenings. They don't so much inform their viewers about what has happened on any specific day as continuously replay variations on their one solitary question: Is our world safe? . . . Although a part of modernity's reflexivity, television newsreaders also perform a comforting ritual. Each night, they run an impressive list of troubles past us, and although these might not be immediately resolved, we are still invited to rest easy.
>
> (68)

Jagtenburg and McKie argue that television news has thus become 'dangerously frivolous'. Paradoxically, it is television comedy, officially a frivolous zone, that is capable of the serious work of exposing the mechanisms of false reassurance. They cite (69) a joke by Lenny Henry: 'The nuclear power plant at Windscale has been renamed Sellafield because it sounds nicer. In future, radiation will be known as magic moonbeams.' Such humour expresses a heartening mistrust of official statements, and encourages a counter-culture of irreverence which at times gathers enough force to challenge the authority of governments. But comedy occupies a well-defined cultural space, and would have to be exceptionally powerful and eerie to break out of that space. Jokes have their own closure. Their formal completeness is its own reward. See, we're not fooled, they proclaim, in a gesture that usually requires no further action.

A character in Don DeLillo's novel *White Noise*, aware that a cloud of dangerous chemicals is moving towards his home, says of his son:

> He continued to watch me carefully, searching my face for some reassurance against the possibility of real danger – a reassurance he would immediately reject as phony.
>
> (117)

Public responses to ecological danger often seem perverse. The abrupt shifts between intensity of fear and resumption of normality (as with BSE) are disconcerting to environmentalists and their opponents. Popular concern about the environment finds numerous cultural expressions in such areas as education and leisure (the extraordinary popularity of television wildlife documentaries, comparatively neglected by Media Studies and Cultural Studies, is only the most obvious example). At times environmentalism seems to be everywhere – yet environmental priorities make so little political headway, so little impression on economic life. It is as if environmentalism has been defined, by the tacit agreement of the majority, as a purely cultural practice, or even a leisure activity. In its many cultural spaces, environmentalism can express and speak to the intensest fears and yearnings, but outside those spaces we are suddenly deaf to environmental arguments. Whether in the lives of individuals or in social policy, environmentalism has great difficulty in moving beyond these cultural spaces. Within them it is permitted the headlong rush of fantasy. The intensity of environmentalist fear and longing derives in part from this confinement, this pent-up, protected condition.

Hence the attractions of the release involved in the climactic endings of thrillers. Peter Hoeg's detective-thriller *Miss Smilla's Feeling for Snow* (1992) is a good example. This novel, a Christmas best-seller in Britain and the United States in 1994, could be called an ecofeminist detective story. Smilla, the heroine, is a Greenlander living in exile in Copenhagen because of the Danish colonialism which has destroyed the hunter-gatherer culture into which she was born. But her cultural position is more complex than this: her mother was an indigenous Greenlander and her father a Danish colonial scientist.

Her special knowledge of snow, retained from childhood, enables her to interpret clues at a murder scene. An ecological perspective therefore solves a murder mystery which has the police baffled. The villain is a criminal scientist, prepared not only to kill but to unleash a lethal and uncontainable ecological catastrophe for the sake of scientific discovery and commercial advantage. Through Smilla, the novel sets up a cautious, uneasy dialogue between her female, colonised perspective – intimate with the ecosystem, aware of consequences – and the masculine, colonialist, scientific perspective which is also part of her identity. A combination of these viewpoints is required to solve the mystery. Smilla can move between the two.

From this cross-cultural position, Smilla offers a model for a general response to environmental crisis. But the seriousness of the novel's environmentalism is called into question by its plot-structure and ending. True to its genre, the novel is drawn continually towards violent showdowns and narrow escapes. Detective stories usually start with simple 'whodunnit' questions which grow into intricate threads of connection, revealing that apparently separate events and characters are interrelated. A kind of ecology is implicit in this uncovering of connection. But at the denouement these stories tend to collapse that intricacy back into a single confrontation. *Miss Smilla* follows this pattern, as do Nevada Barr's and Elizabeth Quinn's overtly environmentalist detective stories, set in American national parks, and Watkins's *Archangel* (1995), as we have seen. Sarah Dunant's *Fatlands* (1993), a

British detective novel in the Sara Paretsky hard-boiled-but-feminist style, in which the detective, Hannah Wolfe, uncovers a BSE-type scandal in pig-farming, also obeys this rule of the genre.

The American ecofeminist and animal liberation activist Marti Kheel has called for a holistic ethics to replace the heroic ethics to which the environmental movement is sometimes drawn:

> Western heroic ethics is designed to treat problems at an advanced stage in their history – namely, at the point at which conflict has occurred. . . . Prevention is simply not a very heroic undertaking. How can you fight a battle if the enemy does not yet exist? It is far more dramatic to allow disease and conflict to develop and then to call in the troops and declare war.
>
> (258)

This points to the limitations of what thrillers tend to do with environmentalism. In all these examples, denouement is violent and sudden, and clears the ground (not such an ecological idea) for at least a temporary restoration of order. Perhaps detective stories couldn't be otherwise; their popularity depends on such releases of emotion. Ecocritics, however, will be looking for the ecological meaning of such endings. They will look for endings which are more than impositions of closure. The need of the detective-novel to condense large diffuse issues into short, tense dramas between a few individuals – to see everything as driven by individual choices – leads to implausibility here. But the difficulty isn't only due to the limitations of the genre. It is the general problem of how to imagine, represent, and begin to effect large-scale change.

These thrillers seem to be recommending a constant environmentalist vigilance, similar to the traditional vigilance of crime-fighters, or even to the vigilance called for in cold-war patriotism. Eco-heroes and heroines are lonely figures at the front-line, maintaining this vigilance, never able to rest for long. Ecocritics may welcome these stories and find them exciting. It's hard not to. But such critics will be wary of the way ecological solutions are replaced by quick, violent fixes: the way these guardians and villains permit the rest of us to be an audience.

WORKS CITED

Adam, Barbara (1998) *Timescapes of Modernity: The Environment and Invisible Hazards*, London: Routledge.

Athanasiou, Tom (1997) *Slow Reckoning*, London: Secker & Warburg.

Barnes, Julian (1989) *A History of the World in 10½ Chapters*, London: Jonathan Cape.

Barr, Nevada (1993) *The Track of the Cat*, London: Headline.

—— (1994) *A Superior Death*, London: Headline.

—— (1995) *Mountain of Bones*, London: Headline.

—— (1996) *Firestorm*, London: Headline.

Byatt, Antonia Susan (1992) *Angels and Insects*, London: Chatto & Windus.

DeLillo, Don (1985) *White Noise*, London: Picador.

Diski, Jenny (1988) *Rainforest*, Harmondsworth: Penguin.

Dunant, Sarah (1994) *Fatlands*, Harmondsworth: Penguin.

Gifford, Terry (1995) *Green Voices: Understanding Contemporary Nature Poetry*, Manchester: Manchester University Press.

Harvey, David (1996) *Justice, Nature and the Geography of Difference*, Oxford: Blackwell.

Herbert, James (1975) *The Fog*, London: New English Library.

Hoeg, Peter (1994) *Miss Smilla's Feeling for Snow* (trans. F. David), London: Flamingo.

Jagtenburg, Tom and McKie, David (1997) *Eco-Impacts and the Greening of Postmodernity*, Thousand Oaks, CA: Sage.

Kheel, Marti (1993) 'From Heroic to Holistic Ethics: The Ecofeminist Challenge', in Greta Gaard (ed.) *Ecofeminism: Women, Animals, Nature*, Philadelphia, PA: Temple University Press, pp. 243–71.

King, Stephen ([1978] 1990) *The Stand*, London: New English Library.

McEwan, Ian (1987) *The Child in Time*, London: Jonathan Cape.

Quinn, Elizabeth (1997) *Killer Whale*, New York: Simon & Schuster Pocket Books.

Swift, Graham (1983) *Waterland*, London: Heinemann.

Watkins, Paul (1995) *Archangel*, London: Faber & Faber.

PART VI

The Nature of the Text

Introduction

With the final part of the reader, 'green reading' moves from general overviews of literary movements and conventions to considerations by ecocritics of specific works or bodies of work. The aim is to get at the 'nature' of the text in a double sense: its possible meaning (conscious that ecocritical interpretation is always provisional) and its specific way of referring to the natural world. But one should not expect the 'close reading' associated with the 'New Criticism' and with the 'deconstruction' which sought to outdo it in its emphasis on 'textuality'. These analyses move freely in and out of their chosen material to debate questions as diverse as representation and responsibility. Nor, in seeking to contextualise these texts, do these critics rely on a solemn invocation of 'History with a capital H', as is often the case with Marxist and even with new historicist interpretations. Rather, the context is likely to be simultaneously geographical and historical, spatial and temporal, climatic and institutional; far from the latter dimensions being denied, they are rendered all the more interesting.

Jonathan Bate's reading of Keats's ode 'To Autumn' as an 'ecosystem' sets the tone. Bate's spirited defence of the poem is, initially, a repudiation of Jerome McGann's remorselessly historicising claim that it was intended to distract its readers from the hard economic facts of bad harvests and food riots in the Regency period. In the second half of the article, which is approximately what is reprinted here, it develops into a defence of Keats's ode as a poem about 'living with the weather', about the inextricability of culture and nature, which works by exploring and affirming 'networks, links, bonds and correspondences'. The ode does not do so crudely or reductively: rather it is a 'thinking' of 'fragile, beautiful, necessary ecological wholeness'. Keats, as presented here, might seem a fitting companion for Thoreau, who certainly emphasised habitat, and also the hidden connections between the human and the non-human; but Louise Westling reminds us that ecocriticism can be 'critical' in the sense of judgemental when she offers her challenging account of the latter's work, indicating an underlying fear of 'bonds'. Her argument, which makes particular sense if one re-reads the extract from 'Walking' reprinted earlier (Chapter 4), is that Thoreau's attitude to nature was deeply ambivalent. Seeing it as his female 'other', and wishing to celebrate it, he kept reverting to the masculine, hierarchical view of it which he had learnt from his master Emerson. Thus we find again and again imagery of distaste intermingled with the rhetoric of celebration, as if Thoreau could not decide whether 'female' nature was there to be subdued or revered.

We are also aware of a profound ambiguity in the 'nature writing' for which Thomas Hardy's fiction is celebrated; but Richard Kerridge argues that Hardy is a positive model for ecocritics in his very ability to problematise the relations between human observer and observed nature, and in turn between the self which wants to stand apart to savour the environment and the self which is implicated in it. In exploring the tension between the 'tourist's' and the 'native's' approach to a locality, Hardy alerts us to the 'situatedness' of our love of nature. Clearly, Kerridge's article opens up infinite possibilities for the ecocritical reading of fiction and modern literature generally. It is worth recalling that, if Hardy was patronised by Henry James and was deemed heretical by T. S. Eliot, he was held in high esteem by both D. H. Lawrence and Virginia Woolf. This goes to show how complex modernism was, and how misleading it is simply to equate it with an anti-mimetic tendency; but it perhaps might also spur us on to reconsider the reputation of the last of these figures. We have seen how much Woolf admired Dorothy Wordsworth's sense of place, her intimate knowledge of her environment. Here Carol H. Cantrell reads *Between the Acts* as an exploration of situated, bodily existence and of nature as a living presence. Cantrell comes to Woolf from the perspective of the philosophy of Maurice Merleau-Ponty, which repudiates the Cartesian dualism of rational ego and mechanical matter in favour of an 'incarnational' approach to perception. One only perceives (and so one only thinks, knows, understands) in the context of an embodied experience in a given place; self, flesh and world are intimately involved in one another. If we read Woolf aright, Cantrell claims, modernism is above all a critique of the model of reason bequeathed by Descartes via the Enlightenment, with its false privileging of mind over matter/body/nature. Thus we see that issues raised by Kerridge in relation to Hardy are enriched when we consider the work of one of his most important admirers.

As we approach our own time, we find ourselves talking less of coherent literary movements such as modernism and more of a variety of discrete forms of writing. Some of the material discussed in our closing chapters might be labelled 'postmodernist', but if so we still need to distinguish that which is 'reconstructive' (*Ceremony*, *Refuge*) from that which is, if not intellectually demanding enough to be 'deconstructive', then certainly evasive and defeatist (*The Silence of the Lambs*). It is worth further noting that, in the former category, the first work mentioned is oriented towards the category of the 'fantastic' and the second queries conventional notions of factuality. 'Writing nature' need not involve a flatly mimetic 'nature writing'. In England, the most celebrated 'fantasist' of the century has been J. R. R. Tolkien, and it is to his major work, *The Lord of the Rings*, that we now turn. Significantly, though it was published well before the era of postmodernism, it is certainly prophetically 'reconstructive' in that it foresees the need to foster human pluralism and natural diversity. Here Patrick Curry argues that, far from encouraging his readers to evade environmental disaster by indulging in dreams of another world, 'Middle-Earth' is presented as a site of struggle, much like our own. Modernity, with its bad 'magic' of unbridled technology, is not simply to be accepted, the novel implies: the destruction of local communities and of ancient forests amount to a 'war on life' which can and must be resisted, as do Tolkien's heroes. If Mordor were to have his way, global destruction would result.

Imagining ecocatastrophe is necessary in order to prevent it, and Leslie Silko's fiction is another model of how to do so. Lawrence Buell celebrates her novel *Ceremony* as a reworking of Eliot's *The Waste Land* in an age when waste lands (wildernesses) are being destroyed and waste lands (devastated regions) are being created; but also he emphasises Silko's ability to revive and revise traditional Laguna storytelling in pursuit of a form with which to encounter and comprehend the new threats to nature. Indeed, she explores the very idea of the breaking of contract between past and present, and between modern humanity and the earth, as the basis of an apocalyptic vision which, simultaneously following and expanding narrative paradigms, attempts to do justice to the planetary trauma on the horizon. In this simultaneous fidelity to received forms and willingness to depart from them where appropriate, Silko's relation to fiction resembles that of Terry Tempest Williams to environmental non-fiction. Cheryll Glotfelty charts the departures made by the author in her *Refuge*, significantly subtitled 'An Unnatural History of Family and Place': for example, its choice of urban as well as rural settings, its self-conscious attention to gender, its fusion of domestic and natural history, its confusion of fact and fiction. All in all, Glotfelty concludes that Williams's writing is both drawing on and destabilising traditional boundaries in accordance with an ecofeminist aesthetic: she is 'breaking the ground' for environmental nonfiction to open it up to new methods and concerns so that it does not fall into disuse. Not that ecological themes are ever likely to prove irrelevant to literary and cultural production: as Jhan Hochman shows, in our closing extract, popular fiction and cinema are often indices of what humanity is doing to the environment and to non-human animals. It is the latter which is the subtext of *The Silence of the Lambs* (significantly popular as both a novel and a film); but Hochman has to remind us that the very symbolism of the film represses the referential dimension of the story, diverts attention from the human exploitation of animals which gives it its resonance. As he starkly puts it, the reality of 'the screaming of the lambs' is displaced: animal suffering is nullified as we are invited to concern ourselves rather with the mental anguish of the human protagonist. Reading even this short extract from Hochman's ingenious article, it is as if our very own time and place, as mediated by the entertainment industry, is suddenly defamiliarised in the larger perspective of nature. Green studies could do worse than follow his example.

43

The Ode 'To Autumn' as Ecosystem

Jonathan Bate*

The world was void,
The populous and the powerful – was a lump,
Seasonless, herbless, treeless, manless, lifeless –
A lump of death – a chaos of hard clay.
The rivers, lakes, and ocean all stood still,
And nothing stirred within their silent depths.

Byron 41

[Byron's poem] 'Darkness' begins ... with the stress of weather. The poem opens, 'I had a dream, which was not all a dream. / The bright sun was extinguished.' Does it stretch credulity too far to suppose that the first clause of the second sentence follows from the second clause of the first sentence? That the extinguished sun was not all a dream? Might the origin of the poem not be the absence of sunshine in June, July and August 1816? ... [The] eruption of Tambora volcano in Indonesia in 1815 killed some 80,000 people on the islands of Sumbawa and Lombok. It was the greatest eruption since 1500. The dust blasted into the stratosphere reduced the transparency of the atomosphere, filtered out the sun and consequently lowered surface temperatures. The effect lasted for three years, straining the growth-capacity of organic life across the planet. Beginning in 1816, crop failure led to food riots in nearly every country of Europe. Only in 1819 were there good harvests again. . . . [Byron's] poem darkly narrates a history in which war temporarily ceases as humankind pulls together in the face of inclement weather but is then renewed on a global scale as a result of the famine consequent upon the absence of sunlight. The global struggle for subsistence leads ultimately to the extinction of mankind. . . . When we read 'Darkness' now, Byron may be reclaimed as a prophet of ecocide. What, I want to ask here, is the legacy of romanticism in our age of eco-crisis? . . . The weather is the primary sign of the inextricability of culture and nature. [Michel] Serres points out in *Le Contrat naturel* that peasants and sailors know the power of the weather in ways that scientists and politicians do not. Romanticism

*From 'Living with the Weather', *Studies in Romanticism*, 35(3), 1996.

listens to the wisdom of sailors and peasants – of [Coleridge's] Mariner and [Wordsworth's] Michael. It challenges the modern separation of culture from nature. Romanticism knows that, in [Bruno] Latour's phrase, a delicate shuttle has woven together 'the heavens, industry, texts, soul and moral law' (Latour 5).

A living reading of Keats's 'To Autumn', in the age of global warming, must begin with the knowledge that we have no choice but to live with the weather. Just as the meteorological reports for July 1816 are the key context for Byron's 'Darkness', so our understanding of 'To Autumn' should begin with the knowledge that the weather was clear and sunny on 38 out of the 47 days from 7 August to 22 September 1819, and that in the week of 15–22 September temperatures were in the mid-sixties, whereas in the corresponding week in each of the three previous years they had been in the mid-fifties. Remember the meteorological and consequent agricultural pattern: the terrible summer and failed harvest of 1816, bad weather and poor harvests continuing in 1817 and 1818, then at last in 1819 a good summer, a full harvest, a beautiful autumn.

'To Autumn' is not an escapist fantasy which turns its back on the ruptures of Regency culture; it is a meditation on how human culture can only function through links and reciprocal relations with nature. For Keats, there is a direct correlation between the self's bond with its environment and the bonds between people which make up society. The link is clear in the letters he wrote around the time of the composition of 'Autumn'. At the end of August 1819, he writes to Fanny Keats:

> The delightful Weather we have had for two Months is the highest gratification I could receive – no chill'd red noses – no shivering – but fair Atmosphere to think in – a clean towel mark'd with the mangle and a basin of clear Water to drench one's face with ten times a day: no need of much exercise – a Mile a day being quite sufficient – My greatest regret is that I have not been well enough to bathe though I have been two Months by the sea side and live now close to delicious bathing – Still I enjoy the Weather I adore fine Weather as the greatest blessing I can have.
> (Keats, *Letters* 2.148)

The measure of human happiness, Keats suggests, is not a matter of government decree, is not determined by the high politics of Fat Louis and Fat Regent, to whom he refers dismissively later in the same letter. There are more basic necessities: good weather, clean water to wash and bathe in, unpolluted air in which to exercise. Keats's residence in Margate and the emergent discourses of sea-bathing and ozone are crucial here.

Then on 21 September 1819 in his journal-letter to George and Georgiana Keats (*Letters* 2.208–9) he moves easily from human bonds ('Men who live together have a silent moulding and influencing power over each other – They interassimilate') to the bond between self and environment ('Now the time is beautiful. I take a walk every day for an hour before dinner and this is generally my walk'). The walk is described: it traces a path from culture to nature, from cathedral and college to meadow and river. Between theorizing about interassimilation and describing his walk in the fresh autumn air, Keats writes 'I am not certain how I should endure loneliness and bad weather together.' Life depends on sociability and warmth: in order to survive, our species needs both social and environmental networks, both human bonds and good weather.

'To Autumn' is a poem about these networks. That it is a weather poem is manifest from the passage describing its genesis in the other famous letter which Keats wrote on Tuesday, 21 September 1819, to J. H. Reynolds:

> How beautiful the season is now – How fine the air. A temperate sharpness about it. Really, without joking, chaste weather – Dian skies – I never lik'd stubble fields so much as now – Aye better than the chilly green of the spring. Somehow a stubble plain looks warm – in the same way that some pictures look warm – this struck me so much in my sunday's walk that I composed upon it. I hope you are better employed than in gaping after weather. I have been at different times so happy as not to know what weather it was.
>
> (*Letters* 2.167)

The consumptive has no choice but to gape after weather. I believe that the key context for this passage is the poor air quality of the years 1816–18 – Byron's 'perpetual density', the effect of Tambora. Health, wrote Keats in his late letters, is the greatest of blessings, the cornerstone of all pleasures (2.289, 306). When his body was finally opened by Dr. Clark, Dr. Luby and an Italian surgeon, 'they thought it the worst possible Consumption – the lungs were intirely destroyed – the cells were quite gone' (Severn to Taylor, *Letters* 2.379). Air quality is of the highest importance for the weak of lung. Keats was killed less by the reviewers than by the weather. I suspect that when he refers to the 'different times' at which he was 'so happy as not to know what weather it was,' he is thinking nostalgically of the time before the bad weather of the immediate post-Tambora years which tragically coincided with the first taking hold of his pulmonary tuberculosis. The good summer and clear autumn of 1819 very literally gave him a new lease of life.

'To Autumn' itself is a poem of networks, links, bonds and correspondences. Linguistically, it achieves its most characteristic effects by making metaphors seem like metonymies. Mist and fruitfulness, bosom-friend and sun, load and bless, are not 'naturally' linked pairs in the manner of bread and butter. One would expect the yoking of them to have the element of surprise, even violence, associated with metaphor. But Keats makes the links seem natural: the progression of one thing to another through the poem is anything but violent or surprising. The effect of this naturalization within the poem is to create contiguity between all its elements.

The world of the poem thus comes to resemble a well-regulated ecosystem. Keats has an intuitive understanding of the underlying law of community ecology, namely that biodiversity is the key to the survival and adaptation of ecosystems. Biodiversity depends on a principle which we might call *illusory excess*. In order to withstand the onslaught of weather an ecosystem needs a sufficient diversity of species to regenerate itself; species which serve no obvious purpose in one homeostasis may play a vital role in changed environmental circumstances. Their superfluousness is an illusion; they are in fact necessary. The wild flowers in the second stanza of 'To Autumn' are an excellent example: in terms of the agricultural economy, the flowers which seed themselves in the cornfield are a waste, an unnecessary excess, but under different environmental conditions they could be more valuable than the corn. The wild-flower which Keats names is the poppy. I believe that this is chosen not only for aesthetic effect – the red dots contrasting with the golden corn, as in Monet's *Wild Poppies* – but also as a reminder of medicinal value. 'The fume of poppies' makes us think of opiates against pain and care. Spare the next swath with your reaping-hook, says Keats, and you might just gain medical benefit; spare the remaining rainforests, say ecologists, and you might just find a vaccine against AIDS among the billions of still unstudied plant species you would otherwise annihilate.

The ecosystem of 'To Autumn' is something larger than an image of agribusiness. Agribusiness sprays the cornfields with pesticides, impatient of poppies and gnats. Agribusiness removes hedgerows, regarding them as wasteful; 'To Autumn', in contrast, listens to hedge-crickets. The poem is concerned with a larger economy than the human one: its bees are there to pollinate flowers, not to produce honey for humans to consume ('later flowers for the bees', not bees for human bee-keepers).

But the imaginary ecosystem of the text is also something larger than a piece of descriptive biology. There are not only links within the biota – flower and bee, the food-chain that associates gnat and swallow – but also links between the discourses which the modem Constitution sought to separate out. The poem not only yokes external and internal marks of biological process (the visible bending of the apple tree, the invisible swelling of the gourd), it also yokes community and chemistry (bosom-friend and sun), physics and theology (load and bless), biology and aesthetics (a link which we may express through the two halves of the word which describes the closing images of the poem: bird-song). And crucially, it refuses to sign the Cartesian constitution which splits apart thinking mind and embodied substance. In contrast to Keats's earlier odes, there is no 'I' listening to a nightingale or looking at an urn: the self is dissolved into the ecosystem. In his journal-letter, Keats wrote of his ideal of interassimilation between men; in the poem he is interassimilated with the environment. Indeed, environment is probably the wrong word, because it presupposes an image of man at the center, surrounded by things; ecosystem is the better word exactly because an ecosystem does not have a center; it is a network of relations.

Insofar as the poem does have a centre and does anthropomorphize, it is distinctively female. The human figures in the central stanza – winnower, reaper, gleaner and cider-presser – embody traditional woman's work. Yet they are not in process of 'working over inorganic nature' in the manner of Marxian man. They are suspended, immobile. The winnower's hair is balanced in the wind, the gleaner balances herself in equilibrium with the eddies of the brook, the reaper is asleep under the influence of the poppy, the cider-presser is winding down in entropic rhythm with the oozings.

In contrast to those feminists who seek to denaturalize traditional images of masculinity and femininity, ecofeminists reappropriate and celebrate the idea of woman's closeness to the rhythms of mother earth. A line of work beginning with Sherry Ortner's 'Is Female to Male as Nature is to Culture?' and best exemplified by Carolyn Merchant's *The Death of Nature*, posits direct links between Enlightenment science, masculinity and technology on the one hand, the exploitation of women and the exploitation of the earth on the other. Keats's images of wise female passivity and responsiveness to nature are prototypically ecofeminist.

If we return to the letter to Reynolds with this in mind, we will notice that it offers more than a weather report. It mediates between meteorology and mythology. The unblemished sky is compared to Diana, mythical goddess of chastity. This allusion fits with the poem's feminized relationship with nature. Keats would have read in Lempriere's *Classical Dictionary* that the poppy was sacred to Diana. Several of the goddess' traditional functions and associations suggest that she may be regarded as a spirit of ecological wholeness: she was supposed to promote the union of communities; she was especially worshipped by women; she seems originally to have been a spirit of the woods and of wild nature who was subsequently brought into friendly accord with early Roman farmers. But this latter shift also reveals the illusion upon which the poem is based. Diana, with her associations of woodland, chase and pool, is preeminently the presider over a pre-agrarian world. The meadows in which she runs are never harvested. Chastity is an ancient image of untouched-virgin-land. It might be said that a more appropriate presider for the poem would be one of Diana's opposites, the fertile Cleopatra: 'he ploughed her and she cropped,' says Enobarbus of Caesar and Cleopatra. The male farmer ploughs, the female land is cropped.

In both letter and poem, Keats celebrates the stubble, that which remains after the cropping and the gathering. This land is worked-over, not virgin. The aestheticized still-point of the poem occurs at the moment when humankind has possessed and emptied the land. But where in the 'Ode on a Grecian Urn' the objective correlative is a human artwork which is celebrated precisely because it transcends time, 'To Autumn' offers only a momentary suspension upon the completion of harvest. At the close of the poem, the gathering swallows and the full-grown lamb are already reminding us of the next spring. Famously, Keats gives up on the earlier odes' quest for aesthetic transcendence, embracing instead the immanence of nature's time, the cycle of the seasons.

'Accidentally or knowingly,' writes Serres, 'the French language uses only one word, *temps*, to speak both of the time that ticks by or flows, and of the weather produced by the clime and by what our ancestors called meteors' (*Le Contrat naturel* I; trans. McCarren). 'To Autumn' is a poem of both time and the weather. In this respect, it mediates between exterior and interior ecologics. Ecosystems evolve in time through the operation of weather; the ecology of the human mind is equally dependent on the two senses of *temps*. Our moods are affected by the weather. Our identities are constituted in both time and place, are always shaped by both memory

and environment. Romantic poetry is especially concerned with these two consti-
tutions. It is both a mnemonic and an ecologic. Weather is a prime means of linking
spatiality and temporality – this, I suggest, is why so many major romantic poems
are weather poems. A romantic poem is a model of a certain kind of being and of
dwelling; whilst always at several removes from the actual moment of being and
place of dwelling in which it is thought and written, the poem itself is an image
of ecological wholeness which may grant to the attentive and receptive reader a
sense of being-at-home-in-the-world.

Let us read 'To Autumn' backwards. The poem ends with an at-homeness-
with-all-living-things (swallow, robin, cricket, sheep, willow, gnat). The final stanza's
river and distant hill are not virgin ecosystems, but they are less touched by
humankind than is the intermediate farmed environment of the middle stanza.
Where the poem has begun is with an intensively managed but highly fertile
domestic economy in a cottage-garden. The movement *of* the poem is thus . . .
from culture to nature. But the movement *through* the poem, with its intricate
syntactical, metrical and aural interlinkings, is not one which divides the culture
from the nature. There is no sense of river, hill and sky as the opposite of house
and garden. Rather, what Keats seems to be saying is that to achieve being-at-home-
ness-in-the-world you have to begin from your own dwelling-place. Think glob-
ally, act locally. . . .

Michel Serres asks: 'In politics or economics, by means of the sciences, we
know how to define power; [but] how can we *think fragility?*' (*Le Contrat naturel*
71; my trans. and emphasis). I ask myself: what might be the legacy of romantic
poetry for us now? And it occurs to me that the answer to Serres' question is the
answer to mine: romantic poetry can enable us to think fragility. Byron's 'Darkness'
proposes that when ecosystems collapse, human bonds do so too. Keats's 'To
Autumn' [is a] thinking of our bonds with each other and the earth, [a] thinking
of fragile, beautiful, necessary ecological wholeness.

WORKS CITED

Byron, Lord (1986) *The Complete Poetical Works* (ed. Jerome J. McGann), Oxford: Oxford
    University Press, Vol. 4.
Keats, John (1958) *Letters* (ed. Hyder E. Rollins), 2 vols, Cambridge, MA: Harvard
    University Press.
—— (1970) *Complete Poems* (ed. Miriam Allott), London: Longman.
Latour, Bruno (1993) *We Have Never Been Modern* (trans. Catherine Porter), Cambridge,
    MA: Harvard University Press.
McCarren, Felicia (1992) '*Le contrat naturel* by Michel Serres, Chapter 2' (translation),
    Critical Inquiry, 19: 1–21.
Merchant, Carolyn (1980) *The Death of Nature: Women, Ecology, and the Scientific
    Revolution*, San Francisco: Harper & Row.
Ortner, Sherry (1974) 'Is Female to Male as Nature is to Culture?', in Michelle Rosaldo
    and Louise Lamphere (eds) *Women, Culture, and Society*, Stanford, CA: Stanford
    University Press.
Serres, Michel (1990) *Le Contrat naturel*, Paris: François Bourin.

44

Thoreau's Ambivalence Toward Mother Nature

LOUISE WESTLING*

Is THOREAU 'A man of Indian wisdom, a person-in-contact with wild nature, with the Great Mother', as Max Oelschlaeger claims in *The Idea of Wilderness* (170)? Or is Richard Slotkin right to see *Walden* as a sublimated hunt, with Thoreau as an intellectualized Natty Bumppo (519)? 1 want to suggest that a major cause of the ambivalence and doubleness of Thoreau's attitude toward the physical world is a gender dynamic embedded in the rich dialogic texture of *Walden*. Because he saw the pond, the earth, and Nature as feminine, Thoreau's essential project was blocked. Instead of showing us the way back to harmony with Nature, Thoreau participated in what Renato Rosaldo calls 'imperialist nostalgia' – creating a sentimental stance toward the land and its creatures that masked and simultaneously erased the conquest and destruction of the 'wild' continent (69–73). In the words of an early colonial commentator, mother nature was 'stript, shorn, and made deformed' while writers pretended to adore her (Kolodny 14).

The problem had a long history before the creation of the American nation and has continued to trouble our literary landscapes down to the present, even in the work of contemporary nature writers. Leo Marx alerted us to the sense of unease that haunted the American pastoral from the beginning, but not until Annette Kolodny's *Lay of the Land* did anyone point to gender as a critical part of the problem. The traditional gendering of Nature and land led Thoreau, like his mentor Emerson, into reactions shaped by contemporary nineteenth-century gender politics. Their era was a time of self-conscious 'manliness' and corresponding distaste for 'effeminacy', which could well be related to the emergence of women into literature and political organizations for the abolition of slavery and for women's rights. But this is just a particular moment in our culture's long tradition of debasing the body and the feminine, Nature and matter in order to exalt the mind and the masculine, culture and spirit. 'Philosophy is constructed on the premise of woman's abasement,' says Hélène Cixous: 'she is the repressed that ensures the system's functioning' (65, 67). Carolyn Merchant and Evelyn Fox Keller have shown how this same premise lies at the base of modern science.

*From 'Thoreau's Ambivalence Toward Mother Nature', *ISLE*, 1(1), 1993.

As Thoreau shaped his journal entries into *Walden*, he exalted the 'father tongue' of the written word and intellectual heritage over the 'mother tongue' of embodied speech which he called 'almost brutish' (101). *Walden* enacts a dramatic dance along a continuum between attraction and repulsion, love and disgust, in the imagined presence of a female Nature from which the author's masculine identity compels him to distinguish himself.

Thoreau's *Journal* unselfconsciously genders the landscape and natural world, as when he refers to the Indian's 'cleanly' use of his 'untrimmed mistress' the earth, in contrast to 'something vulgar and foul' in the white farmer's greater closeness as a tiller of the soil (*J*, 2: 100). The journal also constantly defines his little world at Walden Pond in terms of classical models. On July 7, 1845, for instance, he writes, 'I am glad to remember tonight as I sit by my door that I too am at least a remote descendent of that heroic race of men of whom there is tradition. I too sit here on the shore of my Ithaca, a fellow wanderer and survivor of Ulysses' (*J*, 2: 156). When Thoreau recast his materials for publication, he continued to emphasize the Homeric ideal. He may treat this tradition ironically, as in the famous mock heroic descriptions of the ant battle or the bean field, but he never seriously abandons it as the ground of his manly identity. Time and again he contrasts passive 'effeminacy' to virile action, as Emerson had done before him in the standard formulation of their era. In 'Reading' he champions the reading of Homer and Aeschylus in Greek as a way of avoiding 'dissipation or luxuriousness' (100) and opposes this activity to the degeneracy of the majority of his fellows, 'a race of tit-men' who content themselves by 'sucking the pap' of provincial newspapers and other cheap popular writing (107, 109). High culture is male and heroic; low culture unmistakably feminized.

In shaping a statement of purpose for *Walden*, Thoreau applied violent military imagery to earlier journal material:

> I went to the woods because I wished to live deliberately, to front only the essential facts of life.... I wanted to live deep and suck out all the marrow of life, to live so sturdily and Spartan-like as to put to rout all that was not life, to cut a broad swath and shave close, to drive life into a corner ...
>
> (90–1)

'Life' is here an animal he must kill and eat, or a field he must harvest, or some hunted beast he must drive into a trap.

Man the predator and domesticator of the landscape is only half hidden in these metaphors, as Richard Slotkin noticed some years ago (519). At the heart of Walden is Thoreau's extended meditation on 'The Ponds' describing Walden's shape, exact physical measurements, aspect in various weathers, colors under various skies, and most important for Thoreau, its meaning in the landscape: 'A Lake is the landscape's most beautiful and expressive feature. It is earth's eye; looking into which the beholder measures the depth of his own nature. The fluviatile trees next the shore are the slender eyelashes which fringe it, and the wooded hills and cliffs around are its overhanging brows' (186). Here Thoreau has elaborated the transparent eyeball image of Emerson, transposing the metaphor onto a personified landscape feminized by references to eyelashes, dimples, and 'the heaving of its breast' (188).

This feminine 'other' is beautiful and magnetic but somehow horrifying in its material being, subject to decay like the body. Thoreau's ambivalence toward his body and sensuality in general is most fully displayed in 'Higher Laws', a section whose rhetorical structure seems designed to follow the Platonic progression from physical to higher spiritual realms. "Higher Laws"' begins with Thoreau's Dionysiac urge to snatch up a woodchuck, tear it to pieces, and eat it raw. But very soon he backs away from these impulses almost in horror; they are the antithesis of man's higher, moral being. Eating, drinking – even the Puritan's brown crust and water – are potential experiences of degradation and brutishness. By the end of the section, Thoreau has decided, 'Nature is hard to be overcome, but **she** must be overcome' (188, my emphasis). As Michael West remarks, 'Thoreau remains haunted by a profound ambivalence toward the body and toward those excremental processes that he explicitly undertakes to defend in "Higher Laws"' (1046). This material reality is feminine, and the disease of consumption which was ravaging Thoreau's own body and would cause his early death was blamed by popular medical theory on 'effeminacy' which could be counteracted by an ascetic regimen (West 1054).

It is no wonder that when Thoreau describes his most peaceful and intimate moments of communion with Walden Pond, he is really abstracted from it, as in the emblematic description of fishing in the pond at night. From the outset his purpose is predatory. Separated from the pond by his boat, he only communicates with its life 'by a long flaxen line' (174). Though it may appear that he gives himself over to the forces of Nature by allowing his boat to drift to and fro in the darkness, this movement is circumscribed because the boat is anchored. Not only is Thoreau physically separated from the body of the pond, but he is also abstracted from the life of his own body. He describes his thoughts transcending his physical being and wandering 'to vast cosmogonal themes in other spheres' (175) and needs the jerk of the captured fish, struggling vainly to escape death at his hands, to link him up to Nature again.

Leo Marx excuses Thoreau's maintenance of distance from the life of Walden Pond on grounds of the traditional artificiality of literary pastoral (264–5), but Thoreau's enmeshment in masculine semiotic codes and hero narratives involves him in a sinister project that becomes more obvious in our own era of deforestation and global pollution. Walden's imaginary construct of Nature masks the exploitation of the pond's resources – and in a broader sense of the continent's – for the hero's needs which include the pretense that Nature is still whole and wild, an erotic, healing feminine other that gives access to transcendent spiritual reality.

Many have observed that Thoreau's Walden Pond was no wilderness landscape but instead a colonized space from which Indians and most wildlife had already been removed. Thoreau acknowledges as much, thus destabilizing the ideal he seems to present. During his sojourn at the pond, it was used as a quarry for raw materials like ice and lumber. He can see the village of Concord through a vista opened up by the deforestation of a nearby hill (86–7), he makes his famous bean field in an area cleared fifteen years previously (156), and he indicates that Walden has been destroyed in his lifetime. The pond of his boyhood, 'completely surrounded by thick and lofty pine and oak woods', is by the final writing of Walden circled by denuded shores laid waste by woodchoppers like the Canadian used in the narrative as a model of the natural, heroic man (191–2). In the end, Thoreau was not as interested in a particular place as he was in seeking to use his experiences as rhetoric, 'for the sake of tropes and expression' (162). Most of the experiences he describes in Walden are defined by literary and philosophical allusion in a sort of freefloating Platonic realm of traditional ideas. Nevertheless, Thoreau genuinely sought to negotiate between the blasted landscape of colonial exploitation and the imagined Eden of wilderness. He represents what Donna Haraway would call 'one half of the system of desire mediated by modern science and technology, the half dreaming of reclosing the broken cosmos' (136), but he was trapped within the masculine ethic of heroic assertion and exploitation at the heart of this system that can be traced all the way back to Gilgamesh, destroyer of the wild cedar forest sacred to Innana/Ishtar. Modern science, descending directly from this archaic code, has opposed itself to the traditionally female earth, as Haraway says, 'in order to legitimate deeper penetration by a virile lover/actor/knower' who could hardly afford to identify with the object of his manipulations (136). Like Cooper and Emerson before him, Thoreau expressed an imperialist nostalgia which excused the ravaging of the landscape for profit, even as he lamented it.

At least Thoreau dramatized the problem by the record of his ingenious, multifaceted and passionate efforts to live a different reality than the one his culture imposed upon him. He understood and tried to accept the necessary violence involved in human survival – the sacrificial logic by which we must destroy and eat other living creatures. If he was also horrified by the fact of our decaying materiality, as he says in 'Higher Laws', he was honest enough to articulate the paradox.

Thoreau's version of American pastoral has been reiterated by male writers down to our own time. Hemingway's Nick Adams and Faulkner's Ike McCaslin perform similar escapist nest-building and killing rituals in eroticized landscapes, and gendered responses to Nature motivate environmentally conscious essayists like Edward Abbey and Barry Lopez. Understanding the destructive gender oppositions in *Walden* should help us see that as long as we continue to feminize nature and imagine ourselves apart from the biota, we will continue to enable the 'heroic' destruction of the planet, even as we lament the process and try to erase or deny our complicity in it.

WORKS CITED

Cixous, Hélène and Catherine Clement (1986) *The Newly Born Woman* (trans. Betsy Wing), Minneapolis, MN: University of Minnesota Press.

Haraway, Donna (1989) *Primate Visions: Gender, Race, and Nature in the World of Modern Science*, New York: Routledge.

Kolodny, Annette (1975) *The Lay of the Land: Metaphor as Experience and History in American Life and Letters*, Chapel Hill, NC: University of North Carolina Press.

Marx, Leo (1964) *The Machine in the Garden: Technology and the Pastoral Ideal in America*, New York: Oxford University Press.

Oelschlaeger, Max (1991) *The Idea of Wilderness from Prehistory to the Age of Ecology*, New Haven, CT: Yale University Press.

Rosaldo, Renato (1989) *Culture and Truth: The Remaking of Social Analysis*, Boston, MA: Beacon Press.

Slotkin, Richard (1973) *Regeneration Through Violence: The Mythology of the American Frontier, 1600–1860*, Middletown, CT: Wesleyan University Press.

Thoreau, Henry David (1984) *Journal*, Vol. 2 (ed. Robert Sattelmeyer), Princeton, NJ: Princeton University Press.

—— (1971) *Walden* (ed. J. Lyndon Shanley), Princeton, NJ: Princeton University Press.

West, Michael (1974) 'The Heroic Dimension of Thoreau's Wordplay', *PMLA* 89: 1043–64.

45

Maps for Tourists: Hardy, Narrative, Ecology

RICHARD KERRIDGE*

[IN HIS 'WESSEX novels'] Hardy demands that readers should take seriously the way their presence is implied by the narrative. They should acknowledge that a visitor is not a ghostly, free-moving figure who watches and leaves no imprint, but a bodily presence engaged in an act of consumption which will have material consequences. Tourists are not external to the economy or ecosystem they visit, but part of it, engaged in an activity likely to transform it.

An ecologist studies forms of life not in isolation but as parts of a system, an economy which sustains them and which they constitute. Hardy's narrative forms bring interdependency to the fore. He has a distinctive way of introducing characters which shows them ceaselessly making and remaking each other's identity. Gabriel Oak at the beginning of *Far From the Madding Crowd* seems to be a floating signifier whose perceived 'character' varies not so much because of his own actions as according to the mood of the perceiver:

> Or, to state his character as it stood in the scale of public opinion, when his friends and critics were in tantrums, he was considered rather a bad man; when they were pleased, he was rather a good man; when they were neither, he was a man whose moral colour was a kind of pepper-and-salt mixture.
>
> (*FMC*, 41)

The same formula introduces William Dewy in *Under the Greenwood Tree*. 'Character', here, means not the person occupying the physical space indicated by the narrative but the various impressions people have of that person. Character, in this sense of the word, is environment. Oak's 'character' has no hard boundaries, but is always in flux: always a product of relations with whatever surrounds him.

This remarkable manner of introduction allows the characters to be at once elusively singular and the product of shifting popular opinion. Under the surface

*From 'Ecological Hardy', in Karla Armbruster and Kathleen Wallace (eds) *Beyond Nature Writing*, Charlottesville, VA: University of Virginia Press, 2000.

that reflects our own ideas and moods back at us, the character resides, unreachable, ready to slip away. A contrast is made between the singular character – the physical, vulnerable body that must always be somewhere – and the 'character' as perceived by others, an endlessly changing procession of ideas. To other people, the narrative reminds us at one point, 'Tess was only a passing thought. Even to friends she was no more than a frequently passing thought' (*TD*, 119). The character is clearly located in time and space, but open to unlimited interpretation. Description is denied the power to stabilize character. The meanings people have, which constitute their 'character', are shown to be the product of an environment, a field of meaning in which both readers and characters move.

Character is shown to be a product of continuous interdependency, while a similar emphasis is given to the material interdependencies between places: the flow of goods, information and travelers. The moorland near the barracks in *Far from the Madding Crowd* is marked by 'forms without features; suggestive of anything, proclaiming nothing, and without more character than that of being the limit of something else' (*FMC*, 113): a bit like Gabriel's 'pepper-and-salt mixture'. Tess and Angel deliver milk one morning to a train:

> 'Londoners will drink it at their breakfasts tomorrow, won't they!' she asked. 'Strange people that we have never seen. . . . Who don't know anything of us, and where it comes from; or think how we drove two miles across the moor to-night in the rain that it might reach 'em in time?'
>
> (*TD*, 215)

Tess feels a Wordsworthian pleasure in this glimpse of the infinity of interconnected life. Angel mildly patronizes her, and the moment passes. The reader may be more responsive to her vision, for this is tantalizingly close to a moment of reciprocity: she might almost be imagining the life of her reader. These narrative forms seem especially right for novelists responsive to ecological concerns, since ecology is the study of relationships and interdependencies within shared local environments – and of the relation of such environments to larger ecosystems.

Two forms of pleasure in the natural world appear in Hardy's novels. The unalienated lover of nature *inhabits*; the alienated lover *gazes*. The first is a native, deeply embedded in a stable ecosystem; the second a Romantic, a tourist, a newcomer, a reader. The conventional assumption would be that the transition from pre-industrial to industrial society abolishes the first and produces the second. Many of Hardy's characters are enmeshed in the technological and social changes that produce this transition. His novels are appreciative of both ways of loving nature, and intent on exploring the relationship between them. Environmentalists hope that it may be possible to break the sequence in which estrangement from nature is followed by Romantic regret and desire. They believe in the possibility of sustainable forms of development that will not estrange communities from their natural environments. They seek to build alliances between the tourist and the native, hoping for an eventual society in which everyone will be both of these things.

It is characteristic of the Romantic, alienated viewpoint to attribute unreflective happiness to people seen as living unalienated lives. In a journal entry from 1889, Hardy takes this to a point of splendidly gloomy absurdity:

A woeful fact – that the human race is too extremely developed for its corporeal conditions, the nerves being evolved to an activity abnormal in such an environment. Even the higher animals are in excess in this respect. It may be questioned if Nature, or what we call Nature, so far back as when she crossed the line from invertebrates to vertebrates, did not exceed her mission. This planet does not supply the materials for happiness to higher existences.

(F. E. Hardy, 218)

Happiness is attributed, sardonically, to 'lower' animals, like the maggots Mrs Yeobright watches 'heaving and wallowing with enjoyment' in a heathland pool (*RN*, 285). Embedded in their immediate ecosystem, they lack the equipment to see beyond that system. Nature here is the small-scale life at the margins of human affairs, flourishing in the absence of human intrusion. The activity of small creatures and the immense distances spanned in planetary observation both represent departures from the normal concerns of character and plot. Yet such moments are parts of the very plots they seem to escape. The relinquishing of long perspectives may provide momentary relief from the unhappiness that burdens 'higher existences'. The effect may be obliquely erotic, suggestive of an intense focus on small areas of a person's body. Pauses may be carefully placed to heighten anticipation. The eye that picks out minutiae may belong to a character apprehensive or seeking distraction. Marty, in *The Woodlanders*, sheltering in Giles's cottage, is growing uneasy about his failure to appear, when she hears a rustling outside the window, the sound of a newt moving in the fallen leaves (*TW*, 322). Her heightened, expectant senses catch a sound she would normally miss – an example that seems almost hallucinatory in its extension of normal perception.

For Lawrence Buell, in *The Environmental Imagination* (1995), such techniques are 'a deliberate dislocation of ordinary perception' (Buell, 104). Their purpose is to remind us of neglected non-human perspectives. This is a step towards 'environmental literacy' (Buell, 107). An ecocentric vision would seek not only to assert the value of these perspectives, but also somehow to accommodate them in the human sphere, in 'plot', since they are constitutive of human life. It is not fanciful to credit Hardy with similar aims.

Perhaps Jude is the character with the most highly developed sympathy for non-human creatures. He is punished for allowing hungry birds to feed (*JO*, 39). He tiptoes to avoid crushing earthworms (*JO*, 41). He pities his pig and sacrifices some of its economic value by killing it swiftly (*JO*, 86–9). In all this he is an ironically ineffectual version of an omniscient God who sees even the woe of a sparrow. Jude attempts a Godlike compassion without the advantages of God's position. This human attempt at Godly omniscience is a reproof to a supposedly loving God who has not provided an economy merciful to all forms of life. Unlike Christ's inter-

269

cession, Jude's is ineffectual: he takes the punishment onto himself without saving other victims.

His concern for all creatures is scorned as foolishness or vanity, like his aspiration to study at Christminster. At the pig-killing, Arabella tells him, with moral force, 'Poor folks must live' (*JO*, 88). One conclusion might be that Jude is one of those 'higher existences' whose nerves have evolved to a degree that unfits them for life on this planet. Jude does not draw this conclusion; he does not despair of the planet and retreat into private concerns. Even at his most weary, he rejects the flattering charge that he is unworldly, preferring to find comfort in the idea of incremental progress. 'It takes two or three generations to do what I tried to do in one,' he says (*JO*, 336). 'Our ideas were fifty years too soon to be any good to us' (*JO*, 405).

The other form of intimate attention to the natural world occurs neither in distress nor leisure, but in the course of daily work:

> Winterborne's fingers were endowed with a gentle conjuror's touch in spreading the roots of each little tree, resulting in a sort of caress under which the delicate fibres all laid themselves out in their proper directions for growth.
>
> (*TW*, 93)

To outsiders such as Grace and the reader, Giles's unalienated labour seems a kind of magic or lovemaking. His is the communal knowledge that comes from growing-up, living and working in a stable ecosystem. It is lost when social mobility carries a person away from their community and work. Grace is sent from Little Hintock to be taught the manners of a higher social position. On her return, she has forgotten the names of the different apples grown around her home (*TW*, 72). After Giles's death, Grace feels wistful amazement at the way Giles and Marty were accustomed to work together in the woods. Theirs was a knowledge of minutiae that was not eccentric or self-conscious:

> From the light lashing of the twigs upon their faces when brushing through them in the dark either could pronounce upon the species of the tree whence they stretched; from the quality of the wind's murmur through a bough either could in like manner name its sort afar off. They knew by a glance at a trunk if its heart were sound, or tainted with incipient decay; and by the state of its upper twigs the stratum that had been reached by its roots.
>
> (*TW*, 340–1)

Giles and Marty have a practical knowledge of the woodlands of the type that Ray Dasmann, in *Wildlife Biology* (1964), attributes to the communities he calls 'ecosystem people'. These are communities 'totally dependent, or largely so, on the animals and plants of a particular area' (Dasmann, 21), deeply accustomed to that area and in stable, sustainable relation to the local ecosystem. Gary Paul Nabhan, in *Cultures of Habitat* (1997), explores the interdependency of work, play and story that enables such communities to live in practical intimacy with their environment. Nabhan's examples are the O'odham people of Arizona and the Australian Aboriginals of Alice Springs. Hardy's Wessex villages are not exactly indigenous, pre-industrial communities, but they are the nearest thing to a 'culture of habitat' still to be found in late nineteenth-century England. Little Hintock, in its wooded enclave, is the most secluded and unadulterated; the community most deeply engrossed in its immediate environment. Hardy's plots often turn on the disruptive arrival in such places of forces from outside. New technologies arrive: the seed-drill in *The Mayor of Casterbridge*, the steam-driven threshing-machine in *Tess of the d'Urbervilles*. People arrive or return bringing innovations: Clym, Farfrae, Grace, Fitzpiers, Alec d'Urberville, Angel Clare. Giles and Marty's close association with trees signifies deep-rootedness but also vulnerability. Like trees they are immobile, unable to flee.

Interventions cannot merely be seen as negative, however; since the shifts of narrative position so often remind us that reading itself is a sort of intrusion. And each newcomer is only relatively new. Grace returns to Little Hintock as an alienated outsider, but to Fitzpiers she seems indigenous to that community while he stands outside it. Much of the distress that follows can be traced to the indeterminacy of Grace's position, neither outside nor inside. Tess's calamities follow from the indeterminate position that makes her both aristocrat and poor labourer. Jude's misfortune comes of his unrealistic aspirations. One can almost find in these stories a conservative nostalgia for an idealised feudalism in which people remained in one place and social positions were fixed and clear: a feudalism identified as a natural way of life. 'Social mobility brings disaster: do not long for it', would be the message.

But in Hardy this message is as bitterly ironical as the suggestion that Nature would have done better not to progress from invertebrates to vertebrates. To read Hardy as conservative and hostile to social mobility is to misrepresent him brutally. His novels are profoundly – one might say dangerously – unreconciled to inequalities of wealth and power. Restless desire is the principal source of vitality and pleasure, as well as tragedy. The novels are a record both of the havoc wrought by such desires and the mortifying effect when they are thwarted.

A vision expressed with eloquence by Nabhan is that a creative relationship may be possible between indigenous cultures of habitat and postmodern cultures of technology. Such a relationship would bypass that familiar sequence in which industrialisation destroys the culture of habitat which then becomes an object of nostalgic desire: the perversity which catches so many characters in Hardy and compromises so much nature-writing. In this utopia (to sketch it a little flippantly), a postmodern Giles Winterborne would not die of exposure, nor lose his dwelling because of a feudal property law. He would retain his native understanding of the woods and continue his sustainable forestry, protected by a modern health service and enjoying access to the wider world through television and the internet. Indigenous culture would no longer stand as the binary opposite of modernity, and would no longer be the lost golden age, the innocent primitive, or (the flipside of that) the narrow, ignorant and brutal primitive. Frail as this hope seems, it does attempt the difficult task of properly valuing three things often seen as incompatible: natural environments as loved by tourists and other alienated Romantics, indigenous cultures of habitat, and the material benefits of modernity.

This utopia would require of its inhabitants a high degree of self-consciousness about their own continually shifting positions. Such self-consciousness is required of environmentalists who wish to avoid simple nostalgia for an idealised pre-industrial culture. Nabhan duly situates himself, in *Cultures of Habitat*, telling a story of himself as an Arab-American adolescent lover occupying a complex cross-cultural position (Nabhan, 89–96). He suggests that we might value our own shifts from position to position as a sort of rich diversity, like biodiversity. A famous section of *The Return of the Native* shows us some ways of doing this.

Clym Yeobright is working as a furze-cutter on Egdon Heath. The passage is beautiful because of the intricacy of the sense of relative and interdependent positions it gives the reader:

> This man from Paris was now so disguised by his leather accoutrements, and by the goggles he was obliged to wear over his eyes, that his closest friend might have passed by without recognising him. He was a brown spot in the midst of an expanse of olive-green gorse and nothing more. Though frequently depressed in spirit, when not actually at work, owing to thoughts of Eustacia's position and his mother's estrangement, when in the full swing of labour he was cheerfully disposed and calm.
>
> His daily life was of a curious microscopic sort, his whole world being limited to a circuit of a few feet from his person. His familiars were creeping and winged things, and they seemed to enroll him in their band. Bees hummed around his ears with an intimate air, and tugged at the heath and furze-flowers. . . . The strange amber-coloured butterflies which Egdon produced, and which were never seen elsewhere, quivered in the breath of his lips. . . . Litters of young rabbits came out from their forms to sun themselves upon hillocks, the hot beams blazing through the delicate tissue of each thin-fleshed ear, and firing it to a blood-red transparency in which the veins could be seen. None of them feared him.
>
> (*RN*, 262)

This is nature as paradise temporarily and inadvertently regained. Yeobright's damaged eyesight has forced him to give up his studies. In training to be a schoolteacher he was already contemplating a step of deliberate downward social-mobility. Now he descends even further, and finds an unexpected happiness. By relinquishing a scope of vision beyond the local (as symbolized by reading), he discovers, in work rather than contemplation, a release from self-consciousness and alienation. He has literally come closer to nature. This move is represented by his absorption into the landscape. Simultaneously, he is the man from Paris and a brown spot in an expanse of gorse. This juxtaposition does not merely show us the distance he has come; it positions us where we can see both Yeobrights. Neither perception is to be abandoned.

The 'knowledge' he has cast off is tacitly compared to the 'knowledge' Adam and Eve gained from the forbidden fruit, which caused them to feel shame and to be expelled from Paradise. By renouncing it, Clym is able to return to the Egdon of his childhood and to Paradise. In an unfallen world the animals no longer fear him. He returns, briefly, with a completeness never accomplished by other returners such as Grace and Angel. But Hardy is insistent about the cost of this return. This closeness to nature means loss of vision – loss, for example, of the longer scientific perspectives that may now enable us to foresee and prevent ecological disaster. Yeobright becomes as vulnerable as an animal or insect unable to see further than its immediate surroundings.

That amber-coloured butterfly poses the problem in miniature. It is almost certainly the Lulworth Skipper, *Thymelicus aeteon*. Tom Tolman's *Field Guide to the Butterflies of Britain and Europe* (1997) lists this butterfly as first recorded in Britain in 1832, and gives its range as 'in Britain restricted to the Dorset coast' (Tolman, 275). Hardy's narrator does not give the scientific name, nor even the English name, though elsewhere, as the narrative shifts in register, we have, with *Ulex europaeus*, just the scientific name (*RN*, 89), and with the Cream-Coloured Courser, just the English name (*RN*, 109). If we know the scientific name, we may also know that the butterfly's whole range includes much of Southern Europe and North West Africa. Its rarity is relative. The withholding of these names presents the butterfly as it is known locally, intimately. The narrative keeps both perspectives in play.

Buell identifies Richard Jefferies rather than Hardy as 'Thoreau's English counterpart' (Buell, 105). Hardy he finds problematical as an ecocentric writer because, despite the depth of his portrayal of such environments as Egdon Heath, 'the heath is in the long run ancillary to Clym's story,' and the novel 'is about people in place, not about place itself' (Buell, 255). I have attempted to show that the special value of Hardy to ecocritics is precisely in the way he does not separate place and person. He will not allow anything, place or person, to stabilise in meaning; its meaning is always the product of a shifting set of relations, and always seen in the act of generation by those relations. Paradoxically, this is to create a stronger sense of the elusive, excessive presence of places, since the descriptions and narratives they generate never cohere for long, and are quickly exposed as relative.

WORKS CITED

Buell, Lawrence (1995) *The Environmental Imagination*, Cambridge, MA: Harvard University Press.

Dasmann, Ray (1964) *Wildlife Biology*, New York: John Wiley.

Ebbatson, Roger (1993) *Hardy: The Margin of the Unexpressed*, Sheffield: Sheffield Academic Press.

Hardy, Florence Emily (1972) *The Life of Thomas Hardy 1840–1928*, London: Macmillan.

Hardy, Thomas (1975) *Under the Greenwood Tree*, London: Macmillan. (*UGT*)

—— (1975) *Far from the Madding Crowd*, London: Macmillan. (*FMC*)

—— (1975) *The Return of the Native*, London: Macmillan. (*RN*)

—— (1975) *Two on a Tower*, London: Macmillan. (*TT*)

—— (1975) *The Mayor of Casterbridge*, London: Macmillan. (*MC*)

—— (1975) *The Woodlanders*, London: Macmillan. (*TW*)

—— (1975) *Tess of the d'Urbervilles*, London: Macmillan. (*TD*)

—— (1975) *Jude the Obscure*, London: Macmillan. (*JO*)

Millgate, Michael (1971) *Thomas Hardy: His Career as a Novelist*, London: The Bodley Head.

—— (1982) *Thomas Hardy: A Biography*, Oxford: Oxford University Press.

Nabhan, Gary Paul (1997) *Cultures of Habitat: On Nature, Culture, and Story*, Washington, DC: Counterpoint.

Tolman, Tom (1997) *Field Guide to the Butterflies of Britain and Europe*, London: HarperCollins.

Widdowson, Peter (1989) *Hardy in History: A Study in Literary Sociology*, London: Routledge.

46

The Flesh of the World:
Virginia Woolf's Between the Acts

Carol H. Cantrell*

My entry into the subject of modernism and the natural environment is through the notion of 'place'. Unlike 'landscape' or 'wilderness', 'place' necessarily includes the human presence and in fact is centered around it. At the same time, 'place' is where our embodied selves experience the world, and through which we receive the sources of energy and nurturance which keep us alive and in which our activities make themselves felt most immediately. . . . Yet 'place', like women's traditional work, is usually backgrounded in Western thought, in part because both are intimately connected with the body, the mundane, the ephemeral. Without bodies, without places in which bodies live, none of the human achievements that erase their own conditions of creation would be possible. My conception of place rests on the insight that just as we cannot talk about mind without body, we cannot talk about body without place.

In developing the notion of 'place' I am using in this project, I am drawing on work ranging from geography to perceptual psychology growing out of the work of the phenomenological philosopher Maurice Merleau-Ponty. . . . What Merleau-Ponty does that much ecological thought does not do is put the human perceiver in the picture; indeed, for phenomenologists, the experience of the human observer is the starting point, not an irrelevance or nuisance. At the same time, [he] rejects the notion that the human is all that there is, or all that we can know. His assumption as a philosopher is the same assumption we make in everyday life: that our perceptions are based in a continuity between our bodies and the world. In his words, 'my body is made of the same flesh as the world (it is a perceived), and moreover . . . this flesh of my body is shared by the world' (*The Visible and the Invisible* 248). Furthermore, we share perceptions with other perceivers, who 'have the power to decenter me, to oppose [their] centering to my own' (*V&I* 82). . . .

Merleau-Ponty's double stress on reciprocality and ongoing process gives us a way to describe and understand the interactive nature of human relations with the natural world no less (or more) than with human culture. . . . Because [he] insists

---

* From '"The Locus of Compossibility": Virginia Woolf, Modernism and Place', *ISLE*, 5(2), 1998.

275

on the possibility of exchange between multiple centers of perception, his work has affinities with the ecofeminist dialogics developed by Patrick Murphy: 'The dialogic method is a way to incorporate that decentering recognition of a permanent *in medeas res* of human life and a consistently widening context for human interaction and interanimation within the biosphere and beyond' (Murphy 17). . . . [At the same time, Merleau-Ponty's ideas complement those of] the ecological psychologist James Gibson, whose work explicitly explores the experience of place. . . . Place, for Gibson, is defined by the perceiving subject, for whom horizons and occluded objects shift and change as the perceiver walks or turns her head. Thus the perceiver is literarally the center of the world. At the same time this perceiver looks and walks in the direction she does because the environment prompts these responses in what Gibson calls *affordances*, a word he made up to describe what an environment '*offers* to the animal, what it *provides or furnishes*, whether for good or ill' (33). Different species within the same environment – and different members of the same species as well – will be drawn to different accordances within it . . . [Virginia] Woolf is emphatically an experimental writer; each of her books explores different issues of craft and aesthetics, and even among feminists, who have shown how seriously she took women's issues – and thus addressed real world issues – she is sometimes seen as an aesthete creating what Elaine Showalter called 'uterine environments' (Kaivola 17). My contention, however, is that her writing career can better be described as a series of efforts to find more satisfactory ways of representing human relationships with the real than were available to her in the conventional novel in the realist tradition. My focus will be on her last novel, *Between the Acts*, which I believe is a remarkable culmination to this long process. . . . Indeed, I want to argue that *Between the Acts* can usefully be seen as a detailed and instructive representation of what [Maurice] Merleau Ponty called 'the flesh of the world'. . . .

In contrast with *The Voyage Out* [which depicts a mental journey away from 'place' and a shared environment], Woolf's last novel, *Between the Acts*, is both open-ended and 'thick', woven of multiple layers of life processes, including the human but not restricted to it. The setting of this novel is not merely background but a complex presence – a 'place' in the phenomenological sense. *Between the Acts* takes place on a single day, midsummer 1939, and follows the activities of the three generations of the Oliver family of Pointz Hall which is – as it is every year – the site of a pageant in which the whole community participates. Though the house is not 'rank[ed] among the houses that are mentioned in guide books', there is something about it which makes people ask about it as they drive by. It is an affordance, a place which speaks to people, despite its 'lying unfortunately low on the meadow' (*BA* 7). In fact, it seems to be a place composed of layers and layers of kinds of speech, only some of which are composed of human language. Human history, geological process, the ongoing present life of the biosphere – all are articulate presences lightly felt as part of ordinary life.

The novel opens with talk: 'It was a summer's night and they were talking'; the silences in the human conversation are filled by sounds coming through the open windows: 'a cow coughed' and 'A bird chuckled outside.' To human ears, this chuckle is expressive of place, if nothing else; the bird is not a nightingale because 'nightingales didn't come so far north.' The humans' discussion about a cesspool is in its own ordinary way expressive of place as well; the site is inscribed by history – just as an ordinary human body wears its own life history:

> The old man in the arm-chair – Mr. Oliver, of the Indian Civil Service, retired – said that the site they had chosen for the cesspool was, if he had heard aright, on the Roman road. From an aeroplane, he said, you could still see, plainly marked, the scars made by the Britons; by the Romans; by the Elizabethan manor house; and by the plough, when they ploughed the hill to grow wheat in the Napoleonic wars.
>
> (*BA* 5)

Geological, biological, and human historical processes are foregrounded as part of the weave of 'the present' in which the novel takes place. Bart Oliver's sister, Lucy, taking her tea in the barn set up for refreshments at the pageant's intermission, watches the swallows:

> Excited by the company they were flitting from rafter to rafter. Across Africa, across France they had come to nest here. Year after year they came. Before there was a channel, when the earth, upon which the Windsor chair was planted, was a riot of rhododendrons, and humming birds quivered at the mouths of scarlet trumpets, as the had read that morning in her Outline of History . . .
>
> (*BA* 66)

The inscriptions in the earth, the swallows in the barn, are more than setting and more than symbol; they are affordances acting as a kind of language, providing a weave of information in which the multiple modes of human language participate. In Merleau-Ponty's terms, this is a weave of the visible and the invisible, the literal world registered by the senses as one 'side' of the Moebius strip whose other 'side' simultaneously holds the multiple 'invisible' meanings inhering in the sensible world seen by the human perceiver.

Just as the natural world is foregrounded as participant capable of generating meaning rather than being relegated to mere setting, human language is also foregrounded as a process in itself rather than a mere vehicle for transporting thought or meaning. The reader is constantly made aware of the life of language which exists between people, in large groups and small, a life which exists beyond the intent of any speaker or listener. Woolf's depiction of collective language is so central to this book that I want to provide two examples. The first is the audience discussing the play they've seen:

> . . . I thought it brilliantly clever. . . . O my dear, I though it utter bosh. Did you understand the meaning? Well, he said she meant we all act a part. . . . He said, too, if I caught his meaning, Nature takes part. . . .

> Then there was the idiot. . . . Also, why leave out the Army, as my husband was saying, if it's history? And if one spirit animates the whole, what about the aeroplanes?
>
> (*BA* 117)

> The nurses after breakfast were trundling the perambulator up and down the terrace; as as they trundled they were talking – not shaping pellets of information or handing ideas from one to another, but rolling words, like sweets on their tongues. . . . This morning that sweetness was: 'How cook had told 'im off about the asparagus; how when she ran I said; . . .'
>
> (*BA* 9)

As the comparison of the maids' chit-chat to sweets suggests, language acts in and of themselves are for humans pre-eminent affordances in the environment. Isa Oliver, the young woman married to Bart Oliver's son, finds her attention caught and then betrayed by a newspaper item about a 'A horse with a green tail', and like the woman in the report finds that she has been tricked by fanciful language. For the story goes on to read, "And they dragged her up to the barrack room where she was thrown upon a bed. . . ." That was real' (*BA* 15).

If the focus of *The Voyage Out* is on the unsharable experience of a fevered illness, the focus of *Between the Acts* is on the collective experience of a community event. It is one of the meanings of the title: meaning-making occurs between language acts between participants, and no language act is final. The newspaper account, for example, does not have the last word:

> . . . in the barrack room the bed [Isa reads], and on the bed the girl was screaming and hitting him about the face, when the door (for in fact it was a door) opened and in came Mrs. Swithin carrying a hammer. . . . Not a word passed between them as she went to the cupboard in the corner and replaced the hammer, which she had taken without asking leave. . . .
>
> (*BA* 15)

Gestures and actions are part of the dialogics of the novel; so is the silence of the painting the visitors look at – all are part of the ongoing collective activity of making meaning. But Woolf's dialogic melody is triple, not limited to the human:

> The view repeated in its own way what the tune was saying. . . . The cows, making a step forward, then standing still, were saying the same thing to perfection. Folded in this triple melody, the audience sat gazing. . . .
>
> (*BA* 81)

The pageant ends with 'the present time', represented by mirrors paraded through the audience – who doesn't get it. 'This is death,' thinks the director, 'when illusion fails.' Then rain pours down, leaving 'a fresh earthy smell' and leaving as well a sense of meaningfulness: 'The tune was as simple as could be. But now that the shower had fallen, it was the other voice speaking, the voice that was no one's voice' (*BA* 107).

The dialogics of this novel preclude both the privileged point of view and the finality of closure. The Rev. Streatfield tries to provide a summary of what the pageant meant, and his failure to leave the audience with his stamp of interpretation is part of a general pattern in the novel of 'scraps and orts' of partial or thwarted understanding, interruption, dispersion. Miss LaTrobe's production does indeed satirize, as one critic has put it, 'traits of money-getting, disdain for people seen as inferior . . . and blindness to the waste of young men regarded as expendable' (Phillips 202–3), but the audience reaction is diffuse and obtuse. In the pageant, in responses to the pageant, in conversation at lunch, it is always the same: 'But before they had come to any common conclusion, a voice asserted itself' (*BA* 111). Indeed, interruptions are signs that the world (with its human and non-human elements) is in fact not just looking back, but answering back.

In contrast to the ebb and flow of language and the living landscape, the characters in the novel are virtually caricatures, crammed into the husks of their given roles (Dick 75). To a greater or lesser extent, all these roles (both on and off stage) are defined in relation to the patriarchy governing the human world. Those closest to patriarchal power are most rigidly constrained, but no one escapes. Even 'the wild child of nature', as Mrs. Manresa characterizes herself, is playing a role governed by the task of flaunting propriety. Her stylized performance offers the men of the Oliver household a delightful counterpoint to their own insistence on order and reason. The patriarchal inheritance being passed from father to son to grandson is at least as much an attitude toward property as it is property itself: one of its chief features is that the give and take which Merleau-Ponty characterizes as inherent in our relations with the rest of the world is reduced to the mechanics of possession and control. The Oliver men have learned to respond to affordances in the environment by immediately asserting their right – their duty – to claim possession and maintain order. The importance of this generational pattern is indicated by key passages in the novel which are as disturbing as they are opaque.

In the first of these anti-epiphanies, the youngest Oliver, Isa's young son George, is startled by a flower:

> The flower blazed between the angles of the roots. Membrane after membrane was torn. It blazed a soft yellow, a lambent light under a film of velvet; it filled the caverns behind the eyes with light. All that inner darkness became a hall, leaf smelling, earth smelling, of yellow light. And the tree was beyond the flower; the grass, the flower and the tree were entire.
>
> (*BA* 9–10)

George's response to the flower is to pull it up. His paradoxical action – uniting desire with destruction, comprehension with blindness – is emblematic of a response to an affordance which lacks a sense of the autonomous life of the other, which does not see itself as part of the ongoing life it observes. George's well-meaning destruction bears a family relationship to the grandfatherly prank which destroys his reverie. For when his grandfather Bart sees George with the flower, he terrifies him with a booming 'Good morning, sir' from behind a beak he makes of his newspaper, and then complains that George is a crybaby.

The other landmark anti-epiphany in the novel takes place later in the day when George's father, Giles, also registers the disturbance of an undisciplined natural presence. This time the experience is of revulsion rather than attraction; he sees

> a snake? Dead? No, choked with a toad in its mouth. The snake was unable to swallow; the toad was unable to die. A spasm made the ribs contract; blood oozed. It was birth the wrong way round – a monstrous inversion. So, raising his foot, he stamped on them.
>
> (*BA* 61)

Like his son, Giles finds himself presented with something in the environment that is unspeakable, and like his son, he can't just leave it alone. Instead, he finds a satisfaction in action, in the illusion of control through destruction. Giles is the sole member of the family who is worried about what is happening in Europe, yet the satisfaction he feels in action for the sake of asserting authority is itself ominously akin to the fascism he fears.

This common generational response suggests how vulnerable a place is to the humans who own it. Cultures, histories, and places may be destroyed by the very efforts undertaken to defend them, as Virginia Woolf's delineation of the 'connection between militarism and masculine education' (Beer 180) made clear in *Three Guineas*. Indeed, as Gillian Beer has shown, '[*Between the Acts*] holds the knowledge that cultures and histories are obliterated, that things may not endure.' At the same time, the response of the Oliver males to affordances in the environment is part of a much larger pattern of 'call and response' – that is, of dialogics – which goes on between all the participants, between acts, between people, between human and non-human.

Between the Acts ends with parallel images linking inherently dialogical institutions, the theater and marriage. Putting the pageant behind her, Miss LaTrobe glimpses the possibilities of a new play, a play dominated by the image of 'two figures, half concealed by a rock. The curtain would rise. What would the first words be?' (*BA* 124). In Pointz Hall, the old and the young go to bed, leaving Giles and Isa alone to say the first words to each other they have spoken all day. The last two paragraphs of the novel read:

> Isa let her sewing drop. The great hooded chairs had become enormous. And Giles too. And Isa too against the window. The window was all sky without colour. The house had lost its shelter. It was night before roads

were made, or houses. It was the night that dwellers in caves had watched
from some high place among rocks.

   Then the curtain rose. They spoke.

(BA 130–1)

Both of these moments are poised on the edge of what Merleau-Ponty calls an
'emergent order'; both, significantly, are dialogical. Miss LaTrobe must reach her
audience; Giles and Isa must reach each other. Both will participate in the making
and re-making of their world as part of a project that is beyond their control. And
either or both may fail. Woolf leaves open the possibility of catastrophe, even extinction. But she also leaves open the possibility of making a new life, inventing a new
script, a different plot, perhaps one which will make use of the 'unacted parts' each
of the characters has, perhaps parts of themselves to which the pageant has spoken.
Against the bullying force of fascism, Woolf pits the dialogic process; against the
threat of extinction, she pits the making and remaking of possibility that constitutes the fragility and strength of place.

WORKS CITED

Beer, Gillian (1989) *Arguing with the Past: Essays in Narrative from Woolf to Sidney*, London:
   Routledge.

Dick, Susan (1989) *Virginia Woolf*, London: Edward Arnold.

Gibson, James (1986) *The Ecological Approach to Visual Perception*, Hillsdale, NJ: Lawrence
   Erlbaum.

Kaivola, Karen (1991) *All Contraries Confounded: The Lyrical Fiction of Virginia Woolf, Djuna
   Barnes, and Marguerite Duras*, Iowa City, IA: Iowa University Press.

Merleau-Ponty, Maurice (1969) *The Essential Writings of Merleau-Ponty* (ed. Alden L. Fisher),
   San Diego, CA: Harcourt, Brace.

—— *The Visible and the Invisible* (1968) (ed. Claude Lefort; trans. Alphonso Lingis),
   Evanston, IL: Northwestern University Press.

Murphy, Patrick (1995) *Literature, Nature, and Other: Ecofeminist Critiques*, Albany, NY:
   State University of New York.

Phillips, Kathy J. (1994) *Virginia Woolf against Empire*, Knoxville, TN: Tennessee University
   Press.

Woolf, Virginia (1992) *Between the Acts* (ed. Stella McNichol), Harmondsworth: Penguin.
   (*BA*)

47

Defending Middle-Earth

Patrick Curry*

WHAT IS MOST striking about Tolkien's Middle-earth is the profound presence of the natural world: geography and geology, ecologies, flora and fauna, the seasons, weather, the sky, stars and moon. The experience of these phenonena as comprising a living and meaningful cosmos saturates his entire story. It wouldn't be stretching a point to say that Middle-earth itself appears as a character in its own right. And the personality and agency of this character are none the less so for being non-human; in fact, that is just what allows for a sense of ancient myth, with its feeling of a time when the Earth itself was alive. It whispers: perhaps, therefore, it could be again; perhaps, indeed, it still is.

Animals appear, but Tolkien obviously had a particular affection for flora. There are at least sixty-four species of wild plants mentioned in *The Hobbit* and *The Lord of the Rings* – surely an unusual number for any work of fiction – in addition to several invented kinds. Pride of place, however, goes to trees. Tolkien once referred to *The Lord of the Rings* as 'my own internal Tree'. 'I have among my "papers",' he once wrote, 'more than one version of a mythical "tree", which crops up regularly at those times when I feel driven to pattern-designing. . . . The tree bears besides various shapes of leaves many flowers small and large signifying poems and major legends.'[1] And his personal 'totem' – a birch tree – has long been sacred to indigenous peoples throughout North America, Europe and Asia, the rediscovery and adaptation of whose values is one of the keys to our collective future survival, let alone renewal. (Fully rationalized people, such as our present masters seek, will fall for the first rationalization for exploiting and destroying a disenchanted world that consequently doesn't feel worth defending.)

Tolkien's involvement with trees combined the mythically resonant with the personally poignant in a way which led to an extraordinarily vivid depiction in art. He would have liked John Fowles's avowal that

> If I cherish trees beyond all personal (and perhaps rather peculiar) need and liking of them, it is because of this, their natural correspondence with

*Adapted by the author from *Defending Middle-Earth: Tolkien, Myth and Modernity*, Edinburgh: Floris Books, 1997.

the greener, more mysterious processes of the mind – and because they also seem to me the best, most revealing messengers to us from all nature, the nearest its heart.'[2]

But Tolkien's trees are never just symbols, and in their individuality convey the uniqueness and vulnerability of 'real' trees. One was a 'great-limbed poplar tree' outside his house in the late 1930s, an inspiration for his short story 'Leaf by Niggle', that was 'suddenly lopped and mutilated by its owner, I do not know why. It is cut down now, a less barbarous punishment for any crimes it may have been accused of, such as being large and alive.'[3] Kim Taplin remarks, after Tolkien, 'The wanton felling of trees may have allegorical overtones, but it is also an actual evil . . . and the presence of trees, and the love of trees, are actual as well as symbolic goods.'[4]

Tolkien's trees also have deep historical as well as mythological and psychological roots. Thus, Middle-earth's own Old Forest was not so-called 'without reason, for it was indeed ancient, a survivor of vast forgotten woods . . .'[5] But even in the Third Age, those were already a thing of the past. And at the opening of the story in *The Lord of the Rings* – itself supposedly in the (imaginary) past of our world – even such remnants are on the edge of doom. On the very border of Fangorn Forest, as Treebeard says, Saruman

> is plotting to become a Power. He has a mind of metal and wheels; and he does not care for growing things, except as far as they serve him for the moment. . . . Down on the borders they are felling trees – good trees. Some of the trees they just cut down and leave to rot – orc-mischief that; but most are hewn up and carried off to feed the fires of Orthanc. There is always a smoke rising from Isengard these days.. . . Curse him, root and branch! Many of those trees were my friends, creatures I had known from nut and acorn; many had voices of their own that are lost for ever now. And there are wastes of stump and bramble where once there were singing groves . . .

Indeed, 'it seems that the wind is setting East, and the withering of all woods may be drawing near.'[6] For in what remains of the green garden of Middle-earth, already long tormented by Sauron, has appeared 'the Ring of Power, the foundation of Barad-dûr and the hope of Sauron'. (It is also the hope of Saruman, of course; but he is no more than one of Mordor's imitators and servants.) 'The Ring! What shall we do with the Ring, the least of rings, the trifle that Sauron fancies?' Elrond alone permits himself any irony, even as he too, like all the good and great, acknowledges his helplessness before the Ring on the hand of its maker and master.[7]

Here we must tread carefully, for Tolkien warned repeatedly against an allegorical or topical reading of his story, in which elements receive a more-or-less literal or one-to-one interpretation. His dislike of allegory is well-established: 'I think that many confuse "applicability" with "allegory"; but the one resides in the freedom of the reader, and the other in the purposed domination of the author.'

(Or as he once wonderfully complained, 'To ask if the Orcs "are" Communists is to me as sensible as asking if Communists are Orcs.')[8] Without suggesting that the meaning of the Ring is thereby exhausted, however, I shall avail myself of my right as a reader to perceive 'applicability' – an application that is becoming ever-increasingly difficult to avoid.

Consider that the Ring epitomises the strongest economic and political power in Middle-earth, which already threatens to dominate all others in one vast autocratic realm. Materially, there is none greater. True, it cannot create beauty or understanding or healing, but the three Elven Rings that can 'are ultimately under the control of the One.'[9] And from the point of view of those kinds of considerations, the One Ring's transformative power is unavoidably destructive. Furthermore, this potential will be realised to the full once the Ring is entirely under the control of Sauron. (Such a potential was prefigured in *The Hobbit*, when Tolkien observed of the Goblins, Sauron's chief servants, that 'It is not unlikely that they invented some of the machines that have since troubled the world, especially the ingenious devices for killing large numbers of people at once, for wheels and engines and explosions always delighted them . . .'.)[10]

In his essay 'On Fairy-Stories', Tolkien explicitly links this sort of scientific-technological ingenuity with *magic*, culminating in 'the vulgar devices of the laborious, scientific, magician.'[11] The magic of faërie, by contrast, is what he calls *enchantment*. This is a brilliant and vitally important distinction.[12] He describes the latter as 'the primal desire at the heart of Faërie: the realization, independent of the conceiving mind, of imagined wonder.' 'Realization' here is ambiguous, and properly so; it signifies both the making of the natural world wondrous through the creation of a 'Secondary World . . . artistic in desire and purpose', *and* the realization (through the former) that the Primary or 'real' world actually is wondrous.[13] In the context of *The Lord of the Rings*, enchantment is the art of the elves; and as such, it has a special affinity with nature both as its principal inspiration and as the object of its enhancement: 'Their "magic" is Art, delivered from many of its human limitations: more effortless, more quick, more complete . . .' and even though the Elves 'became sad, and their art (shall we say) antiquarian . . . they also retained the old motive of their kind, the adornment of earth, and the healing of its hurts.'[14]

> Magic too concerns the Earth, but in a completely different way: Enchantment produces a Secondary World into which both designer and spectator can enter, to the satisfaction of their senses while they are inside; but in its purity it is artistic in desire and purpose. Magic produces, or pretends to produce, an alteration in the Primary World. . . . it is not an art but a technique; its desire is *power* in this world, domination of things and wills.[15]

The Enemy is thus 'Lord of magic and machines', who favours '"machinery" – with destructive and evil effects – because "magicians", who have become chiefly concerned to use *magic* for their own power, would do so.'[16] That power rarely starts off as pure self-aggrandisement. Tolkien recognized that 'frightful evil can and does arise from an apparently good root, the desire to benefit the world and others – speedily and according to the benefactor's own plans . . .'. Even Sauron's rise to power at the beginning of the Third Age started 'slowly, beginning with fair motives: the reorganizing and rehabilitation of the ruin of Middle-earth . . .'. And Saruman the collaborator tried to tempt Gandalf with 'Knowledge, Rule, Order'.[17]

On historical grounds alone, Tolkien is quite correct; the appropriation of magic and its transformation into modern science is one of the most important events (and closely-guarded secrets) of the past three centuries.[18] And in contemporary terms, the triumph of highly financed technological magic over enchantment – often through exploiting it in advertising and public relations – is something we see confirmed everywhere in Middle-earth today, just as we continue to hear a great deal about how all this global Progress is not only good for us, but unavoidable in any case. (That exploitation now requires, I feel, a new category, namely glamour: enchantment enslaved in the service of magic.)

Let me be clear: science as a human activity has perfectly honourable antecedents, and is not intrinsically or necessarily perverted by power-as-domination. Even today, some scientists are more oriented to the wonder of the natural world (i.e., enchantment) than its manipulation and exploitation (i.e., magic). This too is discernible within Tolkien's work. In a letter, he observed that the Elves 'have a devoted love of the physical world, and a desire to observe and understand it for its own sake and as "other" . . . not as a material for use or as a power-platform.' The Noldor, or Loremasters, in particular, 'were always on the side of "science and technology", as we should call it . . .'.[19] (On the other hand, it was the Noldor who cooperated with Sauron in forging the Rings of Power, and were thus duped and betrayed by him.)

Nor is technology as such evil, although there is far too much self-interested nonsense about it being 'neutral'; there is nothing morally neutral about a bomb compared, say, with a bicycle. Tolkien admits that 'It would no doubt be possible to defend poor Lotho's introduction of more efficient mills; but not Sharkey and Sandyman's use of them' – and still less, in Treebeard's words, 'orc-work, the wanton hewing . . . without even the bad excuse of feeding the fires . . .'. I think the same point is evident from the Dwarves, who were created by Aulë the Smith, and in their hands 'still lives the skill in works of stone that none have surpassed.' They are also constitutionally prone to greed for gold and precious stones, but when Gimli discovers the Caverns of Helm's Deep, he is adamant, in conversation with Legolas, that 'No dwarf could be unmoved by such loveliness. None of Durin's race would mine those caves for stones or ore, not if diamonds and gold could be got there. Do you cut down groves of blossoming trees in the spring-time for fire-wood?'[20]

Sadly, tragically even, we do. Despite all due qualifications it is true, and must be recognized, that modern science and technology – the ideology (and indeed, cult) of which can be called scientism – is now a very different matter. It has become almost inseparable from both political power and financial profit, and sometimes an object of worship in its own right. As such, it is now as much of a problem in our Middle-earth as it is in Tolkien's literary creation.

Compared to that power, a plea to love and respect for the natural world for its own sake is a slight thing; but it is a potentially powerful one, like a new shoot of green growth amid a crack in concrete. Given the more dominant outlook, of course, those advocating (like Tolkien) or seeking (like a great many of his readers) 'a new communion with nature' are easily accused of 'indulging in fatuous romanticism', a mere childish and sentimental fantasy, in the worst sense of the word.[21] And literary experts and professionals look down on people who read Tolkien in exactly the same way.

Such people have no need to feel ashamed, however; far from it. It was not they, for example, but official 'experts' and 'realists', who decided to feed vegetarian ruminants on animal flesh and douse them with toxic organo-phosphates, only to be astounded when BSE ('mad cow disease') resulted. To take another example, in the words of American forester Gordon Robinson, 'you don't have to be a professional forester to recognize bad forestry any more than you have to be a doctor to recognize ill health. If logging looks bad, it is bad. If a forest appears to be mismanaged, it is mismanaged.' And it takes some serious professional training to be able to ignore the clear and obvious distress and pain of animals you are torturing for trivial or highly questionable reasons in the name of medical science, let alone cosmetics.

Take what abuts the garden of the present Prime Minister of Great Britain (as I write): a 250-acre field, stretching into the distance – and nothing else but electricity poles and a few exposed cottages. It is devoid of life, except for the uniform annual crop. Yet within living memory, there were allotments for local villagers, copses of trees, rose hedges, traditional grassland, all manner of birdlife, ponds with fish, newts and waterfowl. From Essex to Yorkshire, now more typical than not of English agriculture, this is the result of 'chemicals, machines, and the search for profit' (albeit massively subsidised by taxpayers).[22] This is happening almost everywhere, only varying in pace and degree: barbed wire but no orchards; commuters' cars but no buses; wild plants, birds and mammals decimated; privatization and development, while commons and greens disappear; and an enduring legacy of poisons in the soil. Is it really mere 'nostalgia' to point out gross unsustainability (to put it nicely), and ask whether this is really what we want? In even the slightly longer run, who are really the realists here: the official experts, or the amateurs who find such developments appalling and immoral? And it is fitting that Tolkien's own beloved mill and its green environs in Sarehole, where he grew up – and which he was convinced would go under – was saved from the local council and developers by a combination of locals and middle-class incomers: ordinary enough people, all.

As Richard Mabey writes, 'the widespread modern yearning for a relationship with nature and the land based, not on ownership or labour, but on simple delight and sensual and spiritual renewal, is an authentic search for a modern role for the countryside.'[23] Even in huge cities like London, remaining green spaces and 'wild bits' are used, and fellow non-human creatures appreciated, by all classes and sections of the community, who value them as a non-commercialized world, at once natural and communal, to experience and enjoy.[24] And this is just a small but vital part of a deeper truth, what Hazlitt meant by saying that 'Nature is a kind of universal home.'[25] We all participate in nature, so the opportunities it offers to realize, accept (where necessary) and enjoy (where possible) that participation are profoundly democratic.

In Fraser Harrison's words, 'what must be conserved before anything else is the desire in ourselves for Home – for harmony, peace and love, for growth in nature and in our imaginative powers – because unless we keep this alive, we shall lose everything.'[26] This desire is just what Tolkien's work kindles and sustains in his readers.

NOTES

1   J. R. R. Tolkien, *The Letters of J.R.R. Tolkien* (ed. Humphrey Carpenter), London: George Allen & Unwin, 1981, 321, 342.

2   John Fowles, *The Tree*, St Albans: Sumach Press, 1992; first published London: Aurum Press, 1979, 80.

3   J. R. R. Tolkien, *Tree and Leaf* [henceforth *T&L*], London: Unwin Hyman, 1988, 6.

4   Kim Taplin, *Tongues in Trees: Studies in Literature and Ecology*, Bideford: Green Books, 1989, 196.

5   J. R. R. Tolkien, *The Lord of the Rings* [henceforth *LotR*], London: Grafton Books, 1991, I, 179.

6   *LotR*, II, 90–1, 89.

7   *LotR*, III, 184–5; I, 317.

8   *LotR*, I, 11–12; *Letters*, 262.

9   *Letters*, 177.

10 J. R. R. Tolkien, *The Hobbit*, London: Grafton Books, 1991, 69.

11 *T&L*, 15.

12 For an essay exploring and developing this idea, see Patrick Curry, 'Magic vs. Enchantment', *Journal of Contemporary Religion*, 14(3), 1999, 401–12.

13 *T&L*, 18, 49.

14 *Letters*, 151–2.

15 *T&L*, 49–50.

16 *Letters*, 146, 200.

17 *Letters*, 146, 151; *LotR*, I, 339.

18 See, e.g., Charles Webster, *From Paracelsus to Newton: Magic and the Making of Modern Science*, Cambridge: Cambridge University Press, 1982.

19 *Letters*, 236, 190.

20 *Letters*, 200; *LotR*, II, 107; III, 529; II, 189.

21 Fraser Harrison, *The Living Landscape*, London: Mandarin Books, 1991, 13.

22 *Guardian* (12 October 1994).

23 Richard Mabey, *In a Green Shade*, London: Unwin, 1985, 12.

24 Jacqueline Burgess, Carolyn M. Harrison and Melanie Limb, 'People, Parks and the Urban Green: A Study of Popular Meanings and Values for Open Spaces in the City', *Urban Studies*, 25, 1988, 1–19.

25 William Hazlitt, 'On the Love of the Country', 3–8 in *Selected Essays of William Hazlitt* (ed. Geoffrey Keynes), London: Nonesuch Press, 1970, 7.

26 Fraser Harrison, 'England, Home and Beauty', 162–72 in Richard Mabey *et al.* (eds), *Second Nature*, London: Jonathan Cape, 1984, 172.

48

Leslie Silko: Environmental Apocalypticism

LAWRENCE BUELL*

THERE WAS NO end to it; it knew no boundaries; and he had arrived at the point of convergence where the fate of all living things, and even the earth, had been laid. From the jungles of his dreaming he recognised why the Japanese voices had merged with Laguna voices, with Josiah's voice and Rocky's voice; the lines of cultures and worlds were drawn in dark flat lines on fine light sand, converging in the middle of witchery's final ceremonial sand painting. From that time on, human beings were one clan again, united by the fate the destroyers planned for all of them, for all living things; united by a circle of death that devoured people in cities twelve thousand miles away, victims who had never known these mesas, who had never seen the delicate colors of the rocks which boiled up their slaughter.

(Leslie Marmon Silko, *Ceremony*)

[My] epigraph is the climax of Silko's novel.[1] Her GI-protagonist, Tayo, a casualty of the Bataan death march that killed his cousin and foster-brother, Rocky, has been trying to work his way toward mental health following the regime of his medicine man, who foresaw the fatefulness of this night of the autumnal equinox. Tayo has arrived at the abandoned uranium mine on tribal land, from which the ore for Hiroshima and Nagasaki had been quarried and on which his traitorous buddies are about to converge with the intent of turning him over to the authorities as a lunatic. Everything suddenly clicks. Tayo realizes how the global reach of destructive forces connects up everything in his life experience: his reservation to the Pacific Rim, by reason of the bomb, and American Indian to Japanese. What he had experienced as insanity, as the uncontrollable montaging of impressions (seeing the face of his Japanese 'enemy' as the face of his Uncle Josiah, for instance), is sanity. 'He was not crazy. He had only seen and heard the world as it always was: no boundaries, only transitions through all distances and time.' This insight helps give Tayo

*From *The Environmental Imagination: Thoreau, Nature Writing, and the Formation of American Culture*, Cambridge, MA: Harvard University Press, 1995.

288

the strength to resist the 'witchery' that has overtaken his similarly damaged peers. He remains hidden and self-restrained despite his urge to attack the man who has been his chief tormentor, while his peers turn their violence against each other.

One of the most remarkable features of this remarkable book is its fusion of regionalism and globalism, its assertion that 'the fate of all living things' hinges on a minor transaction taking place in a remote cultural niche, a smallish Pueblo tribe of marginal influence within an already marginalized race. Silko capitalizes brilliantly on the historical facts that uranium was mined on Laguna land and that the Laguna – including both Tayo and Silko herself – are an extensively hybridized people. These contingencies allow her to develop a fiction of Tayo's cure both as an intensely particularized story of a reservation lad's retribalization and as a case study of a sickness of global scope. Tayo cannot be cured until he realizes that 'his sickness was only part of something larger, and his cure would be found only in something great and inclusive of everything' (125–6). This realization is forced on him not only in his capacity as a hybrid or world citizen but also as a Laguna: the realization that individual and social pathologies are coextensive. The elders traditionally think of the world as a place-centered continuum of human and nonhuman beings subsisting in the fragile 'intricacies of a continuing process, and with a strength inherent in spider webs woven across paths through sand hills where early in the morning the sun becomes entangled in each filament of web' (35). In Laguna myth, poetically evoked at the start of *Ceremony*, the creator is Spiderwoman.

Thus *Ceremony* becomes a work of ecological ethnopoetics. Although seemingly about people rather than about the environment as such, its vision of human affairs is governed by a sense of their reciprocity with the land. The geography is precise; Silko later affirmed that 'the writing was my way of re-making that place' in compensation for her absence from it; her ordering of physical terrain conforms to the ordering of Laguna sacred geography.[2] Every place signifies; every place, every creature has a story connected with it that forms a web of significance (always in process, not a constant) within which human thought assumes form and meaning. To look at a particular hill or spring, to see it rightly, is to realize where it stands in relation to family history and tribal myth; to look at an insect, rightly, is to connect it with a folktale about the insect's contribution to tribal welfare. This web of associations, which Silko renders schematically through the ceremonial sand painting within which Tayo's mentor performs the first healing ritual, is the antithesis of 'witchery's final ceremonial sand painting', the antiweb of 'the destroyers', of which European conquest and technological transformation are the symptoms.

Ceremony's innovations with cosmic metaphor equal in importance its traditional elements. Its Laguna-style ecocentrism stays very much in the spirit of Tayo's Navajo healer, Betonie, who believes that in a world thrown out of balance ceremonies must evolve in order to remain strong. Simply by incorporating World War II into a mythical narrative, making it part of Laguna ceremonial grammar by absorbing it into a plot of purification, Silko updates the practice of incorporating stories of European (and Mexican) contact into 'traditional' storytelling, which was obviously well in place before the first anthropologists took notes on Laguna culture.

Nor does Silko refrain from tinkering with what would seem to be purely autochthonous motifs. Take the opening invocation:

> Ts'its'tsi'nako, Thought-Woman,
>   is sitting in her room
> and whatever she thinks about
>   appears.

Relative to 'the dynamic, all-comprehensive nature of Thought Woman' in Laguna myth, this image domesticates her, limits her ability to transgress gender, makes her more the magnified image of the writer. The world-web metaphor is another revisionary touch. It makes perfect sense as a consolidation of the image of a Spiderwoman-creator 'who weaves us together in a fabric of interconnection', in Paula Gunn Allen's words;[3] but judging from the anthropological record it is not inevitable for metaphors of weaving and web to be ascribed to Spiderwoman or Thought-Woman, logical though that extension might seem. The revisions produce a somewhat ecofeminized image of the Laguna cosmos that purifies it of certain patriarchal encrustations introduced by Christianity and in other respects modernizes it to accord even more strikingly with feminist and environmentalist presuppositions.

But I want to turn more directly to how Silko's revisionary storytelling leads her to construct a kind of ecological apocalypse. A bit like the protean speaker in *The Waste Land*, one of the first canonical works of modern Anglo-American literature to envision a dying society in the aftermath of world war, Tayo is an initially impotent and inchoate figure who epitomizes and perpetuates the sickness of his culture in a time of aftermath, when the old order of pastoral agrarianism, knit together by the common understandings of ritual and story, has been broken. He has returned home to a drought for which he feels personally accountable. The curse on him, on the land, and on the tribe (whose other young men are also war-damaged) is linked. Only his transformation, as symbolic representative of his generation, by a year-long ceremonial process that simultaneously reintegrates him psychically and retribalizes him can instigate the redemption of the people and the land. Significantly, he recovers his sexuality when reinitiated by the mysterious Ts'eh Montano (literally 'water mountain'), at one level a personification of the land, who offers him reintegration with it. Ts'eh is an avatar of Spider/Thought-Woman and also of the equally mysterious Mexican woman who first initiated him into sex during a symbolic rainstorm that Tayo had 'caused' by an ad hoc prayer ceremony – the first sign in the book that Tayo has the capacity to become a shamanistic hero. (Silko's improvisational multiplication of Spiderwoman's avatars, two of whom are ethnic outsiders, is one of the book's prime examples of her redirection of traditional materials in the interest of a hybridized vision.)

Silko is certainly cosmopolitan enough to have been aware of both *The Waste Land* and its scholarly precursor, Jessie Weston's *From Ritual to Romance*. But whatever the facts of that matter, she also had ready to hand, in the repertoire of Laguna stories, many of the motifs for her rebirth-of-the-hero narrative. One such story is that of Sun Youth, who with the aid of Old Woman Spiderwoman recovers from Kau'ata' the Gambler the clouds that he stole from the people, causing a three-year drought during which 'the earth and the whole ground cracked.' Silko interpolates this story into *Ceremony* at a crucial moment (170–6), when Tayo appears to have recidivized by falling back under the influence of his drunken buddies after his encounter with Betonie. Thereby she both counterpoints Tayo's failure with the mythic hero's success, underscoring in the process the present disjunction between sacred and profane worlds, and foreshadows what Tayo will eventually become.

As in the story of Sun Youth, the fate of the earth is made to hang on Tayo's fate. Silko justifies the portentousness of this burden by investing his saga with mythic, prototypical elements, and by presenting her vision of the inextricable tie between individual and community. *Ceremony's* culminating section oscillates wildly between world as web and world as machine. As Tayo staggers irresolutely toward the mine, he moves through a no-man's-land of barbed wire, another antiweb, the sandstone and dirt extracted by the laborers 'piled in mounds, in long rows, like fresh graves' (245). As a sudden sense of convergence hits him, he becomes aware of 'the delicate colors of the rocks' and utterly antithetical master images collide:

> He knelt and found an ore rock. The gray stone was streaked with powdery yellow uranium, bright and alive as pollen; veins of sooty black formed lines with the yellow, making mountain ranges and rivers across the stone. But they had taken these beautiful rocks from deep within earth and they had laid them in a monstrous design, realizing destruction on a scale only *they* could have dreamed.
>
> (246)

In rapid succession, Tayo sees the world as pristine ecodesign and as 'monstrous design'. A few pages later, the victory of the former gets written in the pattern of the sunrise that ushers him home, the sun 'pushing against the gray horizon hills, sending yellow light across the clouds, and the yellow river sand . . . speckled with the broken shadows of tamaric and river willow' (255). The hill/river, yellow/gray, schematic/kinetic interweave make this epiphany a macrocosmic sequel to the microcosmic rock – a glorious melodrama of human and cultural redemption as a state of ecological grace.

By building on traditional Laguna storytelling Silko thus brings world crisis to an almost utopian closure, at least at the local level. Tayo assumes a place of honor within his family, his domineering aunt no longer disdaining him as her younger sister's half-breed bastard, who ought to have been the one killed in the war instead of her more promising son, Rocky. The place is the one left vacant by Josiah, his uncle and father figure, his first teacher of ceremonial wisdom and of the cattle herding that Tayo will presumably take full charge of. His sick companions either die or flee; the elders are satisfied that Tayo is healed and that 'we will be blessed again' (257). After such a narrow escape ('It had been a close call. The witchery had almost ended the story according to its plan' – 253), the outcome is almost too idyllic. Perhaps Silko herself realized this, for her second full-scale fictional recreation of the southwestern borderlands, *Almanac of the Dead* (1991), is a massive chronicle of social perversions that spares nobody. The continent's modern dispensation began, the text suggests, with an occult collaboration between Montezuma and Cortes, 'members of the same secret clan'; 'Montezuma and his allies had been sorcerers who had called or even invented the European invaders with their sorcery.' Cross-cultural cartels of corrupt entrepreneurs who deal in drugs, arms, and erotica largely control economies and politics. The counterforce, such as it is, resides in a fragmentary native 'almanac' that might contain within it 'a power that would bring all the tribal people of the Americas together to retake the land,' but its inheritors are incapacitated.[4] In an echo of *Ceremony*, *Almanac* ends with one character's return to the Laguna community from which he had been exiled, but he is only one of dozens of figures on Silko's movable stage, and his home-coming is an antiromantic affair compared to Tayo's triumphant return from his ordeal at the uranium mine. On the whole, *Almanac* reads like *Ceremony*'s counterpoint: a dystopian anatomy of the profane, as if *Ceremony* had been redone so as to make the bars of Gallup or the psychiatric ward of the Los Angeles veterans' hospital the center of the novel. The contrast . . . shows the ease with which utopian thinking can become its opposite.

NOTES

1   Here, and below, the text to which I refer is Leslie Marmon Silko, *Ceremony*, New York: Viking, 1977.

2   Silko to James Wright, 1 November 1978, in Silko and Wright, *The Delicacy and Strength of Lace* (ed. Anne Wright), St Paul, MN: Greywolf, 1986, p. 28.

3   Paula Gunn Allen, *The Sacred Hoop: Recovering the Feminine in American Indian Traditions*, Boston: Beacon Press, 1986, p. 11.

4   Leslie Marmon Silko, *Almanac of the Dead*, New York: Simon & Schuster, 1991, pp. 760, 570, 569.

49

Flooding the Boundaries of Form: Terry Tempest Williams's Unnatural History

CHERYLL GLOTFELTY*

BY SUBTITLING *REFUGE* 'An *Un*natural History of Family and Place', Terry Tempest Williams at once alludes to the literary tradition of natural-history writing and announces her departure from the form. At first glance, *Refuge* appears to be conventional natural history. The book's cover design, for example, features an unpeopled natural scene of a bird flying over a lake rimmed by distant mountains. The short biographical note about Williams at the front of the book states that she is naturalist-in-residence at the Utah Museum of Natural History, immediately establishing her authority to write about nature.

Both the prefatory map of the Great Salt Lake and the table of contents, in which chapters are named for different bird species, bespeak familiar literary terrain, territory opened up by the pioneers of American natural history, men like William Bartram, Alexander Wilson, John James Audubon, Henry Thoreau, and John Burroughs. Appearing at the back of the book is a typical list of rare and regular bird species of the Great Salt Lake, arranged phylogenetically and including their Latin scientific names.

From cover to cover, then, *Refuge* initially conforms to our expectations about natural-history writing. Indeed, the text itself follows the nature writing path in many ways, including close observation and detailed description of birds and their habitat, scientific explanations of avian ecology, and the presentation of quantitative data like rainfall and lake level, all enclosed in a first-person, non-fictional form.

What, then, is 'unnatural' about *Refuge*? How does it depart from the traditional genre? Setting is one difference, for Williams describes not only natural areas but also populated urban areas and indoor settings, places such as downtown Salt

---

*From 'Flooding the Boundaries of Form: Terry Tempest Williams' Ecofeminist *Unnatural History*', in Stephen Tchudi (ed.) *Change in the American West: Exploring the Human Dimension*, Reno, NV: University of Nevada Press, 1996. (A book imprint of *Halcyon*, volume 18.)

Lake City, New York City, Bloomingdale's, Nordstrom's, hospital corridors, and the rooms of her family's house. Subject matter is another difference, for the book is about people as much as it is about nature. Williams writes about her family, especially about the strong bonds among generations of women – her grandmother Mimi, her mother, Diane, and herself. Extending her sense of family, Williams probes into Mormon history and culture, unearths information on the ancient Fremont peoples, and visits Mexico to participate in the rituals of the Day of the Dead.

Yet another departure from traditional natural history may be described as the gendered stance of *Refuge*. Where writers like Bartram, Muir, and Leopold, and even Annie Dillard and Ann Zwinger, do not thematize their sex, Williams wears her gender on her sleeve and remains ever-conscious of how being a woman colors every aspect of her experience. Further distinguishing *Refuge* from natural histories of an earlier century are 'unnatural' developments in the world, for Williams comes to believe that the cancer killing the women of her family may have been caused by exposure to radiation during above-ground atomic testing that took place between 1951 and 1962. Although she learns to accept death as 'natural', the knowledge that her mother may have died prematurely – an unsuspecting victim of Cold War militarism – causes Williams to commit civil disobedience, protesting further 'unnatural' abuse of what she calls the 'Motherbody', 'Mother Earth'.

The most striking formal feature of *Refuge*, further distancing it from mainstream natural-history writing is its conflation of natural history with personal, familial history. *Refuge* splices together two stories, the story of the catastrophic flooding of the Bear River Migratory Bird Refuge and the story of Diane Tempest's spreading cancer. Although purists might insist that the two narratives are logically distinct and that their marriage in one book is arbitrary and 'unnatural', nonetheless, emotionally the two are as intertwined as the strands of a rope. As Williams remarks, 'I could not separate the Bird Refuge from my family. Devastation respects no boundaries' (40). Just as the rising Great Salt Lake laps over protective dikes, *Refuge* breaches the conventional boundaries of natural history's subject and form.

Many other traditional boundaries also dissolve; in fact, I argue that this book's mission is to contest boundaries of all sorts. The separation between person and place collapses in statements such as 'I am desert. I am mountains. I am Great Salt Lake' (29). Observer and observed likewise fuse as Williams recalls of her mother, 'I began breathing with her. . . . Mother and I became one. One breathing organism' (230). No longer is there a clear delineation between pleasure and pain or between health and sickness. Even life and death intergrade as Williams refers to birth as our first death and describes death as becoming fully born.

Inside and outside are paradoxically the same when Williams quotes the gnostics, who teach that 'what is inside of you is what is outside of you and the one who fashions you on the outside is the one who shaped the inside of you. And what you see outside of you, you see inside of you' (267). Similarly, matter is imbued with spirit and dreams infuse reality. The closed doors between private and public are thrown open as Williams describes intimate family prayer meetings, reprints her mother's private letters, and publishes her own personal journal entries. Likewise the personal and the political merge as Williams questions patriarchal practices of Mormon home life and as the personal tragedy of cancer in her family prompts Williams to join a political march against nuclear testing.

On a formal level, Williams makes ambiguous the difference between non-fiction and fiction. Birds, for example, are portrayed not just literally, as objects of a naturalist's close observation, but also lyrically and symbolically, as elements contributing to the beauty and meaning of a narrative. Thus, white-faced glossy ibises literally 'eat worms' (18), lyrically flash 'irrdescences of pink, purple, and green' (17), and symbolically 'are the companions of the gods' (18), associated both with death and with birth. In her description of birds and also of landscapes, Williaims maintains the scientific accuracy of a nonfiction writer while she deepens the symbolic resonance of the work, using the techniques of a novelist.

The structure of *Refuge* may appear to lack premeditated design, seeming to simply follow the chronological entries in a nonfiction journal. In actuality, Williams has carefully shaped and paced the material to resemble the plot of a novel and to reproduce a novel's emotional impact. It is this strong sense of plot that makes *Refuge* so much more moving and even cathartic than much of the dry natural-history writing of the past.

One clue to *Refuge*'s novelistic construction can be discovered in the precise measurements of the level of the Great Salt Lake, accurate to the nearest one-hundredth of a foot, that Williams prints after each chapter title. Of what possible relevance are lake-level statistics to the story? If one uses these statistics to construct a graph with chapter numbers on the horizontal axis and lake elevations on the vertical axis, one will find that the resulting curve resembles the plot structure of a traditional novel, with rising action, climaxes, falling action, and denouement. With the skill of a fiction writer, Williams has arranged her factual material so that the highest lake levels correspond to turning points and personal transformations in the family narrative.

In this light, a closer scrutiny of the cover of the book reveals the same fiction/nonfiction fusion. We see a realistic, sharply focussed, full-color photograph of a peregrine falcon superimposed over a dreamlike, blurred-focus, monochromatic photograph of the Bonneville Salt Flats. Are the Flats covered with water, or is that seeming lake really a mirage? We cannot tell. Recalling Marianne Moore's definition of poetry as 'imaginary gardens with real toads in them', here we have an imaginary landscape with a real bird in it. As *Refuge* implies, poetic truth is always a blend of fact and figment.

I believe that what is 'unnatural' about *Refuge* – particularly its gendered stance and its contesting of boundaries – can be attributed to Williams's ecofeminist aesthetic. In *Refuge*, Williams invents a literary art form consonant with ecofeminist philosophy, a philosophy that denounces the hierarchical, dualistic thinking that leads to abuses of power and to alienation from nature. Ecofeminist philosophy and the aesthetic experiments of *Refuge* both deconstruct dualisms such as humanity/nature, self/other, mind/body, and intellect/emotion, replacing them with a holistic vision of connectedness and interdependence. The majority of ecofeminist work has analyzed social, economic, and political structures. Williams is one of the first thinkers to bring an ecofeminist perspective to bear on aesthetics.

The ecofeminist aesthetic informing *Refuge* reveals itself in the contrasting descriptions of two desert sculptures. The first is a nine-story steel-and-concrete structure by Kari Momen entitled 'Metaphor' but jokingly referred to by locals as 'The Tree of Utah'. As Williams writes, 'Its brightly colored spheres (leaves?) resembled enormous tennis *balls*, thirteen feet in diameter, poised on top of an eighty-three-foot lightning *rod*' (127; emphasis mine). The plaque below the towering sculpture explains that Momen, a European architect, saw the West Desert as 'a large canvas with nothing on it' (ibid.) and that 'Metaphor' is his attempt 'to put something out there to break the monotony' (ibid.). Williams points out that 'the man-made tree rose from the salt flats like a small phallus' and that its shadow resembled 'a mushroom cloud' (ibid.). 'The Tree of Utah' represents what might be called masculinist art. The 'tree' – vertical and linear – is an imposition, an arrogant, insensitive, narcissistic, and even aggressive act committed by a foreigner who has never taken the time to learn to appreciate the land on its own terms. The sculpture works against the land rather than with it. Williams's mother dismisses the tree as 'another roadside attraction' (ibid.) and they drive on.

Williams spends much more time experiencing and discussing Nancy Holt's sculpture entitled 'Sun Tunnels', to which Williams and her grandmother Mimi make a pilgrimage. 'Sun Tunnels' is a configuration of four large concrete tunnels laid out on the desert in the shape of an open X. In the top half of the tunnels are cut sets of different-sized holes that correspond to four different constellations. 'During the day, the sun shines through the holes, casting a changing pattern of pointed ellipses and circles of light' (268). The eight-foot-high interior diameter of the tunnels invites the viewer to come inside, and the thick walls ensure that the temperature is fifteen to twenty degrees cooler inside than outside. Holt notes that 'there is also a considerable echo in the tunnels' (ibid.).

To Mimi, the sculpture looks like four pieces of conduit pipe lying on the job site of a construction firm, but as she will discover, this sculpture is not meant to be gazed upon as an object but to be entered into and experienced. The sculpture does not call attention to itself but redirects attention outward to the natural surroundings. As Williams writes, 'The Great Basin landscape is framed within circles and we remember the shape of our planet, the shape of our eyes, our mouth in song and in prayer' (269). In an article excerpted in *Refuge,* Nancy Holt writes that she was personally transformed while conceiving this art. After several days of camping at the site, Holt 'located a particular sound within the land and began to chant. This song became her connection to the Great Salt Lake desert' (268). In an interview, Holt describes her experience to Williams, 'I became like the ebb and flow of light inside the tunnels' (269).

The contrast between 'Metaphor' and 'Sun Tunnels' could hardly be more gender-marked: the one is an erection; the other a conception. For Momen the man, the landscape is mute, a blank canvas upon which to project his own fantasy. For Holt the woman, the landscape has a voice, and art becomes a way of harmonizing with the land, of echoing its sound. The first act of the artist is not to speak but to listen humbly to the land. Connection rather than alienation results. At peace, Williams falls asleep inside one of the tunnels and wakes to find her grandmother standing at the center of the four tunnels, 'turning slowly, looking outward in each direction' (270).

In *Refuge*, Williams creates a literary analog to the kind of art represented by 'Sun Tunnels'. As the pioneer of a new ecofeminist style of nature writing, William expands the boundaries of the nature-writing genre to encompass matters of gender, breaking the ground for natural-history writing to open itself to new methods and concerns.

Yet even as the book breaches conventional boundaries of subject and form, still, there is one boundary that not only remains in tact but is actually reinforced: that is the division between the sexes. In characterizing *Refuge* as an ecofeminist work, I intend this criticism to apply more broadly to the ecofeminist project itself.

Throughout *Refuge* Williams highlights, not the similarities, but the differences between men and women, privileging the special bonds that exist among women. With the exception of her male family members and friends, Williams depicts men as rather dense creatures who need to feel in control and whose motto is 'dollars-and-cents'. Men satirized in this book include not only the 'beergut-over-beltbuckled men' of the Canadian Goose Gun Club (12), but also Mormon leaders, government officials, civil engineers, military officers, and some medical doctors. Even among her loved ones, Williams characterizes individual differences as sexlinked. Thus, Brooke of the 'analytic mind' offers a rational, scientific explanation of a mirage, while Terry prefers to think of it as a symbol of hope on a hot day, and Brooke thinks about the genetic information of a species and the embryology of a curlew, while Terry says a silent prayer for the bird and remembers a special bond that she formed with one. While Diane's impending death causes her husband, John Tempest, to withdraw or burst into fits of rage, daughter Terry enters ever more intimately into what she calls 'the secrecy of sisterhood', 'the privacy of women' (158).

In *Refuge* Williams explores what it means to be 'a woman connected to other women' (51). The book's final dream-vision is one of worldwide sisterhood, with women from all over the globe dancing wildly around a blazing fire in the desert, preparing themselves to reclaim the earth, presumably from its male captors. Williams writes, 'A contract had been made and broken between human beings and the land. A new contract was being drawn by the women, who understood the fate of the earth as their own' (288),

Williams is right to open up natural history to gender issues. But I wish that invoking gender were done in the spirit of bridging differences rather than exaggerating them. I hope that in *Refuge: The Next Generation* the men of the world will also be invited to dance around that blazing fire.

WORKS CITED

Diamond, Irene, and Gloria Orenstein (eds) (1990) *Reweaving the World: The Emergence of Ecofeminism*, San Francisco, CA: Sierra Club Books.

Gaard, Greta (ed.) (1993) *Ecofeminism: Woman, Animals, Nature*, Philadelphia, PA: Temple University Press.

Gray, Elizabeth Dodson (1979) *Green Paradise Lost*, Wellesley, MA: Roundtable Press.

Hypatia (1991) Special issue on ecological feminism, ed. Karen J. Warren, 6(1).

Plant, Judith (ed.) (1989) *Healing the Wounds: The Promise of Ecofeminism*, Philadelphia, PA: New Society.

Plumwood, Val (1986) 'Ecofeminism: An Overview and Discussion of Positions and Arguments', in Janna L. Thompson (ed.) *Women and Philosophy*, special supplement to *Australasian Journal of Philosophy*, 64: 120–38.

Williams, Terry Tempest (1991) *Refuge: An Unnatural History of Family and Place*, New York: Vintage.

50

The 'Lambs' in
The Silence of the Lambs

Jhan Hochman*

A CHARCOAL DRAWING of Clarice [Starling] holding a lamb in the foreground and three Calvaric crucifixes in back lies on Hannibal [Lecter's] table in the Shelby County Courthouse. After hearing of Clarice's failed attempt at rescuing spring lambs, 'were- (meaning 'man') wolf' Hannibal's Last (Passover) Supper before his escape consists of a version of the paschal lamb, 'lamb chops, extra rare.' Curiously, Lieutenant Boyle finds this familiar meat exotic, 'Wonder what he wants for breakfast, a damn thing from the zoo?' perhaps to exaggerate Hannibal's love of flesh. Just after Hannibal kills Lieutenant Boyle, Hannibal hangs him from the prison cage, crucifixion style, bright lights illuminating a gutted and bloody corpse. 'Hannibal' is found dead on top of the elevator but Hannibal, like Dracula and Christ, 'comes back' inside an ambulance (where is its red cross?) going through a tunnel. Hannibal sacrifices and possibly eats a bit of Boyle and Pembry to stage his own death and rebirth. This prototype Mass and crucifixion reconfigures the flock of Christian 'lambs' who eat the Agnus Dei (Lamb of God) into a pack of wolves/vampires/cannibals. After all, lambs don't eat lambs. Wolves do. Christian reference to the Lamb (and the Shepherd – shepherds protect their lambs in order to kill or sell them to be killed) eaten by a Christian flock of innocent lambs, draws attention away from the repugnant human 'cannibalism' of eating 'Christ', and strangely displaces it onto vegetarian lambs. Meanwhile, when Christ is in the guise of the Lamb who quietly accepts his own sacrifice, transubstantiated wine and wafer subtly serve as naturalization and reinforcement of human carnivorism. But it could be worse. Lamb, at least, is not eaten at Communion.

The Mass must not have worked its magic on Clarice, because she is deeply disturbed about lambs being readied for slaughter. These lambs even scream, unlike the Old Testament lamb (synonymous here with the Messiah) who is silent: 'He [the Messiah] was oppressed, and he was afflicted, yet he opened not his mouth: he is brought as a lamb to the slaughter, and as a sheep before her shearers is dumb,

*From 'The Silence of the Lambs: A Quiet Bestiary', ISLE, 1(2), 1993.

299

so he openeth not his mouth' (Isaiah 53:7). From the tradition of this quotation, we might be surprised that lambs scream (or pigs squeal or cows low) when killed. But it's not surprising we're surprised. The slaughterhouse (a.k.a. abattoir, shambles) is isolated so that such terror and suffering needn't be considered. Consideration or feeling stands to threaten the profits of managers and owners made from degraded workers who kill and butcher largely out of desperation of opportunity (cf. the visual work of Sue Coe, especially 'Porkopolis' and John Robbins' *Diet for a New America*). Clarice wasn't lucky enough to be distant from the slaughterhouse; the screaming was right out back. Like a fledgling animal rights guerrilla of recent years, she breaks in to free the lambs, but fumbles her attempt. As a last resort she grabs one lamb and runs. That lamb too is eventually killed and Clarice is 'jailed' and exiled to a *Lutheran* home for orphans, a fitting place for a not-fully interpellated, renegade Christian *and* homo carnarius (flesh lover).

Clarice grows up to accept the killing of lambs (she moves away from the shambles) but not the screaming that's stuck to the 'mushy', 'childish', and 'effeminate' side of her constitution. The 'screaming' *in her head* must be stopped. She attempts this through metaphor, substituting people, Christian lambs, women in need, or just people, for screaming lambs. If she saves Catherine Martin, Clarice might just save herself. Near the film's end when Catherine comes out of Jame [Gumb's] house holding Precious, one of the cops tries to relieve her of the dog. Catherine clutches Precious closer and walks away with precious Precious. It is no mistake Precious looks like a lamb, causing this scenario to look like a more successful reenactment of Clarice's attempt to save the spring lamb years before. On the other hand, with Catherine being readied for slaughter and skinning (she has already been 'fattened') she is the homologue of the spring lamb, just as the unfeeling Jame is the counterpart of Clarice's unsympathetic rancher/uncle with the sheep and horse ranch. Catherine also becomes the lamb surrogate through metonymy, i.e., the contiguity of Precious as lamb. Catherine can therefore be seen as both Clarice (resemblance) and lamb (metonymy). Rescue of Catherine happily relieves the screaming of the lambs *inside Clarice's head*, the kind of silence referred to in the movie's title.

Material lambs, however, continue screaming in the shambles. While Clarice tells Hannibal her story, we are given the opportunity to 'understand' this. But our possible sympathy for lambs is displaced onto our sympathy for Clarice's disturbed nights, and onto the relief that she can sleep once again. Clarice, by being a witness to victimization, becomes a victim, mediating, lessening, or removing the primary victim, the lambs. Carol Adams has already isolated and named the phenomenon whereby human suffering or 'suffering' is substituted for animal suffering. She calls any entity displaced (here, animals) the 'absent referent':

> Metaphorically, the absent referent can be anything whose original meaning is undercut as it is absorbed into a different hierarchy of meaning; in this case the original meaning of animals' fates is absorbed into a human-centered hierarchy. Specifically in regard to rape victims and battered women, the death experience of animals acts to illustrate the

lived experience of women [refers especially to the phrase 'I felt like a piece of meat' stated by a woman describing her own rape].

(42)

Linguistically appropriating animal treatment without appreciating their suffering also occurs in the oft-heard sentence, 'They treated me like an animal.' An animal might serve here as absent referent but, taking Adams further, something more insidious than absence seems likely. Cruel treatment of animals becomes naturalized (the naturalized referent) as *the* way to treat animals. 'They treated me like an animal' could be restated, 'It is, or may be, fitting and natural to treat an animal in such fashion but not me, a human being.' Naturalizing the different treatments of animals and humans gives them the force and veracity of God-given acts. One can be sure that when any person says they were treated like an animal, the treatment was cruel.

Does this film (and novel), besides absenting animals as suffering referents *à la* Adams, naturalize practices of slaughtering and butchering animals, or does it draw critical attention to them? It does seem to criticize lamb killing through Clarice's tale of victimized lambs. However, this seems undercut by the word *silence* from the title. Critical attention to both absented and naturalized lamb cruelty in the world outside the film is replaced by attention to Clarice's mental/emotional experience and its overcoming. The cruelty of humans would have been better brought to the fore by the less happy, anti-Hollywood title, *The Screaming of the Lambs*.

But *screaming* has problems too. The verb usually applies to human vocalization. 'Humanizing' the sound of lambs does serve to elicit sympathy comparable to that for suffering humans, but it also reinforces a suspect, even if understandable and effective, practice of 'humanizing' animals in order to demand decent treatment, or evoke empathy for them. To constitute an entity in human form so its existence, outside our control, can be respected, indicates a problem of imagination – as does the opposite tendency, where animals cannot be seen to feel pain or pleasure in ways similar to us, i.e., what can be called the Cartesian syndrome (see *Discourse on Method*). Autophilia is plausible reason why *The Bleating of the Lambs* wasn't chosen over *The Screaming of the Lambs*, and the well-known Hollywood-reinforced-phobia-against-disturbing-endings is the probable reason both these titles were passed up for *The Silence of the Lambs*.

WORKS CITED

Adams, Carol J. (1991) *The Sexual Politics of Meat: A Feminist-Vegetarian Critical Theory*, New York: Continuum.

Harris, Thomas (1988) *The Silence of the Lambs*, New York: St Martin's Press.

Glossary

anthropocentrism   the assumption that human life is the central fact of the planet.

anthropomorphism   the attribution of human form or personality to nature (as in the 'pathetic fallacy' condemned by John Ruskin).

bioregion   a natural region, exhibiting both stability and diversity, which is defined by its ecological coherence.

biosphere   in its modest, neutral sense, the collective name for all the areas of the earth in which life is found; in its more ambitious, positive sense, the planet and its physical environment as forming one living whole (as in James Lovelock's 'Gaia' hypothesis).

deep ecology   a radical form of ecology which challenges anthropocentrism and which insists that human beings must subordinate their interests to those of the planet.

ecocriticism   the most important branch of green studies, which considers the relationship between human and non-human life as represented in literary texts and which theorises about the place of literature in the struggle against environmental destruction.

ecofeminism   a movement which resists both the domination of nature by humanity and the domination of women by men, exploring the connection between the two processes and seeking a new relationship between woman, man and nature.

ecology   a branch of biology concerned with the relation between living things and their environment; the study of the earth as our home or 'household' (Greek, *oikos*).

ecosystem   the web of connections linking all the animals and plants in a particular environment.

environment   in general, the physical and biological system which supports life; in particular, the surroundings in which living creatures find themselves.

environmentalism   by contrast with 'deep ecology', the belief that the natural world can be 'managed' for the benefit of humanity while causing as little damage to the biosphere as possible within the existing culture–nature relationship.

green studies   an emerging academic movement which seeks to ensure that nature is given as much attention within the humanities as is currently given to gender, class and race.

industrialism   the term used by Andrew Dobson in his *Green Political Thought* (see Bibliography) for the whole political system which is opposed by what he calls 'ecologism'.

nature   the physical, non-human environment, including wildlife and wilderness, flora and fauna, and so on; but also the 'essence' of anything, including humanity, in which case it is often spelt with a capital N and should be used with caution.

pastoral   a literary convention which associates the country with innocence and the court or city with corruption; any literary work contrasting rural and urban life.

weak anthropocentrism   the position advocated by Andrew Dobson in his *Green Political Thought* (see Bibliography): that human beings can dedicate themselves to the welfare of the planet only from a human perspective, and by commitment to a rational political programme; opposed to 'strong anthropocentrism', which views nature instrumentally, but also differing from both the reformism of environmentalism and the absolutism of deep ecology.

Bibliography

Please note:

1   This bibliography does not include primary texts by pre-twentieth-century writers.
2   Readers are recommended to consult back issues of *ISLE* (*Interdisciplinary Studies in Literature and Environment*) for many interesting articles apart from the ones specifically indicated below. ISSN 1076–0962.

Adorno, Theodor W. (1997) *Aesthetic Theory* (ed. G. Adorno and R. Tiedmann; trans. R. Hullot-Kentor), London and Minneapolis, MN: Athlone Press/University of Minnesota Press.

Adorno, Theodor W. and Max Horkheimer (1972) *Dialectic of Enlightenment* (trans. J. Cumming), London: Verso.

Alcorn, John (1977) *The Nature Novel from Hardy to Lawrence*, London: Macmillan.

Armbruster, Karla (1996) 'Blurring Boundaries in Ursula Le Guin's "Buffalo Gals, Won't You Come Out Tonight?": A Poststructuralist Approach to Ecofeminist Criticism', *ISLE*, 3(1): 17–46.

Armbruster, Karla and Kathleen Wallace (eds) (2000) *Beyond Nature Writing*, Charlottesville, VA: University of Virginia Press.

Barnett, Anthony and Roger Scruton (eds) (1998) *Town and Country*, London: Jonathan Cape.

Bate, Jonathan (1991) *Romantic Ecology: Wordsworth and the Environmental Tradition*, London and New York: Routledge.

—— (1996) 'Living with the Weather', *Studies in Romanticism*, 35(3): 431–47.

—— (2000) *The Song of the Earth*, London: Picador.

Berleant, Arnold (1992) *The Aesthetics of Environment*, Philadelphia, PA: Temple University Press.

Berry, Wendell (1983) *Standing by Words*, San Francisco, CA: North Point Press.

Blackwell, Trevor and Jeremy Seabrook (1988) *The Politics of Hope: Britain at the End of the Twentieth Century*, London: Faber & Faber.

Buell, Lawrence (1995) *The Environmental Imagination: Thoreau, Nature Writing, and the Formation of American Culture*, Cambridge, MA: Harvard University Press.

Burke, Kenneth ([1935] 1984a) *Permanence and Change: An Anatomy of Purpose*, Berkeley and Los Angeles: University of California Press.

—— ([1937] 1984b) *Attitudes Towards History*, Berkeley and Los Angeles: University of California Press.

—— (1966) *Language as Symbolic Action: Essays on Life, Literature and Method*, Berkeley and Los Angeles: University of California Press.

—— (1974) 'Why Satire – with a Plan for Writing One', *Michigan Quarterly Review*, 13(4): 307–37.

Cantrell, Carol H. (1998) 'The Locus of Compassibility: Virginia Woolf, Modernism, and Place', *ISLE*, 5(2): 25–40.

Cobb, John B. (1972) *Is It too Late? A Theology of Ecology*, Beverly Hills, CA: Bruce Press.

Conley, Verena Andermatt (1997) *Ecopolitics: The Environment in Post-Structuralist Thought*, London and New York: Routledge.

Coupe, Laurence (1997 onwards) 'Ecocriticism', *Annotated Bibliography for English Studies*, Sassenheim, Netherlands: Swets & Zeitlinger (CD-ROM and Internet).

Curry, Patrick (1997) *Defending Middle-Earth: Tolkien, Myth and Modernity*, Edinburgh: Floris Books.

Danby, John F. ([1948] 1975) *Shakespeare's Doctrine of Nature: A Study of 'King Lear'*, London: Faber & Faber.

—— (1960) *The Simple Wordsworth: Studies in the Poems 1797–1807*, London: Routledge & Kegan Paul.

Dobson, Andrew ([1990] 1995) *Green Political Thought*, London and New York: Routledge.

Ehrenfeld, David (1978) *The Arrogance of Humanism*, New York: Oxford University Press.

Elder, John (1985) *Imagining the Earth: Poetry and the Vision of Nature*, Urbana and Chicago, IL: University of Illinois Press.

Eliot, T. S. (1939) *The Idea of a Christian Society*, London: Faber & Faber.

Garrard, Greg (1996) 'Radical Pastoral?', *Studies in Romanticism*, 35(3): 449–65.

Gifford, Terry (1995) *Green Voices: Understanding Contemporary Nature Poetry*, Manchester: Manchester University Press.

—— (1996) 'The Social Construction of Nature', *ISLE*, 3(2): 27–36.

—— (1999) *Pastoral*, London and New York: Routledge.

Glotfelty, Cheryll (1996) 'Flooding the Boundaries of Form: Terry Tempest Williams' Ecofeminist *Unnatural History*', in Stephen Tchudi (ed.) *Change in the American West: Exploring the Human Dimension*, Reno, NV: University of Nevada Press.

Glotfelty, Cheryll and Harold Fromm (eds) (1996) *The Ecocriticism Reader: Landmarks in Literary Ecology*, Athens, GA and London: University of Georgia Press.

Haraway, Donna J. (1989) *Primate Visions: Gender, Race, and Nature in the World of Modern Science*, New York and London: Routledge.

—— (1991) *Simians, Cyborgs, and Women: The Reinvention of Nature*, New York and London: Routledge.

Harrison, Robert Pogue (1992) *Forests: The Shadow of Civilization*, Chicago and London: University of Chicago Press.

Head, Dominic (1998) 'Problems in Ecocriticism and the Novel', *Key Words*, 1: 60–78.

Heidegger, Martin (1971) *Poetry, Language, Thought* (trans. A. Hofstadter), London and New York: Harper & Row.

Herndl, Varl G. and Stuart C. Brown (1996) *Green Culture: Environmental Rhetoric in Contemporary Culture*, Madison, WI: University of Wisconsin Press.

Hochman, Jhan (1988) *Green Cultural Studies: Nature in Film, Novel, and Theory*, Moscow, ID: University of Idaho Press.

—— (1993) '*The Silence of the Lambs*: A Quiet Bestiary', *ISLE*, 1(2): 57–80.

—— (1997) 'Green Cultural Studies: An Introductory Critique of an Emerging Discipline', *Mosaic*, 30(1): 81–96.

Howarth, William (1996) 'Some Principles of Ecocriticism', in Cheryll Glotfelty and Harold Fromm (eds) *The Ecocriticism Reader: Landmarks in Literary Ecology*, Athens, GA and London: University of Georgia Press.

Kerridge, Richard (1998) 'Ecothrillers: Environmentalism in Popular Culture', *English Review*, 8(3): 32–5.

—— (1999) 'BSE Stories', *Key Words: A Journal of Cultural Materialism*, 2: 111–21.

—— (2000) 'Ecological Hardy', in Karla Armbruster and Kathleen Wallace (eds) *Beyond Nature Writing*, Charlottesville, VA: University of Virginia Press.

Kerridge, Richard and Neil Sammels (eds) (1998) *Writing the Environment: Ecocriticsm and Literature*, London: Zed Books.

Kolodny, Annette (1975) *The Lay of the Land: Metaphor as Experience and History in American Life and Letters*, Chapel Hill, NC: University of North Carolina Press.

Kroeber, Karl (1994) *Ecological Literary Criticism: Romantic Imagining and the Biology of Mind*, New York: Columbia University Press.

Lawrence, D. H. (1936) *Phoenix: The Posthumous Papers of D. H. Lawrence* (ed. E. D. McDonald), London: William Heinemann.

Leavis, F. R. and Denys Thompson ([1933] 1964) *Culture and Environment: The Training of Critical Awareness*, London: Chatto & Windus.

Leopold, Aldo (1949) *A Sand County Almanac*, Oxford: Oxford University Press.

Lévi-Strauss, Claude (1985) *The View from Afar* (trans. J. Neugroschel and P. Hoss), Oxford and New York: Blackwell/Basic Books.

Lopez, Barry (1978) *Of Wolves and Men*, New York: Scribner's.

Lyotard, Jean-François (1984) *The Postmodern Condition: A Report on Knowledge* (trans. G. Bennington and B. Massumi), Manchester: Manchester University Press.

—— (1993) *Political Writings* (trans. B. Readings and K. P. Geiman), London: UCL Press.

McKibben, Bill (1990) *The End of Nature*, Harmondsworth: Penguin.

Marx, Leo (1964) *The Machine in the Garden: Technology and the Pastoral Ideal in America*, London and New York: Oxford University Press.

Meeker, Joseph W. (1997) *The Comedy of Survival: Literary Ecology and a Play Ethic*, Tuscon, AZ: University of Arizona Press.

Merchant, Carolyn (1980) *The Death of Nature: Women, Ecology, and the Scientific Revolution*, San Francisco, CA: Harper & Row.

Merleau-Ponty, Maurice (1968) *The Visible and the Invisible* (trans. A. Lingis), Evanston, IL: Northwestern University Press.

Mies, Maria and Vandana Shiva (1993) *Ecofeminism*, London: Zed Books.

Mitchell, W. J. T. (ed.) (1994) *Landscape and Power*, Chicago and London: University of Chicago Press.

Murphy, Patrick D. (1995) *Literature, Nature, and Other: Ecofeminist Critiques*, Albany, NY: State University of New York Press.

—— (ed.) (1998) *Literature of Nature: An International Sourcebook*, Chicago and London: Fitzroy Dearborn.

Murry, John Middleton (1922) *Countries of the Mind*, London: Hudson.

Plumwood, Val (1993) *Feminism and the Mastery of Nature*, London and New York: Routledge.

Ross, Andrew (1991) *Strange Weather*, London and New York: Verso.

Roszak, Betty and Theodore Roszak (1996) 'Deep Form in Art and Nature', *Resurgence*, 176 (May–June): 20–3.

Roszak, Theodore (1972) *Where the Wasteland Ends: Politics and Transcendence in Post-Industrial Society*, New York: Doubleday.

—— (1993) *The Voice of the Earth: An Exploration of Ecopsychology*, New York: Touchstone.

Roszak, Theodore, Mary E. Gomes and Allen D. Kanner (1995) (eds) *Ecopsychology: Restoring the Earth, Healing the Mind*, San Francisco, CA: Sierra Club Books.

Schama, Simon (1995) *Landscape and Memory*, London: HarperCollins.

Serres, Michel (1995) *The Natural Contract* (trans. E. MacArthur and W. Paulson), Ann Arbor, MI: University of Michigan Press.

Shephard, Paul (1991) *Man in the Landscape: A Historic View of the Esthetics of Nature*, College Station, TX: University of Texas Press.

Simmons, I. G. (1993) *Interpreting Nature: Cultural Constructions of the Environment*, London and New York: Routledge.

Slovic, Scott (1992) *Seeking Awareness in American Nature Writing: Henry Thoreau, Annie Dillard, Edward Abbey, Wendell Berry, Barry Lopez*, Salt Lake City, UT: University of Utah Press.

—— (1999) 'Ecocriticism: Containing Multitudes, Practising Doctrine', *ASLE News*, 11(1): pp. 4–5.

Snyder, Gary (1995) *A Place in Space: Ethics, Aesthetics, and Watersheds*, Washington, DC: Counterpoint.

Soper, Kate (1995) *What is Nature? Culture, Politics and the Non-Human*, Oxford and Cambridge, MA: Blackwell.

Spretnak, Charlene (1991) *States of Grace: The Recovery of Meaning in the Postmodern Age*, San Francisco, CA: HarperCollins.

Stein, Rachel (1997) *Shifting the Ground: American Women Writers' Revisions of Nature, Gender, and Race*, Charlottesville, VA and London: University Press of Virginia.

Tchudi, Stephen (ed.) (1996) *Change in the American West: Exploring the Human Dimension*, Reno, NV: University of Nevada Press.

Thomas, Edward (1909) *The South Country*, London: Dent.

—— (1981) *A Language not to Be Betrayed: Selected Prose* (ed. E. Longley), Manchester: Carcanet.

Wall, Derek (ed.) (1994) *Green History: A Reader in Environmental Literature, Philosophy and Politics*, London and New York: Routledge.

Watts, Alan W. ([1958] 1991) *Nature, Man and Woman*, New York: Vintage.

Westling, Louise H. (1993) 'Thoreau's Ambivalence Towards Mother Nature', *ISLE*, 1(1): 145–50.

—— (1996) *The Green Breast of the New World: Landscape, Gender and American Fiction*, Athens, GA and London: University of Georgia Press.

Williams, Raymond ([1958] 1982) *Culture and Society: Coleridge to Orwell*, London: Hogarth Press.

—— ([1973] 1985) *The Country and the City*, London: Hogarth Press.

—— ([1976] 1981) *Keywords: A Vocabulary of Culture and Society*, London: Fontana.

—— (1980) *Problems in Materialism and Culture*, London: Verso.

—— (1983) *Towards 2000*, London: Hogarth Press.

—— (1989) *Resources of Hope: Culture, Democracy, Socialism* (ed. R. Gable), London and New York: Verso.

BIBLIOGRAPHY

Wilson, Alexander (1992) *The Culture of Nature: North American Landscape from Disney to the Exxon Valdez*, Cambridge, MA: Blackwell.

Woolf, Virginia ([1932] 1986) *The Common Reader: Second Series* (ed. A. McNeillie), London: Hogarth Press.

Index